R for Cloud Computing

A Ohri

R for Cloud Computing

An Approach for Data Scientists

 Springer

A Ohri
Decisionstats.com
Delhi, India

ISBN 978-1-4939-1701-3   ISBN 978-1-4939-1702-0 (eBook)
DOI 10.1007/978-1-4939-1702-0
Springer New York Heidelberg Dordrecht London

Library of Congress Control Number: 2014950411

Printed on acid-free paper

Springer is part of Springer Science+Business Media (www.springer.com)

Dedicated to my six-year-old son Kush.
All that is good in me comes from your love

Preface

I started writing this book on October 10, 2012, and finished its first draft on July 30, 2014, with 54,000 words. I would like to thank my editors and team members at Springer for their patience.

Origin I started learning analytics in 2004, and it was just known as analytics back then. We had moved on from knowledge discovery in databases, and we had not invented the buzzword called data science or Big Data yet. Analytics had two parts, reporting (pulling data, aggregating it, slicing it for a custom view, presenting it in a spreadsheet) and modeling (predictive with regression models and forecasting models). Analytics demanded a secure data environment, and all my clients insisted on retaining data in their premises. Once in a while, I used PGP for encrypting data transfers, and sometimes we used Remote Desktop to connect to remote servers. While working with sensitive data, we used remote submit on remote data warehouses using the analytics stack by the primary analytics player, the SAS Institute.

In the mid-2000s, I came across "cloud computing" as a paradigm in renting hardware and computing via the Internet. A friend of mine, a respected MBA, once called cloud computing as a lot of servers sitting together, and it took me many years to comprehend that simplistic impression. I first came to be involved with the R language in 2007 as I created my own startup, Decisionstats.com, in business analytics writing and consulting. The R language seemed to have a steep learning curve, but it was truly of immense benefit to my fledgling consulting practice.

Once I trained my mind to deal with the vagaries of lists, arrays, and data frames of R, I started off with analyzing projects and doing research. Of course, like anyone who has created a startup, I had help, a lot of help, from some of the best brains on the planet. The developments in technology and in open source software also proved to be of much help. I thank the developers of the R project for this as well as the broader community. One you get familiar with the personalities and their mannerisms, it will prove to be one of the best communities in the technology world. R was associated with some drawbacks in the 2007–2008 era, mainly that it only used data in its memory RAM. This meant it was limited to around 2–3 GB of data, unless one used a database (*those days it meant RDBMS, but now we have many kinds*). The second flaw in my opinion was the speed of processing, especially compared to mainstream analytics software used for business processes.

Around 2009 I first came across the word Big Data. It basically meant data that had bigger volume, faster velocities of refresh and creation, and variety in terms of formats. Volume, Velocity, and Variety are what separate the Big Data people from the rest even today.

Around September 2010, I created an easy-to-use tutorial on my Decision-stats.com blog on using R from Amazon's cloud. While the very first tutorial on the topic was created by Robert Grossman, I simplified it further with a few screenshots. This was primarily for my own use and remembering.

I was a business analytics user, and I sometimes got confused in the online documentation of R, and I found that many other people had exactly the same issue—there was no proper indexed R Online Doc Version 9 to help people like me. It is the huge and ongoing traffic to these tutorials that motivated me to write a book hoping to present a collection of DIY cloud and R for the average common tech geek.

Scope The purpose of the book is to introduce R and cloud computing to the professional practitioner and turn them into data scientists in the process. Chapter 1 gives an Introduction. Chapter 2 describes an approach for people to think like data scientists. Chapter 3 presents choices (some of them confusing) that confront a person navigating R on the cloud. Chapter 4 deals with setting up R on the cloud infrastructure and offers different perspectives and interfaces. Chapter 5 deals with working in R and is aimed at people new to R. Chapter 6 deals with R and Big Data and introduces the reader to the various paradigms in it. Chapter 7 moves beyond Chap. 4's infrastructure as a service and deals with how the R system can interface with Cloud Applications and Services. Chapter 7 is actually a use case chapter for using R on the cloud. Chapter 8 reviews ways to secure cloud as this is a constant insecurity in transitioning to the cloud. Chapter 9 deals with training literature to further help the reader.

Purpose The book has been written from a practical use case perspective. I find that information asymmetry and brand clutter have managed to confuse audiences about the true benefits and costs of a cloud-hosted open source analytics environment. The book is written for R because at the time of publication it remains the most widely used statistical language in the world with the biggest library of open source packages in statistics related to business analytics and the cheapest total cost of ownership including training, transition, and license costs. An earlier book on *R for Business Analytics* has also been written by me and is available at http://www.springer.com/statistics/book/978-1-4614-4342-1.

With over 7000 packages (a very dynamic number) and over 2 million users (a rapidly increasing number), R has a significant lead over other statistical software in terms of a broad library of packages for all analytical needs, and that lead continues to grow, thanks to a highly motivated team of volunteers and developers. R is not going anywhere but up, and for the analytics shop it pays to diversify a bit into the R space.

Plan I will continue to use screenshots as a tutorial device and easy-to-use methods (like graphical User interfaces) to help you analyze much more data at much lower cost. If you use R on the cloud, in an optimum manner, nothing will ever come close in terms of speed, reliability, security, as well as lowered costs (okay, maybe Python will come close—I grant you that, but Pythonistas are still catching up on the statistical libraries). I have tried to make it easy for readers to navigate both R and the cloud. In doing so, I have deliberately adopted a readable everyday conversational style. Every chapter has cited references as well as a few do-it-yourself tutorials.

Intended Audience This is a book for business analysts who are curious about using the cloud. It is also a book for people who use cloud computing and wonder what the buzz on R is all about. Some interviews of well-known practitioners have been included, and these will help decision makers at the CIO level to fine-tune their managerial perspectives on the choices and dilemmas associated with changing to cloud-hosted open source analytics.

Afterthoughts I have focussed on practical solutions. I will therefore proceed on the assumption that the user wants to perform analytics at the lowest cost and greatest accuracy, robustness, and ease possible. I would thus not suggest purely open source solutions when I feel the user is better off with existing software from vendors. I would also recommend in my blog writing and consulting some alternative languages including Python, Scala, Julia, and even SAS for specific use cases. This is because I believe no one software can be suitable for all the user needs, and each user may have their own need based on usage, context, constraints (time, money, training), and flexibility in transitioning to a new solution. I believe new innovation will constantly replace old, legacy solutions, and Andy Grove's advice on "where only the paranoid survive" will be of use to people embarking on a lifelong journey of learning cutting-edge technology which business analytics commits them to.

The instructions and tutorials within this book have no warranty, and using them will be at your own risk. Yet, this is needed because cloud computing can have both existing as well as new security issues as well as constant changes in user interfaces, licensing conditions, regulatory restrictions including those based on user data geography, and price changes besides the usual tendency of unexpected technological changes. One reason I have taken longer to write this book compared to my earlier book is my desire to constantly eliminate what is not needed anymore in the current scenario for enterprises and students wishing to use R and the cloud. As a special note on the formatting of this manuscript, I mostly write on Google Docs, but here I am writing using the GUI Lyx for the typesetting software Latex, and I confess I am not very good at it. However, having written one earlier book on R, *R for Business Analytics* (Springer 2012); 1,900 blog posts; and 100+ paid articles (including 150+ interviews on technology), I hope this book is better formatted and readable than the last one. And yet one more thing—due to a huge number of PDF downloads and torrents of my previous book, I have deliberately made some (but not all) codes within screenshots. This effectively means the print copy of the book would be much better formatted and more easily readable than the electronic version.

I do hope the book is read by both Chief Technology Officers keen to move to open source analytics based on the cloud and students wishing to enter a potentially lucrative career as data scientists. The R Web, the R Apache projects, and demonstration sites by UCLA, Dataspora, and Vanderbilt University are the well-known early implementations of cloud computing and R—as of today, this space is taken by Revolution Analytics (EC2 licensing of their product, RevoDeployR), Open CPU, and RStudio Servers including the Shiny Project.

R is well known for excellent graphics but is not so suitable for bigger data sets in its native easy-to-use open source version. Using cloud computing removes this hurdle very easily; you just increase the RAM on your instance. The enterprise CTO can thus reduce costs incredibly by shrinking software and hardware costs. The book reflects the current landscape of cloud computing providers, so much attention is devoted to Amazon, then to Google, then to Microsoft Azure, with a small mention of IBM and Oracle's efforts as well.

Delhi, India   A Ohri

Acknowledgments I am grateful to many people working in both the cloud and R communities for making this book possible. I would like to thank Anne Milley, JMP; Bob Muenchen, author of *R for SAS and SPSS Users*; Jerooen Ooms; Jan De Leeuw; Gregory Piatetsky Shapiro; Markus Schmidberger; Dr Ingo Miereswa; all readers of Decisionstats.com; Gergely Rapporter; all the R package creators; everyone interviewed by me in DecisionStats.com; and Vignesh Prajapathi and his Decisionstats.com intern Chandan. A writer is a helpless baby in terms of material and practical needs. I would also like to thank my bhais (Kala, Sonu, Micky), my friends (Namy, Tammy, Sam), and my loving family in Delhi, Mumbai, and Calgary.

Contents

About the Author

A Ohri is the founder of the analytics startup Decisionstats.com. He has pursued graduate courses at the University of Tennessee, Knoxville, and completed his master's from the Indian Institute of Management, Lucknow. Ohri also has a mechanical engineering degree from the Delhi College of Engineering. He has interviewed more than 150 practitioners in analytics, including leading members from all the analytics software vendors. Ohri has written almost 2,000 articles on his blog, in addition to writing about APIs for influential websites like ProgrammableWeb. Ohri's current research interests include spreading open source analytics, analyzing social media manipulation with mechanism design, creating simpler interfaces to cloud computing, and investigating climate change manipulation and unorthodox cryptography including visual and quantum. He is currently advising multiple startups in analytics offshoring, analytics services, and analytics education as well as using social media to enhance the buzz for analytics products. Ohri works with R, SAS, Julia, and Python languages and finds beauty in all of them. He is the author of another book on R called R for Business Analytics (Springer 2013). R for Business Analytics is being translated in Chinese.

Chapter 1
Introduction to R for Cloud Computing

1.1 What Is R Really?

R is a language for statistical computing that is widely used in industry in the fields of data mining, business analytics, and data visualization. It is generally considered as the most widely used statistical language with an estimated 2 million users. No official statistics have been released though various estimates of downloads suggest that 2 million users will be a conservative number. The previous champions of the business analytics world were SAS and SPSS languages, but both have been facing stiff competition from R, just like Windows has faced competition from Linux and iOS has faced competition from Android.

This rapid rise in R is primarily because of the fact that R is customizable, is free, and has one of the widest communities of developers creating over 8000 packages for statistical computing. In the open source arena, R has faced some competition from Python, Scala, and other languages like Julia but has largely been able to retain its niche lead in the statistical world, thanks to its huge number of libraries and talented second generation of developers and package creators.

R is well known for excellent graphics but has a perception that it is not so suitable for bigger data sets. This is because R stores data within RAM, so you are constrained by the amount of RAM on your machine. Efforts have been made to work around this limitation by incorporating interfaces to C++, parallel processing, and even new formats like the xfd format used by Revolution Analytics's package RevoScaleR. Using cloud computing removes this memory hurdle very simply and reduces costs by shrinking software and hardware costs. On the cloud you can rent memory by the hour and so do the data intensive aggregation and querying on a virtual machine with a higher RAM. This combines the strengths of R (free and extensive, largest open source library of statistical packages) with the strengths of the cloud (cost effective computing including memory and storage), while cancelling out the biggest perceived weakness of R (in-memory storage limitation).

The cost of traditional licensing for proprietary software in analytics is a big reason for the growth of open source R. Since cloud computing may require multiple

© Springer Science+Business Media New York 2014
A Ohri, *R for Cloud Computing*, DOI 10.1007/978-1-4939-1702-0_1

instances (or virtual machines), a rigidly priced license per core per year does not make any sense. Companies have been recognizing this and introduced on demand pricing for renting the software on an hour usage basis. Some companies have also introduced University Editions of their software for free use to academia, but so far those efforts have been seen as reactive and not proactive, ensuring that the world of analytics will continue to use R for the next few years.

The official definition of what is R is given on the main website at http://www.r-project.org/about.html

R is an integrated suite of software facilities for data manipulation, calculation and graphical display. It includes an effective data handling and storage facility, a suite of operators for calculations on arrays, in particular matrices, a large, coherent, integrated collection of intermediate tools for data analysis, graphical facilities for data analysis and display either on-screen or on hardcopy, and a well-developed, simple and effective programming language which includes conditionals, loops, user-defined recursive functions and input and output facilities. The term "environment" is intended to characterize it as a fully planned and coherent system, rather than an incremental accretion of very specific and inflexible tools, as is frequently the case with other data analysis software.

For the author R is a programming language and a statistical tool, it helps him crunch data and build models for business analytics and make cool graphs.

1.2   What Is Cloud Computing?

There is some confusion in the minds of even experienced analytics practitioners on what constitutes cloud computing and what is time-sharing or just a large collection of remote servers. This confusion is compounded by a large number of service providers who claim to give the best and cheapest computation in the cloud without elucidating how that is different from the desktop generation of computing. Since we believe cloud computing is more than a buzz word, we reproduce here the definition of cloud computing by the reputed NIST.

As per the National Institute of Standards and Technology Definition, Cloud computing is a model for enabling convenient, on-demand network access to a shared pool of configurable computing resources (e.g., networks, servers, storage, applications, and services) that can be rapidly provisioned and released with minimal management effort or service provider interaction.

This cloud model promotes availability and is composed of five essential characteristics

1. On demand self-service
2. Broad Network Access
3. Resource Pooling
4. Rapid Elasticity
5. Measured Service

three service models (SaaS, PaaS, and IaaS) and,
> four deployment models (private, public, community, and hybrid).
> Key enabling technologies include:

1. fast networks,
2. inexpensive computers, and
3. virtualization for commodity hardware.

Major barriers to broader cloud adoption are

- security, interoperability, and portability

This is the NIST definition for cloud computing and it is recommended that the reader can refer to the original document given at the location at the "References" section at the end of this chapter. The original document (also hosted at http://csrc.nist.gov/publications/nistpubs/800-145/SP800-145.pdf) gives a more elaborate definition and explains all the terms involved. Amazon defines this as—the term "Cloud Computing" refers to the on-demand delivery of IT resources via the Internet with pay-as-you-go pricing.

For a layman to be explained in simple short terms, cloud computing is a lot of scalable and custom computing power available by rent/by hour and accessible remotely. It can help in doing more computing at a fraction of the cost

1.2.1   What Is SaaS, PaaS, and IaaS?

Basically infrastructure as a service allows you to hire a virtual server and then use it through a browser. It is a remote machine and you are responsible for installing software and scaling up hardware. Platform as a service provides a platform—the user does not have to worry about managing the hardware but just controlling the software. Software as a service basically means software is rented by the consumer but is hosted and completely managed by the provider.

- Examples of IaaS are Windows Azure Virtual Machines (https://azure.microsoft.com/en-us/) ,Amazon Web Services EC2 (http://aws.amazon.com/ec2/), and Google Compute Engine (https://cloud.google.com/products/compute-engine/).
- Examples of PaaS are Google App Engine (https://developers.google.com/appengine),Salesforce Platform (http://www.salesforce.com/platform/), and Amazon AWS Elastic Beanstalk (http://aws.amazon.com/elasticbeanstalk/)
- Examples of SaaS are Gmail (Messaging) and, Salesforce (CRM).

The following image is from a slide from "Windows Azure Platform: Cloud Development Jump Start". It helps explain the difference between the three terms.

NOTE: While Linux clearly enjoys a lead on the cloud operating systems, Microsoft's Azure platform is a strong contender in the cloud computing space behind Google and Amazon especially given its rich history with working directly with both Service Providers and Enterprise Software Clients.

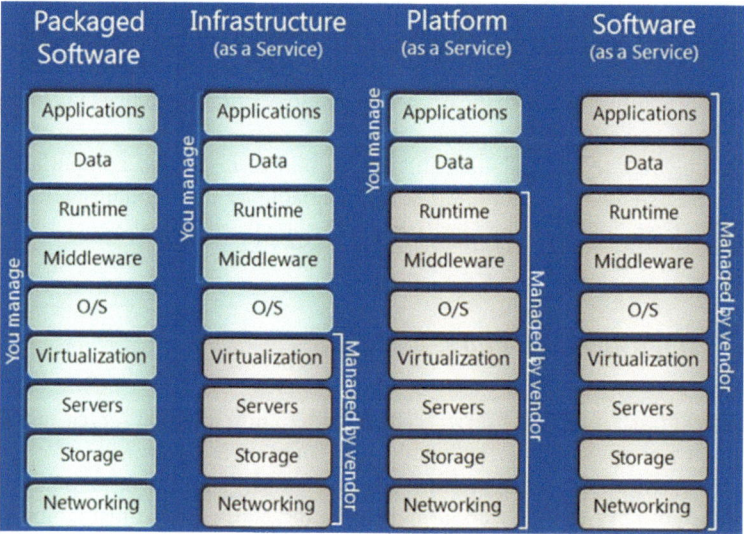

1.3   Why Should Cloud Users Learn More About R?

Some other reasons for cloud computing users to learn R.

1. Bigger Data is the first reason for moving to the cloud and R is the most widely used way to analyse data.
2. The R language is one of the fastest growing languages in the world and the de facto leader in statistical analysis.
3. With packages like ggplot2 it has one of the best visualization and graphical capabilities in analytics software.
4. It is open source and free and the 8000 plus packages can be customized to your business need.
5. It is used and supported by almost everybody in the Business Analytics space including Google, Oracle, Microsoft, SAP, SAS Institute, and IBM.

6. With GUI packages like Deducer and Rattle, it can be easily used for even beginners to start analysing data in R
7. It has one of the healthiest ecosystem of developers, users, community meetups, conferences, help groups, books and startups, and experienced companies in the space offering you cutting edge technological help with R. This includes multiple trainings to learn R for free (including by Coursera and Code School) and graphical user interfaces (like Rattle and Deducer) and IDE like RStudio for helping business users with faster project execution and easier transition to the R platform.
8. For enterprises, there is a healthy ecosystem provided by Revolution Analytics and RStudio for solutions.

NOTE: Some people recommend switching to Python, but the limited number of statistical libraries in Python (now growing thanks to panda, numpy, scipy) is still very less compared to the 5000 statistics related packages in R. That extensive package library and much easier and better graphical capabilities in R compared to Python suggest R remains the leading choice for analytics and statistics. You can see the graphics at https://github.com/hadley/r-python that Python is a formidable alternative to R, pending its successful migration of R libraries and visualization packages.

1.4   Big Data and R

The increasing velocity, variety, and volume of data is why people moved to the cloud for affordable computing. R helps analyse this data further. These 3 V's are the basic pillars of the Big Data analytics movement.

- Volume refers to the hundreds of terabytes and petabytes of stored data inside organizations today.
- Velocity refers to the whole continuum from batch to real time continuous and streaming data.
- Variety refers to multi-structure data from structured to unstructured files, managed and stored in a common platform analysed through common tooling.

A fourth V has been added—it is called Veracity and makes sure data quality is accurate and reliable.

Using R in parallel processing—or in the paradigm of distributed computing is what makes the open source extensive libraries of R an unbeatable combination for Big Data and R.

Big Data was not as easily handled in R in the past but thanks to innovations by package creators, it is now much more easy to handle Big Data in R. For more on Big Data please refer to Chap. 6.

1.5   Why Should R Users Learn More About the Cloud?

R is used in Business Analytics and statistical computing with increasing amounts of data. Since R stores data in memory, it is thus limited to the RAM available in the laptop and server available to the user. This makes transition to R difficult for users who are used to bigger data sizes being processed easily by other analytics software, even though they are much more expensive to license.

There are programmatic ways to help the user with Big Data and we will investigate them further. This includes putting data within databases and using RODBC package, using packages from the Rcpp gallery, using Revolution Analytics Revo Scaler package which converts data into the xdf format, and looking into SAP Hana and Oracle's efforts for in-database analytics.

The cloud offers a way to further cut down the cost of hardware and enhance the ease of using R for bigger datasets. Using R has already cut the cost of software to zero but there is a cost to transitioning to R from existing software packages and cost of retraining analysts. It is also relatively cheaper and easier for people who are business analytics users with limited programming needs to easily start using R with much bigger data sizes. For a more basic, introductory level book on using the R language for purposes of business analytics, you should please refer to "R for Business Analytics" by the same author and publisher.

1.6   How Can You Use R on the Cloud Infrastructure?

This is a simple process to using R on the cloud infrastructure.

1. Sign up with a cloud computing infrastructure provider (refer to the definition of cloud computing). This can be one of the following

    a. Amazon—AWS offers a 1 year free micro instance for you to test.
    b. Microsoft—Azure offers you a 90-day free trial.
    c. Google—Google Compute Engine is currently in private beta. The author is a beta user.
    d. Oracle—Java cloud is currently in beta.

2. Choose your operating system (on the cloud)—Linux or Windows are the two operating systems that are on offer by both Amazon AWS and Microsoft Azure. Google Cloud offers Linux only.
3. Create your computing instance (including the memory and processing needs), and adequate storage (including storage size, type).
4. Install R (we will help you with this in the future chapters) on your cloud instance. Optionally you should install R Studio Server on your cloud instance (Linux only) as it really helps in giving a much better interface.
5. Work with R and other cloud services

   a. Move your data to the cloud storage (whether called blog or bucket) after
      deciding the storage type (including Hadoop, Database, or File System)
   b. use R from your cloud computing instance to the data
   c. create multiple instances of cloud if you need parallel processing or move to
      a bigger memory instance.
   d. Keep an eye on costs. The cloud is billed for how long you use it. This can be
      minimized by automating and batch scripts as well.

1.7   How Long Does It Take to Learn and Apply R on a Cloud?

It takes anything between 30 work hours to 90 work hours for an intermediate
professional to learn and begin using R for Business Analytics on the cloud
(assumed. Variance in learning depends on the user's prior programming resource,
the learning resource used, the context or usage of the end customer of R on the
cloud).In the book Outliers, author Malcolm Gladwell says that it takes roughly
ten thousand hours of practice to achieve mastery in a field but in that time (ten
thousand hours!) both the technology and the cloud computing landscape would
definitely change rendering your knowledge a bit obsolete.

   Once you have learnt how to use R on a cloud computer—it will take less than
5 minutes or the time it takes for your local computer to boot up, to start doing
business analytics on the cloud.

1.8   Commercial and Enterprise Versions of R

The following companies are working in R commercially from a product
perspective.

Revolution   Analytics is the leading vendor of software products in R for
   Enterprises. They have embraced Big Data Analytics with their investments in
   RevoScaleR package and RHadoop, and cloud computing by enabling their

software as a rentable service on Amazon Ec2 and through RevoDeployR. Their website is at http://www.revolutionanalytics.com/ and software is available from http://www.revolutionanalytics.com/downloads/

Cloud   versions of Revolution Analytics software are available from https://aws.amazon.com/marketplace/pp/B00KKDR3VQ/ and https://aws.amazon.com/marketplace/pp/B00IO6H6KE/. At the time of writing this there was a 14-day free trial for Revolution Analytics products on Amazon AWS.

The   cost of as July 2014 is reproduced here. You can see details on what Amazon EC2 instance types are in Chap. 3.

EC2 Instance Type	EC2 Usage	Software	Total
hi1.4xlarge	$3.23/hr	$11.20/hr	$14.43/hr
hs1.8xlarge	$4.73/hr	$5.60/hr	$10.33/hr
cc2.8xlarge	$2.13/hr	$11.20/hr	$13.33/hr
i2.xlarge	$0.913/hr	$1.40/hr	$2.313/hr
i2.2xlarge	$1.835/hr	$2.80/hr	$4.635/hr
i2.4xlarge	$3.54/hr	$5.60/hr	$9.14/hr
i2.8xlarge	$6.95/hr	$11.20/hr	$18.15/hr
c3.8xlarge	$1.81/hr	$11.20/hr	$13.01/hr

R   for Excel —This helps integrate R with Microsoft Excel. The website is at http://www.statconn.com/ and software can be downloaded—http://rcom.univie.ac.at/download.html. You can also integrates R with Word, Open Office, and Excel with Scilab.

Oracle   R Enterprise—Oracle has been a leading investor in the R ecosystem. You can see more from here— http://www.oracle.com/technetwork/topics/bigdata/r-offerings-1566363.html

In addressing the enterprise and the need to analyse Big Data, Oracle provides R integration through four key technologies

Oracle R Distribution *Oracle's supported redistribution of open source R, provided as a free download from Oracle, enhanced with dynamic loading of high performance linear algebra libraries. website icon*

Oracle R Enterprise *Integration of R with Oracle Database. A component of the Oracle Advanced Analytics Option. Oracle R Enterprise makes the open source R statistical programming language and environment ready for the enterprise with scalability, performance, and ease of production deployment. website icon*

Oracle R Advanced Analytics for Hadoop *High performance native access to the Hadoop Distributed File System (HDFS) and Map Reduce programming framework for R users. Oracle R Advanced Analytics for Hadoop is a component of Oracle Big Data Connectors software suite. website icon*

ROracle An open source R package, maintained by Oracle and enhanced to use the Oracle Call Interface (OCI) libraries to handle database connections—providing a high-performance, native C-language interface to Oracle Database.

Tibco   Enterprise Runtime for R (TERR)—This is available from https://tap.tibco.com/storefront/trialware/tibco-enterprise-runtime-for-r/prod15307.html. It is embedded in the TIBCO Spotfire platform to provide predictive analytic capabilities and is available for integration into other applications through various APIs. Developing in R and then deploying on TIBCO® Enterprise Runtime for R enable much wider acceptance in the enterprise software space.

Yhat   ScienceBox—Yhat Sciencebox is a data science platform that allows you to configure and manage R and Python environments. Sciencebox comes preloaded with your favorite R and Python packages and libraries. Users can easily create and switch between custom environments, manage data science project workflows and add custom packages such as Rstudio, iPython Notebook, pandas and ggplot. It is available at https://aws.amazon.com/marketplace/pp/B00KQY1T32/

1.9 Other Versions of R

Some other versions of R or forks exist in the open source world. They can be evaluated for enterprises for customized needs

- pqR—pqR is a new version of the R interpreter. It is based on R-2.15.0, distributed by the R Core Team (at r-project.org), but improves on it in many ways, mostly ways that speed it up, but also by implementing some new features and fixing some bugs. You can see more at https://github.com/radfordneal/pqR/wiki and http://www.pqr-project.org/
- Renjin is a new JVM-based interpreter for the R language. It is intended to be 100% compatible with the original interpreter, to run on the Google AppEngine platform, and generally to open new opportunities for embedding libraries and programs written in R. Renjin enables R developers to deploy their code to Platform-as-a-Service providers like Google App engine, Amazon Beanstalk, or Heroku without worrying about scale or infrastructure. Renjin is pure Java—it can run anywhere. You can read more at http://www.renjin.org/ and https://github.com/bedatadriven/renjin.
- Riposte, a fast interpreter and JIT for R. It can be seen at https://github.com/jtalbot/riposte but has not been updated in some time.

1.10   Cloud Specific Packages of R

Some cloud specific packages of R are given here for the convenience of the reader.

- RAmazonS3 Package that allows R programmers to interact with Amazon's S3 storage server, uploading and downloading and generally managing files. It is available at http://www.omegahat.org/RAmazonS3/
- RAmazonDBREST—This package provides an interface to Amazon's Simple DB API (http://aws.amazon.com/simpledb/). It is available at http://www. omegahat.org/RAmazonDBREST/
- AWS.tools R package to use Amazon Web Serviceshttps://github.com/armstrtw/ AWS.tools
- segue—An R Language package for parallel processing on Amazon's Web Services. Includes a parallel lapply is a function for the Elastic Map Reduce (EMR) engine https://code.google.com/p/segue/
- cloudRmpi is means for doing parallel processing in R, using MPI on a cloud-based network. It currently supports the use of Amazon's EC2 cloud computer service. cloudRmpi provides a mechanism to launch and manage a cloud-based network and to access an R session on the network's master MPI node (using the rreval package). http://norbl.com/cloudrmpi/cloudRmpi.html. However package "cloudRmpi" was removed from the CRAN repository.

However the Python Package boto offers a much more complete solution to interfacing the cloud (Amazon) but it is from the Python language. It can be seen at https://github.com/boto/boto

1.11   Examples of R and Cloud Computing

The R Web, the R Apache projects, and demonstration sites by UCLA, Dataspora, and Vanderbilt University are the well-known early implementations of cloud computing and R—though there are private implementations of R for research consulting. Dataspora is closed as of June 2011. In March 2011, Dataspora was acquired by Via Science. However you can see the original site for baseball statistics at Venderbilt University at http://data.vanderbilt.edu/rapache/bbplot/

Note this is a surprisingly good interactive visualization leveraging R on a web server, though of course in time it will be greatly superseded by the appeal of Javascript enhanced R Shiny projects.

Jeroen Ooms has done seminal work in porting R for Web Applications. An older version of his application can be seen at http://rweb.stat.ucla.edu/ggplot2/

We will be using the datasets available at UCI Machine Learning Repository(a popular website for datasets used for demonstration and teaching purposes). Downloading the dataset from https://archive.ics.uci.edu/ml/machine-learning-databases/

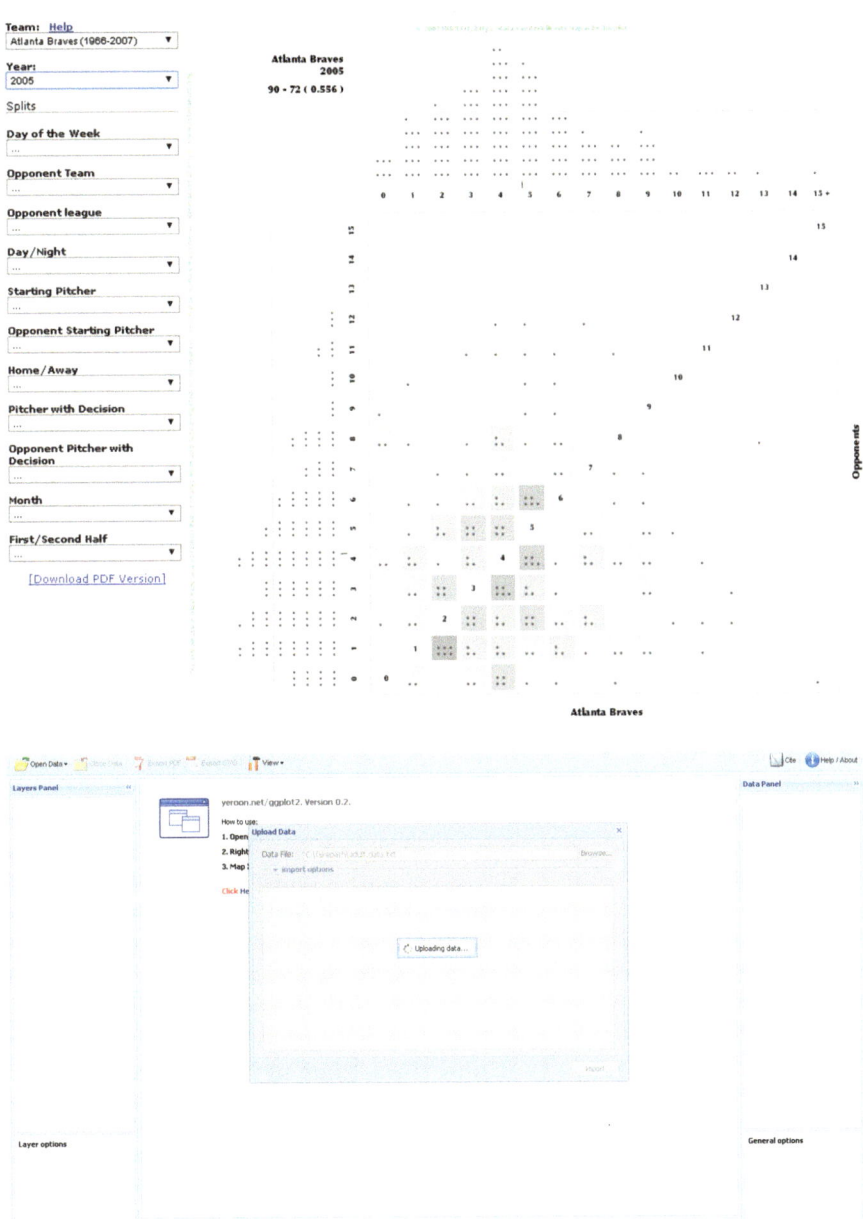

adult/adult.data we find that Jeroen's application can be used for surprisingly powerful analysis, which can be a very good replacement for BI Visualization Tools. This application is being ported currently to the OPENCPU System (which we will discuss later).

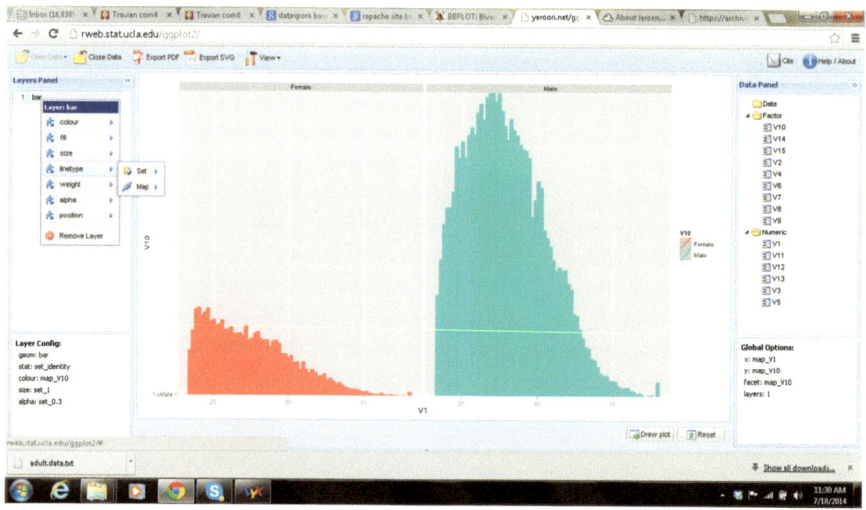

The recent addition of the Shiny package can be used for creating interactive web visualization from R. The complete list of examples can be seen at http://shiny. rstudio.com/gallery. We reproduce here one of the applications which can be used for demonstrating KMeans Clustering at http://shiny.rstudio.com/gallery/kmeans-example.html. Thus the R Shiny project is the second generation of interactive visualization projects using web servers and R continuing the work of the R Apache project which was incubated out of Venderbilt University and further enhanced by UCLA.

Other usage of R and the cloud is in conjunction with databases like SAP Hana or Oracle. IBM Netezza has a couple of packages that help in connecting R to IBM Netezza. R is integrated with such as IBM SPSS® and InfoSphere®, as well as Mathematica and you can read an article at https://www.ibm.com/developerworks/opensource/library/bd-learnr/ on how Infosphere streams can work with a R toolkit.

1.12 How Acceptable Is R and the Cloud to Enterprises?

The following interviews are meant to highlight the complete acceptance of R in enterprise software. The specific use cases are with SAP Hana and TIBCO.

1.12.1 SAP Hana with R Interview 1 (7 June 2012)

Alvaro Tejada Galindo aka Blag is a developer working with SAP Hana and R at SAP Labs, Montreal. SAP Hana is SAP's latest offering in BI, it is also a database and a computing environment, and using R and HANA together on the cloud can give major productivity gains in terms of both speed and analytical ability, as per preliminary use cases.

Ajay—Describe how you got involved with databases and R language.

Blag—I used to work as an ABAP Consultant for 11 years, but has also been involved with programming since the last 13 years, so I was in touch with SQLServer, Oracle, MySQL, and SQLite. When I joined SAP, I heard that SAP HANA was going to use a statistical programming language called "R". The next day I started my "R" learning.

Ajay—What made the R language a fit for SAP HANA? Did you consider other languages? What is your view on Julia/Python/SPSS/SAS/Matlab languages?

Blag—I think "R" is a must for SAP HANA. As the fastest database in the market, we needed a language that could help us shape the data in the best possible way. "R" filled that purpose very well. Right now, "R" is not the only language as "L" can be used as well (http://wiki.tcl.tk/17068) and not forgetting "SQLScript" which is our own version of SQL (http://goo.gl/x3bwh). I have to admit that I tried Julia, but could not manage to make it work. Regarding Python, it is an interesting question as I am going to blog about Python and SAP HANA soon. About Matlab, SPSS, and SAS I have not used them, so I got nothing to say there.

Ajay—What is your view on some of the limitations of R that can be overcome with using it with SAP HANA?

Blag—I think mostly the ability of SAP HANA to work with Big Data. Again, SAP HANA and "R" can work very nicely together and achieve things that were not possible before.

Ajay—Do you have a case study on an actual usage of R with SAP HANA that led to great results?

Blag—Right now the use of "R" and SAP HANA is very preliminary, I do not think many people have started working on it, but as an example that it works, you can check this awesome blog entry from my friend Jitender Aswani "Big Data, R and HANA: Analyze 200 Million Data Points and Later Visualize Using Google Maps" (http://allthingsr.blogspot.com/#!/2012/04/big-data-r-and-hana-analyze-200-million.html).

1.12.2   SAP Hana with R Interview 2–14 June 2012

This is Jason Kuo who worked with SAP Analytics as Group Solutions Marketing Manager. Jason answered questions on SAP Analytics and its increasing involvement with R statistical language.

Ajay—What made you choose R as the language to tie important parts of your technology platform like HANA and SAP Predictive Analysis? Did you consider other languages like Julia or Python?

Jason—It is the most popular. Over 50 % of the statisticians and data analysts use R. With 3, 500+ algorithms it is arguably the most comprehensive statistical analysis language. That said, we are not closing the door on others.

Ajay—When did you first start getting interest in R as an analytics platform?

Jason—SAP has been tracking R for 5+ years. With R's explosive growth over the last year or two, it made sense for us to dramatically increase our investment in R.

Ajay—Can we expect SAP to give back to the R community like Google and Revolution Analytics does—by sponsoring Package development or sponsoring user meets and conferences? Will we see SAP's R HANA package in this year R conference User 2012 in Nashville?

Jason—Yes. We plan to provide a specific driver for HANA tables for input of the data to native R. This was planned for the end of 2012. We will then review our event strategy. SAP has been a sponsor of Predictive Analytics World for several years and was indeed a founding sponsor. We may be attending the year R conference in Nashville.

Ajay—What has been some of the initial customer feedback to your analytics expansion and offerings?

Jason—We have completed two very successful Pilots of the R Integration for HANA with two of SAP's largest customer

You can create your SAP HANA Developer Edition in the cloud by using the instructions from http://scn.sap.com/docs/DOC-28294.

1.12.3   TIBCO TERR

An interview with Louis Bajuk-Yorgan, from TIBCO. TIBCO which was the leading commercial vendor to S Plus, the precursor of the R language makes a commercial enterprise version of R called TIBCO Enterprise Runtime for R (TERR). Louis also presented at User2014 http://user2014.stat.ucla.edu/abstracts/talks/54_Bajuk-Yorgan.pdf

DecisionStats(DS)—How is TERR different from Revolution Analytics or Oracle R? How is it similar?

Louis Bajuk-Yorgan (Lou)—TERR is unique, in that it is the only commercially developed alternative R interpreter. Unlike other vendors, who modify and extend the open source R engine, we developed TERR from the ground up, leveraging our 20+ years of experience with the closely related S-PLUS engine. Because of this, we were able to architect TERR to be faster, more scalable, and handle memory much more efficiently than the open source R engine. Other vendors are constrained by the limitations of the open source R engine, especially around memory management. Another important difference is that TERR can be licensed to customers and partners for tight integration into their software, which delivers a better experience for their customers. Other vendors typically integrate loosely with open source R, keeping R at arms length to protect their IP from the risk of contamination by R's GPL license. They often force customers to download, install, and configure R separately, making for a much more difficult customer experience. Finally, TIBCO provides full support for the TERR engine, giving large enterprise customers the confidence to use it in their production environments. TERR is integrated in several TIBCO products, including Spotfire and Streambase, enabling customers to take models developed in TERR and quickly integrate them into BI and real-time applications.

DS—How much of R is TERR compatible with?

Lou—We regularly test TERR with a wide variety of R packages and extend TERR to greater R coverage over time. We are currently compatible with ~1800 CRAN packages, as well as many bioconductor packages. The full list of compatible CRAN packages is available at the TERR Community site at tibcommunity.com.

DS—Describe Tibco Cloud Compute Grid? What are its applications for data science?

Lou—Tibco Cloud Compute Grid leverages the Tibco Gridserver architecture, which has been used by major Wall Street firms to run massively parallel applications across tens of thousands of individual nodes. TIBCO CCG brings this robust platform to the cloud, enabling anyone to run massively parallel jobs on their Amazon EC2 account. The platform is ideal for Big Computation types of jobs, such as Monte Carlo simulation and risk calculations. More information can be found at the TIBCO Cloud Marketplace at https://marketplace.cloud.tibco.com/.

DS—What advantages does TIBCO's rich history with the S project give it for the R project?

Lou—Our 20+ years of experience with S-PLUS gave us a unique knowledge of the commercial applications of the S/R language, deep experience with architecting, extending and maintaining a commercial S language engine, strong ties to the R community, and a rich trove of algorithms we could apply on developing the TERR engine.

DS—Describe some benchmarks of TERR with open source of R.

Lou—While the speed of individual operations will vary, overall TERR is roughly 2–10x faster than open source R when applied to small data sets, but 10–100x faster when applied to larger data sets. This is because TERR's efficient memory management enables it to handle larger data more reliably, and stay more linear in performance as data sizes increase TERR.

DS—TERR is not open source. Why is that?

Lou—While open sourcing TERR is an option we continue to consider, we have decided to initially focus our energy and time on building the best S/R language engine possible. Running a successful, vibrant open source project is a significant undertaking to do well, and if we choose to do so, we will invest accordingly. Instead, for now we have decided to make a Developer Edition of TERR freely available, so that the R community at large could still benefit from our work on TERR. The Developer Edition is available at tap.tibco.com.

DS—How is TIBCO giving back to the R Community globally? What are its plans on community?

Lou—As mentioned above, we make a free Developers Edition of TERR available. In addition, we have been sponsors of UseR for several years, we contribute feedback to the R Core team as we develop TERR, and we often open source packages that we develop for TERR so that they can be used with open source R as well. This has included packages ported from S-PLUS (such as sjdbc) and new packages (such as tibbrConnector).

DS—As a sixth time attendee of UseR, describe the evolution of R ecosystem as you have observed it?

Lou—It has been fascinating to see how the R community has grown and evolved over the years. The useR conference at UCLA this year was the largest ever (700+ attendees), with more commercial sponsors than ever before (including enterprise heavyweights like TIBCO, Teradata, and Oracle, smaller analytic vendors like RStudio, Revolution and Alteryx, and new companies like plot.ly). What really struck me, however, was the nature of the attendees. There were far more attendees from commercial companies this year, many of whom were R users. More so than in the past, there were many people who simply wanted to learn about R.

1.13   What Is the Extent of Data that Should Be on Cloud Versus Local Machines?

Moore's law is the observation that, over the history of computing hardware, the number of transistors in a dense integrated circuit doubles approximately every two years. The law is named after Gordon E. Moore, co-founder of Intel Corporation and is credited with the still declining prices and increasing power of local computing.

Unlike cloud providers who advise you to move ALL your data to the cloud, this book and its author will advise a guided, optimized, and heterogeneous approach for cloud computing. This is because even cloud providers do have outages (though much less than your local computing) and are prone to security issues as well as regulatory issues (especially related to data on European Union citizens). While cloud providers have tried to overcome this by providing servers across the globe, the recent revelations that internet software providers are forced to share data with governments in secret legal orders, reduces the move to full-fledged cloud computing as the only option for businesses and corporations globally. Thus the transition from the desktop is toward heterogeneous computing including a mix of onsite compute and remote computing and not just pure cloud computing. In addition Moore's law and the continuous decline in hardware prices mean that your local laptop and desktop are more powerful than a server was a decade ago.

1.14 Alternatives to R

1. R for SAS and SPSS Users—A free document is available at https://science. nature.nps.gov/im/datamgmt/statistics/R/documents/R_for_SAS_SPSS_users. pdf while the best resource for this is a book by Bob Muenchen at http://www. springer.com/statistics/computational+statistics/book/978-1-4614-0684-6
2. A presentation at http://www.cytel.com/pdfs/CC02.pdf argues that R graphics are better than in SAS but can be used from within SAS System software.
3. An alternative book is SAS and R: Data Management, Statistical Analysis, and Graphics http://www.amazon.com/gp/product/1420070576.
4. Python—pandas is an open source, BSD-licensed library providing high-performance, easy-to-use data structures, and data analysis tools for the Python programming language (http://pandas.pydata.org/). Scikit-learn library offers Machine Learning in Python http://scikit-learn.org/stable/.
5. Julia is a new language. It provides a sophisticated compiler, distributed parallel execution, numerical accuracy, and an extensive mathematical function library. The library, largely written in Julia itself, also integrates mature, best-of-breed C and Fortran libraries for linear algebra, random number generation, signal processing, and string processing.(http://julialang.org/).
6. IJulia is a Julia-language back-end combined with the IPython interactive environment. This combination allows you to interact with the Julia language using IPython's powerful graphical notebook, which combines code, formatted text, math, and multimedia in a single document (https://github.com/JuliaLang/IJulia.jl).
7. Clojure—Clojure is a dynamic programming language that targets the Java Virtual Machine (and the CLR and JavaScript). It is designed to be a general-purpose language, combining the approachability and interactive development of a scripting language with an efficient and robust infrastructure for multithreaded programming. Clojure is a compiled language—it compiles directly to JVM bytecode, yet remains completely dynamic. Every feature supported by Clojure is supported at runtime (http://clojure.org/).
8. Scala—Scala is an acronym for "Scalable Language". It is available at http://www.scala-lang.org/. You can also test it out in the browser at http://www.simplyscala.com/.

An interview with a BigML.com employee shows how clojure can be an alternative to R at least on the JVM. This is a partial extract from an interview with Charlie Parker, head of large scale online algorithms at http://bigml.com.

Ajay—You use clojure for the back end of BigML.com. Are there any other languages and packages you are considering? What makes clojure such a good fit for cloud computing?

Charlie—Clojure is a great language because it offers you all of the benefits of Java (extensive libraries, cross-platform compatibility, easy integration with things like Hadoop, etc.) but has the syntactical elegance of a functional language. This makes our code base small and easy to read as well as powerful.

We have had occasional issues with speed, but that just means writing the occasional function or library in Java. As we build towards processing data at the Terabyte level, we are hoping to create a framework that is language-agnostic to some extent. So if we have some great machine learning code in C, for example, we will use Clojure to tie everything together, but the code that does the heavy lifting will still be in C. For the API and Web layers, we use Python and Django, and Justin is a huge fan of HaXe for our visualizations.

1.15   Interview of Prof Jan De Leeuw, Founder of JSS

Here is a partial extract of a July 2014 Interview with one of the greatest statisticians and educator of this generation, Prof Jan de Leeuw.

DecisionStats(DS) Describe your work with Gifi software and nonlinear multivariate analysis.

Jan De Leeuw(JDL)—I started working on NLMVA and MDS in 1968, while I was a graduate student researcher in the new Department of Data Theory. Joe Kruskal and Doug Carroll invited me to spend a year at Bells Labs in Murray Hill in 1973–1974. At that time I also started working with Forrest Young and his student Yoshio Takane. This led to the sequence of "alternating least squares" papers, mainly in Psychometrika. After I returned to Leiden we set up a group of young researchers, supported by NWO (the Dutch equivalent of the NSF) and by SPSS, to develop a series of Fortran programs for NLMVA and MDS. In 1980 the group had grown to about 10–15 people, and we gave a successful postgraduate course on the "Gifi methods", which eventually became the 1990 Gifi book. By the time I left Leiden most people in the group had gone on to do other things, although I continued to work in the area with some graduate students from Leiden and Los Angeles. Then around 2010 I worked with Patrick Mair, visiting scholar at UCLA, to produce the R packages smacof, anacor, homals, aspect, and isotone.

DS—You have presided over almost 5 decades of changes in statistics. Can you describe the effect of changes in computing and statistical languages over the years, and some learning from these changes?

JDL—I started in 1968 with PL/I. Card decks had to be flown to Paris to be compiled and executed on the IBM/360 mainframes. Around the same time APL came up and satisfied my personal development needs, although of course APL code was difficult to communicate. It was even difficult to understand your own code after a week. We had APL symbol balls on the Selectrix typewriters and APL symbols on the character terminals. The basic model was there as you develop in an interpreted language (APL) and then for production you use a compiled language (FORTRAN). Over the years APL was replaced by XLISP and then by R. Fortran was largely replaced by C, and I never switched to C + + or Java. We discouraged our students to use SAS or SPSS or MATLAB. UCLA Statistics promoted XLISP-STAT for quite a long time, but eventually we had to give it up. See http://www.stat.ucla.edu/~deleeuw/janspubs/2005/articles/deleeuw_A_05.pdf.

(In 1998 the UCLA Department of Statistics, which had been one of the major users of Lisp-Stat, and one of the main producers of Lisp-Stat code, decided to switch to S/R. This paper discusses why this decision was made, and what the pros and the cons were.) Of course the WWW came up in the early nineties and we used a lot of CGI and PHP to write instructional software for browsers.

Generally, there has never been a computational environment like R so integrated with statistical practice and development, and so enormous, accessible, and democratic. I must admit I personally still prefer to use R as originally intended: as a convenient wrapper around and command line interface for compiled libraries and code. But it is also great for rapid prototyping, and in that role it has changed the face of statistics. The fact that you cannot really propose statistical computations without providing R references and in many cases R code has contributed a great deal to reproducibility and open access.

DS—Does Big Data and Cloud Computing, in the era of data deluge require a new focus on creativity in statistics or just better application in industry of statistical computing over naive models?

JDL—I am not really active in Big Data and Cloud Computing, mostly because I am more of a developer than a data analyst. That is of course a luxury. The data deluge has been there for a long time (sensors in the road surface, satellites, weather stations, air pollution monitors, EEG's, MRI's) but until fairly recently there were no tools, both in hardware and software, to attack these data sets. Of course Big Data sets have changed the face of statistics once again, because in the context of Big Data the emphasis on optimality and precise models becomes laughable. What I see in the area is a lot of computer science, a lot of fads, a lot of ad-hoc work, and not much of a general rational approach. That may be unavoidable.

DS—How can we make the departments of Statistics and departments of Computer Science work closely for better industry relevant syllabus especially in data mining, business analytics, and statistical computing?

JDL—That is hard. The cultures are very different as CS is so much more aggressive and self-assured, as well as having more powerful tools and better trained students. We have tried joint appointments but they do not work very well. There are some interdisciplinary programs but generally CS dominates and provides the basic keywords such as neural nets, machine learning, data mining, cloud computing, and so on. One problem is that in many universities statistics is the department that teaches the introductory statistics courses, and not much more. Statistics is forever struggling to define itself, to fight silly battles about foundations, and to try to control the centrifugal forces that do statistics outside statistics departments.

Chapter 2
An Approach for Data Scientists

What is a data scientist? A data scientist is one who had inter-disciplinary skills in both programming, statistics, and business domains to create actionable insights based on experiments or summaries from data. One of the most famous definitions is from Drew Conway.

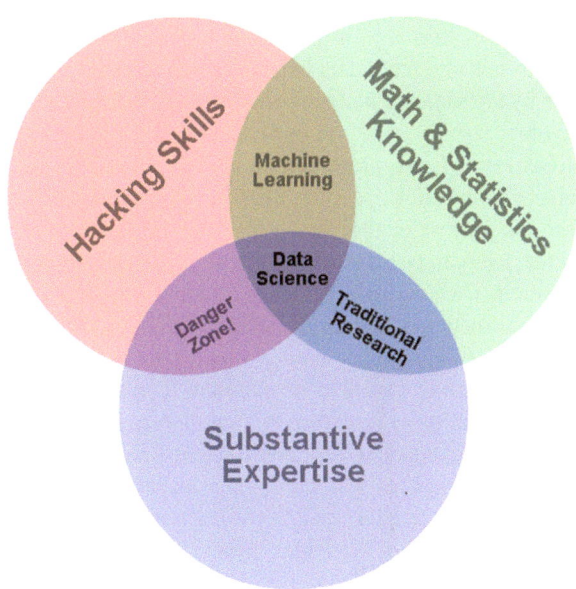

© Springer Science+Business Media New York 2014
A Ohri, *R for Cloud Computing*, DOI 10.1007/978-1-4939-1702-0_2

On a daily basis, a data scientist is simply a person

- who can write some code
  - in one or more of the languages of R, Python, Java, SQL, Hadoop (Pig, HQL, MR)
- for
  - data storage, querying, summarization, visualization efficiently, and in time
- on
  - databases, on cloud, servers, and understand enough statistics to derive insights from data so business can make decisions

What should a data scientist know? He should know how to get data, store it, query it, manage it, and turn it into actionable insights. The following approach elaborates on this simple and sequential premise.

2.1 Where to Get Data?

A data scientist needs data to do science on, right! Some of the usual sources of data for a data scientist are:

APIs—API is an acronym for Application Programming Interface. We cover APIs in detail in Chap. 7. APIs is how the current Big Data paradigm is enabled, as it enables machines to talk and fetch data from each other programmatically. For a list of articles written by the same author on APIs—see https://www.programmableweb.com/profile/ajayohri.

Internet Clickstream Logs—Internet clickstream logs refer to the data generated by humans when they click specific links within a webpage. This datum is time stamped, and the uniqueness of the person clicking the link can be established by IP address. IP addresses can be parsed by registries like https://www.arin.net/whois or http://www.apnic.net/whois for examining location (country and city), internet service provider, and owner of the address (for website owners this can be done using the website http://who.is/). In Windows using the command ipconfig and in Linux systems using ifconfig can help us examine IP Address. You can read this for learning more on IP addresses http://en.wikipedia.org/wiki/IP_address. Software like Clicky from (http://getclicky.com) and Google Analytics(www.google.com/analytics) also helps us give data which can then be parsed using their APIs. (See https://code.google.com/p/r-google-analytics/ for Google Analytics using R).

Machine Generated Data—Machines generate a lot of data especially for sensors to ensure that the machine is working properly. This datum can be logged and can be used with events like cracks or failures to have predictive asset maintenance of M2M (Machine to Machine) Analytics.

Surveys—Surveys are mostly questionnaires filled by humans. They used to be administered manually over paper, but online surveys are now the definitive trend. Surveys reveal valuable data about current preferences of current and potential customers. They do suffer from the bias inherent from design of questions by the creator. Since customer preferences evolve surveys help in getting primary data about current preferences. Coupled with stratified random sampling, they can be a powerful method for collecting data. SurveyMonkey is one such company that helps create online questionnaires (https://www.surveymonkey.com/pricing/).

Commercial Databases—Commercial Databases are proprietary databases that have been collected over time and are sold/rented by vendors. They can be used for prospect calling, appending information to existing database, and refining internal database quality.

Credit Bureaus—Credit bureaus collect financial information about people, and this information is then available for marketing organizations (subject to legal and privacy guidelines). The cost of such information is balanced by the added information about customers.

Social Media—Social media is a relatively new source of data and offers powerful insights albeit through a lot of unstructured data. Companies like Datasift offer social media data, and companies like Salesforce/Radian6 offer social media tools (http://www.salesforcemarketingcloud.com/). Facebook has 829 million daily active users on average in June 2014 with 1.32 billion monthly active users. Twitter has 255 million monthly active users and 500 million Tweets are sent per day. That generates a lot of data about what current and potential customers are thinking and writing about your products.

2.2 Where to Process Data?

Now you have the data. We need computers to process it.

- Local Machine—Benefits of storing the data in local machine are ease of access. The potential risks include machine outages, data recovery, data theft (especially for laptops) and limited scalability. A local machine is also much more expensive in terms of processing and storage and gets obsolete within a relatively short period of time.
- Server—Servers respond to requests across networks. They can be thought of as centralized resources that help cut down cost of processing and storage. They can be an intermediate solution between local machines and clouds, though they have huge capital expenditure upfront. Not all data that can fit on a laptop should be stored on a laptop. You can store data in virtual machines on your server and connected through thin shell clients with secure access.
- Cloud—The cloud can be thought of a highly scalable, metered service that allows requests from remote networks. They can be thought of as a large bank of servers but that is a simplistic definition. The more comprehensive definition is given in Chapter 1.

This chapter and in fact this book holds that the cloud approach benefits data scientists the most because it is cheap, secure, and easily scalable. The only hindrance to adoption to the cloud is conflict within existing IT department whose members are not trained to transition and maintain the network over cloud as they used to do for enterprise networks.

2.2.1   Cloud Processing

We expand on the cloud processing part.

- **Amazon** EC2—Amazon Elastic Compute Cloud (Amazon EC2) provides scalable processing power in the cloud. It has a web-based management console, has a command line tool, and offers resources for Linux and Windows virtual images. Further details are available at http://aws.amazon.com/ec2/. Amazon EC2 is generally considered the industry leader. For beginners a 12-month basic preview is available for free at http://aws.amazon.com/free/ that can allow practitioners to build up familiarity.
- **Google** Compute—https://cloud.google.com/products/compute-engine/
- **Microsoft** Azure—https://azure.microsoft.com/en-us/pricing/details/virtual-machines/ Azure Virtual Machines enable you to deploy a Windows Server, Linux, or third-party software images to Azure. You can select images from a gallery or bring your own customized images. Charge for Virtual Machines is by the minute. Discounts can range from 205 to 32 % depending if you prepay 6 months or 12 month plans and based on usage tier.
- **IBM** shut down its SmartCloud Enterprise cloud computing platform by Jan. 31, 2014 and will migrate those customers to its SoftLayer cloud computing platform, which was an IBM acquired company https://www.softlayer.com/virtual-servers
- **Oracle** Oracle's plans for the cloud are still in preview for enterprise customers as of July 2014. https://cloud.oracle.com/compute

2.3   Where to Store Data?

We need to store data in a secure and reliable environment for speedy and repeated access. There is a cost of storing this data, and there is a cost of losing the data due to some technical accident.

You can store data in the following way

- csv files, spreadsheet, and text files locally especially for smaller files. Note while this increases ease of access, it also creates problems of version control as well as security of confidential data.
- relational databases (RDBMS) and data warehouses

- hadoop based storage
- noSQL databases—These are the next generation of databases. They are non-relational, distributed, open-source, and horizontally scalable. A complete list of NoSQL databases is at http://nosql-database.org/. Notable NoSQL databases are MongoDB, couchDB, etc.

  - key-value store—Key-value stores use the map or dictionary as their fundamental data model. In this model, data is represented as a collection of key-value pairs, such that each possible key appears at most once in the collection.

    · Redis—Redis is an open source, BSD licensed, advanced key-value store. It is often referred to as a data structure server since keys can contain strings, hashes, lists, sets, and sorted sets (http://redis.io/). Redis cloud is a fully managed cloud service for hosting and running your redis dataset (http://redislabs.com/redis-cloud). rredis: An R package for the Redis persistent key-value database available from http://redis.io.http://cran.r-project.org/web/packages/rredis/index.html
    · Riak is an open source, distributed database. http://basho.com/riak/. Riak CS (Cloud Storage) is simple, open source storage software built on top of Riak. It can be used to build public or private clouds
    · MemcacheDB is a persistence enabled variant of memcached, a general-purpose distributed memory caching system often used to speed up dynamic database-driven websites by caching data and objects in memory. The main difference between MemcacheDB and memcached is that MemcacheDB has its own key-value database system based on Berkeley DB, so it is meant for persistent storage rather than as a cache solution

- column oriented databases
- cloud storage

2.3.1   Cloud Storage

- Amazon—Amazon Simple Storage Services (S3)—Amazon S3 provides a simple web-services interface that can be used to store and retrieve any amount of data, at any time, from anywhere on the web. http://aws.amazon.com/s3/. Cost is a maximum of 3 cents per GB per month. There are three types of storage: Standard Storage, Reduced Redundancy Storage, Glacier Storage. Reduced Redundancy Storage (RRS) is a storage option within Amazon S3 that enables customers to reduce their costs by storing non-critical, reproducible data at lower levels of redundancy than Amazon S3 standard storage. Amazon Glacier stores data for as little as $0.01 per gigabyte per month and is optimized for data that is infrequently accessed and for which retrieval times of 3 to 5 hours are suitable. These details can be seen at http://aws.amazon.com/s3/pricing/

- Google—Google Cloud Storage https://cloud.google.com/products/cloud-storage/. It also has two kinds of storage. Durable Reduced Availability Storage enables you to store data at lower cost, with the tradeoff of lower availability than standard Google Cloud Storage. Prices are 2.6 cents for Standard Storage (GB/Month) and 2 cents for Durable Reduced Availability (DRA) Storage (GB/Month). They can be seen at https://developers.google.com/storage/pricing#storage-pricing.
- Azure—Microsoft has different terminology for its cloud infrastructure. Storage is classified into three types with a fourth type (Files) being available as a preview. There are three levels of redundancy: Locally Redundant Storage (LRS),Geographically Redundant Storage (GRS), Read-Access Geographically Redundant Storage (RA-GRS): You can see details and prices at https://azure.microsoft.com/en-us/pricing/details/storage/.
- Oracle Storage is available at https://cloud.oracle.com/storage and costs around 30$ / TB per month.

2.3.2   Databases on the Cloud

- Amazon

    - Amazon RDS—Managed MySQL, Oracle, and SQL Server databases. http://aws.amazon.com/rds/. While relational database engines provide robust features and functionality, scaling a workload beyond a single relational database instance is highly complex and requires significant time and expertise.
    - DynamoDB—Managed NoSQL database service. http://aws.amazon.com/dynamodb/. Amazon DynamoDB focuses on providing seamless scalability and fast, predictable performance. It runs on solid state disks (SSDs) for low-latency response times, and there are no limits on the request capacity or storage size for a given table. This is because Amazon DynamoDB automatically partitions your data and workload over a sufficient number of servers to meet the scale requirements you provide.
    - Redshift—It is a managed, petabyte-scale data warehouse service that makes it simple and cost-effective to efficiently analyse all your data using your existing business intelligence tools. You can start small for just $0.25 per hour and scale to a petabyte or more for $1,000 per terabyte per year. http://aws.amazon.com/redshift/.
    - SimpleDB—It is highly available and flexible non-relational data store that offloads the work of database administration. Developers simply store and query data items via web services requests http://aws.amazon.com/simpledb/. A table in Amazon SimpleDB has a strict storage limitation of 10 GB and is limited in the request capacity it can achieve (typically under 25 writes/second); it is up to you to manage the partitioning and re-partitioning of

your data over additional SimpleDB tables if you need additional scale. While SimpleDB has scaling limitations, it may be a good fit for smaller workloads that require query flexibility. Amazon SimpleDB automatically indexes all item attributes and thus supports query flexibility at the cost of performance and scale.

- Google

  - Google Cloud SQL—Relational Databases in Google's Cloud https:// developers.google.com/cloud-sql/
  - Google Cloud Datastore—Managed NoSQL Data Storage Service https:// developers.google.com/datastore/
  - Google Big Query—Enables you to write queries on huge datasets. BigQuery uses a columnar data structure, which means that for a given query, you are only charged for data processed in each column, not the entire table https:// cloud.google.com/products/bigquery/.

- Databases—This is expanded more in Chap. 6

  - RDBMS
  - Document DBs
  - Monet DB
  - Graph Databases

- How to query data?

  - SQL—we can use SQL within R using the sqldf package.
  - Pig
  - Hive QL

- Prepackaged R packages or Python Libraries that do the job:

  - AWS.tools: R package to use Amazon Web Services (http://cran.r-project.org/ web/packages/AWS.tools/index.html)
  - The bigrquery provides a read-only interface to Google BigQuery. It makes it easy to retrieve metadata about your projects, datasets, tables and jobs, and provides a convenient wrapper for working with bigquery from R. (https:// github.com/hadley/bigrquery)

2.4 Basic Statistics for Data Scientists

Some of the basic statistics that every data scientist should know are given here. This assumes rudimentary basic knowledge of statistics (like measures of central tendency or variation) and basic familiarity with some of the terminology used by statisticians.

- Random Sampling—In truly random sampling, the sample should be representative of the entire data. Random sampling remains of relevance in the era of Big Data and Cloud Computing
- Distributions—A data scientist should know the distributions (normal, Poisson, Chi Square, F) and also how to determine the distribution of data.
- Hypothesis Testing—Hypothesis testing is meant for testing assumptions statistically regarding values of central tendency (mean, median) or variation. A good example of an easy-to-use software for statistical testing is the "test" tab in the Rattle GUI.
- Outliers—Checking for outliers is a good way for a data scientist to see anomalies as well as identify data quality. The box plot (exploratory data analysis) and the outlierTest function from car package (Bonferroni Outlier Test) are how statistical rigor can be maintained to outlier detection.

2.5 Basic Techniques for Data Scientists

Some of the basic techniques that a data scientist must know are listed as follows:

- Text Mining—In text mining, text data are analysed for frequencies, associations, and correlation for predictive purposes. The tm package from R greatly helps with text mining.
- Sentiment Analysis—In sentiment analysis the text data are classified based on a sentiment lexicography (e.g., which says happy is less positive than delighted but more positive than sad) to create sentiment scores of the text data mined.
- Social Network Analysis—In social network analysis, the direction of relationships, the quantum of messages, and the study of nodes, edges, and graphs is done to give insights.
- Time Series Forecasting—Data is said to be auto regressive with regards to time if a future value is dependent on a current value for a variable. Techniques such as ARIMA and exponential smoothing and R packages like forecast greatly assist in time series forecasting.
- Web Analytics
- Social Media Analytics

2.6 How to Store Output?

Congratulations, you are done with your project! How do we share it so that both code and documentation are readable and reproducible. While the traditional output was a powerpoint, a spreadsheet, or a word document, some of the newer forms of output are.

- Markdown—a minimalistic form of HTML.
- You can read the cheat sheet on Markdown at http://shiny.rstudio.com/articles/rm-cheatsheet.html

  - HTML 5—see the slidify package
  - Latex—see sweave (for typesetting)

2.7 How to Share Results and Promote Yourself?

Data scientists are known when they publish their results internally and externally of their organization with adequate data hygiene safeguards. Some of the places on the internet to share your code or results are:

- github

  - Rpubs
  - meetups
  - twitter
  - blogs and linkedin

2.8 How to Move or Query Data?

We use utilities like wget, winscp, or curl to move massive amounts of data.

2.8.1 Data Transportation on the Cloud

This typically referred to as Network Costs or Ingress/Egress costs for data, and these can be critical components for costing when large amounts of data are being transferred. While traditional approach was ETL for data warehouses, we can simplify the data transportation costs on the cloud, extract, transform, and load

ETL(extract, transform, and load) refers to a process in database usage and especially in data warehousing that: extracts data from outside sources, transforms it to fit operational needs, which can include quality levels, loads it into the end target (database, more specifically, operational data store, data mart, or data warehouse). We will cover more on databases in Chap. 6.

2.9   How to Analyse Data?

The concept of Garbage In, Garbage Out (GiGo) stems from the fact that computers can only produce output that is dependent on quality of input. So data quality is an important factor for the production of quality analysis. The concept of tidy data further helps us in gauging and refining data quality.

2.9.1   Data Quality—Tidy Data

The most common problems with messy datasets

1. column headers are values, not variable names
2. multiple variables are stored in one column
3. variables are stored in both rows and columns
4. multiple types of observational units are stored in the same table
5. a single observational unit is stored in multiple tables

In tidy data:

1. Each variable forms a column.
2. Each observation forms a row.
3. Each type of observational unit forms a table.

For more on tidy data, refer to the paper by Hadley Wickham in "References" section of this chapter. In addition a new package called tidyr has been introduced.

You can read about this new package at http://blog.rstudio.org/2014/07/22/ introducing-tidyr/

tidyr is new package that makes it easy to "tidy" your data. Tidy data is data that is easy to work with: it is easy to munge (with dplyr), visualize (with ggplot2 or ggvis), and model (with R's hundreds of modeling packages).

tidyr provides three main functions for tidying your messy data: gather(), separate() and spread().

- gather() takes multiple columns, and gathers them into key-value pairs: it makes "wide" data longer.
- Sometimes two variables are clumped together in one column. separate() allows you to tease them apart

2.9.2   Data Quality—Treatment

The following treatments are done on data to improve quality.

1) **Missing Value Treatment** deals with missing and incomplete data. This is usually done by deletion, imputation by (mean, median, or correlation) or creation of a categorical value (missing value flag) which indicates whether value was missing or not.
2) **Outlier Treatment** deals with extreme values of data, usually by capping the maximum and creating a minimum. For example age of adults may be capped at 20 years minimum, and 80 years maximum and any values below 20 may be imputed to be rounded off to 20, and any data indicating age above 80 may be capped at 80.

2.9.3 Data Quality—Transformation

The following transformations can help in creating new variables that make more coherent sense than doing analysis on original data. If the input data is X, the transformed value can be X^2 (square), $X^{0.5}$ (Square Root), $\log(X)$, $\exp(X)$, and $1/X$ (inverse).

2.9.4 Split Apply Combine

In the split-apply-combine strategy you split the data into smaller number of parts, you apply a function to it, then you combine these parts together. It is computationally easier than applying the function to the whole data at once. The R package plyr is based on this and greatly helps with simplifying data structures. For more on split apply combine see the *Journal of Statistical Software* paper in the "References" part of this chapter.

2.10 How to Manipulate Data?

We need to bring data into the desired shape, dimension so as to analyse and represent it.

Some of the standard ways of manipulating data are:

- Grouping
- Selecting
- Conditional Selecting
- Transforming
- Slicing and Dicing Data

The book Data Manipulation with R by Phil Spector deals more with this topic. http://www.springer.com/mathematics/probability/book/978-0-387-74730-9. You can also see the R Tutorial in Chap. 5 for basic data manipulation.

2.10.1   Data Visualization

Data visualization is a new branch of descriptive statistics. Some of the points to remember in this topic are:

Grammar of Graphics was a book written by Leland Wilkinson and implemented in R by Dr Hadley Wickham for the ggplot2 package. The ggplot2 package gives considerable aesthetic lift over native graphics in R. Basically a graph is considered a mix of axis, plot type, statistical transformation, and data.

Types of Graphs—The following graph shows the basic types of graphs. Most data scientists are expected to know basic as well as advanced graphs. A good guide is available at http://www.statmethods.net/graphs/.

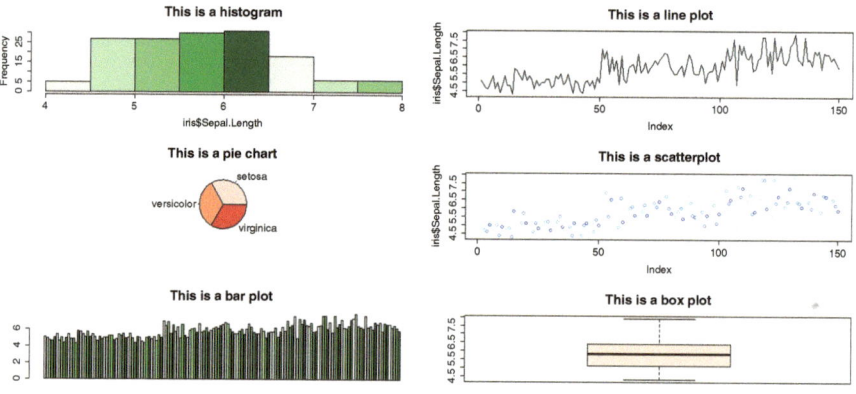

2.11   Project Methodologies

Knowledge discovery in databases (KDD) is the process of (semi-)automatic extraction of knowledge from databases which is valid, previously unknown, and potentially useful. Project methodologies help to break down complex projects into manageable chunks. The three most commonly used methodologies are:

- DMAIC—This is expanded as Define, Measure, Analyse, Improve and Control and is part of the six sigma methodology for sustained quality improvement. Define the problem needs to be solved, measure the capability of the process, analyse when and where do defects occur, improve process capability by

reducing the process variation and looking at the vital factors, and lastly by putting in place controls to sustain the gains.
- SEMMA—This stands for Sample, Explore, Modify, Model, and Assess. It was developed by the SAS Institute and is considered a logical and sequential methodology for carrying out data mining.
- CRIPS-DM—Cross Industry Standard Process for Data Mining was created by ESPRIT from European Union. Its constituents and methodology can be shown as follows.

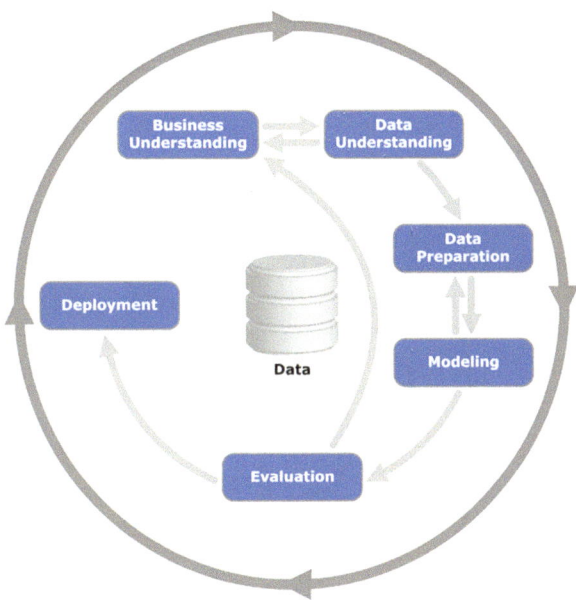

2.12 Algorithms for Data Science

An **algorithm** is simply a step by step procedure for calculations. It is thus a procedure or formula for solving a problem. Some of the most widely used algorithms by data scientists are

- **Kmeans (Clustering)**—An illustration is shown below.

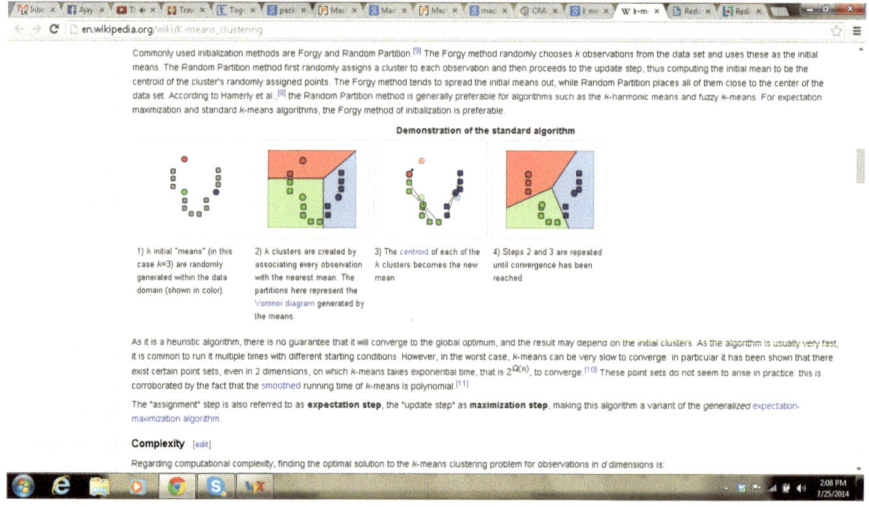

Commonly used initialization methods are Forgy and Random Partition.[9] The Forgy method randomly chooses k observations from the data set and uses these as the initial means. The Random Partition method first randomly assigns a cluster to each observation and then proceeds to the update step, thus computing the initial mean to be the centroid of the cluster's randomly assigned points. The Forgy method tends to spread the initial means out, while Random Partition places all of them close to the center of the data set. According to Hamerly et al.,[9] the Random Partition method is generally preferable for algorithms such as the k-harmonic means and fuzzy k-means. For expectation maximization and standard k-means algorithms, the Forgy method of initialization is preferable.

Demonstration of the standard algorithm

1) k initial "means" (in this case k=3) are randomly generated within the data domain (shown in color).

2) k clusters are created by associating every observation with the nearest mean. The partitions here represent the Voronoi diagram generated by the means.

3) The centroid of each of the k clusters becomes the new mean.

4) Steps 2 and 3 are repeated until convergence has been reached.

As it is a heuristic algorithm, there is no guarantee that it will converge to the global optimum, and the result may depend on the initial clusters. As the algorithm is usually very fast, it is common to run it multiple times with different starting conditions. However, in the worst case, k-means can be very slow to converge: in particular it has been shown that there exist certain point sets, even in 2 dimensions, on which k-means takes exponential time, that is $2^{\Omega(n)}$, to converge.[10] These point sets do not seem to arise in practice: this is corroborated by the fact that the smoothed running time of k-means is polynomial.[11]

The "assignment" step is also referred to as **expectation step**, the "update step" as **maximization step**, making this algorithm a variant of the generalized expectation-maximization algorithm.

Complexity [edit]

Regarding computational complexity, finding the optimal solution to the k-means clustering problem for observations in d dimensions is:

- **Ordinary Least Squares (Regression)**—This method minimizes the sum of squared-vertical distances between the observed responses in the dataset and the responses predicted by the linear approximation.
- **Apriori Algorithm** is used in Association Rules and Market Basket Analysis to find which combination of transactions appears most frequently together over a minimum threshold support. A good example and demonstration is given in the "References" part of this chapter.
- **K Nearest Neighbours**—An object is classified by a majority vote of its neighbours, with the object being assigned to the class most common among its k nearest neighbours (k is a positive integer, typically small). If k = 1, then the object is simply assigned to the class of that single nearest neighbour.
- **Support Vector Machines**—An SVM model is a representation of the examples as points in space, mapped so that the examples of the separate categories are divided by a clear gap that is as wide as possible. New examples are then mapped into that same space and predicted to belong to a category based on which side of the gap they fall on.
- **Naive Bayes** classifier—Bayes theorem says The probability P(A|B) of "A assuming B" is given by the formula P(A|B) = P(AB) / P(B). A naive Bayes classifier assumes that the value of a particular feature is unrelated to the presence or absence of any other feature, given the class variable. For example, a fruit may be considered to be an apple if it is red, round, and about 3″ in diameter.
- **Neural Nets**—These were inspired by how nature and human brain works. An example system has three layers. The first layer has input neurons which send data via synapses to the second layer of neurons, and then via more synapses to

the third layer of output neurons. More complex systems will have more layers of neurons with some having increased layers of input neurons and output neurons. The synapses store parameters called "weights" that manipulate the data in the calculations.

For a more exhaustive list see http://en.wikibooks.org/wiki/Data_Mining_Algorithms_In_R. It has the following chapters and algorithms covered.

- **Dimensionality Reduction**—Principal Component Analysis, Singular Value Decomposition, Feature Selection
- **Frequent Pattern Mining**—The Eclat Algorithm, arulesNBMiner, The Apriori Algorithm, The FP-Growth Algorithm
- **Sequence Mining**—SPADE, DEGSeq
- **Clustering**—K-Means, Hybrid Hierarchical Clustering, Expectation Maximization (EM),Dissimilarity Matrix Calculation,Hierarchical Clustering,Bayesian Hierarchical Clustering,Density-Based Clustering, K-Cores, Fuzzy Clustering— Fuzzy C-means, RockCluster, Biclust, Partitioning Around Medoids (PAM), CLUES,Self-Organizing Maps (SOM), Proximus,CLARA
- **Classification**—SVM, penalizedSVM,kNN, Outliers, Decision Trees, Naive Bayes, adaboost, JRip
- **R Packages**—RWeka, gausspred, optimsimplex, CCMtools, FactoMineR, nnet

Machine Learning is defined as the science of getting computers to act without being explicitly programmed A complete list is defined at http://en.wikipedia.org/wiki/List_of_machine_learning_algorithms.

It has the following constituents:

- **Supervised learning**—Statistical classification
- **Unsupervised learning**—Artificial neural network, Association rule learning, Hierarchical clustering, Cluster analysis, Outlier Detection
- **Reinforcement learning**
- **Deep learning**

A nice book for understanding machine learning in R is Machine Learning in R (Packt Publishing). The Machine Learning View in R (http://cran.r-project.org/web/views/MachineLearning.html) has a great collection of all R packages dealing with Machine Learning.

In R, rattle is a package and GUI that allows the user to use a lot of algorithms with comparative ease. It has cluster analysis, regression models, classification models, SVM, neural nets, random forests, decision trees, and association analysis, all done using a few clicks and with very good documentation and lucid examples.

2.13 Interview of John Myles White, co-author of Machine Learning for Hackers

A partial extract from an interview of John Myles White, co-author of Machine Learning for Hackers.

Ajay—How can academia and private sector solve the shortage of trained data scientists (assuming there is one)?

John—There is definitely a shortage of trained data scientists: most companies are finding it difficult to hire someone with the real chops needed to do useful work with Big Data. The skill set required to be useful at a company like Facebook or Twitter is much more advanced than many people realize, so I think it will be some time until there are undergraduates coming out with the right stuff. But there is a huge demand, so I am sure the market will clear sooner or later.

The changes that are required in academia to prepare students for this kind of work are pretty numerous, but the most obvious required change is that quantitative people need to be learning how to program properly, which is rare in academia, even in many CS departments. Writing one-off programs that no one will ever have to reuse and that only work on toy data sets does not prepare you for working with huge amounts of messy data that exhibit shifting patterns. If you need to learn how to program seriously before you can do useful work, you are not very valuable to companies who need employees that can hit the ground running. The companies that have done best in building up data teams, like LinkedIn, have learned to train people as they come in since the proper training is not typically available outside those companies. Of course, on the flipside, the people who do know how to program well need to start learning more about theory and need to start to have a better grasp of basic mathematical models like linear and logistic regressions. Lots of CS students seem not to enjoy their theory classes, but theory really does prepare you for thinking about what you can learn from data. You may not use automata theory if you work at Foursquare, but you will need to be able to reason carefully and analytically. Doing math is just like lifting weights: if you are not good at it right now, you just need to dig in and get yourself in shape.

About—John Myles White is a Phd Student in Ph.D. student in the Princeton Psychology Department, where he studies human decision-making both theoretically and experimentally. Along with the political scientist Drew Conway, he is the author of a book published by OReilly Media entitled Machine Learning for Hackers, which is meant to introduce experienced programmers to the machine learning toolkit.

Chapter 3
Navigating the Choices in R and Cloud Computing

3.1 Which Version of R to Use?

You should always use the latest version of R unless it breaks one of your packages that is needed for critical usage. In that case you are advised to both write to package maintainer as well as keep multiple versions of R. Some other versions of R are pqR Renjin and Riposte but they are not as mature right now. To help you keep your software updated, consider the installr package (covered later in this chapter)

We also show you two other forks of R or non-mainstream versions of R. Maybe they suit your needs or you can contribute to them!

3.1.1 *Renjin*

Upcoming is a project called Renjin. Renjin is a new implementation of the R language and environment for the Java Virtual Machine (JVM), whose goal is to enable transparent analysis of Big Data sets and seamless integration with other enterprise systems such as databases and application servers. See the demo at http://renjindemo.appspot.com/. However, Renjin is not yet production ready.

3.1.2 *pqR*

pqR is a new version of the R interpreter. It is based on R-2.15.0, distributed by the R Core Team (at r-project.org), but improves on it in many ways, mostly ways that speed it up, but also by implementing some new features and fixing some bugs.

One notable improvement is that pqR is able to do some numeric computations in parallel with each other, and with other operations of the interpreter, on systems with multiple processors or processor cores. It is created by Radford Neal (http://www.

© Springer Science+Business Media New York 2014

A Ohri, *R for Cloud Computing*, DOI 10.1007/978-1-4939-1702-0_3

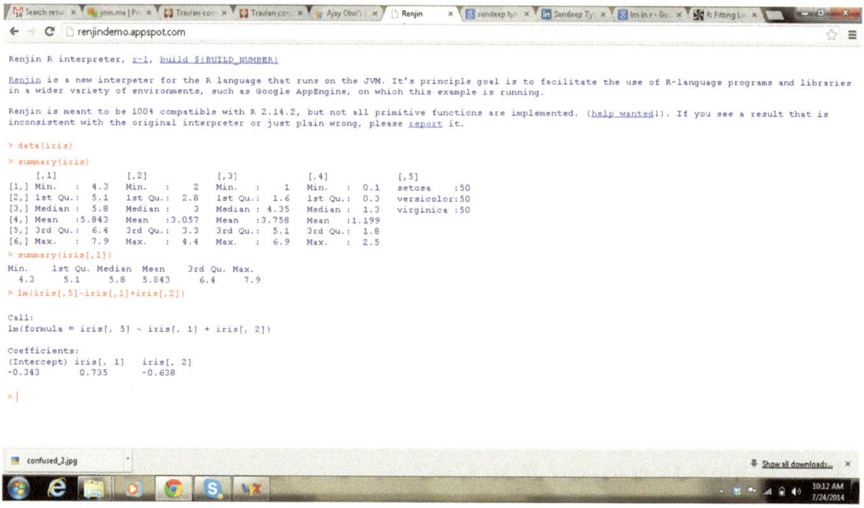

cs.utoronto.ca/~radford/homepage.html) and is available at http://www.pqr-project.
org/

In addition to this there is the Riposte project (see Riposte: a trace-driven
compiler and parallel VM for vector code in R http://dl.acm.org/citation.cfm?id=
2370825). However, the github repository has not been updated in a year

3.2 Which Interface of R to Use

http://rforanalytics.wordpress.com/useful-links-for-r/code-enhancers-for-r/

- Integrated Development Environment (IDE)

  - RStudio—One of the most popular IDEs used by developers in the R
    community, and it makes developing R code extremely easy and professional.
  - Eclipse with statet http://www.walware.de/goto/statet StatET is an Eclipse
    based IDE (integrated development environment) for R. It offers a set of
    mature tools for R coding and package building. This includes a fully
    integrated R Console, Object Browser, and R Help System, whereas multiple
    local and remote installations of R are supported. StatET is provided as plug-in
    for the Eclipse IDE.
  - Revolution Analytics—Revolution R Enterprise DevelopR (earlier R Produc-
    tivity Environment) created by Revolution Analytics is a sturdy enterprise
    grade software environment. A notable innovation is the use of code snippets
    to help write code. A partial screenshot is shown here showing the snippets
    facility.

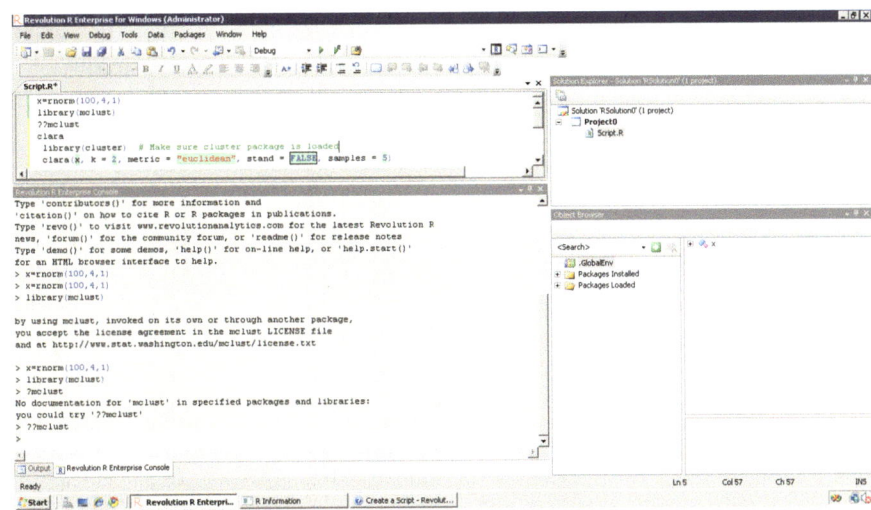

- Console—This is the default interface.
- GUIs

  - Rattle—Rattle is a GUI focused at data mining. We cover an example of Rattle in Chap. 5.
  - R Commander—This is one of the most widely used GUIs in R project. It is excellent for beginners. In addition it has a huge number of plug-ins that extend its capability. Notable plug-ins are epack (for time series) and kmggplot2 (for enhanced data visualization).

  - Deducer—Deducer is a GUI focused at data visualization. We cover an example of Deducer in Chap. 5.

- Online Versions of R-

  - Statace
  - R Fiddle
  - OpenCPU

- Commercial Versions

  - Revolution R
  - Oracle R
  - Tibco R

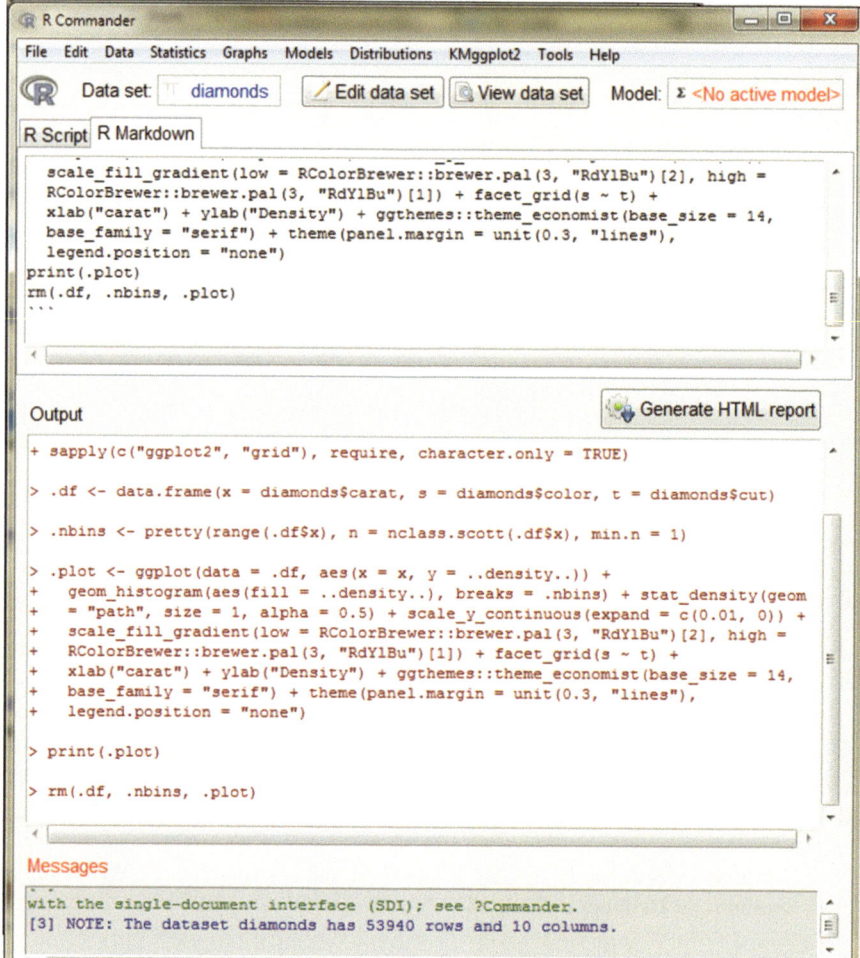

3.3   Using R from the Browser

3.3.1   Statace

Statace is a web-based platform that empowers data scientists to collaborate with each other and build graphical self-service applications for people with no knowledge of statistics. Each application is automatically available through an API for easy integration with existing systems.

is an extract from an interview with its CEO, Christian Mladenov.

Ajay Ohri (AO)—What is the difference between using R by StatAce and using R by RStudio on a R Studio server hosted on Amazon EC2?

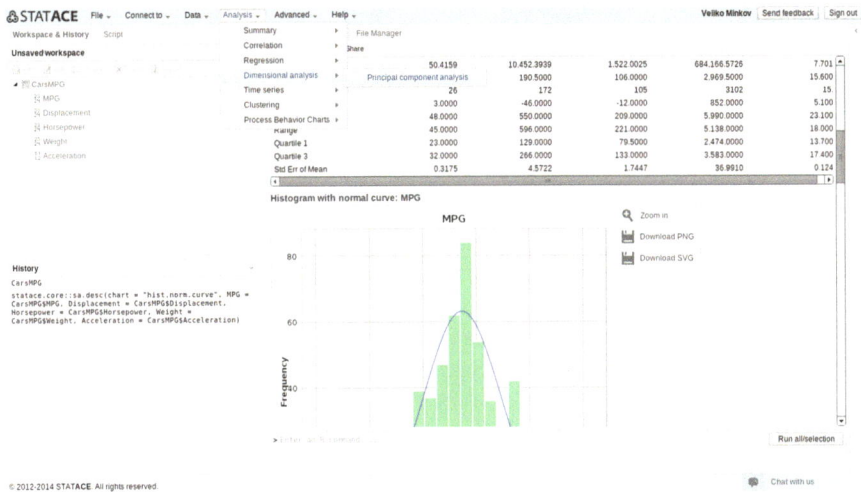

Christian Mladenov (CM)—There are a few ways in which I think StatAce is better:

You do not need the technical skills to set up a server. You can instead start straight away at the click of a button.

You can save the full results for later reference. With an RStudio server you need to manually save and organize the text output and the graphics.

We are aiming to develop a visual interface for all the standard stuff. Then you will not need to know R at all.

We are developing features for collaboration, so that you can access and track changes to data, scripts, and results in a team. With an RStudio server, you manage commits yourself, and Git is not suitable for large data files.

AO—How do you aim to differentiate yourself from other providers of R based software including Revolution, RStudio, Rapporter, and even Oracle R Enterprise?

CM—We aim to build a scalable, collaborative and easy to use environment. Pretty much everything else in the R ecosystem is lacking one, if not two of these. Most of the GUIs lack a visual way of doing the standard analyses. The ones that have it (e.g., Deducer) have a rather poor usability. Collaboration tools are hardly built in. RStudio has Git integration, but you need to set it up yourself, and you cannot really track large source data in Git.

Revolution Analytics have great technology, but you need to know R and you need to know how to maintain servers for large scale work. It is not very collaborative and can become quite expensive.

Rapporter is great for generating reports, but it is not very interactive—editing templates is a bit cumbersome if you just need to run a few commands. I think it wants to be the place to go to after you have finalized the development of the R code, so that you can share it. Right now, I also do not see the scalability.

With Oracle R Enterprise you again need to know R. It is targeted at large enterprises and I imagine it is quite expensive, considering it only works with Oracle's database. For that you need an IT team. Screenshot from 2013-11-18 21:31:08

AO—How do you see the space for using R on a cloud?

CM—I think this is an area that has not received enough quality attention—there are some great efforts (e.g. ElasticR), but they are targeted at experienced R users. I see a few factors that facilitate the migration to the cloud:

Statisticians collaborate more and more, which means they need to have a place to share data, scripts, and results.

The number of devices people use is increasing, and now frequently includes a tablet. Having things accessible through the web gives more freedom.

More and more data lives on servers. This is both because it is generated there (e.g., click streams) and because it is too big to fit on a user's PC (e.g., raw DNA data). Using it where it already is prevents slow download/upload.

Centralizing data, scripts, and results improves compliance (everybody knows where it is), reproducibility, and reliability (it is easily backed up).

For me, having R to the cloud is a great opportunity.

AO—What are some of the key technical challenges you currently face and are seeking to solve for R based cloud solutions?

CM—Our main challenge is CPU use, since cloud servers typically have multiple slow cores and R is mostly single-threaded. We have yet to fully address that and are actively following the projects that aim to improve R's interpreter— pqR, Renjin, Riposte, etc. One option is to move to bare metal servers, but then we will lose a lot of flexibility.

Another challenge is multi-server processing. This is also an area of progress where we do not yet have a stable solution.

3.3.2   R Fiddle

R Fiddle is another project that enables people to start using R from within the browser. Here is a partial extract from an interview with Dr Jonathan Cornelissen, CEO of Datamind which also makes RDocumentation and R-fiddle.

Ajay—Congrats for making on the first page of hacker news with R-Fiddle. What were your motivations for making http://www.r-fiddle.org/?

Jonathan—Thank you. I must admit it was very exciting to be mentioned on Hacker News, since a lot of people were exposed to the R-fiddle project immediately. In addition, it was a first good test on how our servers would perform.

The motivation for building R-fiddle was simple; our CTO Dieter frequently uses the popular sitehttp://jsfiddle.net/ to prototype webpages, and to share his coding ideas with us. We were looking for something similar for R but it turned out a website allowing you to quickly write, run, and share R-code right inside your browser that did not exist yet. Since we were convinced a fiddle-like tool for R

would be useful, we just started building it. Based on the positive reactions and the fast adoption of R-fiddle, I think we were right. That being said, this is a first version of R-fiddle, and we will definitely improve it over the coming months. Check out our blog for updates. (http://blog.datamind.org/)

Ajay—Why did you make http://www.rdocumentation.org/ given that there is so much #Rstats documentation all around the internet including http://www. inside-r.org/?

Jonathan—When we started working on the www.datamind.org platform, we did an online survey to find out whether there would be interest in an interactive learning platform for R and statistics. Although the survey was not on this topic, one of the most striking findings was that a large percentage of R users apparently is frustrated about the documentation of R and its packages. This is interesting since it not only frustrates current users, but it also increases the barrier to entry for new R users and hence puts a brake on the growth and adoption of R as a language. It is mainly for the latter reason we started building Rdocumentation. The whole focus is on usability and letting all users contribute to make the documentation stronger. By the end of next week, we will launch a new version of Rdocumentation, that introduces advanced search functionality for all R functions, shows the popularity of R packages and much more. So make sure to www.Rdocumentation.org for updates.

Ajay—What have been your responses to http://www.datamind.org/#/. Any potential content creation partners or even corporate partners like statistics.com, Revolution, RStudio, Mango etc.

Jonathan—The response to the beta version of DataMind has been great, thousands of learners signed up and took the demo course. We are talking to some of the leading companies in the space and some very well-known professors to develop courses together. It is too soon to disclose details, but we will put regular updates on www.datamind.org. Corporates interested in what we do should definitely get in contact with Martijn@datamind.org.

Ajay—Would it be accurate to call http://www.r-fiddle.org/#/ a browser based GUI for R on the cloud? What enhancements can we expect in the future?

Jonathan—R-fiddle is indeed a browser based GUI for R on the cloud. We have a lot of ideas to improve and extend it. Some of the ideas are: the ability for users to concurrently make changes to a fiddle (Google-docs-style), support for loading data sets, github integration, better security management, lists of popular fiddles, or fiddles from popular people, etc. However, the strong point about R-fiddle is that it is really simple and there is absolutely no friction to start using it. In that respect, we want to differentiate R-fiddle from more advanced solutions such as StatAce or Rstudio Server, which focus on more advanced R users or R usage.

Ajay—You described your architecture for datamind.org at http://blog.datamind.org/ which is very open and transparent of you. What is the architecture for http://www.r-fiddle.org/#/ and what is it based out of?

Jonathan—That is an easy one. Although some details differ obviously, from a high-level perspectiveDataMind.org and R-fiddle.org have exactly the same IT architecture.

Ajay—http://www.datamind.org/#/dashboard describes course creation. How many courses are in the pipeline and how many users and corporate training clients do you foresee in the next 12 months?

Jonathan—Since we launched DataMind, we were inundated by requests from teachers and industry experts eager to contribute their own coursework on the site. But up until last week, it was only possible to take courses instead of creating them yourself. We decided to change this since we do not want to be solely a content company, but also a platform for others to create courses.

Furthermore, by expanding DataMind with a content creation tool, we go beyond our naturally limited in-house ability to create courses. Now DataMind is ready to become a full on ecosystem to facilitate education between our users.

Ajay—What do you think of R in the cloud for teaching (http://blog.datamind.org/2013/07/23/how-to-run-r-in-the-cloud-for-teaching/) ?

Jonathan—We are convinced that cloud solutions are the future of teaching and learning in general. The main problem with the first wave of online education solutions (such as Coursera, EdX, Udacity, etc.) is that they "only" make a copy of the classroom online instead of leveraging technology to create a more engaging and efficient learning experience and interface. Therefore, I do not think the future is in generic learning solutions. Learning interfaces will differ from domain to domain.

Good examples are: Duolingo.com to learn languages, or Codeschool.com to learn web development. We are on a mission to build the best learning solutions for statistics and data science.

Ajay—What are some of the other ways we can help make R more popular on the cloud?

Jonathan—I really like the vision behind StatAce.com, and I think something like it will definitely increase further adoption of R. It is somewhat surprising that Rstudio is not offering something like that, but my assumption is they are working on it. That being said, what would be really cool is a very easy-to-use graphical user interface with R under the hood. Whether you like it or not, R has quite a steep learning curve for most people, and allowing them to analyse data with R through a graphical user interface on the web as a first step could start the adoption of R in less technical areas.

3.3.3 RShiny and RStudio

Shiny is a web application framework for R that helps turn analytics into interactive web apps (without HTML, CSS, or JavaScript knowledge). It is available at http://shiny.rstudio.com/. An example of an application from its gallery is below.

Here is an interview with Jeff Allen who works with R and the new package Shiny in his technology startup. His RShiny application can be seen at http://trestletechnology.net:3838/grn/.

Ajay—Describe how you started using R. What are some of the benefits you noticed on moving to R?

Jeff—I began using R in an internship while working on my undergraduate degree. I was provided with some unformatted R code and asked to modularize the code and then wrap it up into an R package for distribution alongside a publication.

To be honest, as a Computer Science student with training more heavily emphasizing the big high-level languages, R took some getting used to for me. It was not until after I concluded that initial project and began using R to do my own data analysis that I began to realize its potential and value. It was the first scripting language which really made interactive use appealing to me—the experience of exploring a dataset in R was unlike anything I would been taught in my University courses.

Upon gaining familiarity with the syntax and basics of the language, I began to see the immense value in the vast array of R packages which had already been created and made publicly available. I found repeatedly that many of the "niche" functions I would been coding myself in more traditional languages had already been developed and shared freely on CRAN or Bioconductor.

Ajay—Describe your work in computational biology using R

Jeff—I work in the Quantitative Biomedical Research Center (QBRC) at UT Southwestern Medical Center. My group is involved in analysing and mining massive biological datasets, much of which is now coming from different sequencing

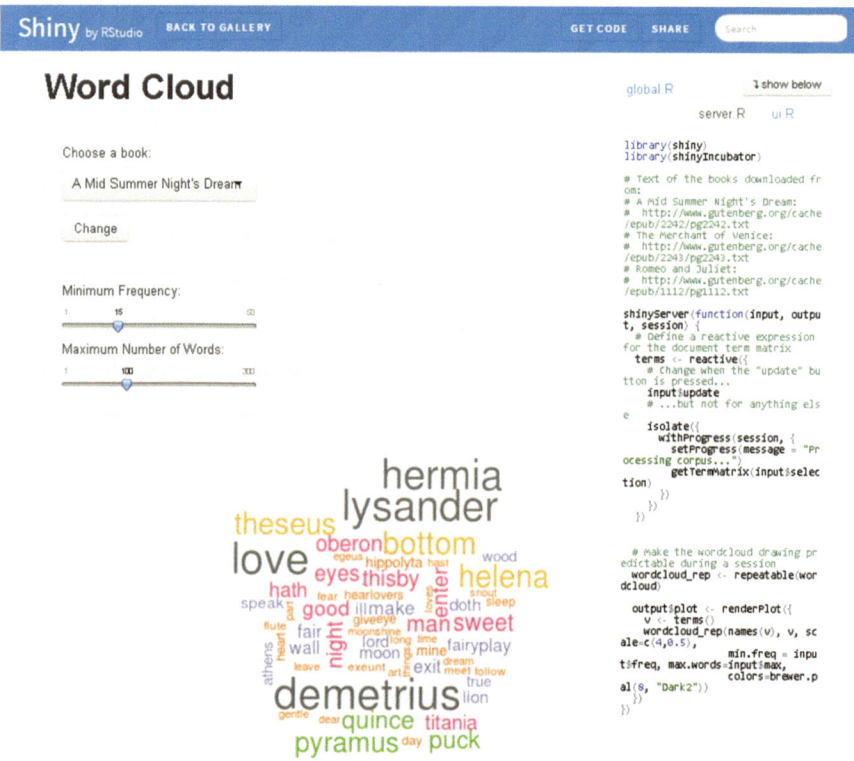

technologies (DNA-seq, RNA-seq, etc.) which generate many Gigabytes of data with each experiment. Unfortunately, due to the sheer volume of that data, R is often unfit for the initial analysis and pre-processing of the data. However, once the data has been processed and reduced, we use R to identify statistically and (hopefully) biologically interesting trends or anomalies.

Personally, most of my research lately has focused on reconstructing the interactions between genes based on the patterns and behaviours we can observe. Thankfully, most of the data we work with here fits in memory, so I use R almost exclusively when doing analysis in this area. My most recent work was in "Ensemble Network Aggregation" (ENA), the package of which is now available in CRAN.

Ajay—Describe your work in web applications using R

Jeff—I was initially tasked with developing software packages which encapsulated the new statistical methodologies being developed within the group (which, at the time, were largely focused on microarray data). I continued developing R packages and began investigating how I might be able to integrate my prior experience with web development into these projects. We ended up developing a handful of different web applications which typically required that we use R to precompute any data which ultimately made its way (statically) into the application.

Reconstruct Gene Networks

File URL:

/sampleExp.csv

Unfortunately, Shiny isn't playing nicely with file uploads at the time of writing, so I've disabled the custom file uploads temporarily. However, you can post your expression file online using any one of the free file hosting sites now available and provide the URL here to process it in this app!

You can also download the sample dataset here.

One row represents a single:

Sample ▾

Method to use to reconstruct the network:

GeneNet ▾

Connection threshold:

0   0.15

Use the slider to set the number of connections which will be displayed in the graph. Higher, more stringent thresholds will include fewer connections, while lower thresholds will display more connections

More recently, we have been developing sites which take advantage of dynamic or real-time R analysis, such as our upcoming release of the Lung Cancer Explorer—a tool which allows for the interactive exploration of lung cancer data within a browser. We went to great lengths to develop the IT and software infrastructure that would allow us to interact with R remotely for these applications.

I have been taking some time on the side to play with RStudio's new Shiny application which, like most everything else that group has put out, represents a massive leap forward in this space. We have already begun looking at how we can supplement or replace some of our in-house systems with Shiny to start taking advantage of some of its capabilities.

Ajay—What is Trestle Technology focused on?

Jeff—I initially was doing a lot of web development, and helping small-medium businesses integrate and automate various software systems. Once R got added to my resume, however, I started finding more interesting work helping start-ups get their IT and analytics infrastructures off the ground.

My hope is to continue living at the intersection of data and software development and grow this company in that space. It is quite difficult to find groups doing good analysis and proper software development under one roof—especially in Academia. I thoroughly enjoy the process of enriching data analysis tools with more comprehensive, user-friendly interfaces which allow for more efficient exploration of the underlying datasets.

Ajay—Compare R and Python, What are some of the ways you think R can be further improved?

Jeff—I must confess that I am a fairly late-comer to the Python world. I had tinkered with Perl and Python a few years back and ended up feeling more comfortable with Perl for my needs at that point, so I have used it for most of my scripting. Only recently have I started revisiting Python and getting introduced to some of the neat tools available. To me, Python offers a more intuitive Object-Orienting framework than either Perl or R provides, which helps me stay more organized as my "scripts" inevitably grow into "software".

Aside from OO, I still feel there is much room for improvement in R's "Big Data" capabilities. The community has certainly been making huge strides in bypassing memory limitations (with packages like ff) and speeding up the code (with code compilation, etc). Nonetheless, I find that my motivation in leaving R for any part of my data analysis is typically motivated by performance concerns and a desire to avoid having to nest any C++ code in my R scripts (though the recent improvements in the Rcpp and devtools packages are making that a much less painful process).

About—

Jeffrey D Allen is a computational biologist at UT Southwestern Medical Center at Dallas.

To know more on the Shiny package and use it for interactive visualization please refer to the cheat sheet at http://shiny.rstudio.com/articles/cheatsheet.html.

3.4   The Cloud Computing Services Landscape

There are 3 main players in the infrastructure provider space for cloud computing world for data sciences. They are:

1. Amazon AWS
2. Microsoft Azure
3. Google Compute Cloud

Others are Oracle Java Cloud and IBM Softlayer

The easiest way to convince someone to start using R on the cloud remains using the Amazon Web Services with Windows Operating System and using a Remote Desktop Player to connect, and then use a graphical user interface (GUI) package of R like Deducer (data visualization), R Commander, or Rattle (Data Mining). This is the opinion of the author and it is based on his impression of the relative penetration of Linux in the world of business analytics as well as some of the issues that transitioning to Linux does on users. It is recommended that the user change one thing at a time, from hardware (PC or Cloud), operating system (Windows or Linux), and analytics software (R versus prior software). However the best option for a potential data science centre of excellence is to use Linux on the cloud albeit with the R Studio Server to make the transition easier.

3.4.1   *Choosing Infrastructure Providers*

When it comes to choosing Infrastructure as a service, we can choose using the following options:

Cloud Provider	Strengths	Weakness
Amazon AWS (EC2)	Widest Range of Instances and Regions, Great Documentation	Loss of control
Microsoft Azure	Best Interface Design	Comparatively Expensive
Google Cloud (Compute Engine)	Secure, Cheap for Technically Advanced Users	No Windows Instances

If we do not want to use the cloud for our entire analytical needs, we can use it for computationally intensive things like running simulations or scoring models. This is where software that is offered as a service can help us. Note both Amazon, Microsoft, and Google offer more than just the cloud infrastructure as a service. It is quite useful to look at the complementary services that a cloud infrastructure provider provides, and choose based on suitability.

3.4.1.1   Amazon Cloud

There are many kinds of instances in Amazon at http://aws.amazon.com/ec2/instance-types/. To remove confusion we have represented this in a mildly modified table.

	vCPU	ECU	RAM(GiB)	Storage (GB)	$ per Hour	Type -Linux Usage	Provider
t2.micro	1	Variable	1	EBS Only	$0.01	General Purpose - Current Generation	Amazon (North Virginia)
t2.small	1	Variable	2	EBS Only	$0.03	General Purpose - Current Generation	Amazon (North Virginia)
t2.medium	2	Variable	4	EBS Only	$0.05	General Purpose - Current Generation	Amazon (North Virginia)
m3.medium	1	3	3.75	1 x 4 SSD	$0.07	General Purpose - Current Generation	Amazon (North Virginia)
m3.large	2	6.5	7.5	1 x 32 SSD	$0.14	General Purpose - Current Generation	Amazon (North Virginia)
m3.xlarge	4	13	15	2 x 40 SSD	$0.28	General Purpose - Current Generation	Amazon (North Virginia)
m3.2xlarge	8	26	30	2 x 80 SSD	$0.56	General Purpose - Current Generation	Amazon (North Virginia)
c3.large	2	7	3.75	2 x 16 SSD	$0.11	Compute Optimized - Current Generation	Amazon (North Virginia)
c3.xlarge	4	14	7.5	2 x 40 SSD	$0.21	Compute Optimized - Current Generation	Amazon (North Virginia)
c3.2xlarge	8	28	15	2 x 80 SSD	$0.42	Compute Optimized - Current Generation	Amazon (North Virginia)
c3.4xlarge	16	55	30	2 x 160 SSD	$0.84	Compute Optimized - Current Generation	Amazon (North Virginia)
c3.8xlarge	32	108	60	2 x 320 SSD	$1.68	Compute Optimized - Current Generation	Amazon (North Virginia)
g2.2xlarge	8	26	15	60 SSD	$0.65	GPU Instances - Current Generation	Amazon (North Virginia)
r3.large	2	6.5	15	1 x 32 SSD	$0.18	Memory Optimized - Current Generation	Amazon (North Virginia)
r3.xlarge	4	13	30.5	1 x 80 SSD	$0.35	Memory Optimized - Current Generation	Amazon (North Virginia)
r3.2xlarge	8	26	61	1 x 160 SSD	$0.70	Memory Optimized - Current Generation	Amazon (North Virginia)
r3.4xlarge	16	52	122	1 x 320 SSD	$1.40	Memory Optimized - Current Generation	Amazon (North Virginia)
r3.8xlarge	32	104	244	2 x 320 SSD	$2.80	Memory Optimized - Current Generation	Amazon (North Virginia)
i2.xlarge	4	14	30.5	1 x 800 SSD	$0.85	Storage Optimized - Current Generation	Amazon (North Virginia)
i2.2xlarge	8	27	61	2 x 800 SSD	$1.71	Storage Optimized - Current Generation	Amazon (North Virginia)
i2.4xlarge	16	53	122	4 x 800 SSD	$3.41	Storage Optimized - Current Generation	Amazon (North Virginia)
i2.8xlarge	32	104	244	8 x 800 SSD	$6.82	Storage Optimized - Current Generation	Amazon (North Virginia)
hs1.8xlarge	16	35	117	24 x 2048	$4.60	Storage Optimized - Current Generation	Amazon (North Virginia)

AWS Terminology:

- Instances—AMIs—An instance is like a virtual computer dedicated to you running remotely. Think of it as a combination of hardware choices (like how much RAM) and operating system choices (Windows, Red Hat Linux, or Ubuntu Linux). Each instance has a unique id called AMAZON INSTANCE ID.
- Elastic Block Storage (EBS)—Volumes—A volume is like a hard disk, or ROM Storage. Once you terminate an instance everything on the volume would be deleted. You can however stop and restart an EBS backed Instance
- Elastic Block Storage—Snapshots—Snapshots are like stored or saved volumes for further reference.
- Network and Security—Security Groups—Security groups are used for giving access to certain Ports, to certain access types (SSH, or HTTP, or HTTPS, or RDP). We will discuss these in further detail later.
- Network and Security—Elastic IPs—You can choose to refer to your amazon instance by its IP Address, by attaching an Elastic IP. This is free if attached to a running instance, but costs a small sum if reserved without a running instance. Once you release a certain IP address, it goes back to the pool of available IP addresses for Elastic IP on AWS.
- Amazon has s3 storage (http://aws.amazon.com/s3/) and glacier storage (http://aws.amazon.com/glacier/)

Storage Pricing

Region: US Standard			
	Standard Storage	**Reduced Redundancy Storage**	**Glacier Storage**
First 1 TB / month	$0.095 per GB	$0.076 per GB	$0.010 per GB
Next 49 TB / month	$0.080 per GB	$0.064 per GB	$0.010 per GB
Next 450 TB / month	$0.070 per GB	$0.056 per GB	$0.010 per GB
Next 500 TB / month	$0.065 per GB	$0.052 per GB	$0.010 per GB
Next 4000 TB / month	$0.060 per GB	$0.048 per GB	$0.010 per GB
Over 5000 TB / month	$0.055 per GB	$0.037 per GB	$0.010 per GB

Request Pricing

3.4.1.2   Other Components of Amazon Cloud

Amazon Simple Storage deals with data storage. The vast offerings by Amazon can be summed up in this webpage http://aws.amazon.com/products/.

3.4.1.3 Google Cloud Services

A lucid infographic from https://cloud.google.com/developers/articles/storage-overview helps you understand various components of Google 's cloud offerings.

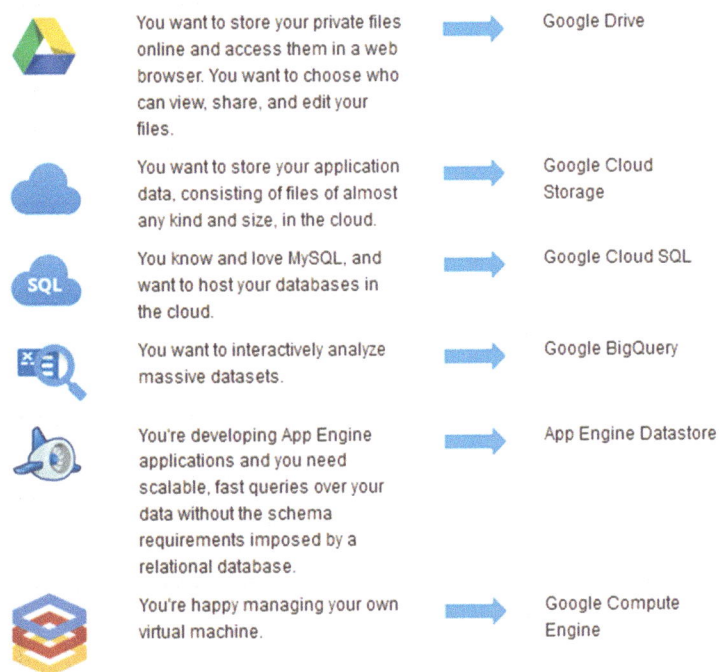

At a glance, here are the options for storing and analyzing your data in Google's Cloud Platform:

You want to store your private files online and access them in a web browser. You want to choose who can view, share, and edit your files. → Google Drive

You want to store your application data, consisting of files of almost any kind and size, in the cloud. → Google Cloud Storage

You know and love MySQL, and want to host your databases in the cloud. → Google Cloud SQL

You want to interactively analyze massive datasets. → Google BigQuery

You're developing App Engine applications and you need scalable, fast queries over your data without the schema requirements imposed by a relational database. → App Engine Datastore

You're happy managing your own virtual machine. → Google Compute Engine

This can be seen at https://cloud.google.com/. It has the following components.

1. Application Platforms

   a. Google App Engine—Used for building web applications, mobile applications, gaming, as well as websites. You can see your existing Google Cloud Projects at https://cloud.google.com/console.

2. Computing Infrastructure

   a. Google Compute Engine—This is primary cloud infrastructure offering by Google. It was in limited preview at the time of writing this book, though the author is grateful to the team for the free access. However it is likely to change based on competition as well as feedback from users once it comes out of preview. One notable disadvantage is that the Windows operating system is completely ignored by Google Compute Engine. The pricing of Google

Compute Engine remains one of the most cost effective—as this chart shows for pricing dated 27 February 2013. Note that prices of cloud instances change after every few months, usually becoming cheaper.

				Standard	
Instance type	**Virtual Cores**	**Memory**	**Local disk**	**Price (US$)/Hour (US hosted)**	**Price (US$)/Hour (Europe hosted)**
n1-standard-1-d	1	3.75GB *	420GB *	$0.14	$0.15
n1-standard-2-d	2	7.5GB	870GB	$0.28	$0.30
n1-standard-4-d	4	15GB	1770GB	$0.55	$0.60
n1-standard-8-d	8	30GB	2 x 1770GB	$1.10	$1.21
n1-standard-1	1	3.75GB	Diskless (0 GB) **	$0.12	$0.13
n1-standard-2	2	7.5GB	Diskless (0 GB)	$0.24	$0.26
n1-standard-4	4	15GB	Diskless (0 GB)	$0.48	$0.53
n1-standard-8	8	30GB	Diskless (0 GB)	$0.96	$1.06

High Memory Machines for tasks that require more memory relative to virtual cores					
n1-highmem-2-d	2	13GB	870GB	$0.32	$0.36
n1-highmem-4-d	4	26GB	1770GB	$0.64	$0.72
n1-highmem-8-d	8	52GB	2 x 1770GB	$1.27	$1.43
n1-highmem-2	2	13GB	Diskless (0 GB) **	$0.25	$0.29
n1-highmem-4	4	26GB	Diskless (0 GB)	$0.51	$0.57
n1-highmem-8	8	52GB	Diskless (0 GB)	$1.02	$1.14

High CPU Machines for tasks that require more virtual cores relative to memory					
n1-highcpu-2-d	2	1.80GB	870GB	$0.17	$0.19
n1-highcpu-4-d	4	3.60GB	1770GB	$0.34	$0.38
n1-highcpu-8-d	8	7.20GB	2 x 1770GB	$0.68	$0.77
n1-highcpu-2	2	1.80GB	Diskless (0 GB) **	$0.14	$0.15
n1-highcpu-4	4	3.60GB	Diskless (0 GB)	$0.27	$0.30
n1-highcpu-8	8	7.20GB	Diskless (0 GB)	$0.54	$0.61
			* 1GB is defined as 2^30 bytes	** diskless includes boot disk	

Google Cloud Storage is available at https://cloud.google.com/pricing/cloud-storage. It has two types of pricing including durable reduced availability storage and standard storage. It is Google's offering for cloud storage, but is different from the file storage offered by Google Drive. Durable Reduced Availability Storage enables you to store data at lower cost, with the tradeoff of lower availability than standard Google Cloud Storage.

Storage Pricing (per GB per month)*

Monthly Usage	Standard Storage	Durable Reduced Availability Storage
First 0-1 TB	$0.085	$0.063
Next 9TB	$0.076	$0.054
Next 90TB	$0.067	$0.049
Next 400TB	$0.063	$0.045
Next 4500TB	$0.054	$0.042

3.4.1.4 Windows Azure

1. Windows Azure storage provides two levels of redundancy: Locally Redundant Storage (LRS)—provides highly durable and available storage within a single sub region. Geo Redundant Storage (GRS)—provides highest level of durability by additionally storing data in a second sub-region within the same region.

STORAGE CAPACITY	GEOGRAPHICALLY REDUNDANT	LOCALLY REDUNDANT
First 1 TB / Month	$.095 per GB	$.070 per GB
Next 49 TB / Month	$.08 per GB	$.065 per GB
Next 450 TB / Month	$.07 per GB	$.06 per GB
Next 500 TB / Month	$.065 per GB	$.055 per GB
Next 4,000 TB / Month	$.06 per GB	$.045 per GB
Next 4,000 TB / Month	$.055 per GB	$.037 per GB
Over 9,000 TB / Month	Contact us	Contact us

Storage transaction costs are shown below.

STORAGE TRANSACTIONS	PRICE
100,000 Transactions	$.01 per 100,000

2. Querying or Data Access on the Cloud:

    a. Google Big Query is available at https://cloud.google.com/products/big-query. BigQuery supports analysis of datasets up to hundreds of terabytes. BigQuery uses a columnar data structure and is a cloud enabled massively parallel query engine. You can read more on this at https://cloud.google.com/files/BigQueryTechnicalWP.pdf.

3.5   Interview Ian Fellows Deducer

Here is an interview with Dr Ian Fellows, creator of acclaimed packages in R like Deducer and the Founder and President of Fellstat.com

Ajay—Describe your involvement with the Deducer Project and the various plug-ins associated with it. What has been the usage and response for Deducer from R Community.

Ian—Deducer is a graphical user interface for data analysis built on R. It sprung out of a disconnect between the tool chain used by myself and the tool chain of the psychologists that I worked with at the University of California, San Diego. They were primarily SPSS user, whereas I liked to use R, especially for anything that was not a standard analysis. I felt that there was a big gap in the audience that R serves. Not all consumers or producers of statistics can be expected to have the computational background (command-line programming) that R requires. I think it is important to recognize and work with the areas of expertise that statistical users have. I am not an expert in psychology, and they did not expect me to be one. They are not experts in computation, and I do not think that we should expect them to be in order to be a part of the R tool chain community.ian. This was the impetus behind Deducer, so it is fundamentally designed to be a familiar experience for users coming from an SPSS background and provides a full implementation of the standard methods in statistics, and data manipulation from descriptives to generalized linear models. Additionally, it has an advanced GUI for creating visualizations which has been well received, and won the John Chambers award for statistical software in 2011.

Uptake of the system is difficult to measure as CRAN does not track package downloads, but from what I can tell there has been a steadily increasing user base. The online manual has been accessed by over 75,000 unique users, with over 400,000 page views. There is a small, active group of developers creating add-on packages supporting various sub-disciplines of statistics. There are 8 packages on CRAN extending/using Deducer, and quite a few more on r-forge. Ajay—Do you see any potential for Deducer as an enterprise software product (like R Studio et al) Ian Like R Studio, Deducer is used in enterprise environments but is not specifically geared towards that environment. I do see potential in that realm, but do not have any particular plan to make an enterprise version of Deducer.

Ajay—Describe your work in Texas Hold'em Poker. Do you see any potential for R for diversifying into the casino analytics—which has hitherto been served exclusively by non open source analytics vendors?

Ian—As a Statistician, I am very much interested in problems of inference under uncertainty, especially when the problem space is huge. Creating an Artificial Intelligence that can play (heads-up limit) Texas Hold'em Poker at a high level is a perfect example of this. There is uncertainty created by the random drawing of cards, the problem space is $10^{\{18\}}$, and our opponent can adapt to any strategy that we employ. While high level chess A.I.s have existed for decades, the first viable program to tackle full scale poker was introduced in 2003 by the incomparable

Computer Poker Research group at the University of Alberta. Thus poker represents a significant challenge which can be used as a test bed to break new ground in applied game theory. In 2007 and 2008 I submitted entries to the AAA's annual computer poker competition, which pits A.I.s from universities across the world against each other. My program, which was based on an approximate game theoretic equilibrium calculated using a co-evolutionary process called fictitious play, came in second behind the Alberta team.

Ajay—Describe your work in social media analytics for R. What potential do you see for Social Network Analysis given the current usage of it in business analytics and business intelligence tools for enterprise?

Ian—My dissertation focused on new model classes for social network analysis (http://arxiv.org/pdf/1208.0121v1.pdf and http://arxiv.org/pdf/1303.1219.pdf). R has a great collection of tools for social network analysis in the statnet suite of packages, which represents the forefront of the literature on the statistical modeling of social networks. I think that if the analytics data is small enough for the models to be fit, these tools can represent a qualitative leap in the understanding and prediction of user behaviour. Most uses of social networks in enterprise analytics that I have seen are limited to descriptive statistics (what is a user's centrality; what is the degree distribution), and the use of these descriptive statistics as fixed predictors in a model. I believe that this approach is an important first step, but ignores the stochastic nature of the network, and the dynamics of tie formation and dissolution. Realistic modeling of the network can lead to more principled, and more accurate predictions of the quantities that enterprise users care about. The rub is that the Markov Chain Monte Carlo Maximum Likelihood algorithms used to fit modern generative social network models (such as exponential-family random graph models) do not scale well at all. These models are typically limited to fitting networks with fewer than 50,000 vertices, which is clearly insufficient for most analytics customers who have networks more on the order of 50,000,000. This problem is not insoluble though. Part of my ongoing research involves scalable algorithms for fitting social network models. Ajay—You decided to go from your Phd into consulting (www.fellstat.com). What were some of the options you considered in this career choice? Ian I have been working in the role of a statistical consultant for the last 7 years, starting as an in-house consultant at UCSD after obtaining my MS. Fellows Statistics has been operating for the last 3 years, though not fulltime until January of this year. As I had already been consulting, it was a natural progression to transition to consulting fulltime once I graduated with my Phd. This has allowed me to both work on interesting corporate projects and continue research related to my dissertation via sub-awards from various universities.

Ajay—What does Fellstat.com offer in its consulting practice?

Ian—Fellows Statistics offers personalized analytics services to both corporate and academic clients. We are a boutique company that can scale from a single statistician to a small team of analysts chosen specifically with the client's needs in mind. I believe that by being small, we can provide better, close-to-the-ground responsive service to our clients. As a practice, we live at the intersection of mathematical sophistication and computational skill, with a hint of UI design thrown into the mix. Corporate clients can expect a diverse range of analytic skills from the development of novel algorithms to the design and presentation of data for a general audience. We have worked with Revolution Analytics developing algorithms for their ScaleR product, the Center for Disease Control developing graphical user interfaces set to be deployed for world-wide HIV surveillance, and Prospectus analysing clinical trial data for retinal surgery. With access to the cutting edge research taking place in the academic community, and the skills to implement them in corporate environments, Fellows Statistics is able to offer clients world-class analytics services.

Ajay—How does Big Data affect the practice of statistics in business decisions?

Ian—There is a big gap in terms of how the basic practice of statistics is taught in most universities, and the types of analyses that are useful when data sizes become large. Back when I was at UCSD, I remember a researcher there jokingly saying that everything is correlated rho=.2. He was joking, but there is a lot of truth to that statement. As data sizes get larger everything becomes significant if a hypothesis test is done, because the test has the power to detect even trivial relationships.

Ajay—How is the R community including developers coping with the Big Data era? What do you think R can do more for Big Data?

Ian—On the open source side, there has been a lot of movement to improve R's handling of Big Data. The bigmemory project and the ff package both serve to extend R's reach beyond in-memory data structures. Revolution Analytics also has the ScaleR package, which costs money, but is lightening fast and has an ever growing list of analytic techniques implemented. There are also several packages integrating R with hadoop.

Ajay—Describe your research into data visualization including word cloud and other packages. What do you think of Shiny, D3.Js and online data visualization?

Ian—I recently had the opportunity to delve into d3.js for a client project and absolutely love it. Combined with Shiny, d3, and R one can very quickly create a web visualization of an R modeling technique. One limitation of d3 is that it does not work well with internet explorer 6–8. Once these browsers finally leave the ecosystem, I expect an explosion of sites using d3.

Ajay—Do you think word cloud is an overused data visualization type and how can it be refined?

Ian—I would say yes, but not for the reasons you would think. A lot of people criticize word clouds because they convey the same information as a bar chart, but with less specificity. With a bar chart you can actually see the frequency, whereas you only get a relative idea with word clouds based on the size of the word. I think this is both an absolutely correct statement, and misses the point completely. Visualizations are about communicating with the reader. If your readers are statisticians, then they will happily consume the bar chart, following the bar heights to their point on the y-axis to find the frequencies. A statistician will spend time with a graph, will mull it over, and consider what deeper truths are found there. Statisticians are weird though. Most people care as much about how pretty the graph looks as its content. To communicate to these people (i.e., everyone else) it is appropriate and right to sacrifice statistical specificity to design considerations. After all, if the user stops reading you have not conveyed anything. But back to the question I would say that they are over used because they represent a very superficial analysis of a text or corpus. The word counts do convey an aspect of a text, but not a very nuanced one. The next step in looking at a corpus of texts would be to ask how are they different and how are they the same. The word cloud package has the comparison and commonality word clouds, which attempt to extend the basic word cloud to answer these questions (see: http://blog.fellstat.com/?p=101).

About—Dr. Ian Fellows is a professional statistician based out of the University of California, Los Angeles. His research interests range over many sub-disciplines of statistics. His work in statistical visualization won the prestigious John Chambers Award in 2011, and in 2007–2008 his Texas Hold'em AI programs were ranked second in the world.

Applied data analysis has been a passion for him, and he is accustomed to providing accurate, timely analysis for a wide range of projects, and assisting in the interpretation and communication of statistical results. He can be contacted at info@fellstat.com.

3.6 Notable R Projects

Some of the notable R projects have contributed greatly in the past and present to making the R environment more friendly for web applications. Some other projects which are of note:

3.6.1 Installr Package

R is great for installing software. Through the "installr" package you can automate the updating of R (on Windows, using updateR()) and install new software. Software installation is initiated through a gui (just run installr()), or through functions such as: install.Rtools(), install.pandoc(), install.git(), and many more. The updateR() command performs the following: finding the latest R version, downloading it, running the installer, deleting the installation file, copy and updating old packages to the new R installation. It was created by Tal Gallili, who is also the creator of the R-Bloggers website that aggregates 500 plus blogs on R language through RSS feeds.

3.6.2 Rserve

Rserve is a TCP/IP server which allows other programs to use facilities of R (see
www.r-project.org) from various languages without the need to initialize R or link
against R library. Every connection has a separate workspace and working directory.
Client-side implementations are available for popular languages such as $C/C++$,
PHP and Java. Rserve supports remote connection, authentication, and file transfer.
Typical use is to integrate R back end for computation of statistical models, plots,
etc. in other applications. Here, Rserve acts as a socket server (TCP/IP or local
sockets) which allows binary requests to be sent to R.

http://cran.r-project.org/web/packages/Rserve/index.html

3.6.3 RApache

rApache is a project supporting web application development using the R statistical
language and environment and the Apache web server. The current release runs on
UNIX/Linux and Mac OS X operating systems. It is available at http://rapache.net/.
Please do read the fine manual at http://rapache.net/manual.html.

3.6.4 Rook

This package contains the Rook specification and convenience software for building
and running Rook applications. It borrows heavily from Ruby's Rack project
A Rook application is literally an R function that takes an R environment as input,
and returns a list of HTTP-relevant items as output. You can write and run Rook
apps within R using the built-in Rhttpd web server and deploy them on rApache.

*Rook is both a web server interface and an R package. The idea behind the
former is to separate application development from server implementation. Thus,
when a web server supports a web server interface, an application written to its
specifications is guaranteed to run on that server.*

3.6.5 RJ and Rservi

Note RServi is a confusing name (from Rserve) but it is a distinct project. RJ is an
open source library providing tools and interfaces to integrate R in Java applications.
RJ project also provides a pool for R engines, easy to setup and manage by a web-
interface or JMX. One or multiple client can borrow the R engines (called RServi)
see http://www.walware.de/it/rj/ and https://github.com/walware/rj-servi.

3.6.6 R and Java

- rJava is a simple R-to-Java interface. It is comparable to the .C/.Call C interface. rJava provides a low-level bridge between R and Java (via JNI). It allows to create objects, call methods, and access fields of Java objects from R.
- JRI is a Java/R Interface, which allows to run R inside Java applications as a single thread. Basically it loads R dynamic library into Java and provides a Java API to R functionality. It supports both simple calls to R functions and a full running REPL. JRI is now part of rJava.
- The JGR project makes the full use of both JRI and rJava to provide a full Java GUI for R.http://cran.r-project.org/web/packages/JGR/.
- iPlots is a package for the R statistical environment which provides high interaction statistical graphics, written in Java. http://cran.r-project.org/web/packages/iplots/index.html.

3.7 Creating Your Desktop on the Cloud

If you have been using the Windows Operating System on your desktop, when moving to the cloud you may choose the following software to minimize any issues in transition to cloud computing. Download and install the following

1. Chrome Browser www.google.com/chrome
2. Adobe Acrobat Reader http://get.adobe.com/reader/
3. Libre Office www.libreoffice.org/download or Open Office http://www.openoffice.org/download/
4. 7 zip http://www.7-zip.org/download.html
5. Java http://www.java.com/en/download/index.jsp

Additional Software for your statistical computing environment

1. Python http://www.python.org/download/
2. R http://cran.stat.ucla.edu/bin/windows/ or other locations at http://cran.r-project.org/mirrors.html
3. R Studio IDE http://www.rstudio.com/ide/download/desktop

Chapter 4
Setting Up R on the Cloud

The basic process of setting up your R based analytics in the cloud can be summarized as follows:

1. We create an account with the cloud services provider
2. We sign into the cloud account
3. We choose various options to create the remote virtual machine (commonly called an instance)
4. We customize attached storage based on computational needs. The name and storage cost of this varies as per the cloud service provider. There are also multiple layers or an hierarchy of storage options based on how frequently the stored data will be accessed.
5. We fire up (or start) the instance (cloud virtual machine).
6. Once a Linux Cloud instance is started we use SSH to login. (note—other connectivity options are below this list) and can use SCP to transfer data
7. We configure firewalls on instances so we can use ports (like 22 for SSH, 80 for HTTP, 8787 for R Studio Server)
8. We install R on the cloud instance using the installation instructions for the remote cloud operating system. We also install appropriate packages.
9. We install R Studio (Server) on Linux cloud instances and R Studio (Desktop) on Windows cloud instances.
10. We save the instance and the data in permanent storage like an image/snapshot to prevent loss of data and to ensure process is one time.
11. We turn off/delete the instance when we do not need to work on it.
12. We use more than one instance when we need a lot more work to be done in parallel processing.

© Springer Science+Business Media New York 2014

A Ohri, *R for Cloud Computing*, DOI 10.1007/978-1-4939-1702-0_4

4.1   Connecting to the Cloud Instance Easily

1. **PuTTY** is used to connect from Windows (local machine) to Linux (Cloud machine), where as a terminal window can be used for Linux (local machine) to Linux (cloud machine).

   - Download and Install PuTTY from http://www.chiark.greenend.org.uk/~sgtatham/putty/download.html
   - Use PuTTYgen to convert your .pem file (i.e., from Amazon cloud) to a .ppk format
   - Use PuTTY to login to your cloud Ubuntu machine.
   - You can save your credentials in PuTTY

2. You can use Windows Remote Desktop (RDP) to connect from Windows (local machine) to Windows (cloud machine). If our local machine's operating system is Windows, we use Putty to connect for SSH to Linux (cloud machine).
3. Ultimately we can use RStudio Server on the cloud (Linux) instance to create an easier coding environment especially for people transitioning from using Windows on desktops and servers to using Linux on the cloud, with minimal transition issues.
4. **WinSCP** can be used to upload and download data easily from your local Windows machine to your remote Linux Machine.

   - WinSCP can be downloaded from http://winscp.net/eng/download.php
   - You can then login to your session.

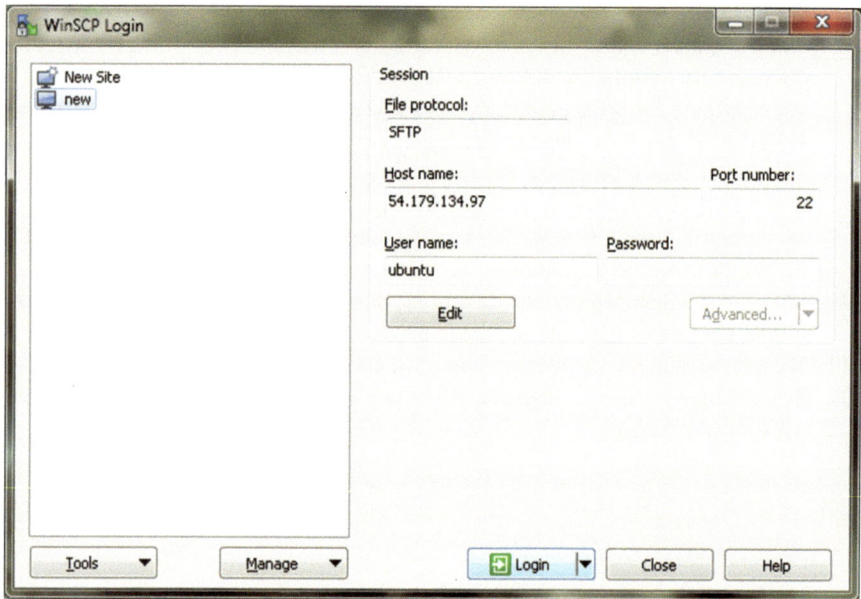

- The WinSCP can import your saved settings from PuTTY.

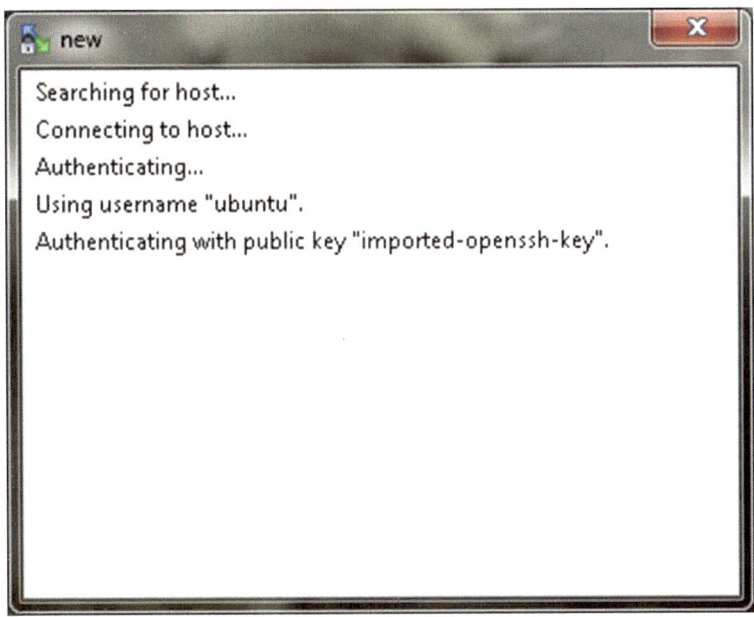

- You can simply drag and drop your files from your local machine to your cloud machine.

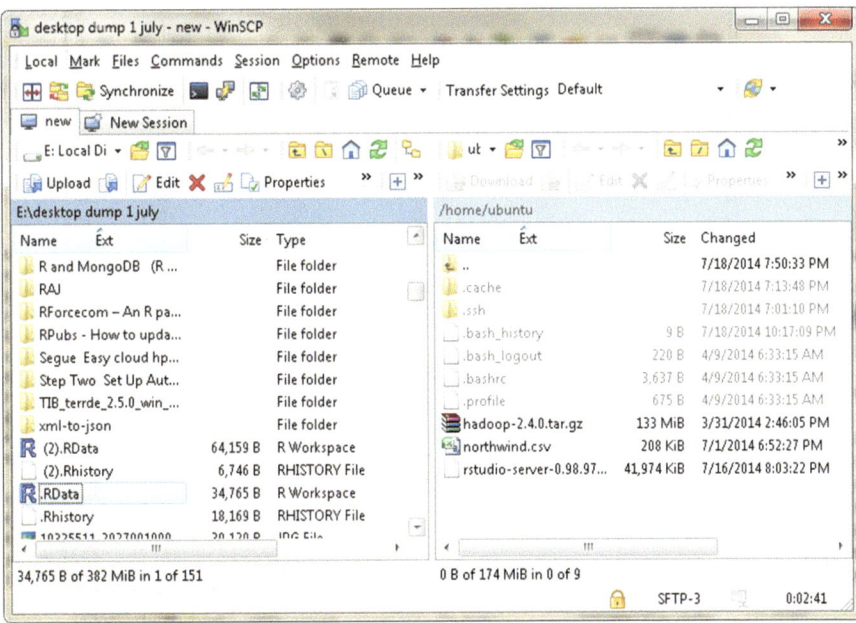

You can please see this article on how to connect to Amazon EC2 Instance from a Windows OS Computer Using PuTTY. Note, detailed instructions are available from http://docs.aws.amazon.com/AWSEC2/latest/UserGuide/putty.html.

4.2 Setting Up R in Amazon's Cloud

The following are tutorials for setting up R on the Amazon cloud.

4.2.1 Local Computer (Windows) Cloud (Linux)

When you log into the AWS Console Dashboard, this is what you see if you click EC2 Dashboard.

1. Note on the right margin that EC2 Dashboard is highlighted.
2. Note that on the top margin, you can see your account ids (we will take more on account management).
3. Note that on the top margin you can see the region. You can click on this drop-down menu item to change the region.

Some notation of the basic terminology used by Amazon in its EC2 Dashboard. You need to know these at a minimum if you are new to the cloud.
    Instances-

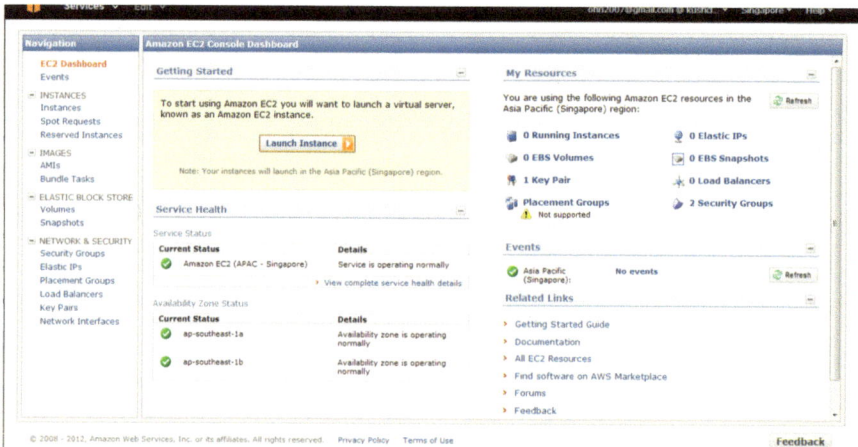

2. We click on Launch Instance button above and we see three options for launching an instance. We choose Quick Launch Wizard.

In this, we do the following:

- Name the instance
- Create a new security pair (it will help us in secure access). We will download the new key pair to our local computer in the next step by clicking the Download Button.
- Choose an Operating System in the Launch Configuration (Note there are prepackaged bundles called AMIs which we can choose if we want a preinstalled software)

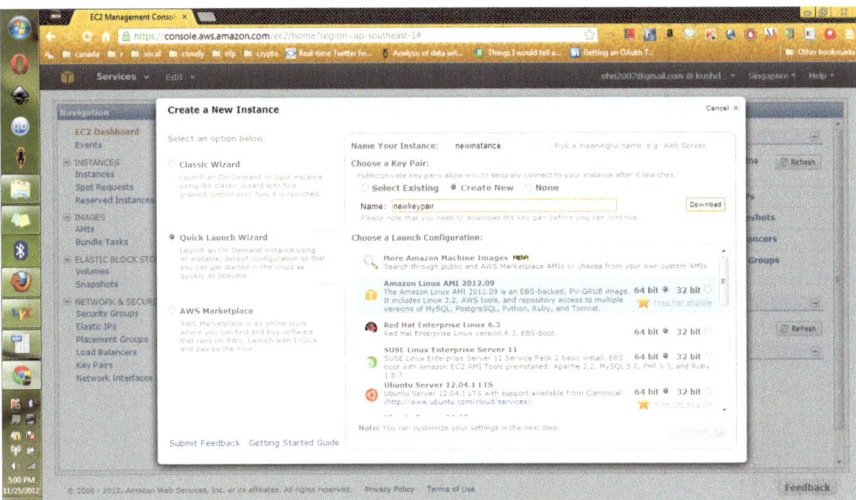

3. Next we download the new key pair (a .PEM file) to our local computer.

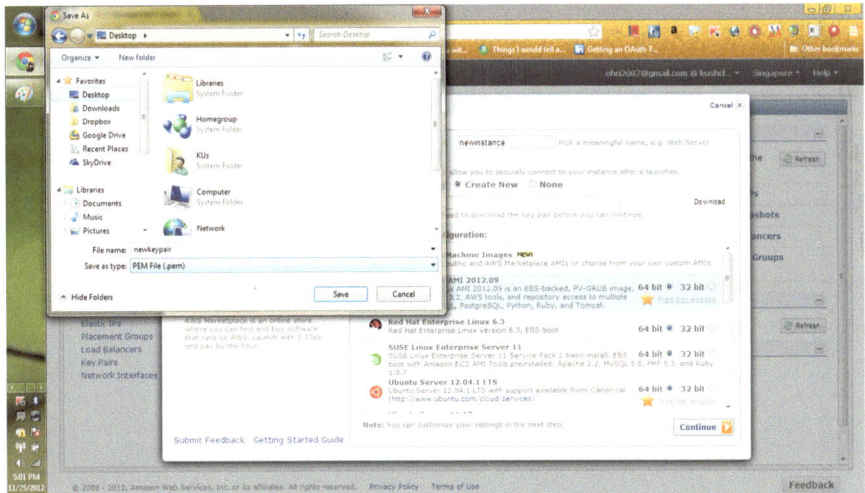

4. The downloaded key pair or .pem file should be saved to a secure location. We
   need it to logon to out cloud computer securely, and such that no one else can
   log on.
5. I have chosen Ubuntu Server 64 bit as my operating system in the previous screen
   and I choose type as t1.micro (note, this is the free tier that Amazon gives for free
   usage for 1 year). There were other operating systems available as you have seen,
   but there are also other Instance Types. They differ in terms of Processing Power
   (Number of Cores), Memory (RAM), and obviously per hour usage costs.

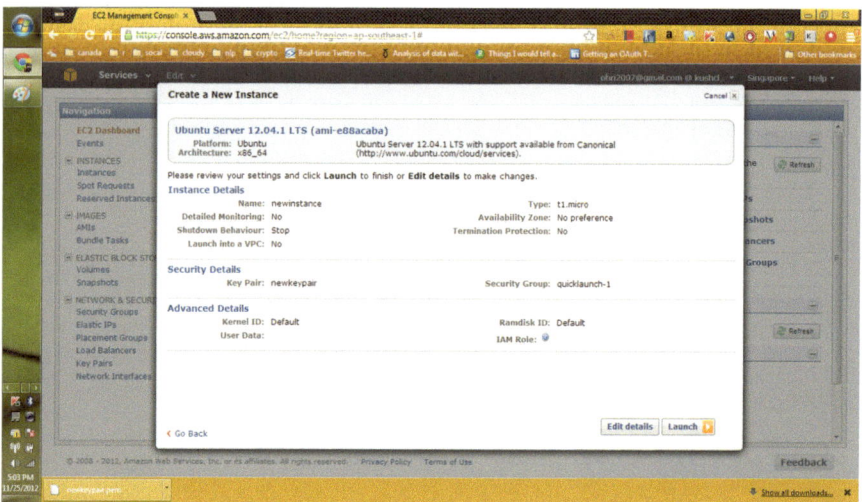

6. Next we click launch. While the instance is launching we see this wait window.

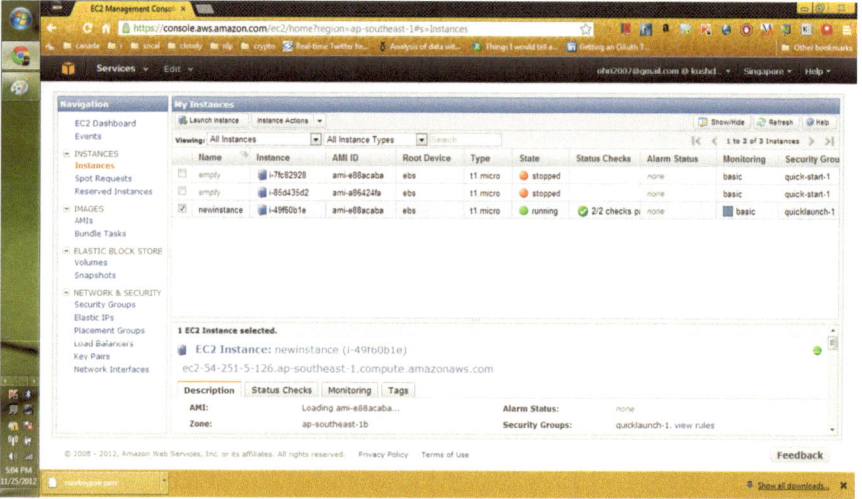

7. Next we can check the status of our remote cloud computer (or instance) in the right margin (Navigation). The tab instances are highlighted. It shows the status of current instances as well as any past instances we have used. Note that we have unique AMI id for instance, and it has a separate column on Root Device which says ebs (we explain EBS backed instances in Chap. 4).

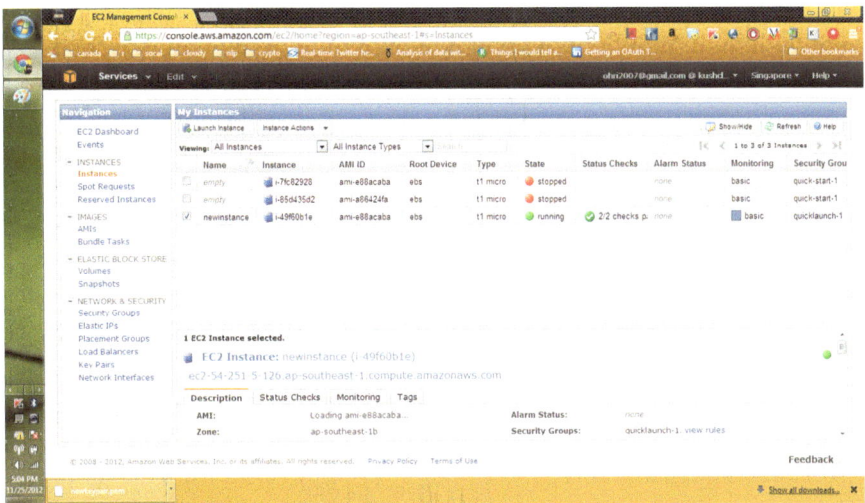

8. Next we see more details within the Instance tab, when we check on the check box of our instance. We see many actions in Instance Management an in Instance Actions (including Terminate, Reboot, Stop). Note the item—Change Termination Protection. We can enable Termination Protection so an accidental click does not terminate our instance.

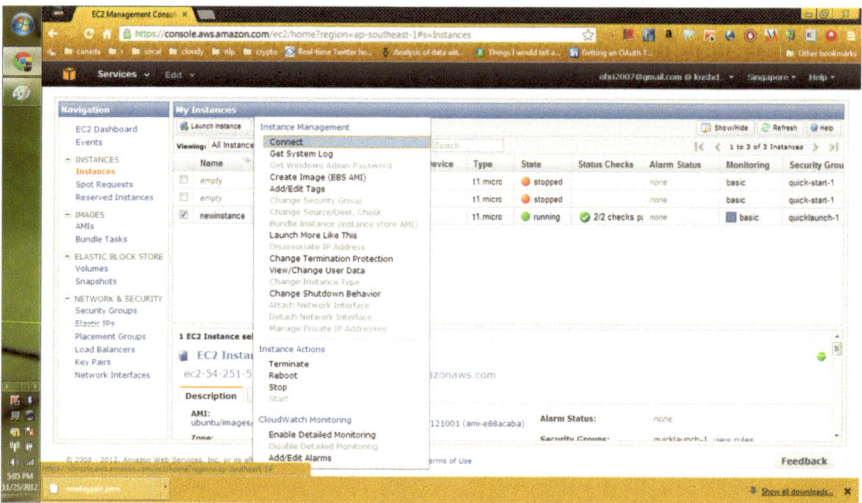

9. Next we click connect on the menu items we saw in the previous step. This is the window that greets us. It shows us how to access our remote instance using SSH.

WHAT IS SSH? We explain here for its definition at http://en.wikipedia.org/wiki/Secure_Shell.

Secure Shell (SSH) is a cryptographic network protocol for secure data communication, remote command-line login, remote command execution, and other secure network services between two networked computers. It connects, via a secure channel over an insecure network, a server, and a client running SSH server and SSH client programs, respectively. [67] The protocol specification distinguishes between two major versions that are referred to as SSH-1 and SSH-2

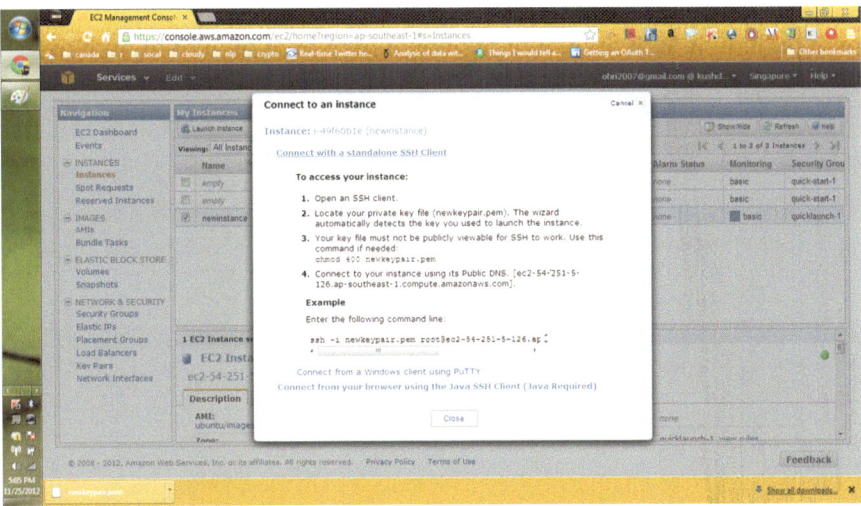

10. I use my local computer, Windows terminal window to connect. Note I need to change the instructions slightly, instead of logging in as root, I log in as ubuntu. Just copy and paste the line ssh -i new. . ..) in notepad, replace the word root by the word ubuntu. Note you may also put a -X flag after "ssh -i" if you want graphical capabilities, but be warned that X Windows forwarding is slow. If you are completely comfortable in Windows and or need heavy graphical interaction, maybe you should start the instance using Windows on the cloud, and then simply follow the instructions at the next section to connect using Remote DeskTop.

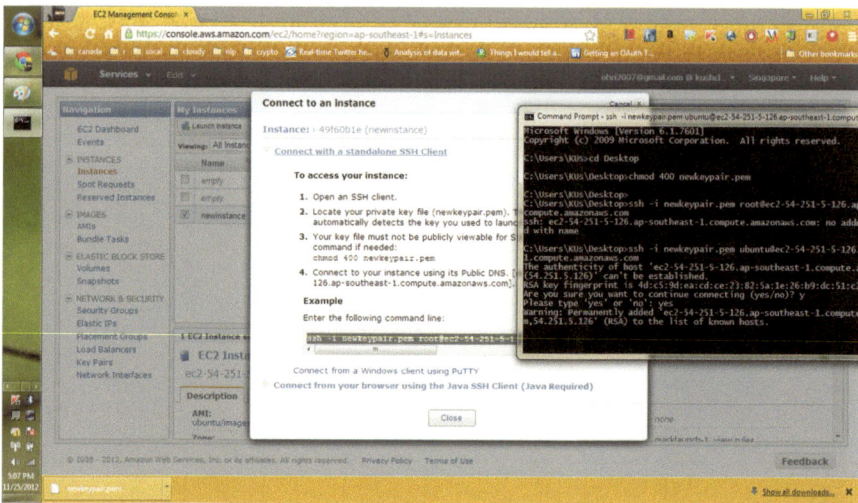

I follow the following steps—change the properties of my downloaded keyfile, and then try, and connect. Note I will need to change the name of user from "root" as in Amazon's instructions to Ubuntu. Additionally, I am not using Putty but installed a copy of OpenSSL for Win32 on my Windows 7 local computer.

```
Microsoft Windows [Version 6.1.7601]
Copyright (c) 2009 Microsoft Corporation.  All rights reserved.

C:\Users\KUs>cd Desktop

C:\Users\KUs\Desktop>chmod  400 newkeypair.pem

C:\Users\KUs\Desktop>ssh -i newkeypair.pem root@ec2-54-251-5-126.ap-southeast-1.
compute.amazonaws.com
Please login as the user "ubuntu" rather than the user "root".

^[[A

^[[A^[[A^[[AConnection to ec2-54-251-5-126.ap-southeast-1.compute.amazonaws.com
closed.

C:\Users\KUs\Desktop>ssh -i newkeypair.pem ubuntu@ec2-54-251-5-126.ap-southeast-
1.compute.amazonaws.com
```

11. ELASTIC IP ADDRESS—I see this when I am logged on.

Using Elastic IP Address in Amazon AWS

Next I have attached an elastic ip address to shorten the remote address of my instance. Now I can connect using ssh directly on the IP address. We use the right margin to allocate an elastic IP address to our instance.

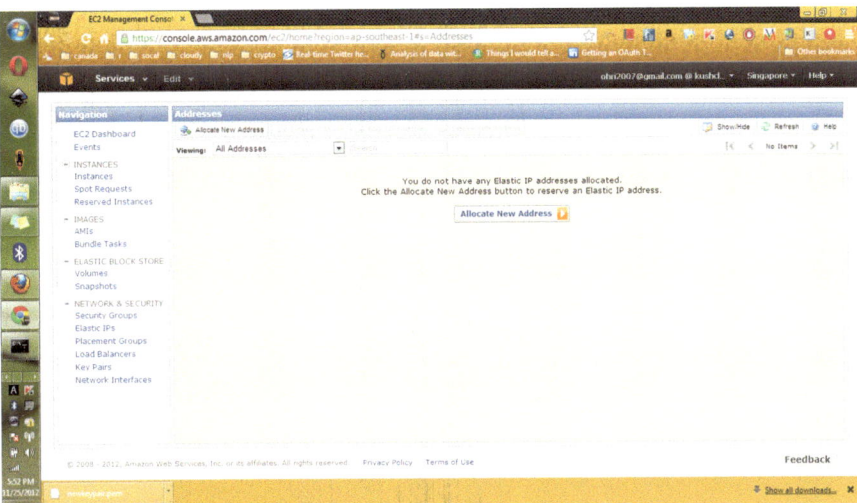

Note in order to do that I must have enabled the SSH method and that port for access.

Next I allocate the IP address to the correct instance.

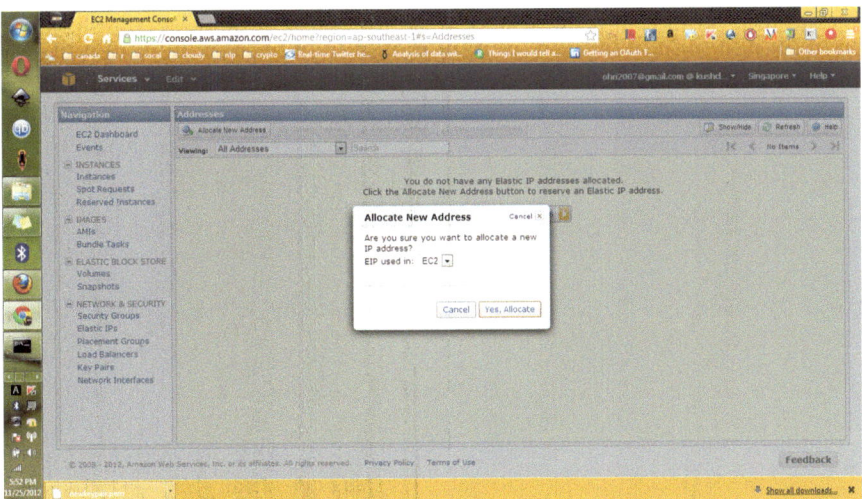

Next we check on that IP address's check box to associate address.

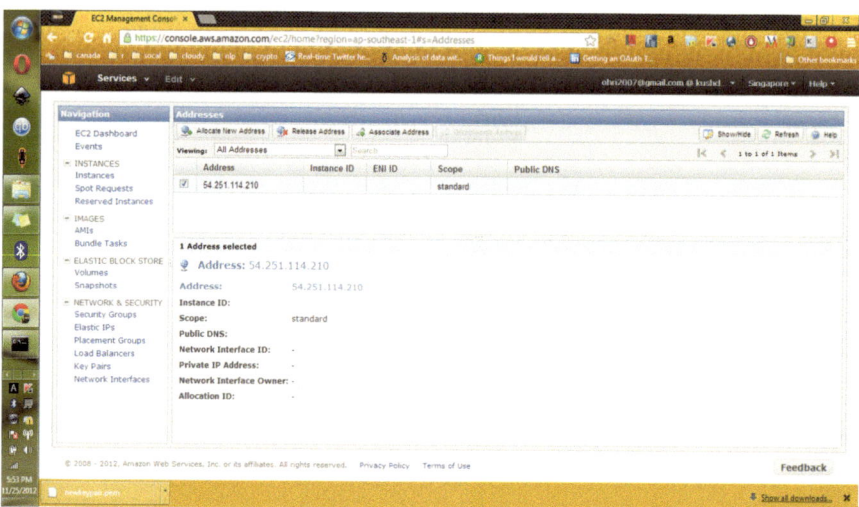

Next we associate the IP address to our instance.

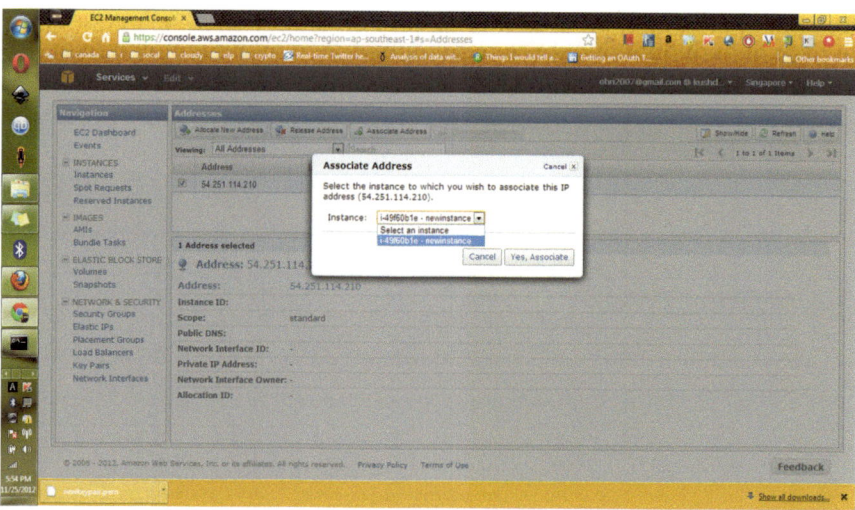

We see that the IP address is correctly allocated (this step maybe very critical for handling multiple instances and multiple IP addresses).

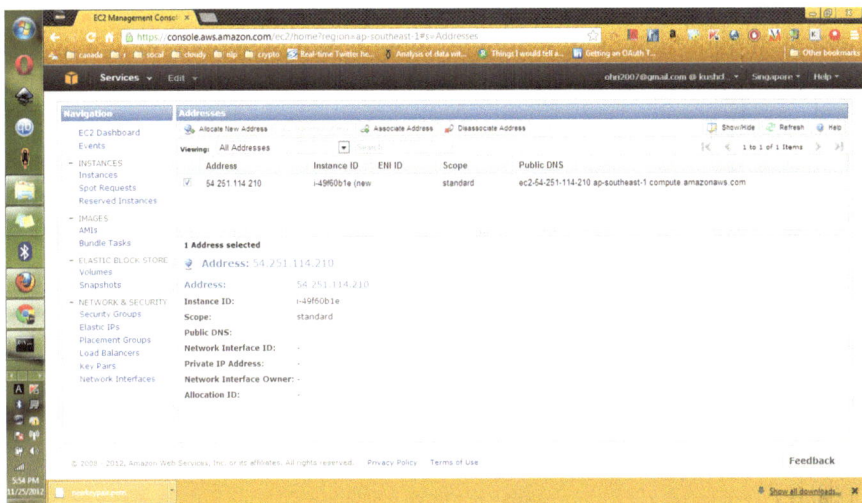

NOW that is my cloud instance! Hello Cloud Sky!

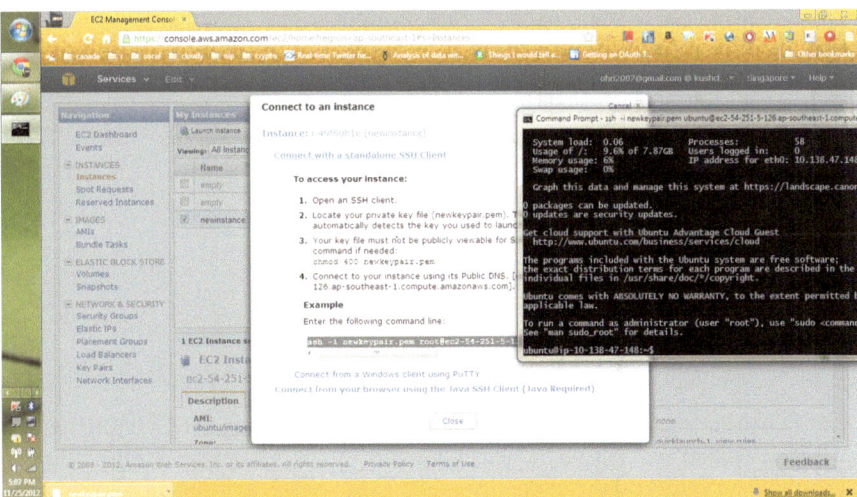

12. Next we move to installing R and RStudio software in our remote Amazon Instance. The procedure is the same even for any other cloud because basically after the connection step we are using the virtual machine.

    We will use the following commands in the console

- Install latest version of R

sudo apt-get install r-base

- Install in order to use RCurl

sudo aptitude install libcurl4-openssl-dev

- Install a few background files.

This will help us in case of troubleshooting library dependencies, or other software that may be needed to help our software run.
   sudo apt-get install gdebi-core
   sudo apt-get install libapparmor1

- Download RStudio Server

wget http://download2.rstudio.org/rstudio-server-0.97.336-amd64.deb

- Install RStudio Server

sudo gdebi rstudio-server-0.97.336-amd64.deb
   NOTE:

1. *sudo* gives administrative rights
2. *wget* gets data
3. *apt-get install* helps install software
4. *apt-get update* helps update software

- We need to create a new user for RStudio.

sudo adduser newuser1

- We need to change its password

sudo passwd newuser1

- Now just login to IPADDRESS:8787 with user name and password above

NOTE—Moving Data from Amazon Storage (s3) to Amazon Compute (ec2)
   To download an Amazon S3 object, use the following command, substituting the URL of the object to download. This method requires that the object you request is public.
   wget http://s3.amazonaws.com/my_bucket/my_folder/my_file.ext

The difference between EBS backed instances versus normal storage is here. http://docs.aws.amazon.com/AWSEC2/latest/UserGuide/ComponentsAMIs.html# storage-for-the-root-device.

You can stop an Amazon EBS-backed instance, but not an Amazon EC2 instance store-backed instance.

Stopping causes the instance to stop running (its status goes from running to stopping to stopped). A stopped instance persists in Amazon EBS, which allows it to be restarted. Stopping is different from terminating; you can't restart a terminated instance. Because Amazon EC2 instance store-backed AMIs can't be stopped, they're either running or terminated. While the instance is stopped, you can treat the root volume like any other volume, and modify it (for example, repair file system problems or update software). You just detach the volume from the stopped instance, attach it to a running instance, make your changes, detach it from the running instance, and then reattach it to the stopped instance. Make sure you reattach it to the correct storage device (whichever device name is specified as the root device in the instance's block device mapping)

Storage for the Root Device

All AMIs are categorized as either *backed by Amazon EBS* or *backed by instance store*. The former means that the root device for an instance launched from the AMI is an Amazon EBS volume created from an Amazon EBS snapshot. The latter means that the root device for an instance launched from the AMI is an instance store volume created from a template stored in Amazon S3. For more information, see Root Device Volume.

This section summarizes the important differences between the two types of AMIs. The following table provides a quick summary of these differences.

Characteristic	Amazon EBS-Backed	Amazon instance store-backed
Boot Time	Usually less than 1 minute	Usually less than 5 minutes
Size Limit	1 TiB	10 GiB
Root Device Volume	Amazon EBS volume	Instance store volume
Data Persistence	Data on Amazon EBS volumes persists after instance termination; you can also attach instance store volumes that don't persist after instance termination	Data on instance store volumes persists only during the life of the instance; you can also attach Amazon EBS volumes that persist after instance termination
Upgrading	The instance type, kernel, RAM disk, and user data can be changed while the instance is stopped.	Instance attributes are fixed for the life of an instance
Charges	Instance usage, Amazon EBS volume usage, and Amazon EBS snapshot charges for AMI storage	Instance usage and Amazon S3 charges for AMI storage
AMI Creation/Bundling	Uses a single command/call	Requires installation and use of AMI tools
Stopped State	Can be placed in stopped state where instance is not running, but the instance is persisted in Amazon EBS	Cannot be in stopped state; instances are running or terminated

Size Limit

Amazon EC2 instance store-backed AMIs are limited to 10 GiB storage for the root device, whereas Amazon EBS-backed AMIs are limited to 1 TiB. Many Windows AMIs come close to the 10 GiB limit, so you'll find that Windows AMIs are often backed by an Amazon EBS volume.

Note

All Windows Server 2008, Windows Server 2008 R2, and Windows Server 2012 AMIs are backed by an Amazon EBS volume by default because of their larger size.

4.3 Using Revolution R on the Amazon Cloud

The enterprise and professional customer can use R on the Amazon cloud using The Revolution R ami that is listed at https://aws.amazon.com/marketplace/seller-profile?id=3c6536d3-8115-4bc0-a713-be58e257a7be. We can boot it up using the standard way for a Amazon Machine Image (AMI) and especially use the Big Data package called RevoScaleR as well as ramp up the RAM for faster data processing. The cost of the software is thus licensed by the hour and also by the type of instance used (since that is considered a proxy metric for size of data crunched).

This kind of pricing is definitely more convenient for customers to test out software before they commit to not so inexpensive annual licenses.

4.4   Using the BioConductor Cloud AMI

The bioconductor project has some prebuilt Amazon Machine Images available at http://www.bioconductor.org/help/bioconductor-cloud-ami/#ami_ids

Using this approach launches an Amazon Instance within a few minutes

Amazon Machine Image (AMI) that is optimized for running Bioconductor in the Amazon Elastic Compute Cloud (or EC2) for sequencing tasks. Here are a few reasons you could use it:

- *You do not want to install Bioconductor on your own machine.*
- *You have a long-running task and you don't want it to tie up the CPU on your own machine.*
- *You have a parallelizable task and would like to run it (either on multiple CPUs on a single machine or in a cluster of many machines).*
- *You want to run R in your web browser (using RStudio Server).*
- *The AMI contains many packages which can be very difficult to install and configure.*

You can read the complete document at http://www.bioconductor.org/help/ bioconductor-cloud-ami/.

- Click on the link provided at http://www.bioconductor.org/help/bioconductor-cloud-ami/ (it is at *"Obtain an Amazon Web Services account and start the **AMI**. Additional instructions below."*).

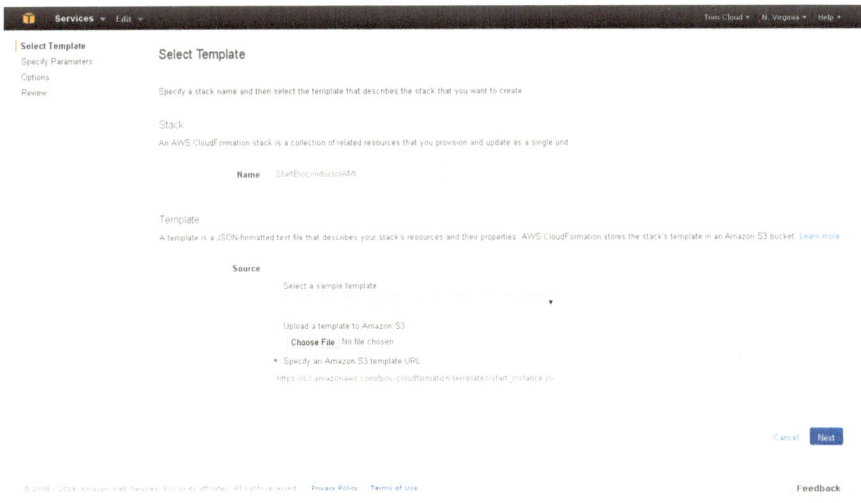

- Specify Parameters—Note the t1.micro is free

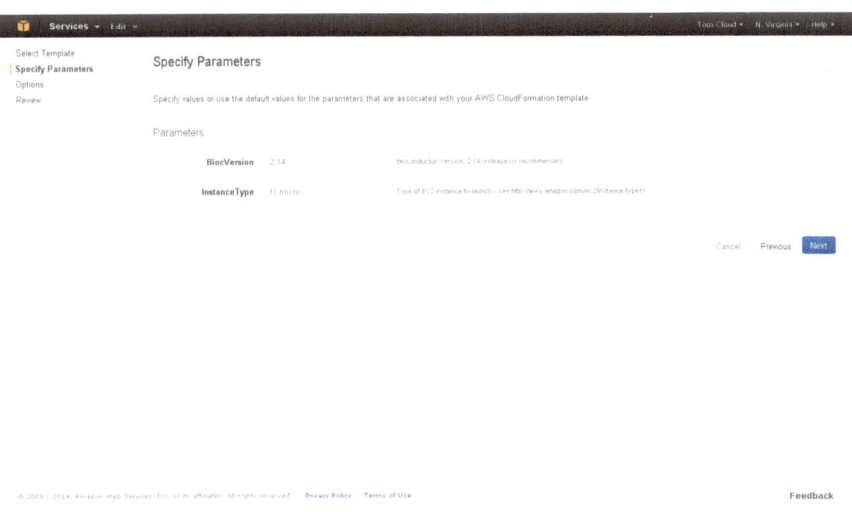

- You can keep clicking *Next* as the options are prefilled. It takes some time to boot up the system.

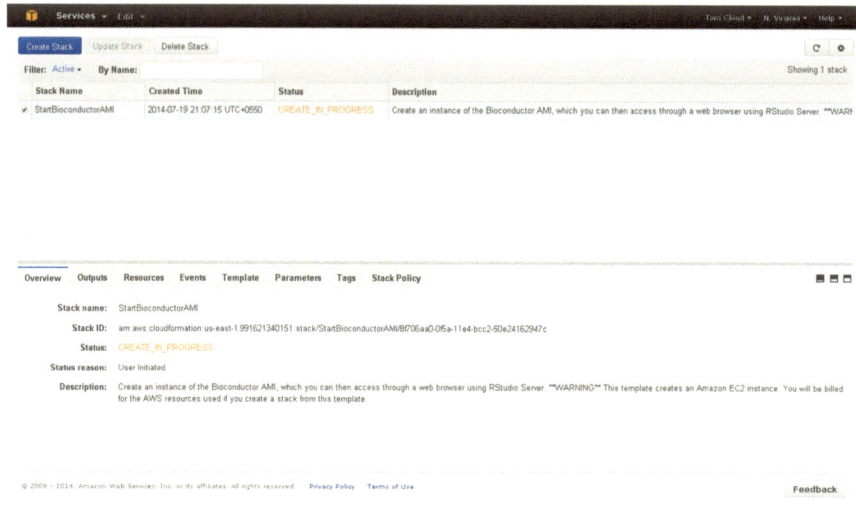

• Now note the connection url and password for the RStudio Server

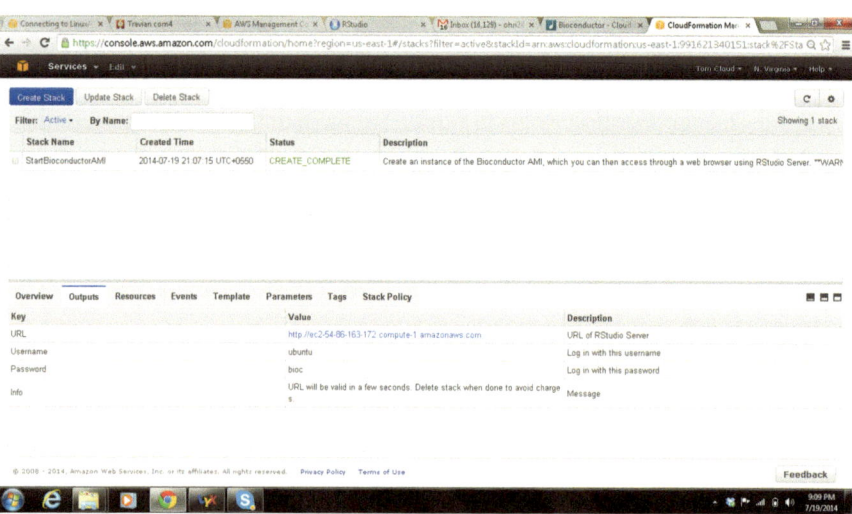

- Now you can see RStudio interface in the browser and run demos. A great advantage of using RStudio server is the easier access to graphical output than compared to command line. Even a Windows user can thus run the Linux operating system with ease using the RStudio interface. Even a cloud computing beginner can start this using the Bioconductor AMI.

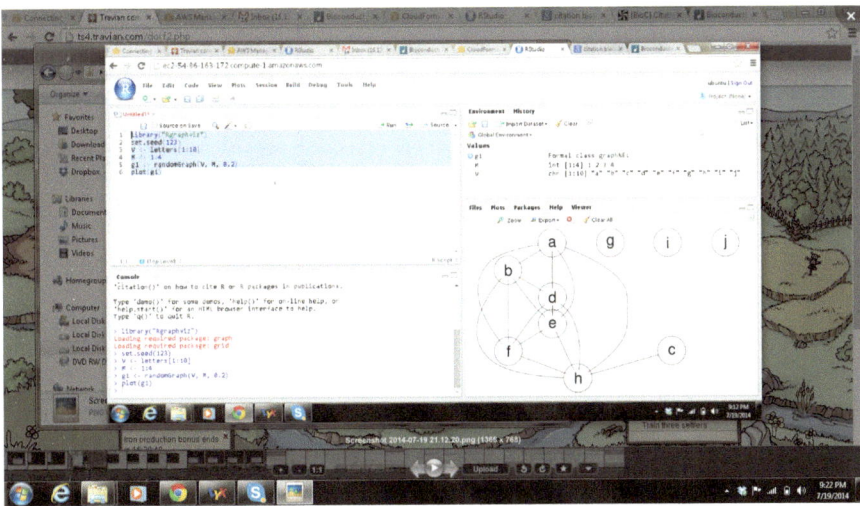

- This was made possible using the Amazon Web Services using Cloud Formation option. In this case we used the Bioconductor template.

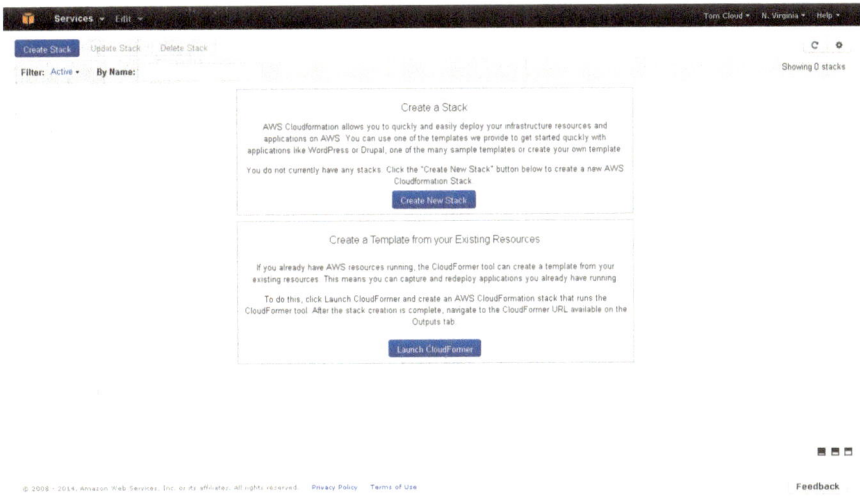

4.5   R in Windows Azure Cloud

A tutorial for using R on the amazing Windows Azure cloud follows. The Windows Azure cloud does offer Linux instances and has the best user interface and professional documentation for an enterprise software.

- Go to https://manage.windowsazure.com
- Login using your Windows Account (or create one—it is like john-doe@hotmail.com or johnfoe@live.com).

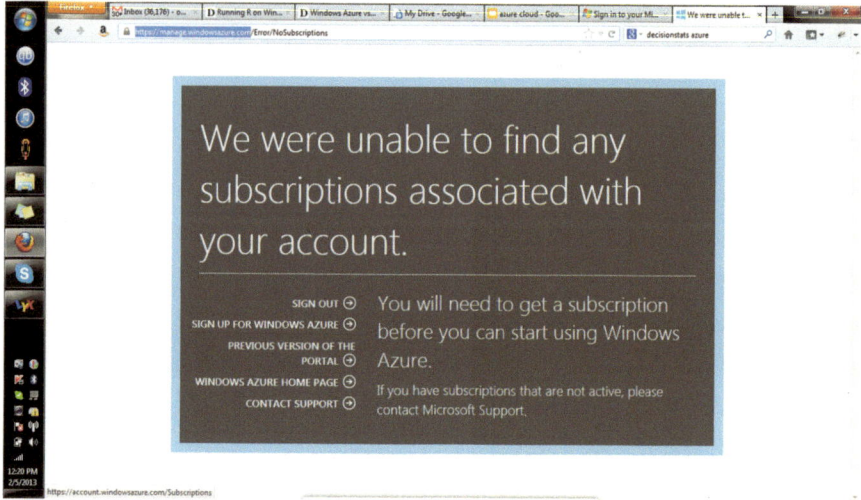

- Sign up for Windows Azure
- Sign up for a free 3-month Trail (or the current discount or trial offer)

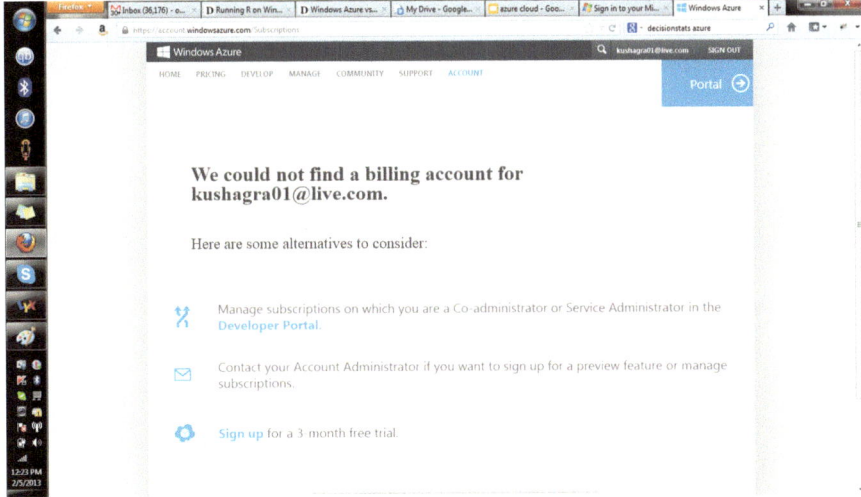

- These are the details for your free trial.

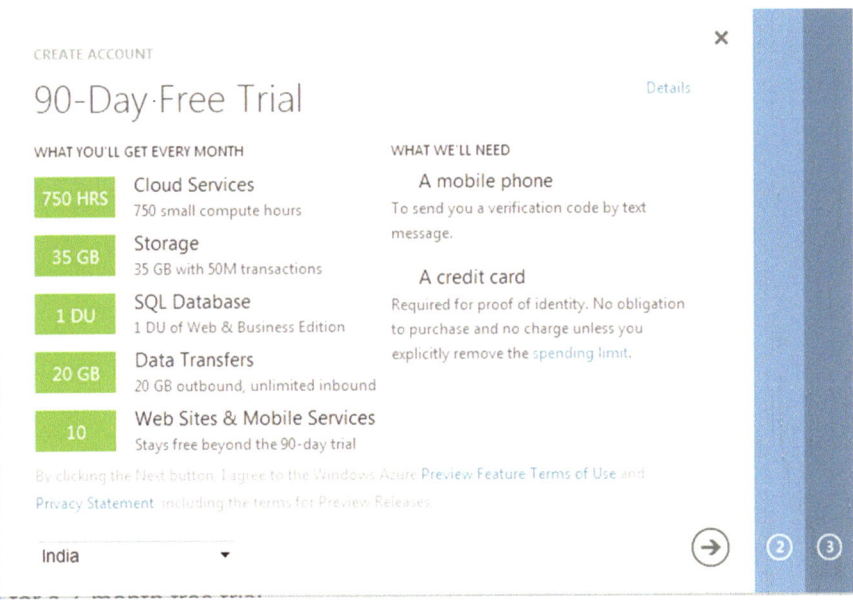

- Verify your phone.

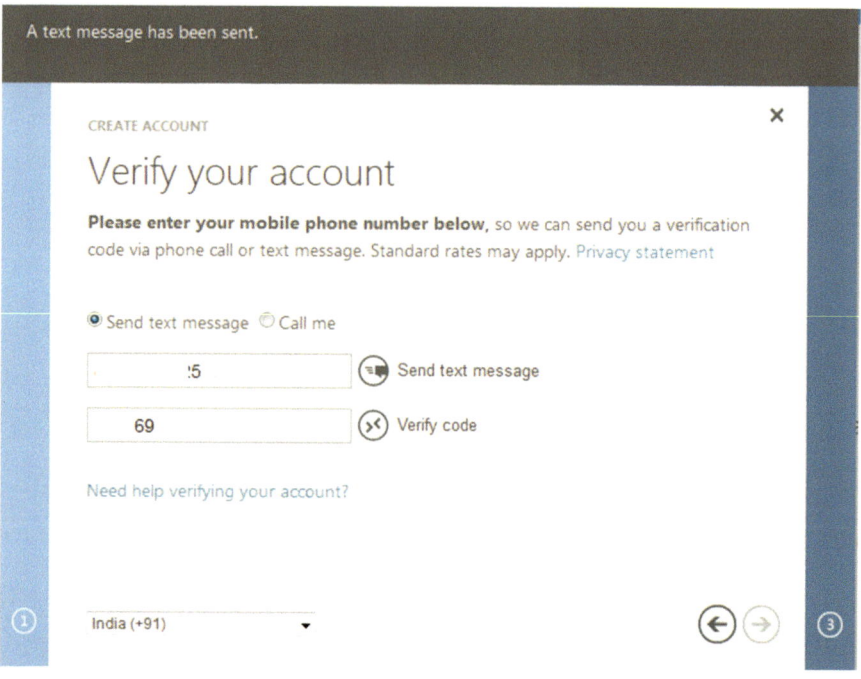

• Phone verified.

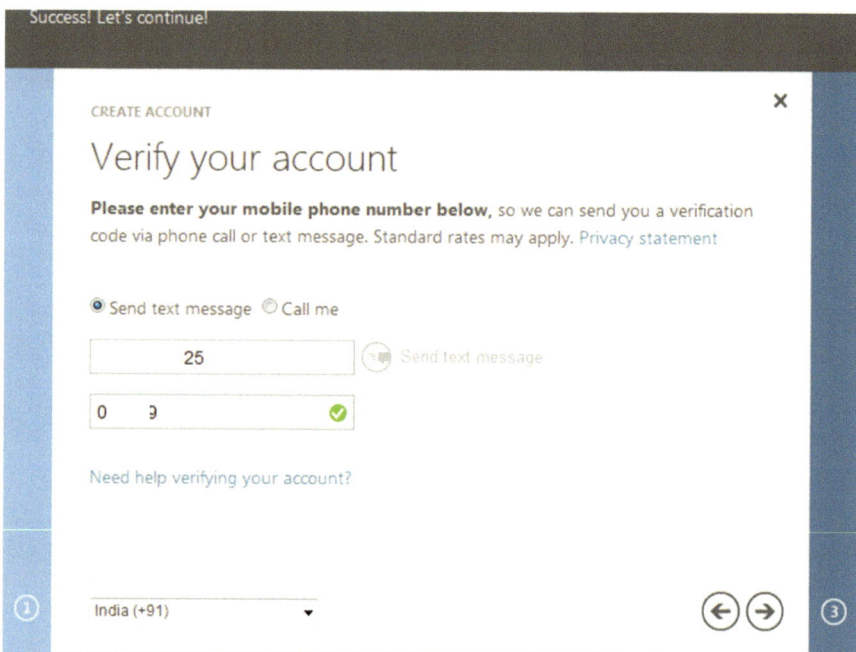

- Enter Credit Card Details (your own please).
- You get this screen if everything goes well. Click on the blue portal button.

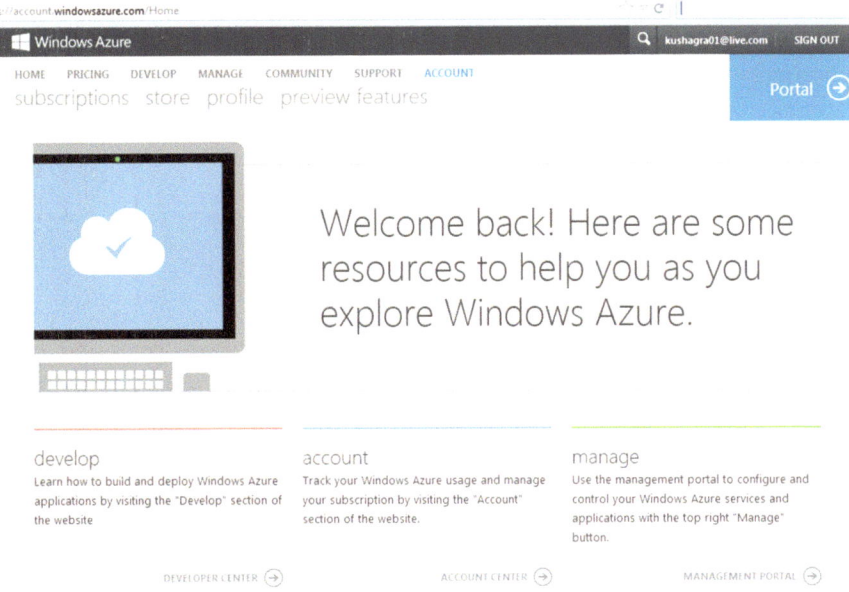

- Now you are in the Azure Dashboard.

The first time takes the 30 s tour that pops up.

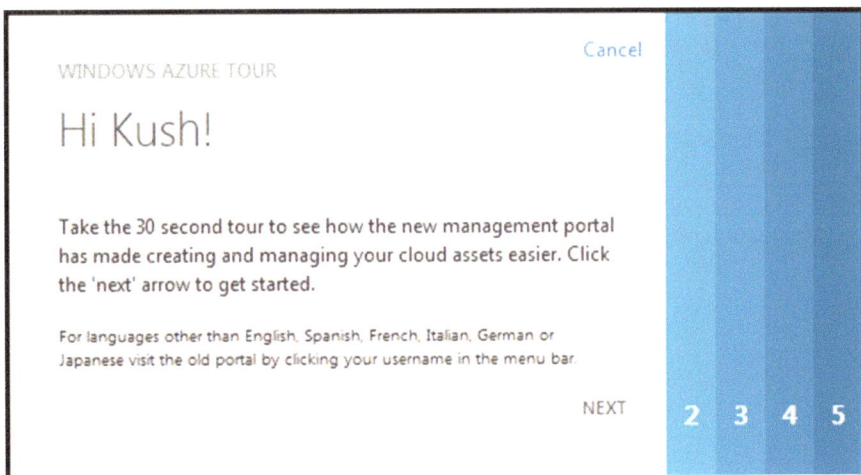

- This is the Windows Azure Dashboard.

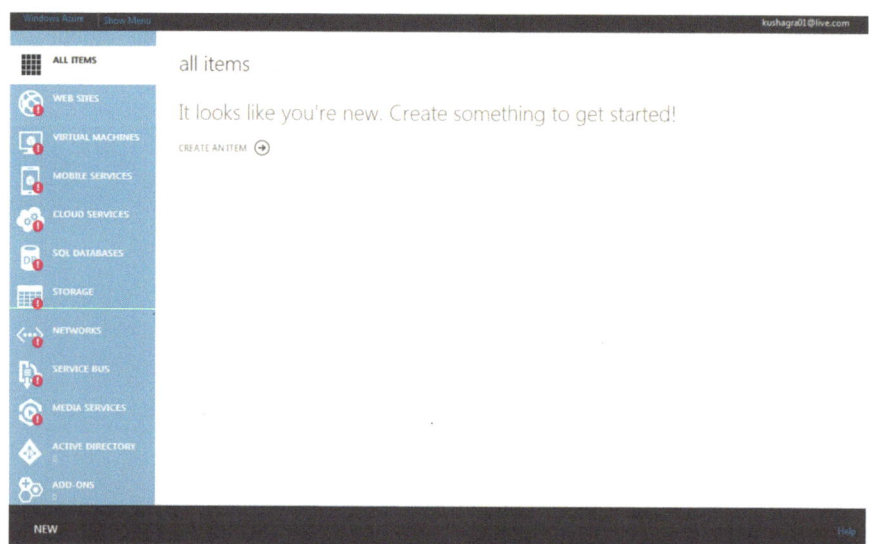

• Lets create a new Virtual Instance in Compute since we want to install R.

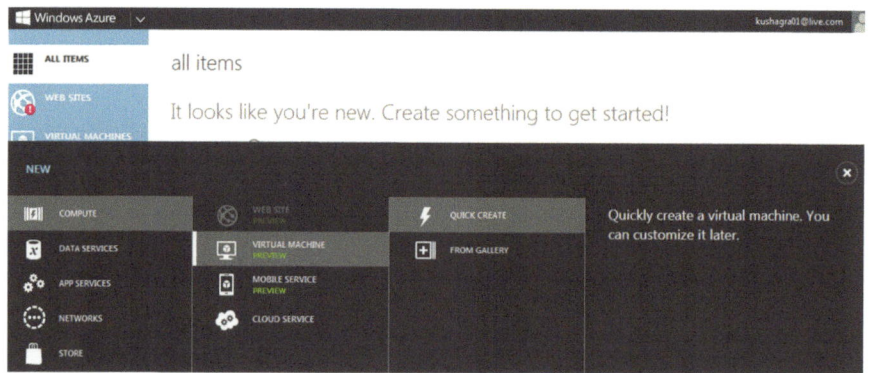

• Specify a DNS name as per the hint given

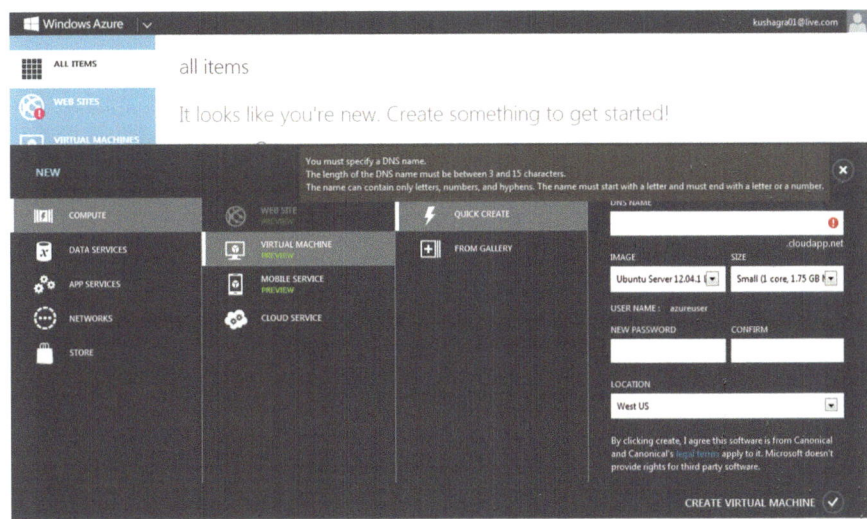

- Choose an operating system from the image drop down

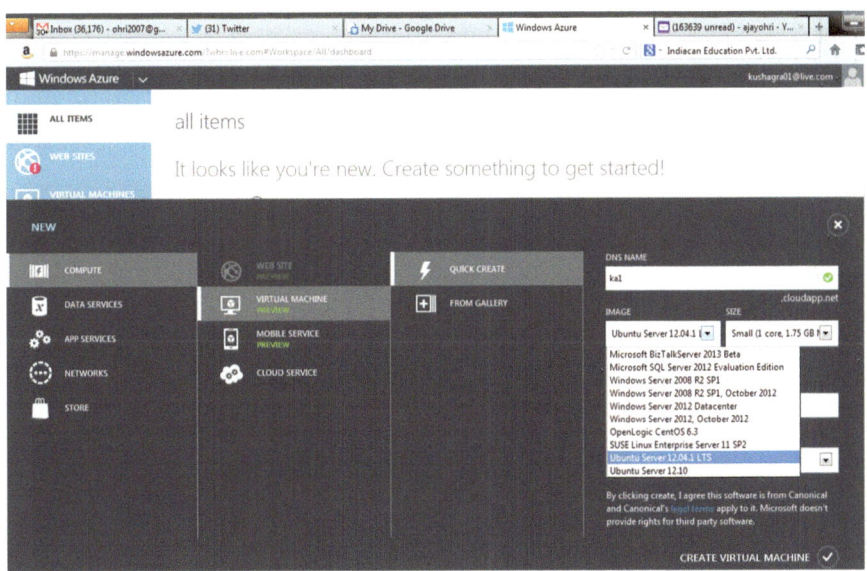

- Choose size of instance (which shows number of cores and memory).

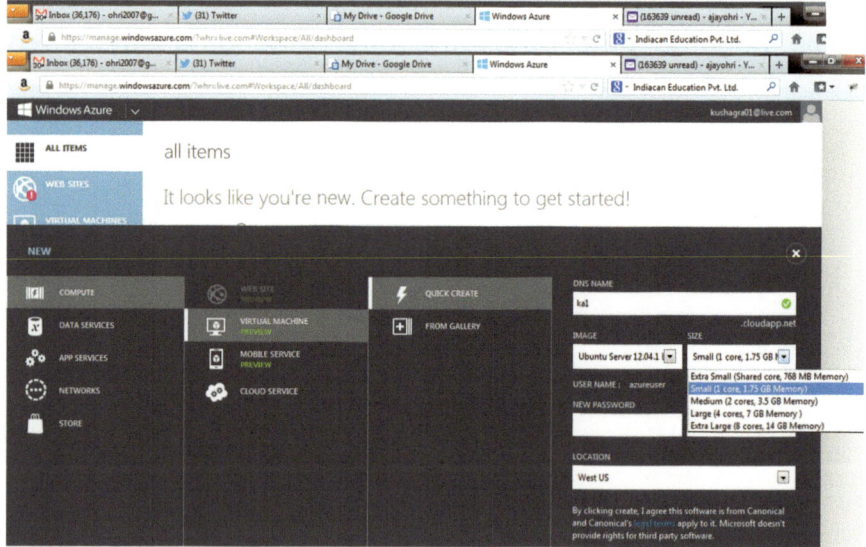

- Choose the password for accessing your remote instance.

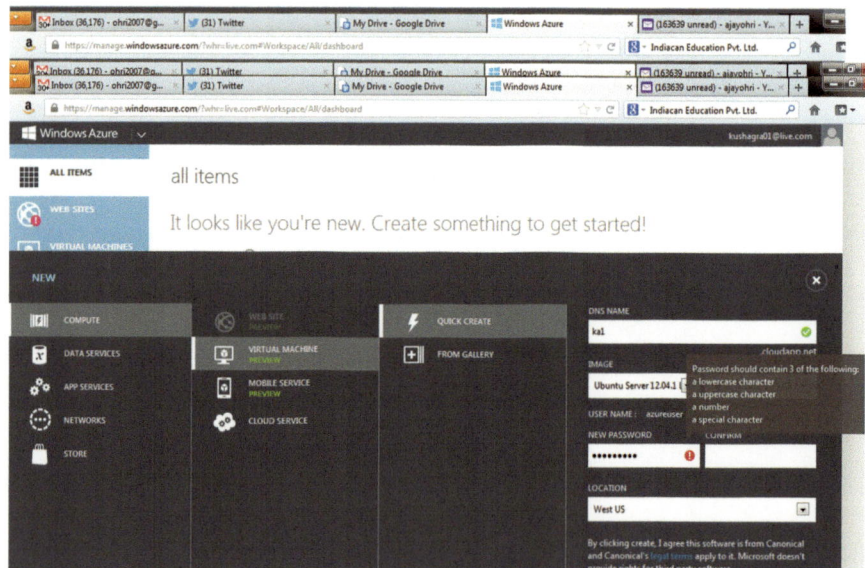

- You also need to choose the region for the instance. This is crucial because of regulations regarding export of privacy sensitive data across national borders as well as proximity of your own location. Then click on the **create virtual machine** button.

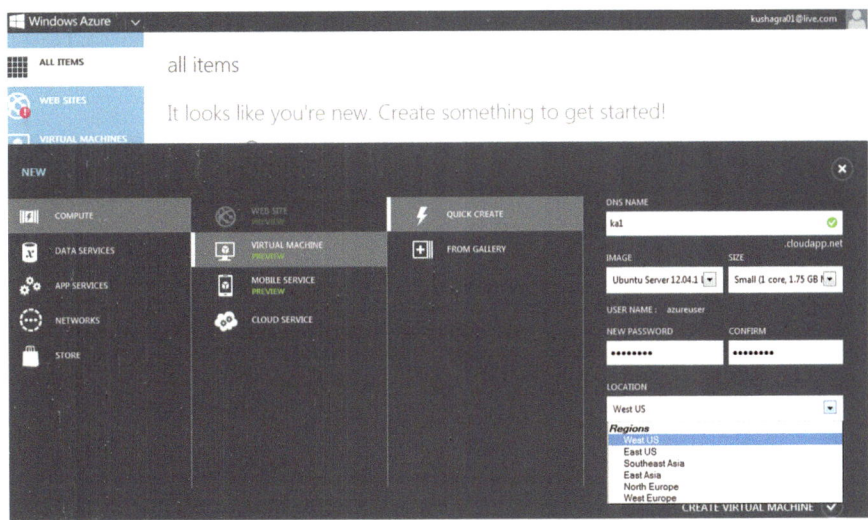

- This is the screen shown while Azure provisions the cloud instance. Note on the bottom notifications including details can be seen.

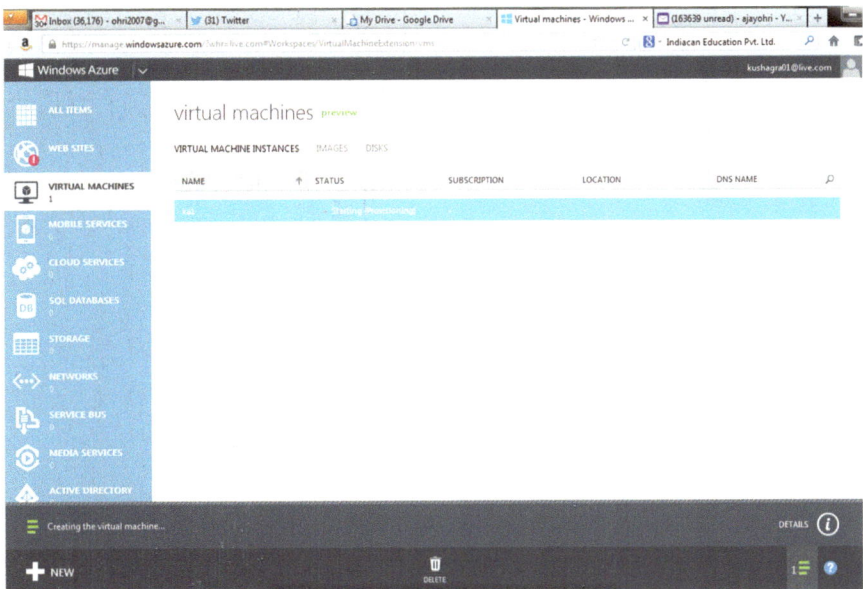

- Download Putty from http://www.chiark.greenend.org.uk/~sgtatham/putty/download.html (if not downloaded earlier!)
- The log window below shows the virtual machine is created.

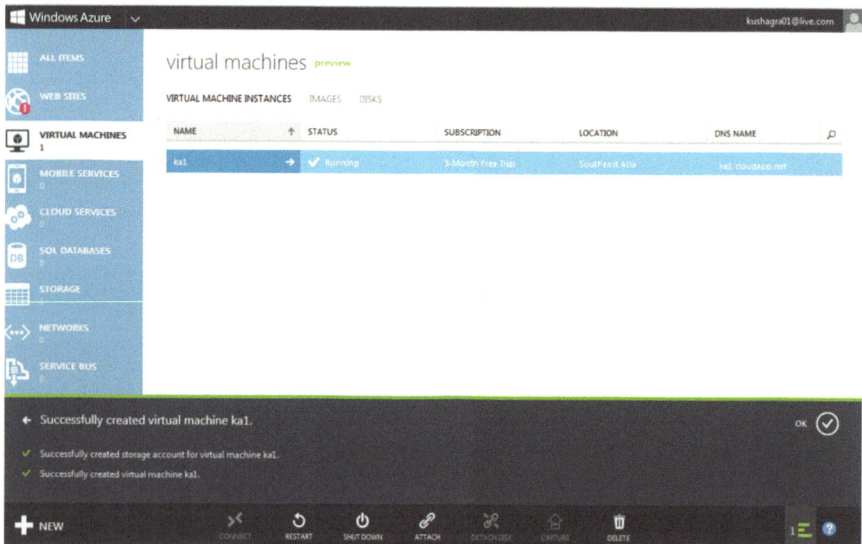

• We see a storage account also has been attached to the virtual machine.

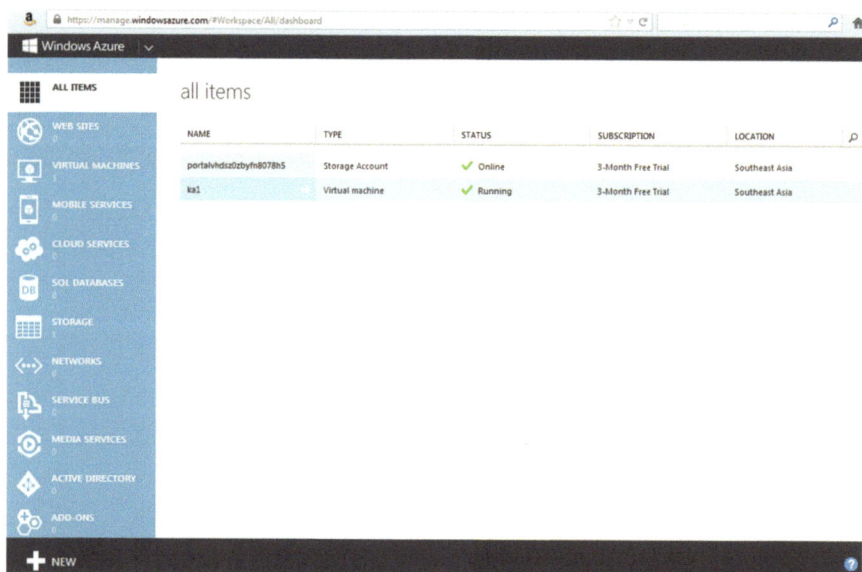

• If we click on the virtual machine name (here ka1) we can see the preview
  including Dashboard (or log), Endpoints, and Configure options.

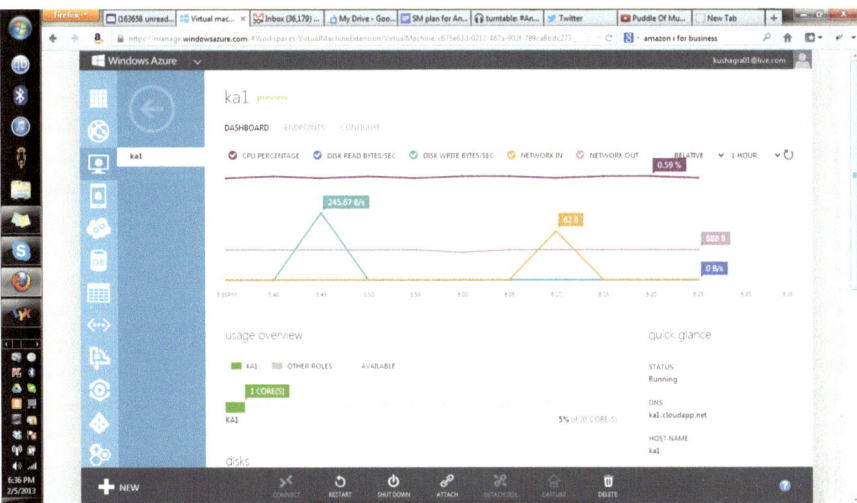

- We see the details of IP Addresses and details for SSH by scrolling down within this screen.

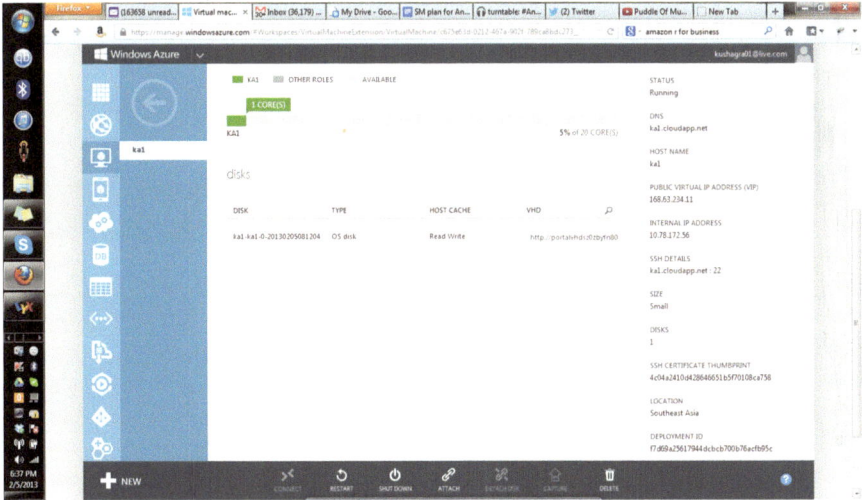

- Endpoints show the ports and protocols for connection.

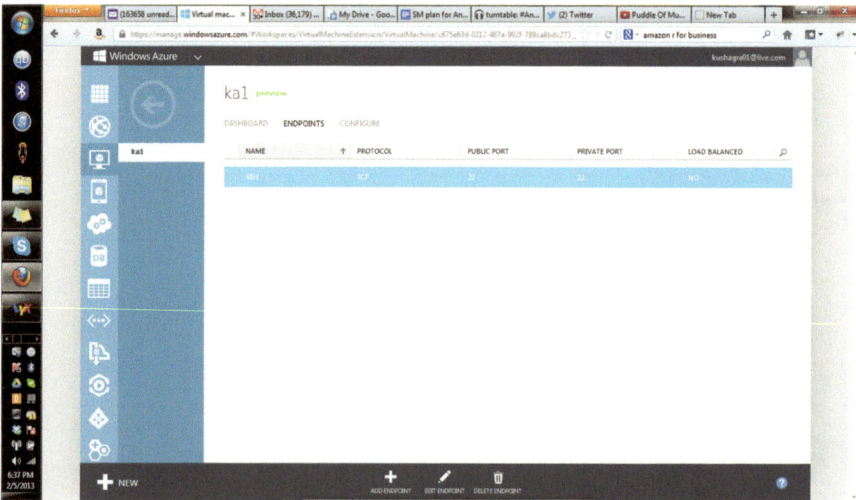

• We can configure endpoints.

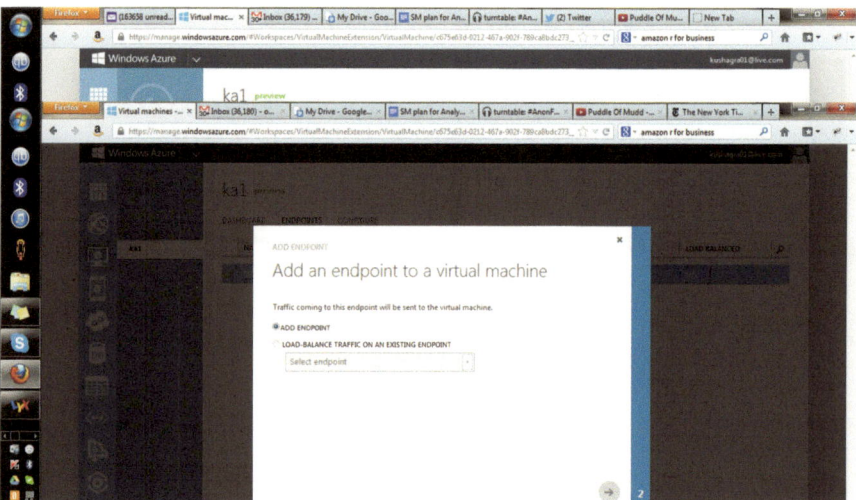

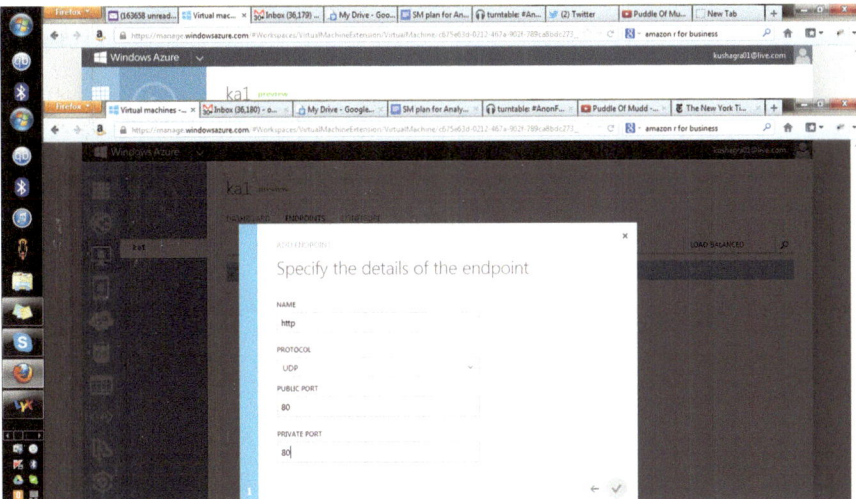

- Using the help we see the methods to connect.

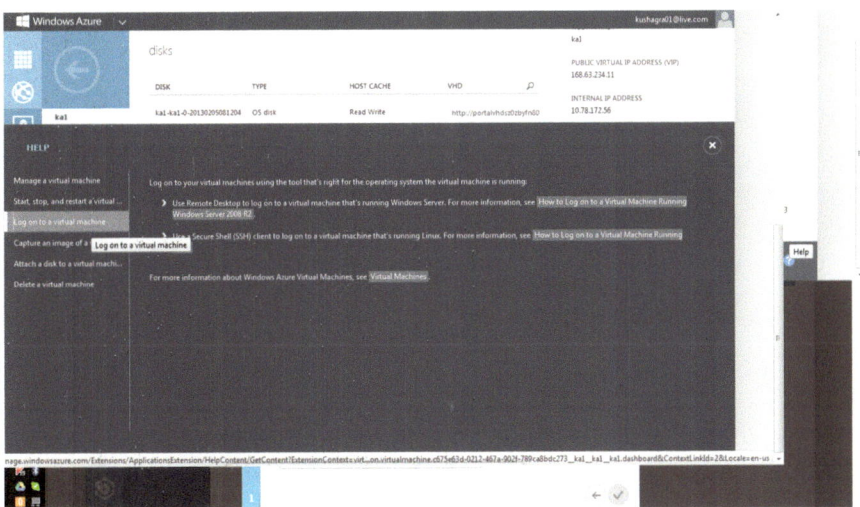

- We configure the connection options in PuTTY

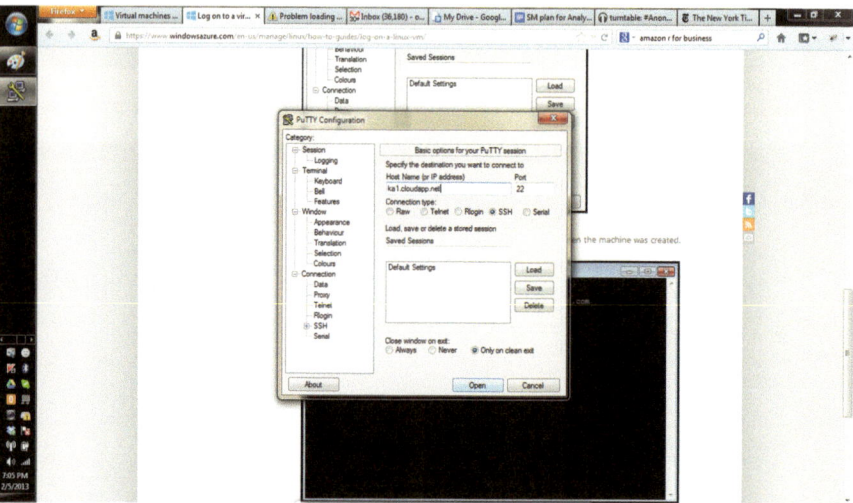

- Note the rsa2 key fingerprint and compare it from the one in previous step. It should be the same.

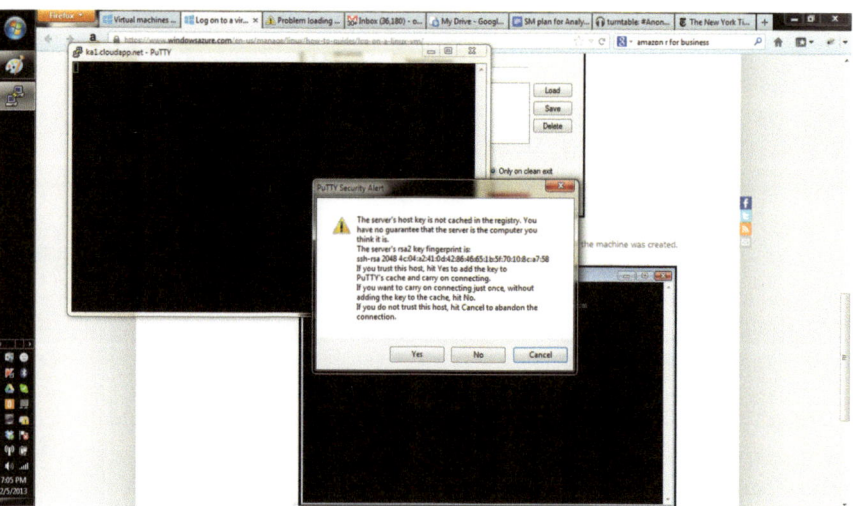

- A successful login! We used the username and password we chose above.

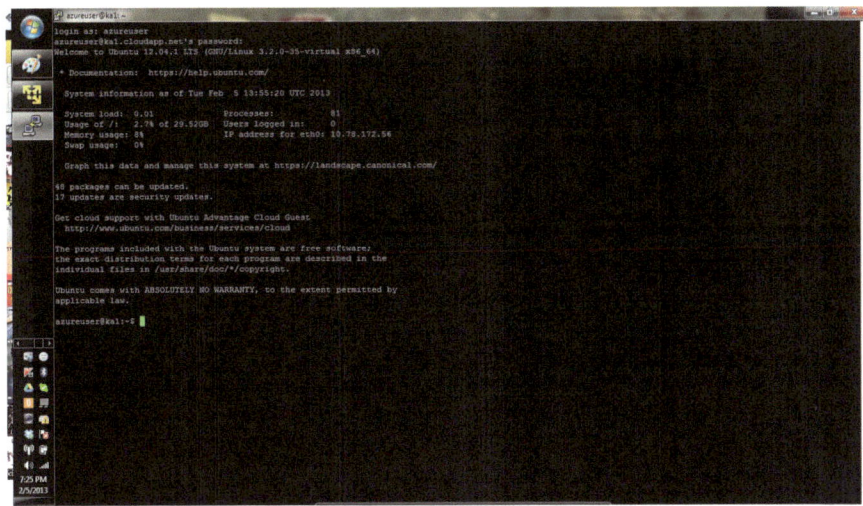

Now we install R, RStudio Server, and connect to port 8787.

Additionally, Microsoft Azure offers Machine Learning as a Service.

Azure Machine Learning is also designed for seasoned data scientists. It supports R, the popular open-source programming environment for statistics, and data mining. You can drop existing R code directly into your workspace, or write your own in ML Studio, which securely supports more than 350 R packages.

4.6   R in the Google Cloud

A tutorial for using R in the Google Cloud follows. Google Cloud does not offer the Windows operating system as an option for customers.

- The Google APIs console is at https://code.google.com/apis/console. We need to activate Google Cloud Compute Engine and Google Cloud Storage APIs.

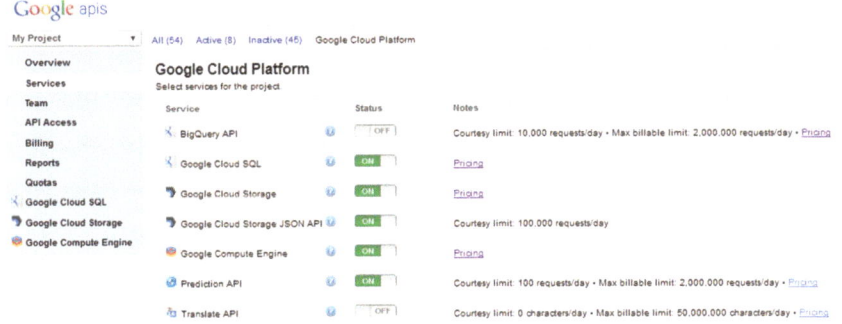

- Create Project

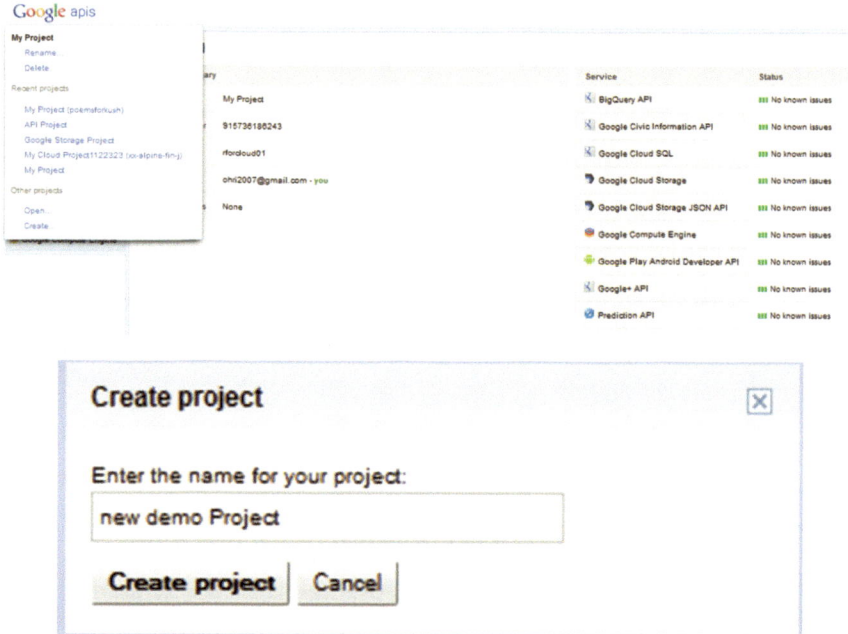

- Register Project ID

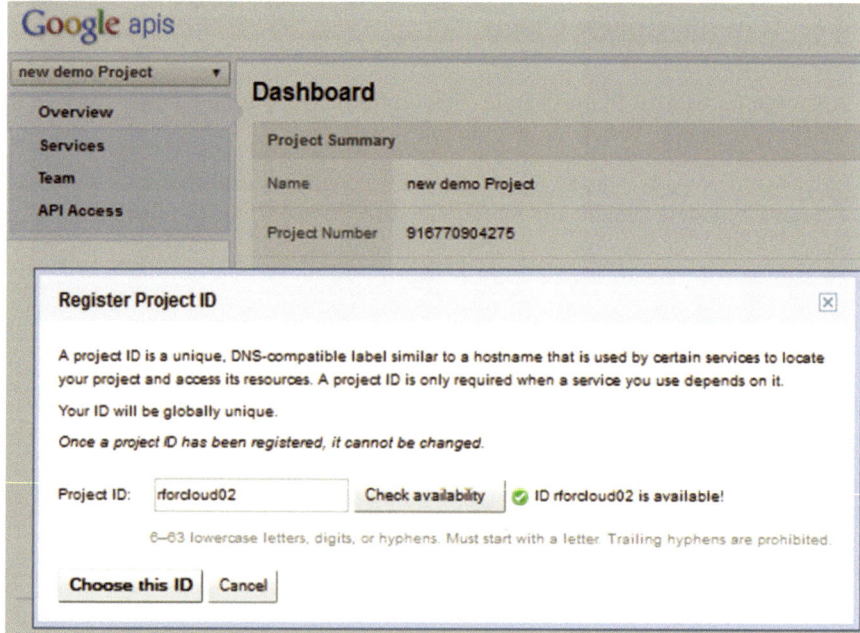

- **Note Access Keys**
- Create OAuth Keys

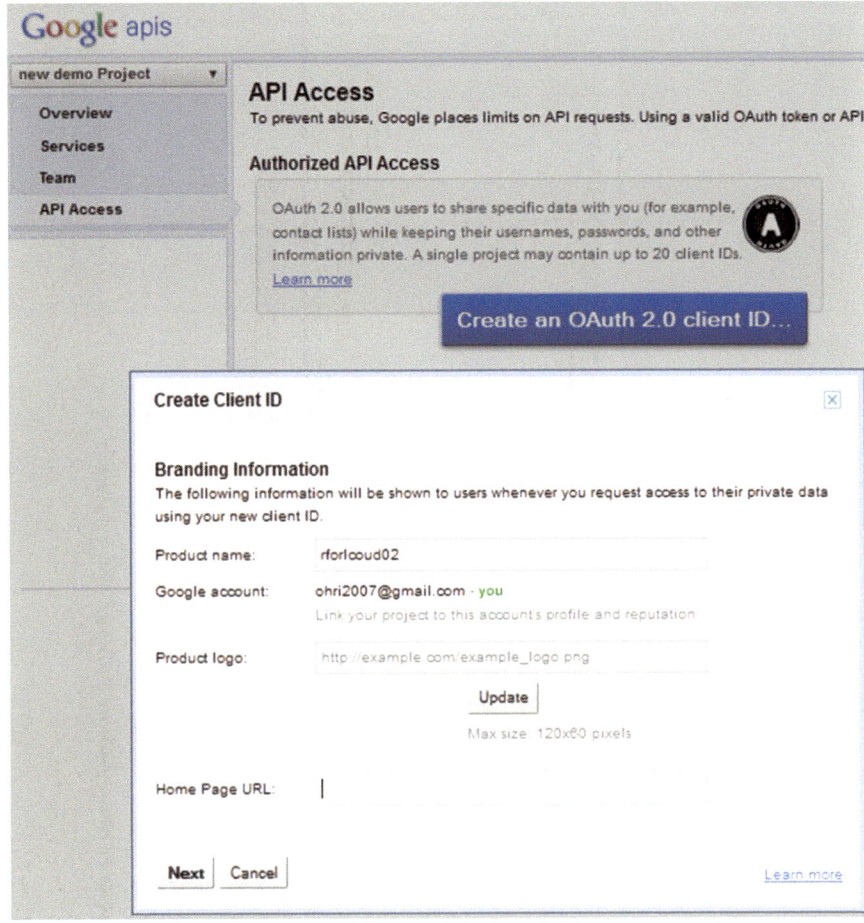

- Choose Application Type

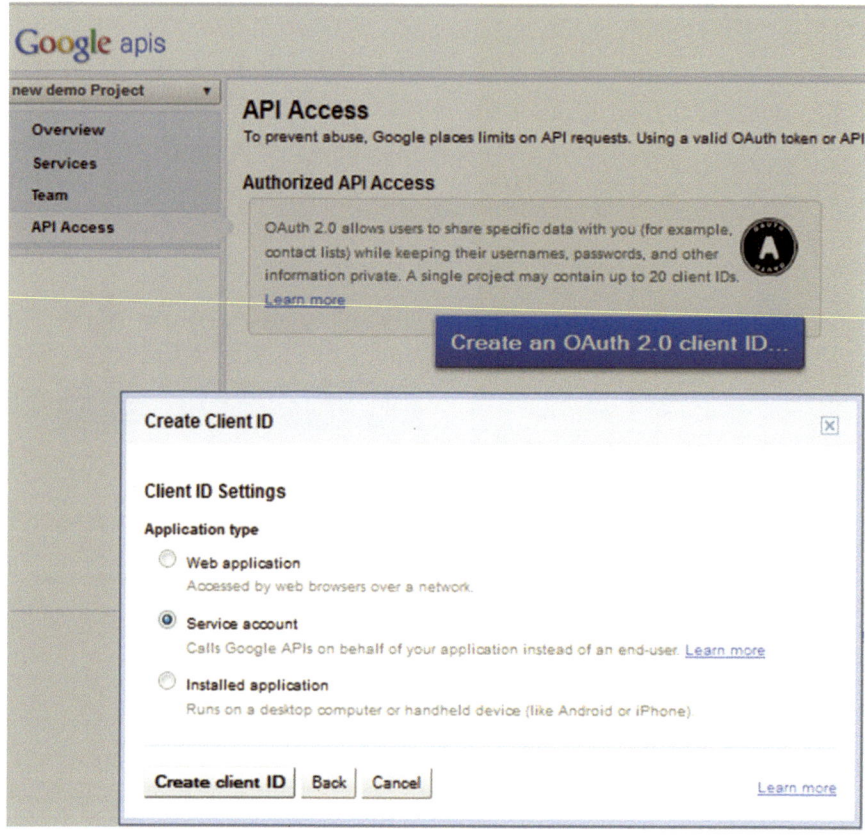

• Download Keys

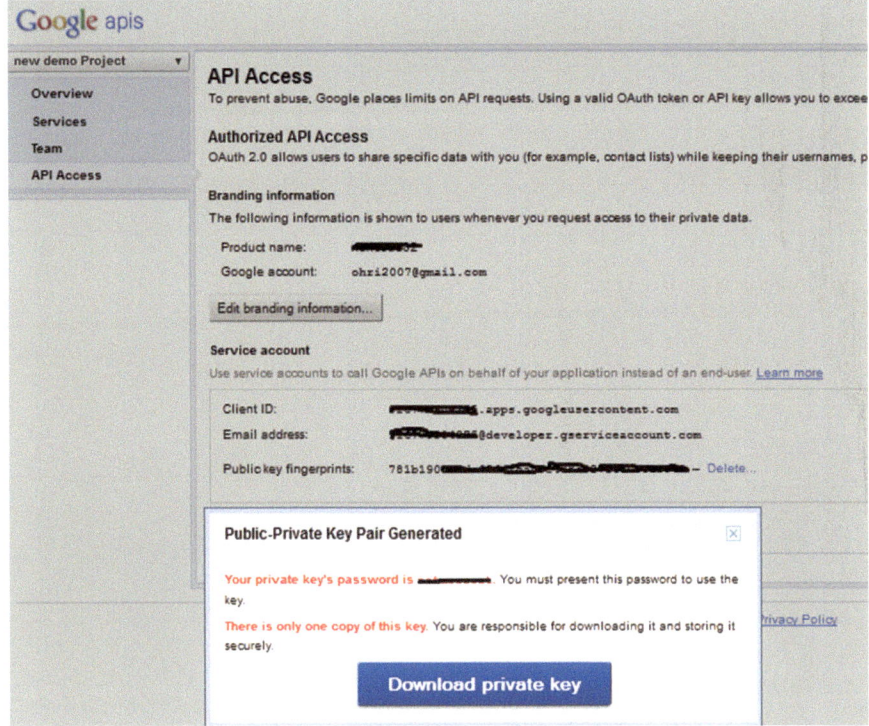

And this is how the final console will look

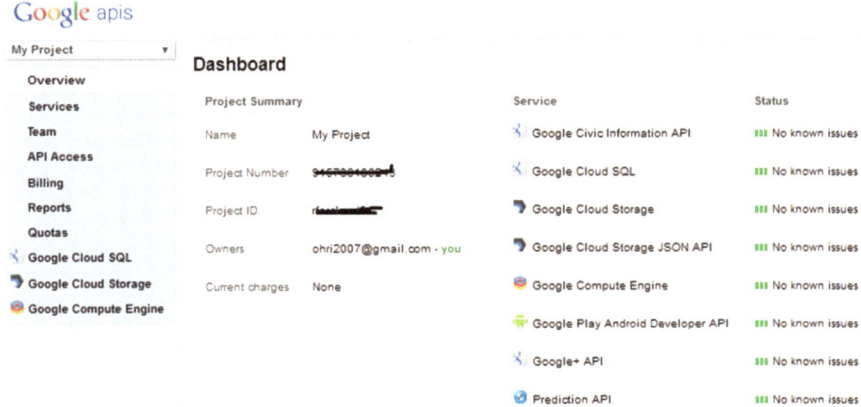

- Upload Data to Google Storage. The Google Storage Manager is at https://storage.cloud.google.com/. Uploading can be done by a web interface.

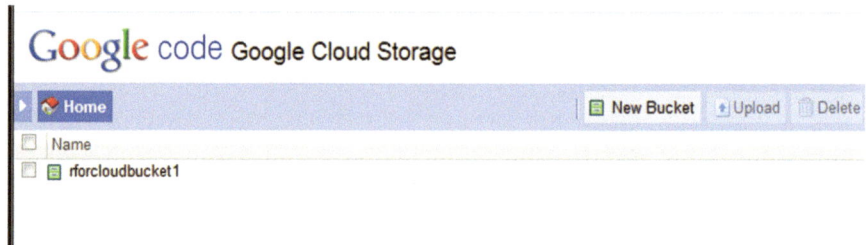

- Create a New Bucket

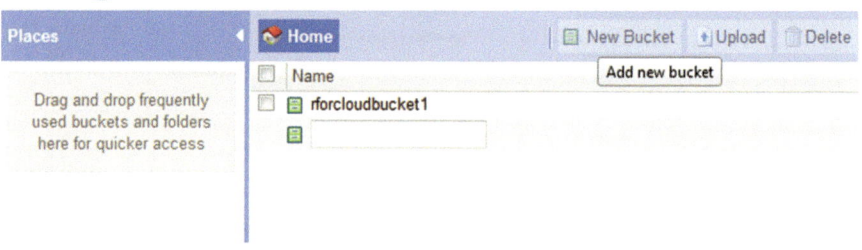

- Choose an (Available) Name!

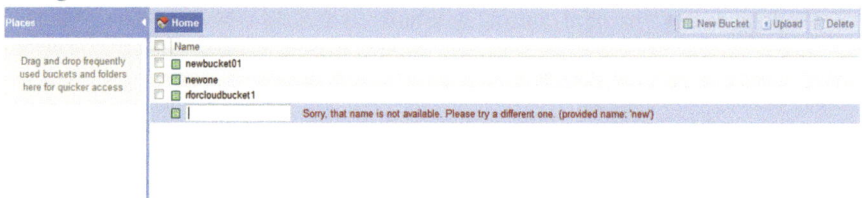

- Upload Data

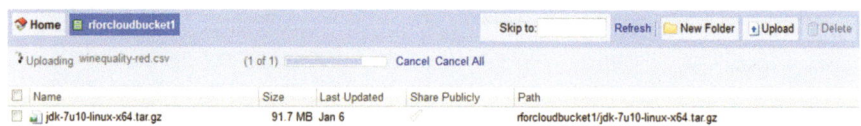

Note—For Google Storage

- Go to bucket
- Browse Local Files
- Upload and Wait
- Note the location path for the GS file (after enabling public sharing)

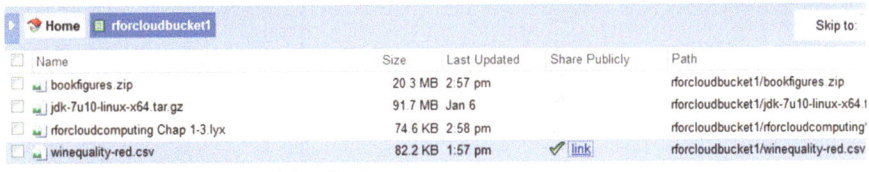

- Google Compute. The Google Compute tab is in the Google APIs console
. • We create a new disk by going to the Disks Tab

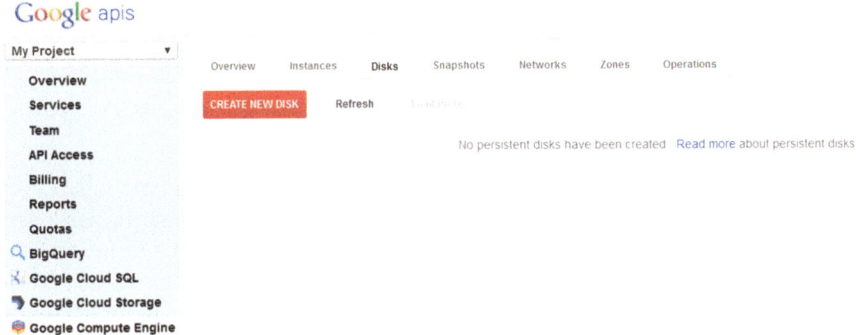

- Create New Disk—specifying the zone and size (GB). Note the REST console helps us in crafting the REST request in real time if we wanted to use REST for creating the Disk. Snapshots are presaved images of data stored that we can use to create disks.

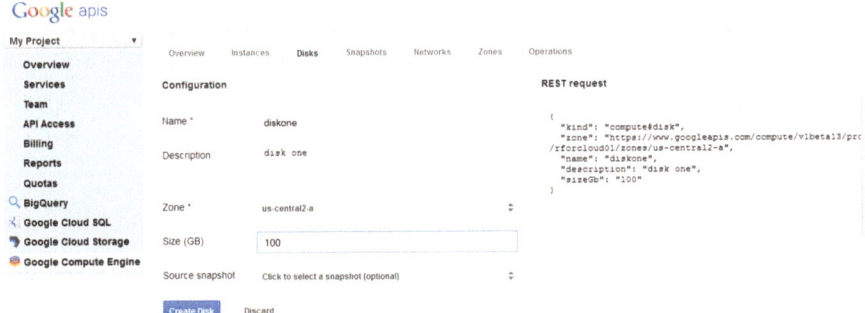

- This is shown when the disk is ready.

- Now we move to create the computing, processing part of our cloud. This is known as the instance. Click the instances tab on the top margin.
- Click on create new instance.

- Not we have many different regions to create our instance in. For regulatory and data hygiene purposes it is best advised to create the instance in the same zone as which the data is collected from—particularly if it is privacy sensitive data
- Note that Machine Specifications get populated simultaneously as we are crafting our instance type. This ensures we create exactly what we want, and any error by scrolling down drop downs is avoided.

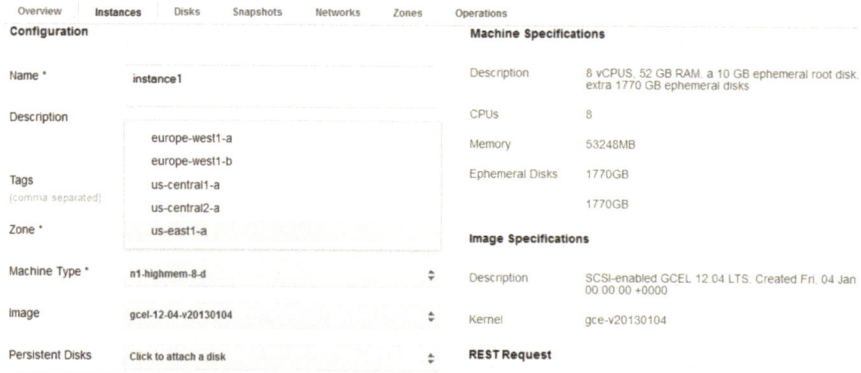

- Note the various types of instances in machine type—the number here refers to number of CPUs, while the rest of the designations stand for high memory, standard memory, and high cpu type. Note again the Machine Specifications on the right enable us to fine tune and control exactly what we want to create, and that depends on our computational load. RAM is critical to us as we are using R.

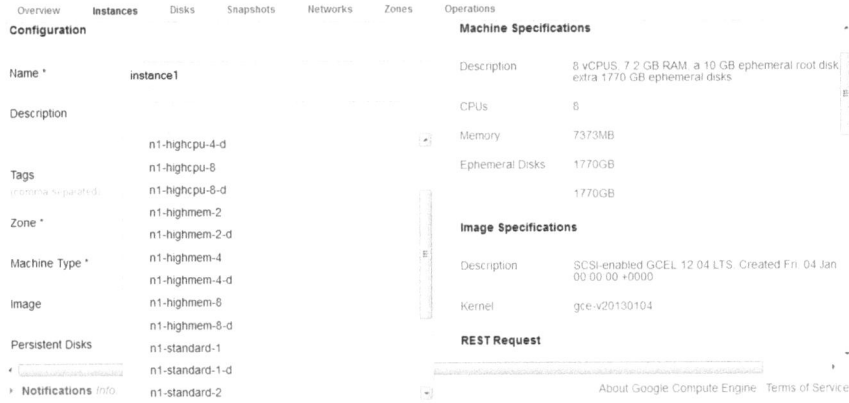

- When we click on the image, we get the preloaded images. These are mostly plain vanilla Operating Systems including Cent OS, Ubuntu, and GCEL. Note Google Compute supports only Linux. You could also create your own custom image/snapshot by taking a standard OS, and installing your custom software. This is useful as the user does not want to install the same set of software (R, etc) each time.

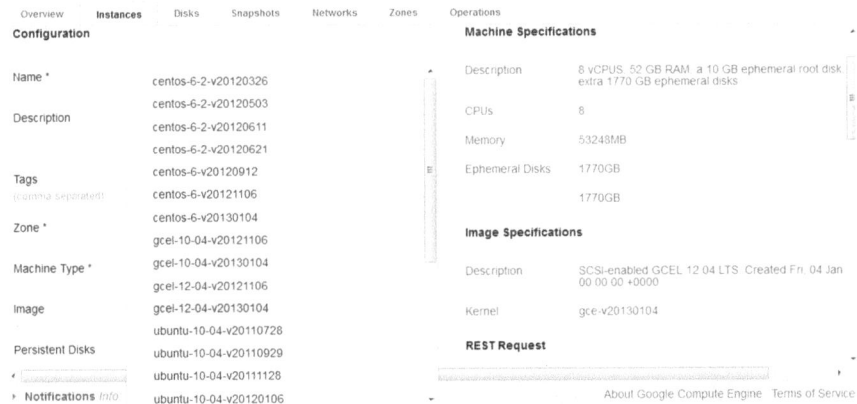

- Note that we get an error if our disk storage and our compute instance are in different zones. Also note that the REST console is crafting our request simultaneously based on our inputs in the Graphical User interface within the browser.

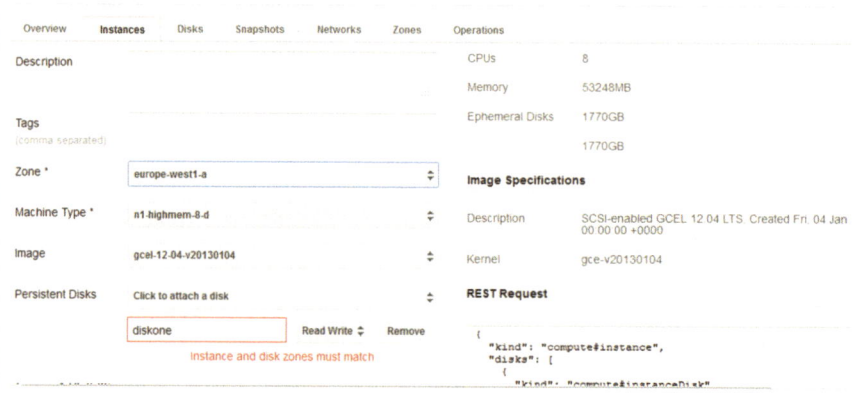

- We can also choose whether we want the disk to be Read Only or Read-Write.

- We could also specify IP addresses (if we have a previous ip address). Note the REST console is creating the request on the right as we fine tune inputs.

- Below the REST console is our command line utils in case we needed to do the same things we did in the GUI from command line using the GC util tool. That is often the case when we are trying to automate repeatable tasks. Also note on the left side, we can enable our service request and also enable access to other members of the Google Cloud Platform.

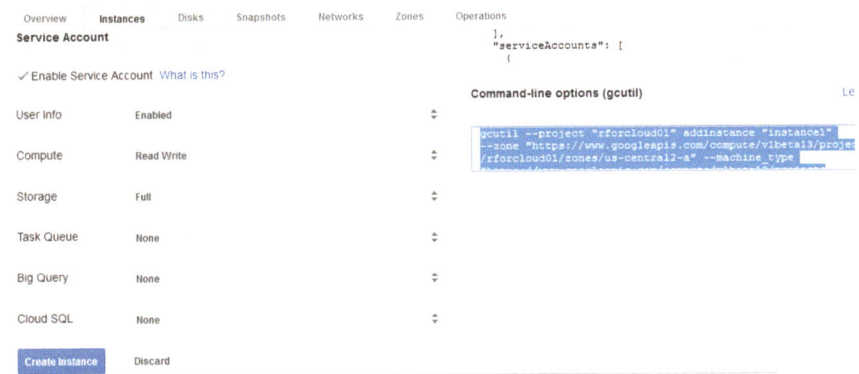

- We can enable access to other Google Cloud Services.

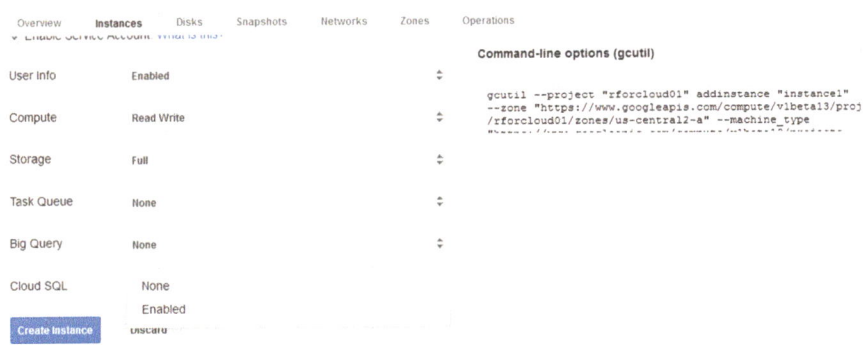

- We clicked on Create Instance—blue tab.
- The instance shows first PROVISIONING, then STAGING, then READY. It also shows us the external IP address, machine type, zone.

- If we click on the instance name (in blue above left) this is what we see, note we can also see the SSH instructions for using gcutil. gcutil is a command line utility created by Google for developers to access its cloud.

- If you are interested in reading the booting log (which is useful when troubleshooting) you can click on serial console—show output.

- Now we move to the Networks tab in the upper margin. This is where we enable ports for access and security.

- Now we are ready to install R, RStudop Server, and Connect to it. We can then move the data using the Google Storage in our Google Cloud Instance.

4.6.1   Google Big Query

- The Google Big Query Console is at https://bigquery.cloud.google.com/.

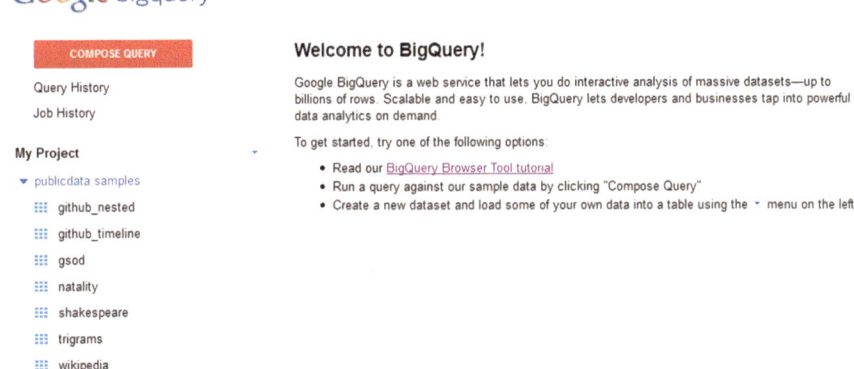

An R package for Google Big Query is https://github.com/hadley/bigrquery.

4.6.2   Google Fusion Tables API

Google Fusion Tables is an experimental application that lets you store, share, query, and visualize data tables. GFusionTables is an R package that acts interface for Fusion Tables from R and is available at http://gfusiontables.lopatenko.com/.

Example—Using the code from https://gist.github.com/felixhaass/5766725#file-drone_data-r we can plot the drone strikes and fatalities using R. and Fusion Tables. This can be presented as a time series line plot in R and presented visually in Google Fusion Tables. Dotted line shows change in US political system at Presedential level.

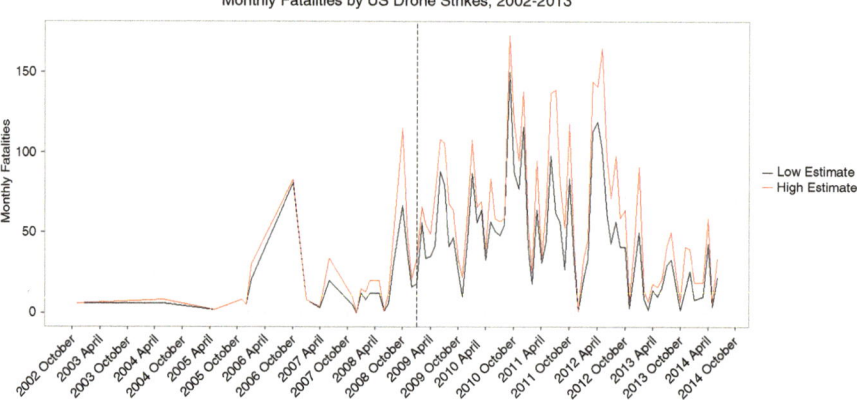

The **Spatial Map** is below

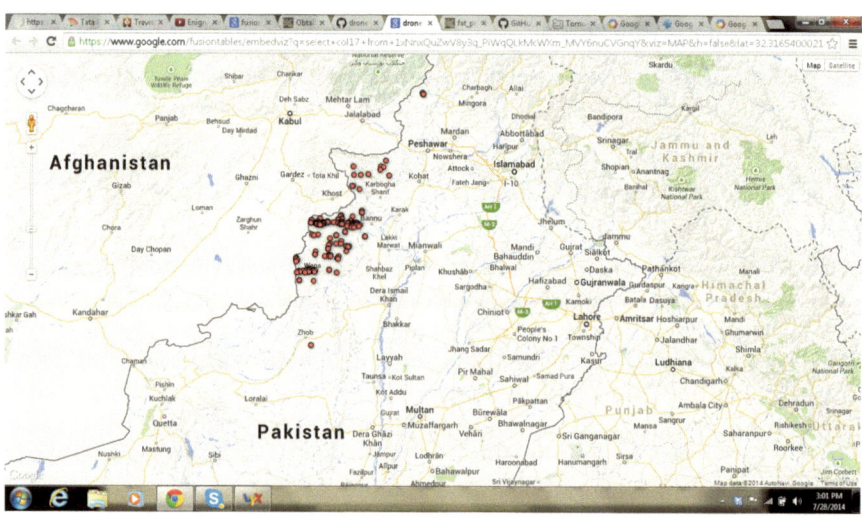

This is an example of reproducible research in which I could recreate the analysis using the code given at http://bretterblog.wordpress.com/2013/06/20/obtaining-and-mapping-us-drone-strike-data-with-r-and-google-fusion-tables/ exactly. This was enabled by sharing the code on github. The dynamic graph is at http://goo.gl/y9v2V9 and it can be zoomed out (to see Yemen strikes) or zoomed in to see the pattern of strikes.

4.6.3 Google Cloud SQL

Google Cloud SQL is a managed cloud instance of mySQL (mySQL is one of the most popular relational databases).

4.6.4 Google Prediction API

The Google Prediction API is at https://developers.google.com/prediction/. It can be used for prediction tasks and classification. Some of the use cases are for

- Customer sentiment analysis
- Spam detection
- Document and email classification
- Churn analysis
- Fraud
- Recommendation systems

You can use the R package for it at https://code.google.com/p/google-prediction-api-r-client/ and https://code.google.com/p/r-google-prediction-api-v12/. You can make training calls to the Prediction API against data in the Google Storage or a local CSV file.

4.7 R in IBM SmartCloud

As of 2014, IBM has shut down SmartCloud as a public cloud however it offers it for enterprises. This tutorial is for IBM SmartCloud, and it may or may not be relevant to current or future users of IBM SmartCloud Enterprise. IBM Smart Cloud is evolving very fast so some of these instructions may seem outdated. However I was given a free account and I am showcasing my experiences here. Currently IBM is using Softlayer as a public cloud infrastructure product (Softlayer is an another acquisition by IBM to offer cloud computing). You can see IBM's current offerings on the cloud at http://www.ibm.com/developerworks/cloud/services.html.Due to the still evolving nature of IBM's cloud offerings, this section will cover nearly all there is to be covered about IBM's cloud.

4.7.1 IBM SmartCloud Enterprise

- Go to https://www-147.ibm.com/cloud/enterprise/dashboard (or Google for the IBM SmartCloud Enterprise Dashboard link if available presently. As of now public and hybrid clouds are available at http://www.ibm.com/cloud-computing/us/en/private-cloud.html).

• Login and Click on Add Instance

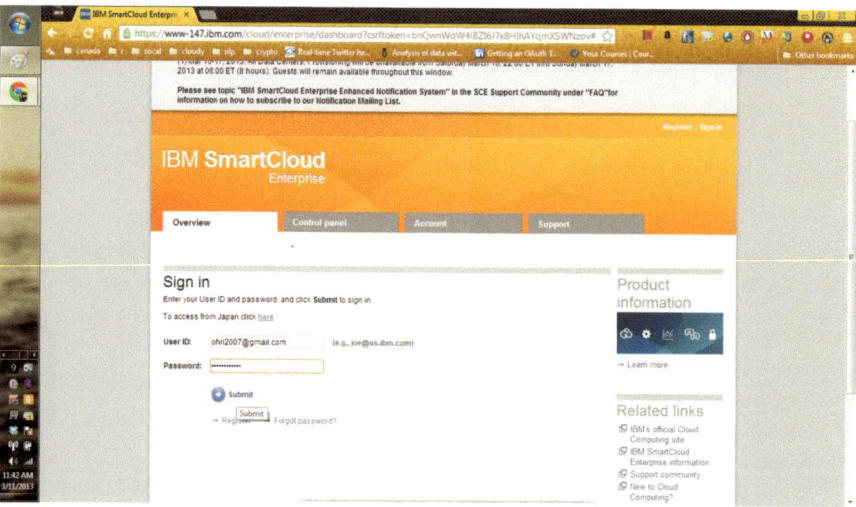

• Choose Public Cloud.

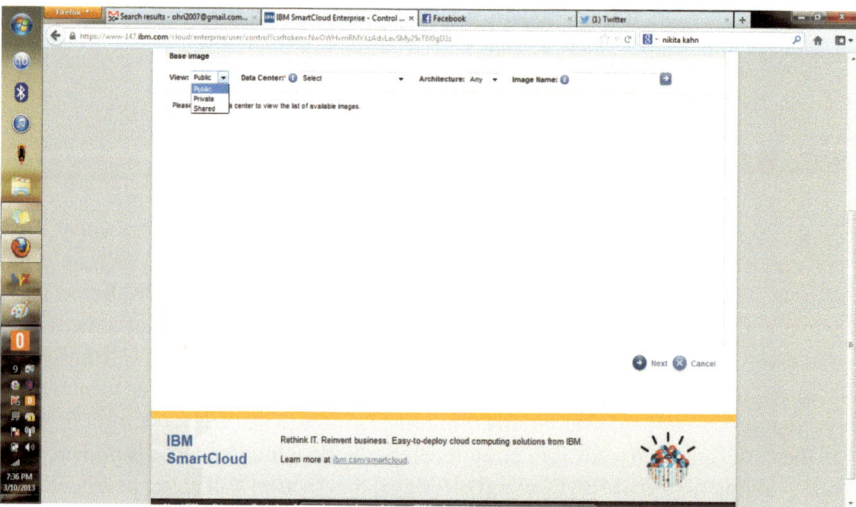

• Choose an appropriate location based on your data compliance and your own location.

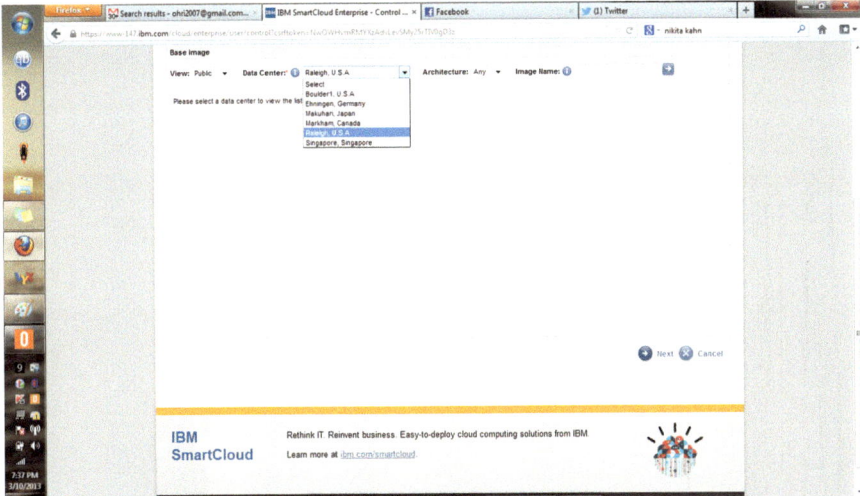

- Choose between 32-bit and 64-bit architecture based on your computing needs.

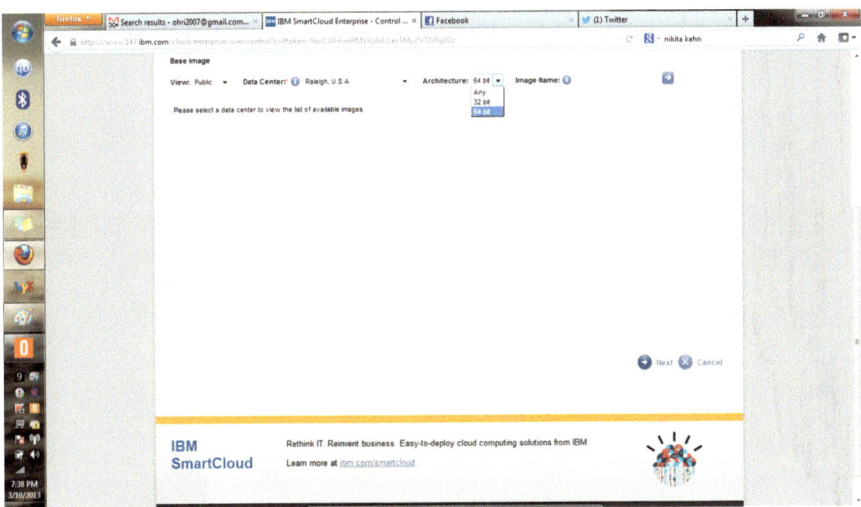

- You can choose wild card characters or part of name of instance to search.

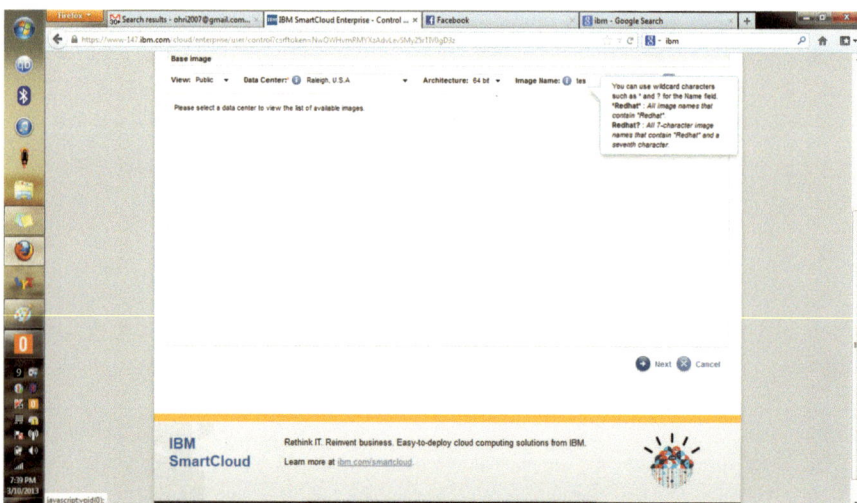

- We can put * and then click on the blue arrow in the right.

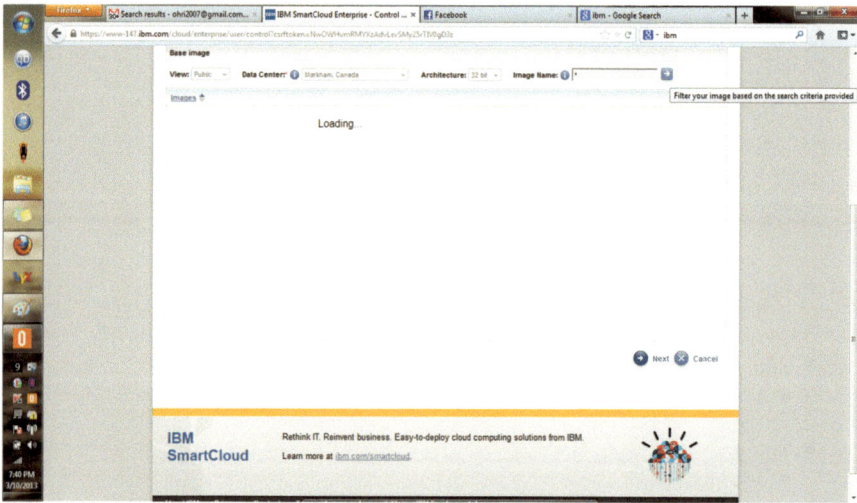

- From the search results, we choose one image (here RHEL 64-bit Linux) and
  then click next.

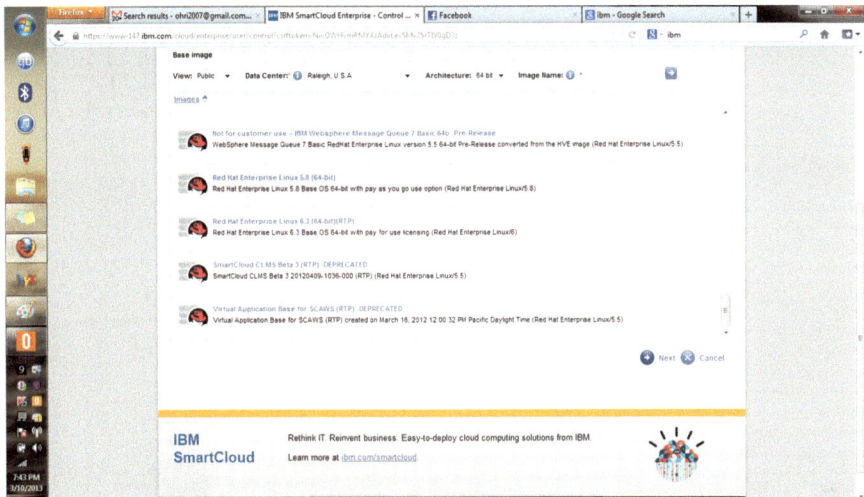

- We choose an appropriate configuration from the drop down in Server Configuration. Note the price is updated automatically.

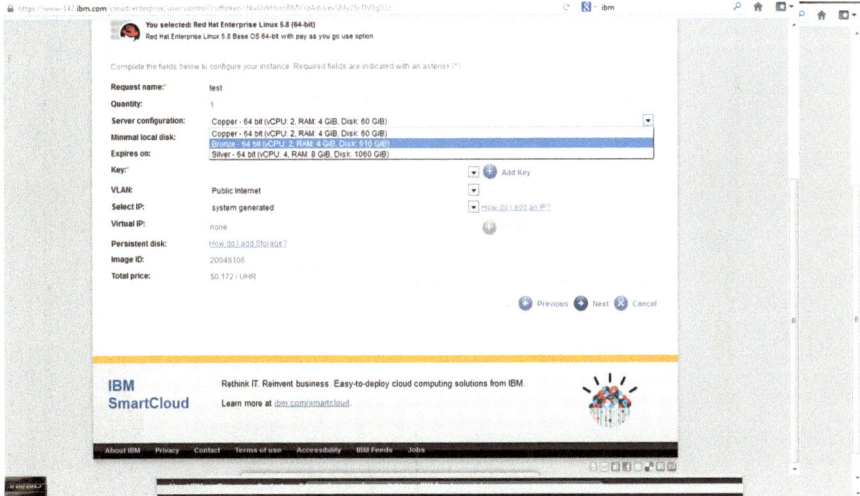

- We need to login securely—so we click on the blue + sign to add a new secure key.

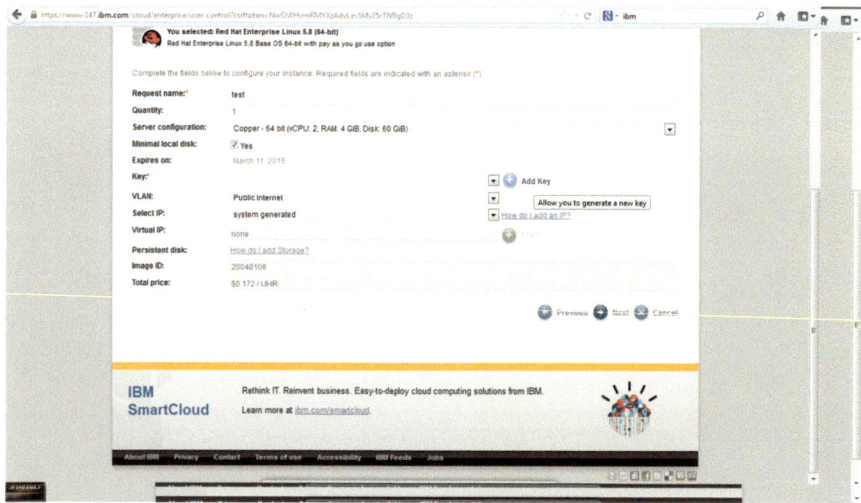

- In the next popup window, choose a name and click on generate new key pair

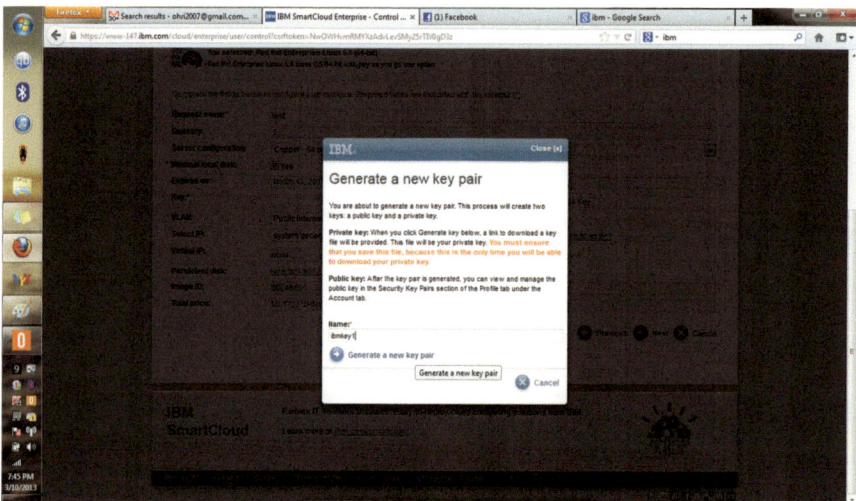

- Download the key

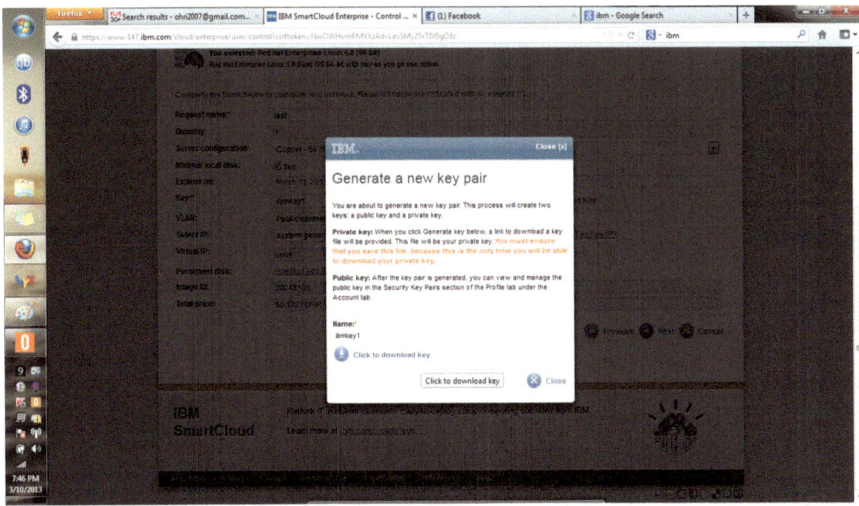

- This is a RSA file which we save to our local computer

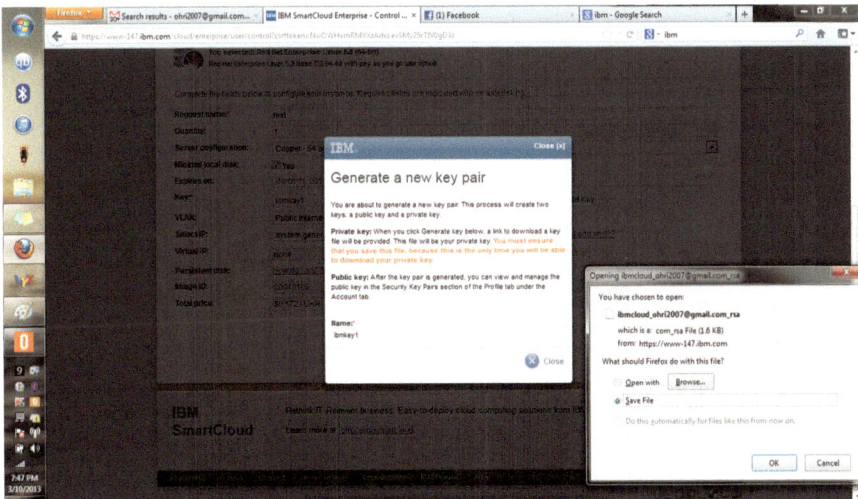

- Note we will have to modify the file format (from RSA to PPK) to make it useable. We will do this step later using PuTTyGen on our local machine.
- Additional Note—we can now configure additional options including storage from **Persistent disk** and fixed-IP addresses from **select IP.**

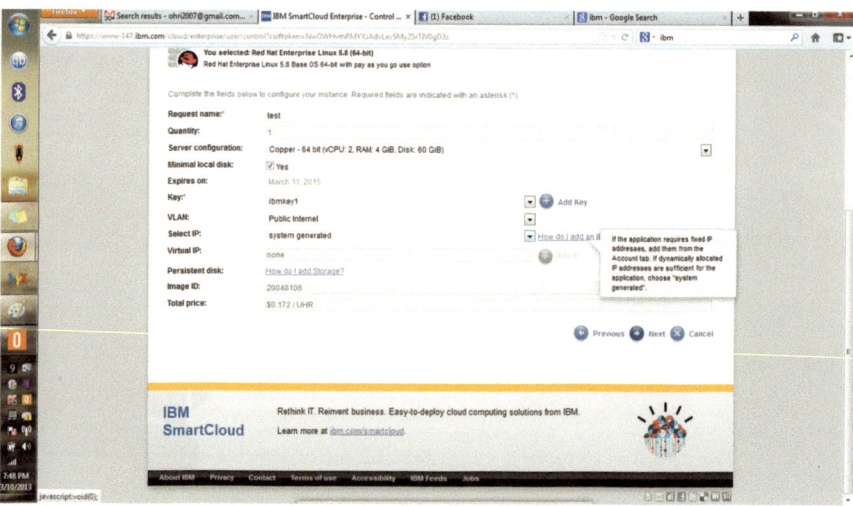

- Storage is also added through the Storage view of Control Panel (we are in the instance panel).

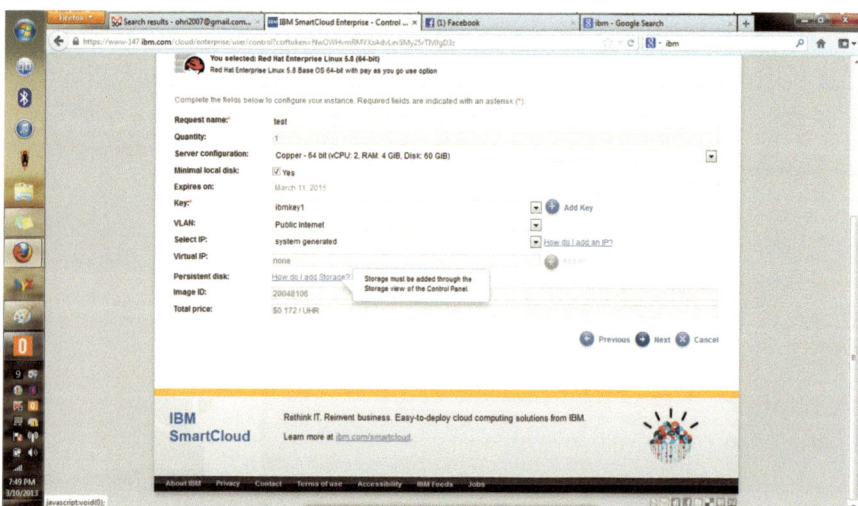

- We verify the instance configuration in the last step before launching the instance.

• One more thing, accept the Service terms before launching.

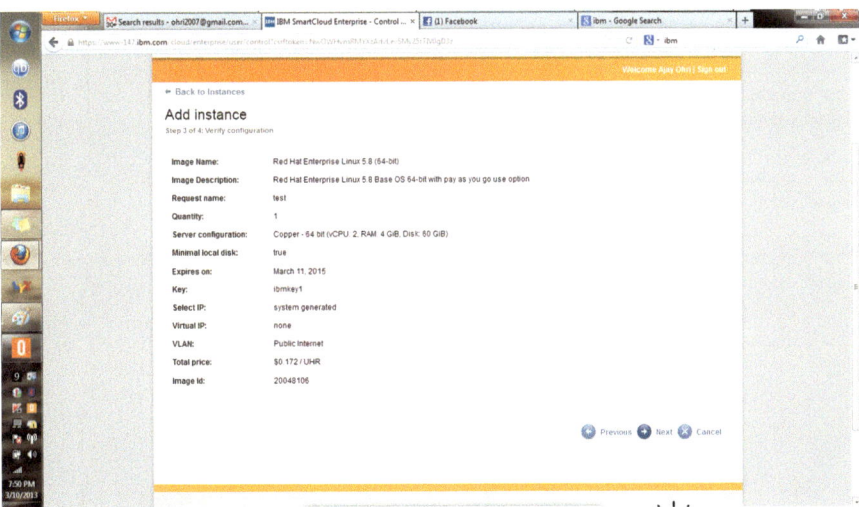

• The instance takes a small time to begin.
• You can check status using the control panel while waiting.

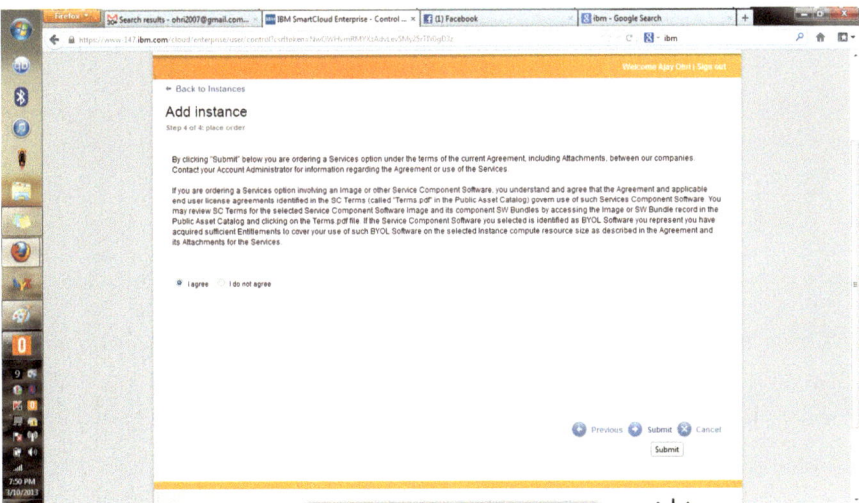

• Connecting to IBM SmartCloud using Putty.

Instructions to getting started in connecting to your instance are given below the Notifications. You can scroll down to read them.

   Note that the user id is **idcuser** for your SSH private key.

   You can download WinSCP from http://winscp.net/eng/download.php. You can read detailed instructions using the Tutorial Videos in the Support Tab.

Now—note the IP Address from the Instance tab.

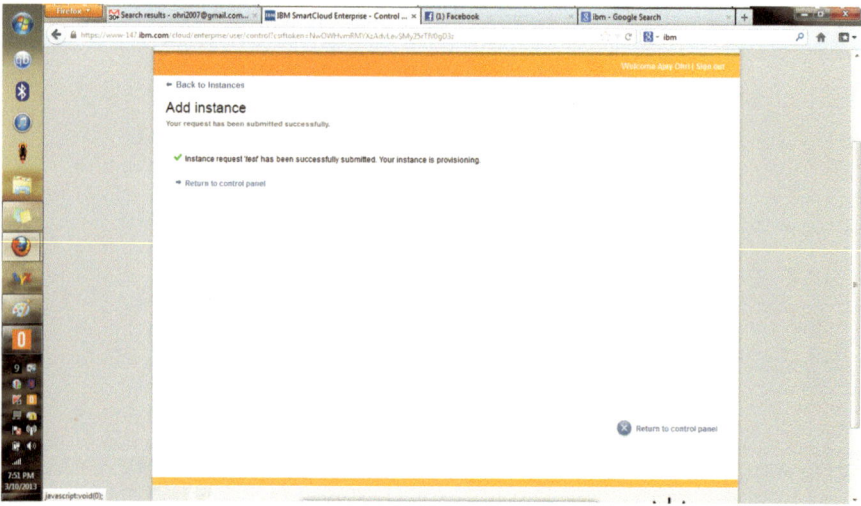

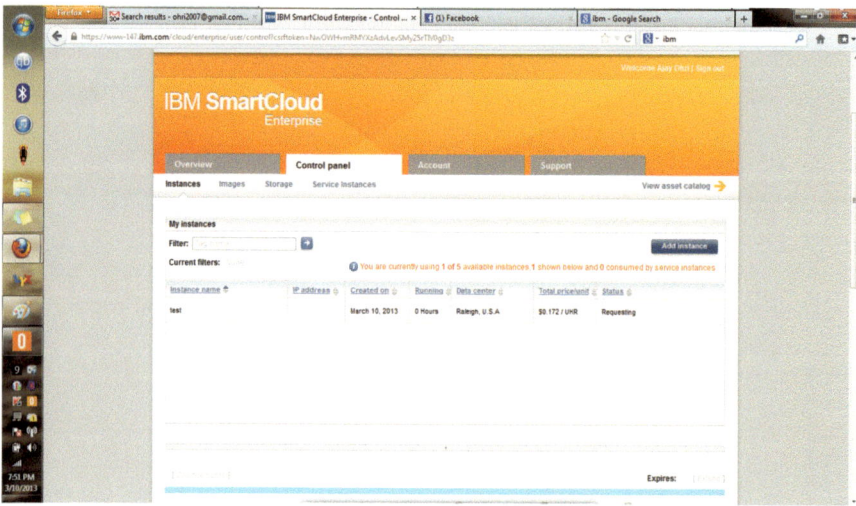

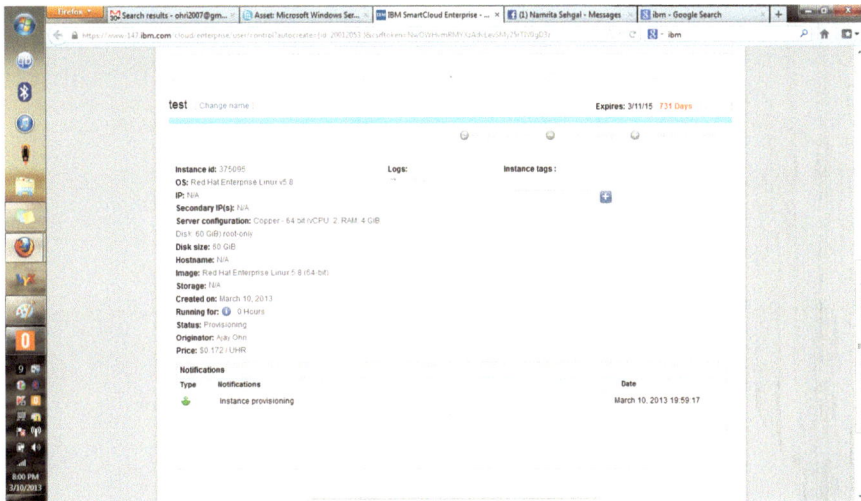

Download Putty from http://www.chiark.greenend.org.uk/~sgtatham/putty/download.html.

Use PuttyGEN to convert the downloaded RSA file into a .ppk file and save it.

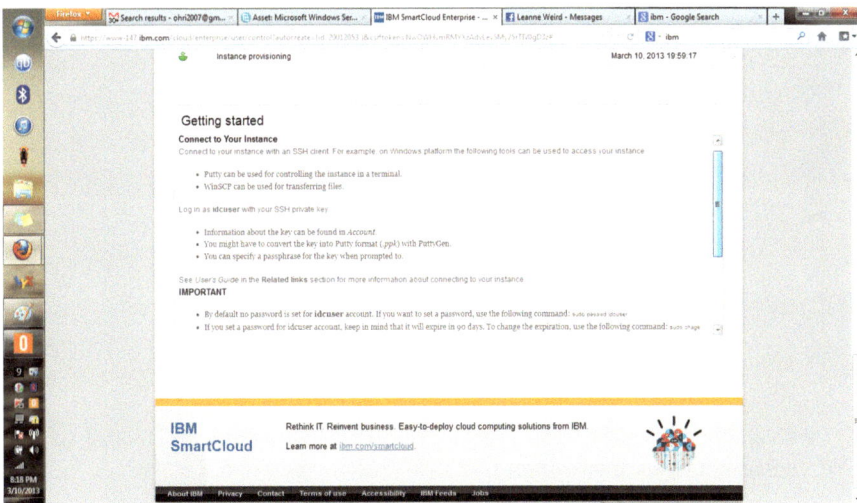

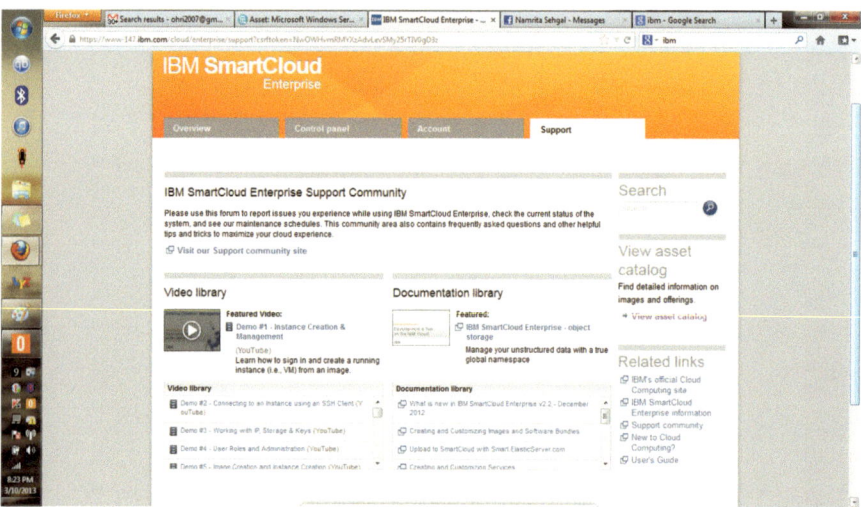

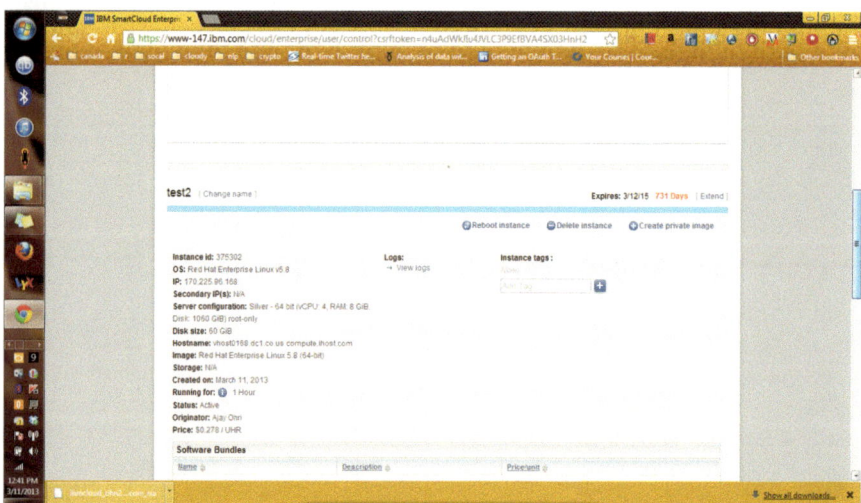

We can choose a passphrase for this key file as an additional layer of security. We choose not to use a passphrase.

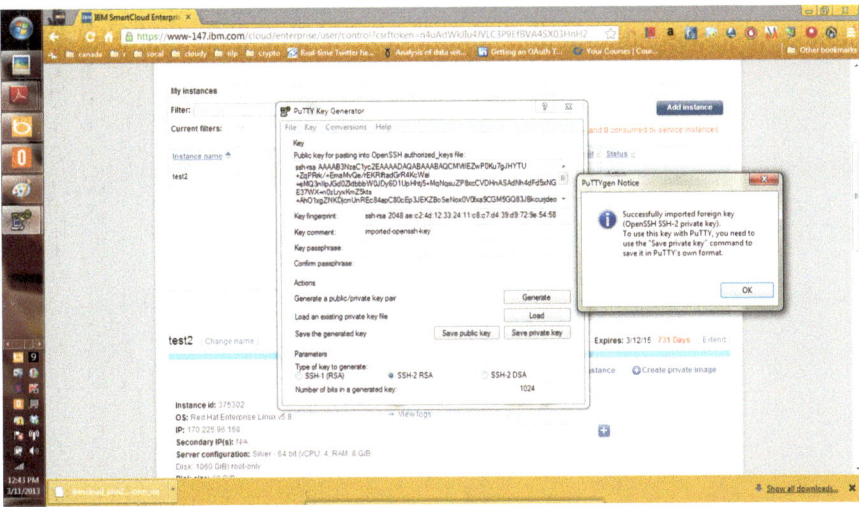

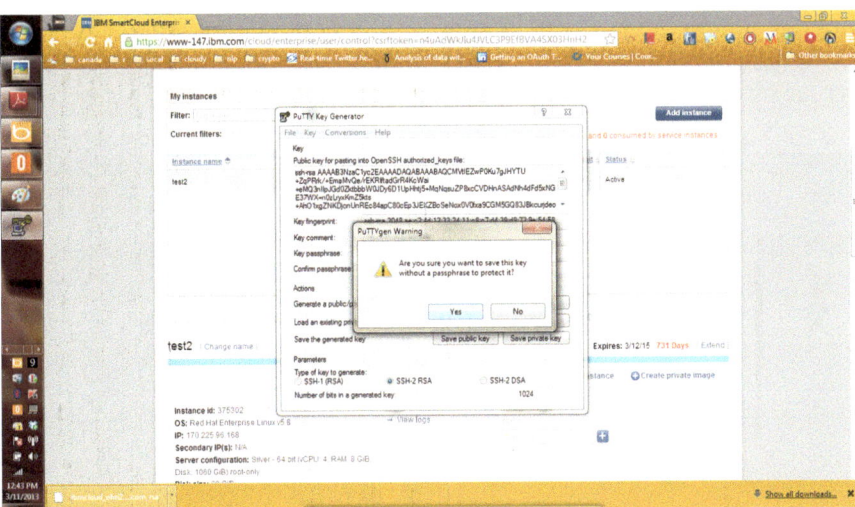

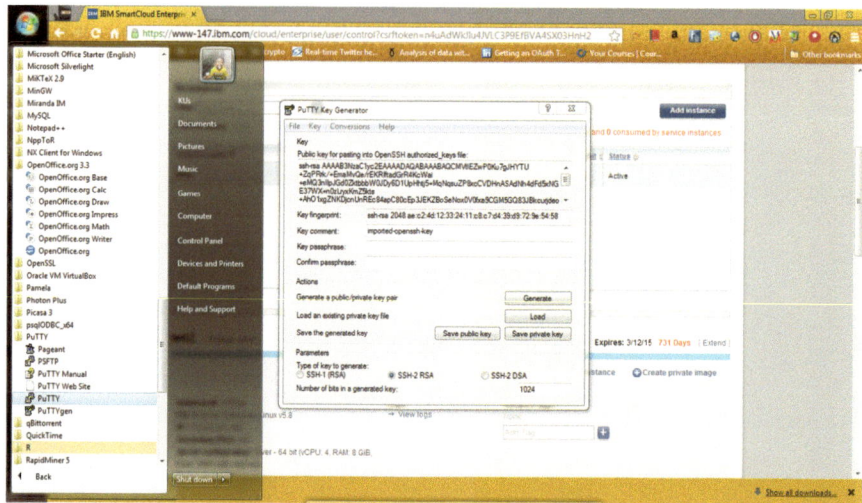

And now we use PuTTY to connect (while we used PuTTYgen to generate the key).

We paste the IP Address we noted above in the space shown, and we choose port 22 for SSH connections.

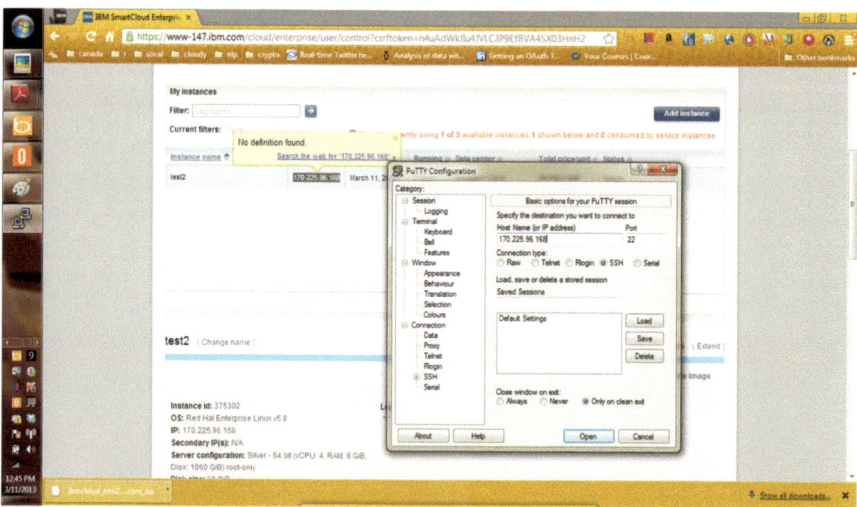

In the **SSH>data** options we choose the username we saw before (idcuser).

We add the location of the .ppk file (the key file for authentication) in the **SSH>auth** options.

Then click open to open the connection. Click Yes to add the key to carry on connecting.

Installing R and RStudio on the RHEL (Red Hat Enterprise Linux) Cloud Instance.

• Installing R-
• Install epel

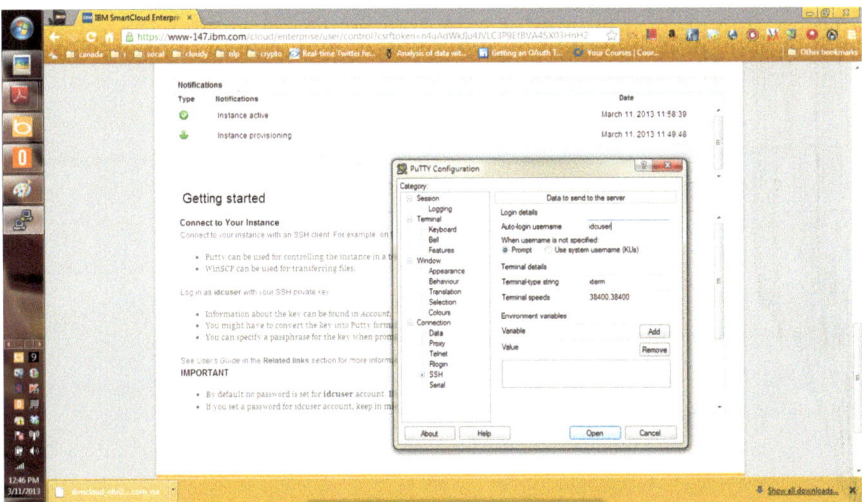

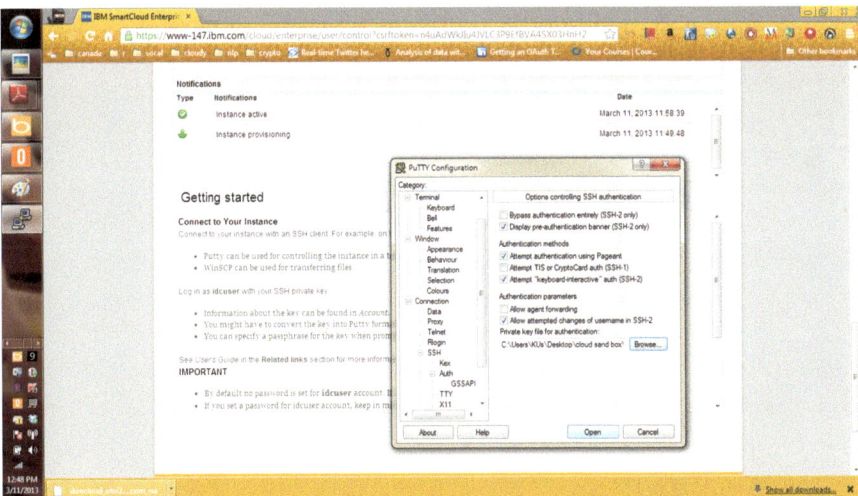

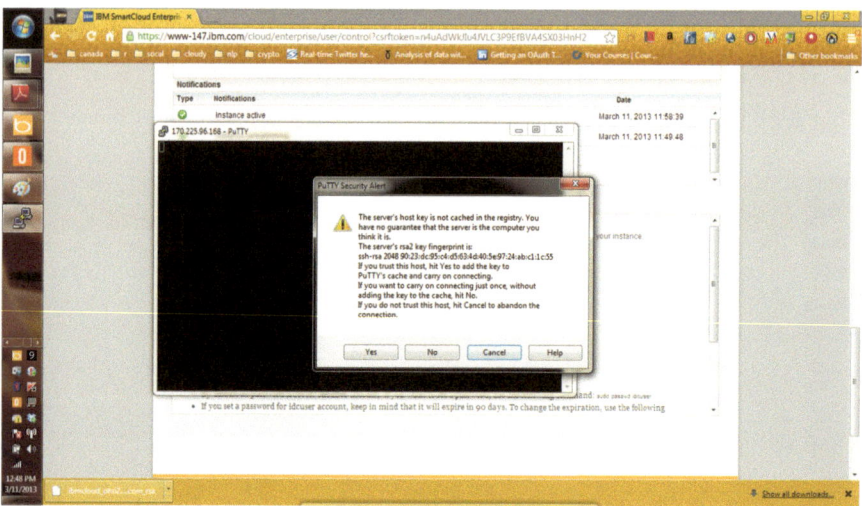

(Type the following commands in the Terminal Window. You may change the version number from 6–8 to the latest)

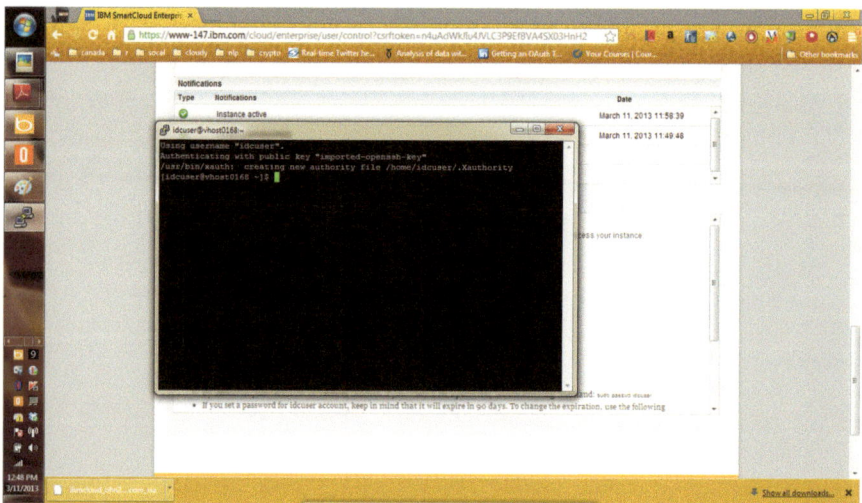

sudo rpm-ivh http://dl.fedoraproject.org/pub/epel/6/i386/epel-release-6-8.noarch.rpm

And we are now within the cloud instance.

(OR sudo rpm-ivh http://dl.fedoraproject.org/pub/epel/6/x86_64/epel-release-6-8.noarch.rpm)

• Install R

sudo yum install R

- Start R

sudo R
  HINT (to paste urls in Linux Window—use Shift + Insert)
  To Install RStudio Server
  (Instructions from http://www.rstudio.com/ide/download/server. You may change the version number from 0.97.320 to the latest)

- Download Install 64-bit RStudio Server.

wget http://download2.rstudio.org/rstudio-server-0.97.320-x86_64.rpm
     sudo yum install –nogpgcheck rstudio-server-0.97.320-x86_64.rpm

- Verify the Installation

sudo rstudio-server verify-installation
  Changing Firewalls in your RHEL

- Change to Root

sudo bash

- Change directory

cd etc/sysconfig

- Read Iptables (or firewalls file)

vi iptables
  (Hint—to Quit vi, press escape, then colon : then q)

- Change Iptables to open port 8787 (*RStudio's Default Port*)

/sbin/iptables -A INPUT -p tcp —dport 8787 -j ACCEPT

- Add new user name (here newuser1)

sudo useradd newuser1

- Change password in new user name

sudo passwd newuser1

- Now just using a browser, go to IPADDRESS:8787. Login with user name and password above. You can now use R from a visual IDE environment.
- Additionally you can create new users (even non Linux Users) to give them access to this cloud instance to start using R.

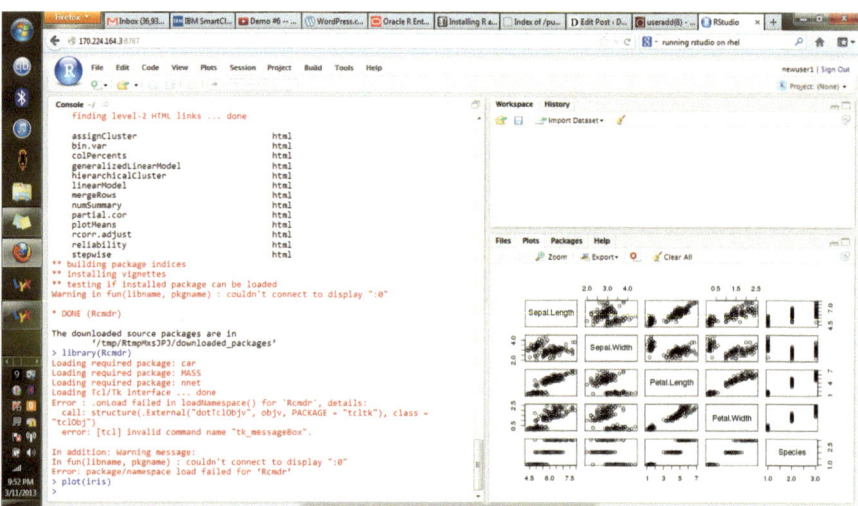

After doing your work, finally delete the instance.

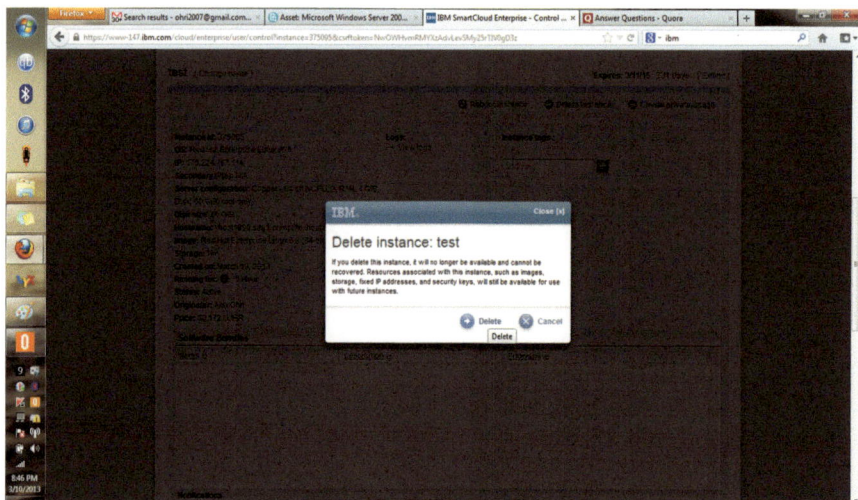

4.7.2   IBM Softlayer

The IBM softlayer interface is slightly different but the overall process remains the same. You can use the password created to login as user root. However an added feature is solution designer by which we can configure additional solutions (like Hadoop from Cloudera or MongoDB).

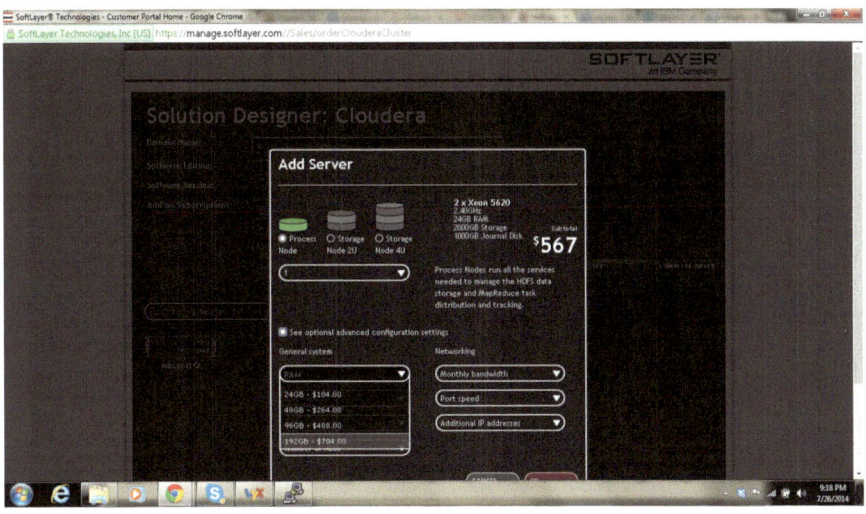

4.7.3   Using R with IBM Bluemix

The article titled "**Using R with databases A speedy combination: DB2 10.5 with BLU Acceleration and R**" (http://www.ibm.com/developerworks/data/library/techarticle/dm-1402db2andr/index.html?ca=drs) explains how to use R with data that's housed in relational database servers including accessing data stored in DB2 with BLU Acceleration and IBM BLU Acceleration for Cloud environments.

BLU Acceleration for Cloud is a product by IBM, it is a data warehousing, and analytics solution available in the Cloud and available at http://bluforcloud.com/.

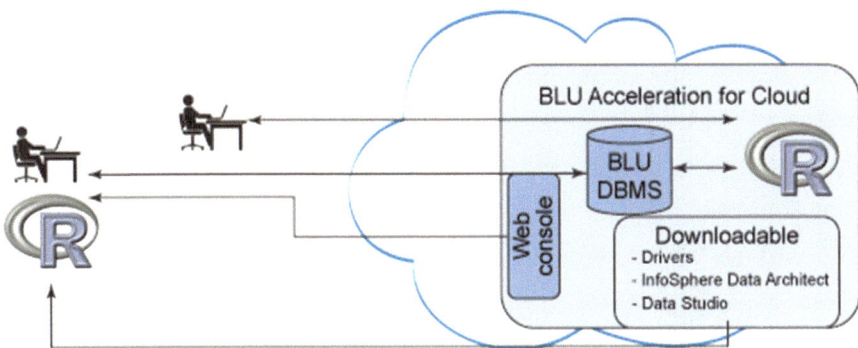

IBM Bluemix is an open-standards, cloud-based platform for building, managing, and running applications of all types (web, mobile, Big Data, new smart devices) or IBM's offering as a **Platform as a Service**. Capabilities include Java, mobile back end development, data acquisition and analytics, as well as capabilities from ecosystem partners and open source all through an as-a-service model in the cloud. It is available at https://ace.ng.bluemix.net/. The article "**Build a data mining app using Java, Weka, and the Analytics Warehouse service**"at http://www. ibm.com/developerworks/library/bd-dataminingblu-app/ shows how to potentially create an app for statistical analysis with options for including R.

In Bluemix, the Java application is deployed and takes advantage of the Analytics Warehouse (formerly BLU Acceleration) service to perform analysis.

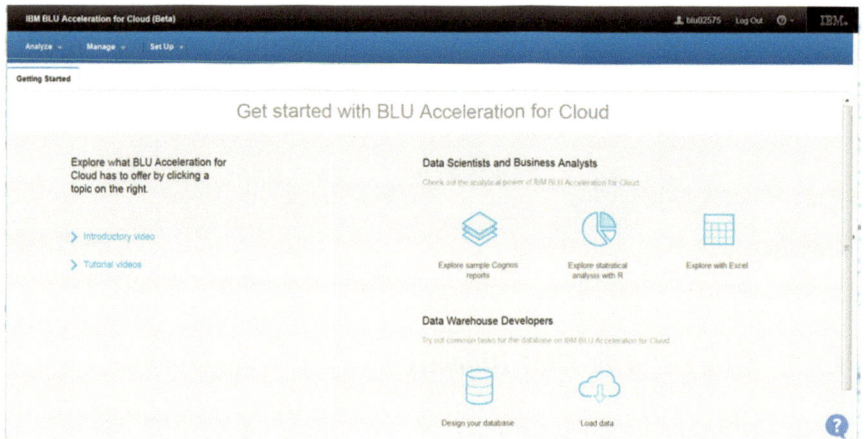

Chapter 5
Using R

Now that we have R setup and installed on your cloud instance, let us explore some ways we can use R usefully. In the following case studies I have chosen use cases for examples that would typically require a lot of hardware (read-cloud) and sometimes even specialized software. However the examples are not necessarily Big Data—they are limited by the author's access to practical data sets, the time required to fully explain all such examples, and the vast scope of the rich canvas R offers.

5.1 A R Tutorial for Beginners

To quickly boot strap the average user's R skills, here is a tutorial. It is based on extract article the author wrote some time back on his Decisionstats.com blog. In this the intention is to cut down on your learning time of a new language (here R) by identifying the most commonly used syntax and listing them in order a business analyst (or data scientist or statistical researcher or whatever buzzword the industry is coining post 2014) may need for data analysis.

Comments in R

To write comments in R, we use the # sign in front of the comment. This ensures that the part of code, text coming after # is ignored. Making comments is useful for readability of code and sharing it with other people. It also helps in the eventual and inevitable documentation process.

Packages

Packages are modules to help load up specific functions for defined tasks.

install.packages("Hmisc"İ) #installs package Hmisc

library(Hmisc) #loads package Hmisc

update.packages( ) #Updates all packages

Data Input

This lists the methodology with which a basic data input from file system to R is done.

© Springer Science+Business Media New York 2014   127
A Ohri, *R for Cloud Computing*, DOI 10.1007/978-1-4939-1702-0_5

getwd( ) # Gets you the current working directory

setwd("C:/Path"Ì) #Sets the working directory to the new path , here C:/Path

dir( ) Lists all the files present in the current working directory

a=read.csv("1.csv"Ì,header=T,sep=",",stringsAsFactors=T)

here

a= read.csv (**assigns** the object name a to whatever comes to the right side)

You can also explicitly assign a character name to a data object using assign)

read.csv is a type of input command derived from read.table to read in a rectangular object (rows and columns)

header specifies whether the first line has variable names or not

sep denotes separator (generally a comma for CSV files but can be space or tab for text files)

stringsAsFactors=T reads in strings as character values and not factor levels

To get help on all the options in input please type *?read.table* at the R console.

Example—

Download NorthWind Database as a csv file from https://github.com/tmcnab/northwind-mongo

Using the following options we are able to read the file correctly.

northwind=read.csv("northwind.csv",header=T,sep=",",row.names=NULL, stringsAsFactors=F)

str(northwind)

Object Inspection

Since R is an object-oriented language, we need to be sure of how to inspect objects and address parts of them.

ls( ) gives all the objects loaded in R

rm(poo) removes object named poo

str(iris) # Gives the structure of object named including class, dimensions, type of variables, names of variables, and a few values of variables as well.

#The only drawback of the str command is that it can throw up a lot of information for a Big Data set

names(iris) # Gives the names of variables of the object *iris*

class(a) # Gives the class of *a* object like data.frame, list,matrix, vector, etc.

dim(a) # Gives the dimension of object (rows, column)

nrow(a) #Gives the number of rows of object *a*—useful when used as an input for another function

ncol(a) # Gives the number of columns of object *a*

length(a) # Gives the length of object—useful for vectors, for a data frame it is the same as ncol

a[i,j] # Gives the value in ith row and jth column

a[i,] # Gives all the values in ith row

a[,j] # Gives all the values in jth column

a$var1 #Gives the variable named var1 in object a. This can be treated as a separate object on its own for inspection or analysis

Data Inspection

head(a,10) #gives the first ten rows of object a

tail(a,20) gives the last twenty rows of object a

*b=**ajay**[sample(nrow(**ajay**),replace=F,size=**0.05***nrow(**ajay**)),]* #gives a **5%** random sample of the data in data frame **ajay**

Here,

[] uses the subset to give value in the specified row

sample is the function for choosing random sample

nrow(ajay) =total number of rows to be sampled,

size= Size of sample =5% of above,

replace =F means each row number is selected only once

Basic Math Functions

sum(a)—sum of numbers in object *a*

sqrt(a)—square root sum of numbers in object *a*

sd(a)—standard deviation of numbers in object *a*

log(a)—log of numbers in object *a*

mean(a)—mean of numbers in object *a*

median(a)—median of numbers in object *a*

Additional—

cumsum —# Cumulative Sum for a column

diff—#Differencing for a column

lag—#Lag

Data Manipulation

paste(a$Var) #converts Var from Factor/Numeric variable to Character Variable

as.numeric(a$Var2) #Converts a character variable into a numeric variable

is.na(a) # returns TRUE whenever it encounters a Missing Value within the object

na.omit(a) #Deletes all missing values (denoted by NA within R)

na.rm=T # (this option enables you to calculate values Ignoring Missing Values) 4

nchar(abc) gives the values of characters in a character value

substr("ajay"Í,1,3) #gives the substring from starting place 1 to ending place 3. Note in R index starts from 1 for first object

Date Manipulation

The package *lubridate* helps in date manipulation and parsing dates from text data.

```
library(lubridate)
> a="20Mar1987"
> dmy(a)
[1] "1987-03-20 UTC"
> b="20/7/89"
> dmy(b)
[1] "1989-07-20 UTC"
> c="October 12 93"
> mdy(c)
[1] "1993-10-12 UTC"
```

Data Analysis

summary(a) #Gives summary of object including min,max,median,mean, 1st quartile, 3rd Quartile) for numeric objects, and frequency analysis of Factor variables

table(a) #Gives Frequency Analysis of variable or object

table(a$var1,a$var2) # Gives cross tabs of Var1 with respect to Var 2 of object a

library(Hmisc) #loads HMisc which enables us to use the following describe and summarize function

describe(a$var1) #gives a much more elaborate and concise summary of the variable Var 1—it is a better version of summary

summarize(a$var1,a$var2,FUN) #applies a function (like sum, median, summary, or mean) on Var 1, as GROUPED by Var2

cor(ajay) gives correlation between all numeric variables of object *ajay*

Data Visualization

plot(a$var1,a$var2) #Plots Var 1 with Var 2

boxplot(a) #boxplot

hist(a$Var1) #Histogram

plot(density(a$Var1) #Density Plot

pie #(pie chart)

Modeling

a=lm(y~x) #creates model

summary(a) gives model summary including parameter estimates when a is a model object created by lm

vif(a) #gives Variance Inflation (library(car) may help)

outlierTest(a) #gives Outliers

Write Output

write.csv(a) #Write output as a csv file

png("graph.png"Ì) # Write plot as png file

q() -# Quits R Session

R is a huge language with 5000 packages and hundreds of thousands of functions. To help the reader, we have created a set of important functions as a reference card. Note this differs slightly from the example shown above—as it is basically a card to help memorize syntax.

My first 25 R Commands

What's here?
- ls()
- getwd()
- setwd()
- dir()
- rm()

What's in my object?
- str()
- class()
- dim()
- length()
- names()
- nrowl() # and ncol()

Packages
- install.package("FOO")
- library(FOO)
- update.package()

Math
- log(x)
- mean(x)
- sd(x)
- median(x)
- exp(x)

How do I select or change stuff
- data.frame.name$variable
- data.frame[row,column]
- subset(df,df.name$var1 > X & df$var2 <Y | df$var3 ==" text")

Function
- function1=**function(x,y,z)**{x^2+2x*y+(z/10)-23}

What can I do?
- read.table()
- write.table()
- summary()
- table()
- plot()
- hist()
- boxplot()
- library(Hmisc) describe()
- library(Hmisc) summarize()

and

My next 25 R Commands

What's missing? Operators
- is.na()
- na.omit()
- na.rm=T

- diff
- lag
- cumsum

System
- system.time()
- Sys.Date()
- Sys.time()

Modeling
- cor(x)
- lm(x)
- vif(a)
- outlierTest(a)

Data Mining
- kmeans
- arules::apriori
- tm::tm_map

References-

http://www.statmethods.net/advstats/cluster.html
http://cran.r-project.org/web/packages/arulesViz/vignettes/arulesViz.pdf
http://cran.r-project.org/web/packages/tm/vignettes/tm.pdf
http://www.rdatamining.com/examples/association-rules

Data Manipulation
- as operator
- substr
- nchar
- paste
- difftime
- strptime
- lubridate::mdy
- apply functions

What more can I do?
- b=ajay[**sample**(nrow(ajay),**replace**=F, **size**=0.05*nrow(ajay)),]
- **png("graph.png")** Write plot as png file
- **dev.off**

5.2 Doing Data Mining with R

Data mining is defined as using statistical and programming tools to investigate and explore data (or mine them) to identify patterns, insights, and decision support strategies. The leading project methodology for doing Data Mining is CRISP-DM (Cross Industry Standard Process for Data Mining) and a visual representation of CRISP-DM is given here. This will help in quality control and process checks during data mining projects.

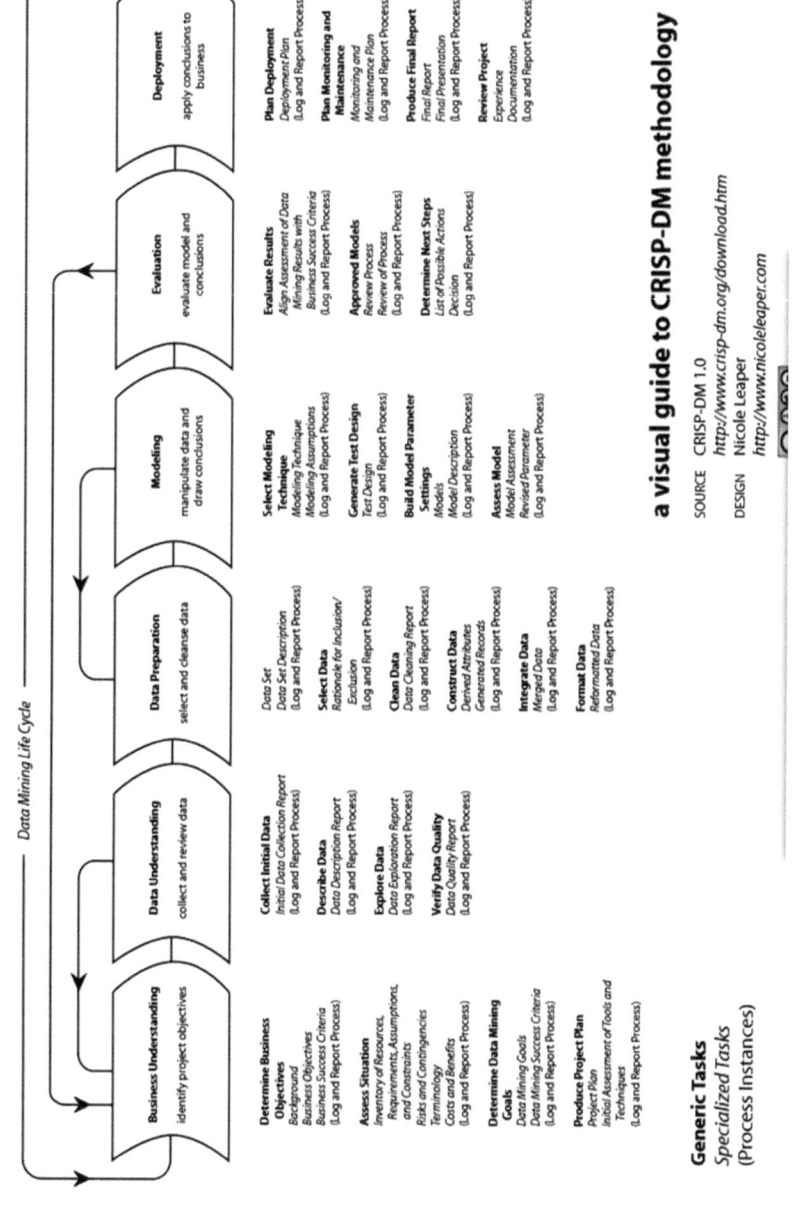

a visual guide to CRISP-DM methodology

SOURCE   CRISP-DM 1.0
         http://www.crisp-dm.org/download.htm
DESIGN   Nicole Leaper
         http://www.nicoleleaper.com

To simplify the usage of data mining through R, we will make use of the excellent graphical user interface (GUI) package "rattle". We install Rattle using the procedure for installing packages given in section above. For troubleshooting any issues, please refer to the website at http://rattle.togaware.com/.

Invoking Rattle

```
R R Console
ISBN 3-900051-07-0
Platform: x86_64-w64-mingw32/x64 (64-bit)

R is free software and comes with ABSOLUTELY NO WARRANTY.
You are welcome to redistribute it under certain conditions.
Type 'license()' or 'licence()' for distribution details.

  Natural language support but running in an English locale

R is a collaborative project with many contributors.
Type 'contributors()' for more information and
'citation()' on how to cite R or R packages in publications.

Type 'demo()' for some demos, 'help()' for on-line help, or
'help.start()' for an HTML browser interface to help.
Type 'q()' to quit R.

[Previously saved workspace restored]

> library(rattle)
Rattle: A free graphical interface for data mining with R.
Version 2.6.25 r42 Copyright (c) 2006-2013 Togaware Pty Ltd.
Type 'rattle()' to shake, rattle, and roll your data.
> rattle()|
```

Data Input Options—Note we use the library option here, but we have multiple options including spreadsheet and ODBC (for databases)

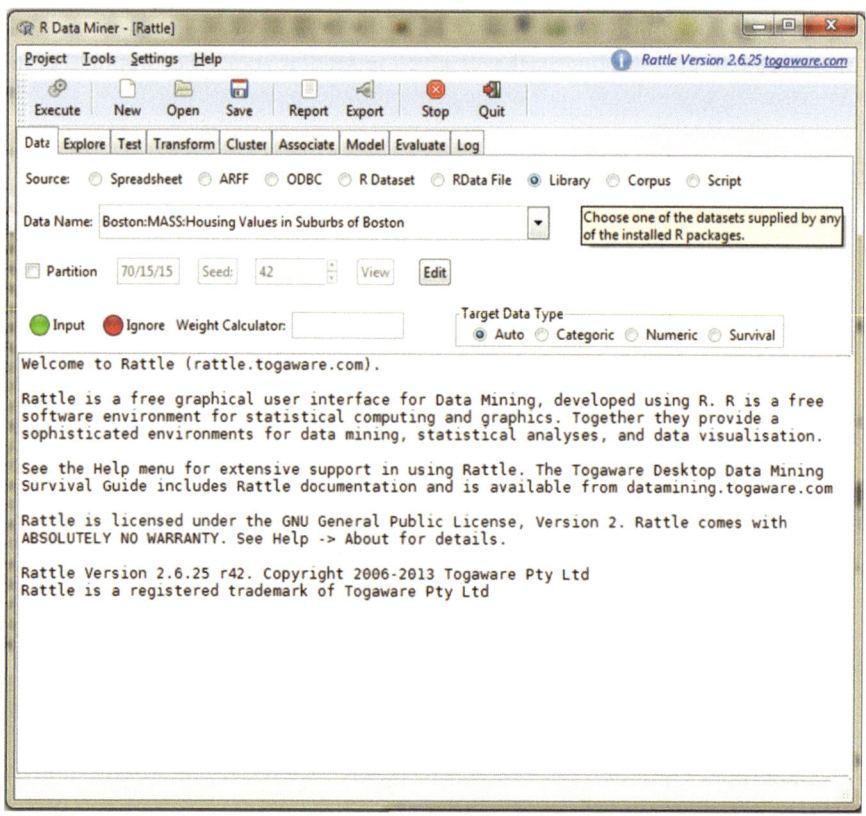

Now we click the **Execute Button** to run the current tab. The Execute button needs to be pressed every time a new change is done.

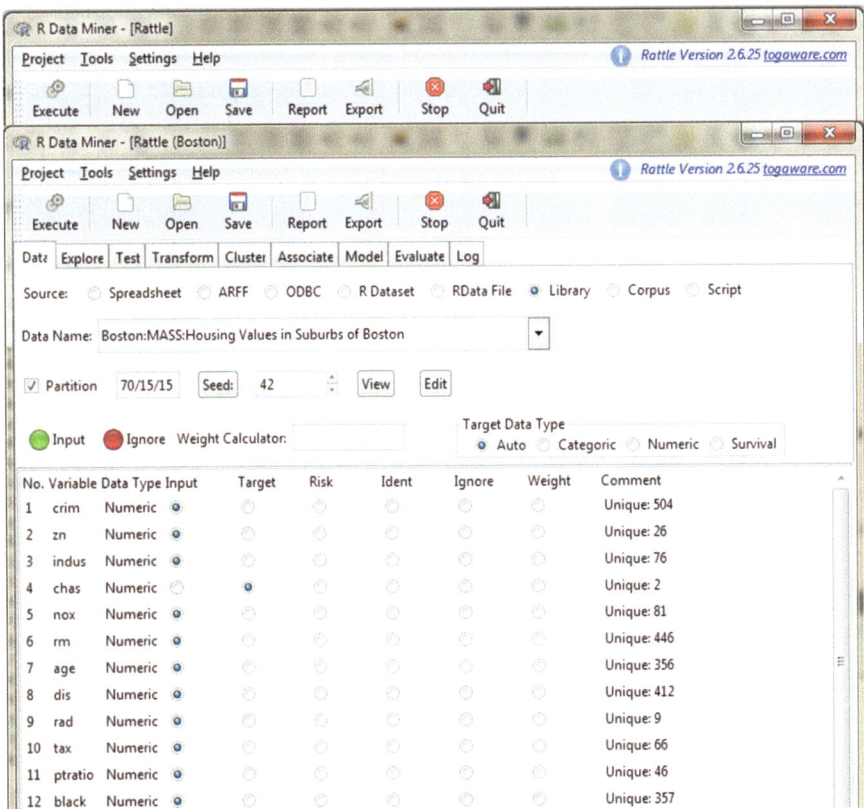

Note we can use a random seed to split the data into train/validate/test datasets which will help with building a model, and then validating for overfitting.

Rattle automatically has assigned **chas** variable as target variable, which we will like to change to **medv** variable. Again the author would like to emphasize the professional nature of this GUI using the extremely easy to read hover help cards when a mouse pointer comes on a tab.

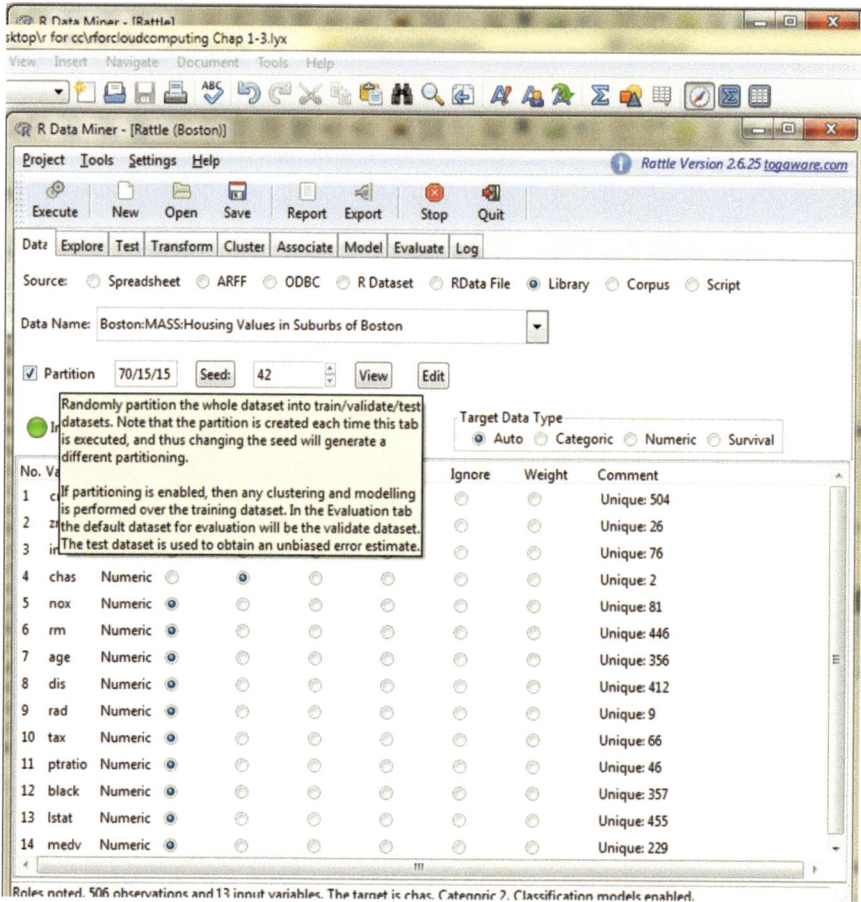

Now we use the radio buttons to change the target variable to **medv** and then click Execute button.

We note that the **bottom bar** in the following figure gives us a prompt for what kind of models are now enabled.

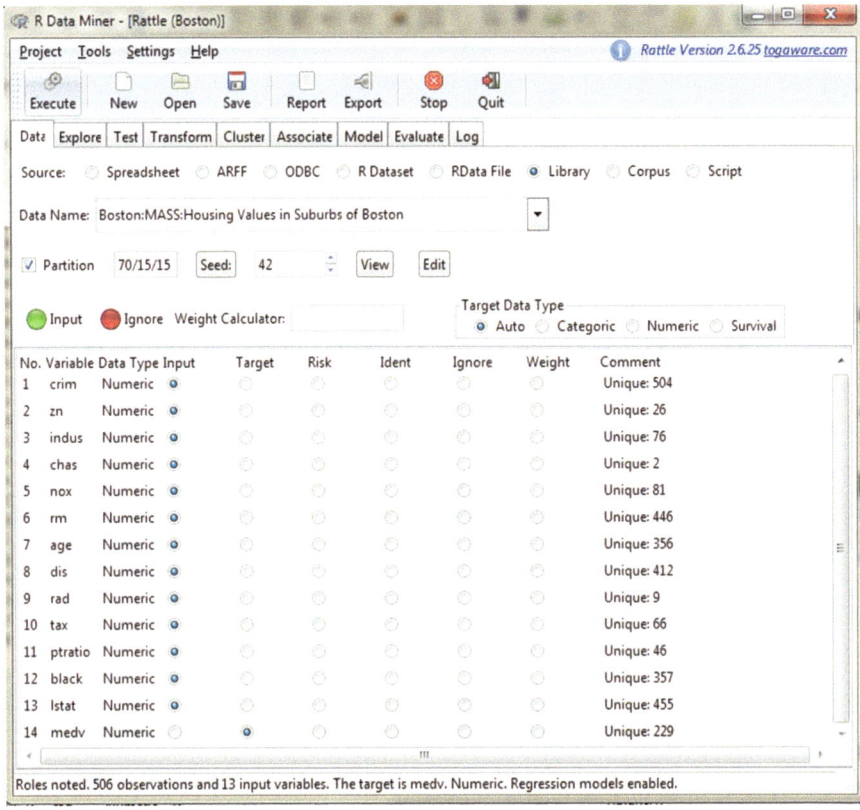

Building Decision Trees

Lets click the Model Tab from the Data Tab. Note some options are greyed out. This is because **rattle** package is designed to prevent junk analysis by reckless clicking unlike some other badly designed Graphical User Interfaces.

We click the **tree** radio button and then choose the appropriate options in **algorithm**, and splits/buckets/depth/complexity

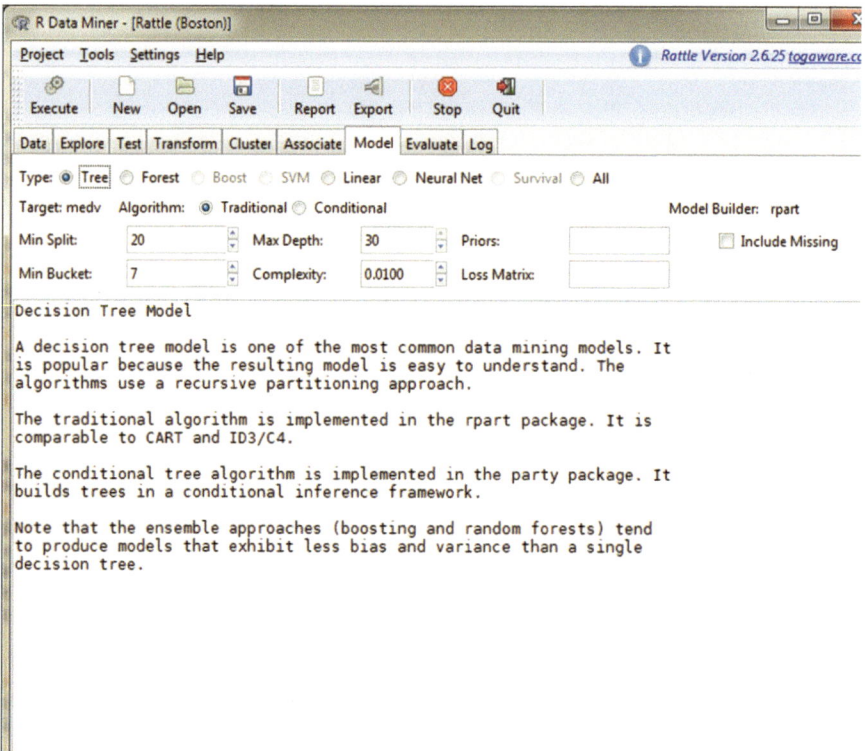

and this is the result

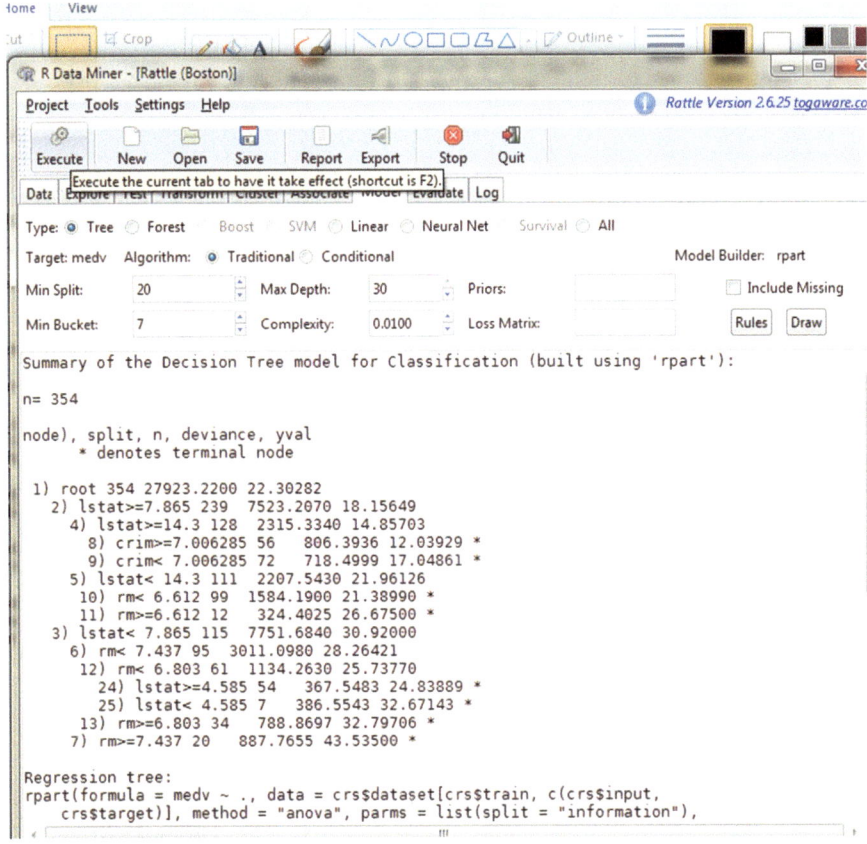

```
R Data Miner - [Rattle (Boston)]

Project   Tools   Settings   Help                                    Rattle Version 2.6.25 togaware.co

  Execute   New   Open   Save   Report   Export   Stop   Quit
            Execute the current tab to have it take effect (shortcut is F2).
  Data  Explore  Test  Transform  Cluster  Associate  Model  Evaluate  Log

Type: ⊙ Tree  ○ Forest    ○ Boost    ○ SVM  ○ Linear  ○ Neural Net   ○ Survival  ○ All

Target: medv   Algorithm:  ⊙ Traditional ○ Conditional              Model Builder:  rpart

Min Split:      20          Max Depth:    30      Priors:                 ☐ Include Missing

Min Bucket:     7           Complexity:   0.0100  Loss Matrix:            Rules    Draw

Summary of the Decision Tree model for Classification (built using 'rpart'):

n= 354

node), split, n, deviance, yval
      * denotes terminal node

 1) root 354 27923.2200 22.30282
   2) lstat>=7.865 239  7523.2070 18.15649
     4) lstat>=14.3 128  2315.3340 14.85703
       8) crim>=7.006285 56   806.3936 12.03929 *
       9) crim< 7.006285 72   718.4999 17.04861 *
     5) lstat< 14.3 111  2207.5430 21.96126
      10) rm< 6.612 99  1584.1900 21.38990 *
      11) rm>=6.612 12   324.4025 26.67500 *
   3) lstat< 7.865 115  7751.6840 30.92000
     6) rm< 7.437 95  3011.0980 28.26421
      12) rm< 6.803 61  1134.2630 25.73770
        24) lstat>=4.585 54   367.5483 24.83889 *
        25) lstat< 4.585 7   386.5543 32.67143 *
      13) rm>=6.803 34   788.8697 32.79706 *
     7) rm>=7.437 20   887.7655 43.53500 *

Regression tree:
rpart(formula = medv ~ ., data = crs$dataset[crs$train, c(crs$input,
    crs$target)], method = "anova", parms = list(split = "information"),
```

we click on the **Rules** and **Draw** Button on the right top corner (below the check
box **Include Missing**)

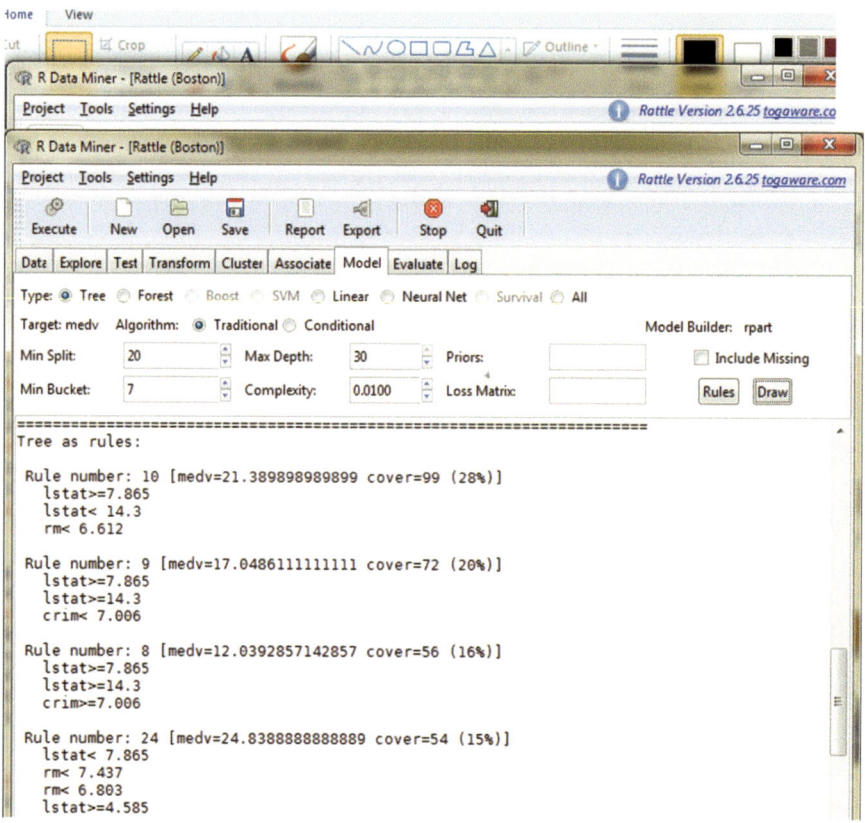

and

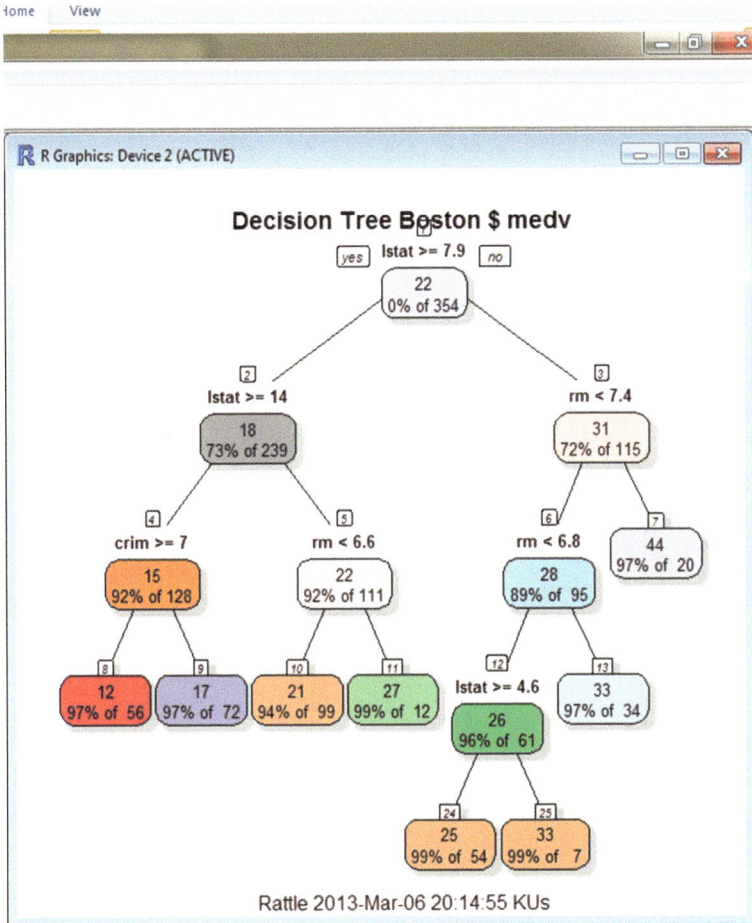

Congrats—you just built your first Decision Tree Model in R, without knowing any R code, and clicking just a few times.

You can do the following with just a few clicks in Rattle:

- statistical tests
- ensemble models (and regression, neural net, etc.)
- clustering
- association analysis

The intuitive design with the lucid help makes it one of the hidden aces in R's packages for potential analysts. The documentation is also one of the best and is available at http://rattle.togaware.com/.

5.3   Web Scraping Using R

For this exercise we are using R for downloading cricket scores just for academic purposes. ESPN Cricinfo is the best site for cricket data and using the XML package in R we can easily scrape and manipulate data. Data from the ESPN Cricinfo website is available from the STATSGURU website. The url is of the form:

http://stats.espncricinfo.com/ci/engine/stats/index.html?class=1;team=6; template=results;type=batting

or an example

http://stats.espncricinfo.com/ci/engine/stats/index.html?class=1;team=6; template=results;type=batting

If you break down this URL to get more statistics on cricket, you can choose the following parameters.

class

1=Test 2=ODI 3=T20I 11=Test+ODI+T20I

team

1=England 2=Australia 3=South America 4-West Indies 5=New Zealand 6=India 7=Pakistan and 8=Sri Lanka

type

batting bowling fielding allround for official team aggregate

Note—*You should always check any website for terms of use before trying any automated web scraping. In this case Terms of Use are here—you may need to check this before trying any heavy duty or nonacademic web scraping.* http://www. espncricinfo.com/ci/content/site/company/terms_use.html.

Here is the code for scraping the website and doing a small analysis on it. Note we use the XML package in R and in particular the readHTMLTable function.

library(XML)

url= "http://stats.espncricinfo.com/ci/engine/stats/index.html?class=1;team= 6;template=results;type=batting"

#Note—I can also break the url string and use paste command to modify this url with parameters

tables=readHTMLTable(url)

tables$"Overall figures"

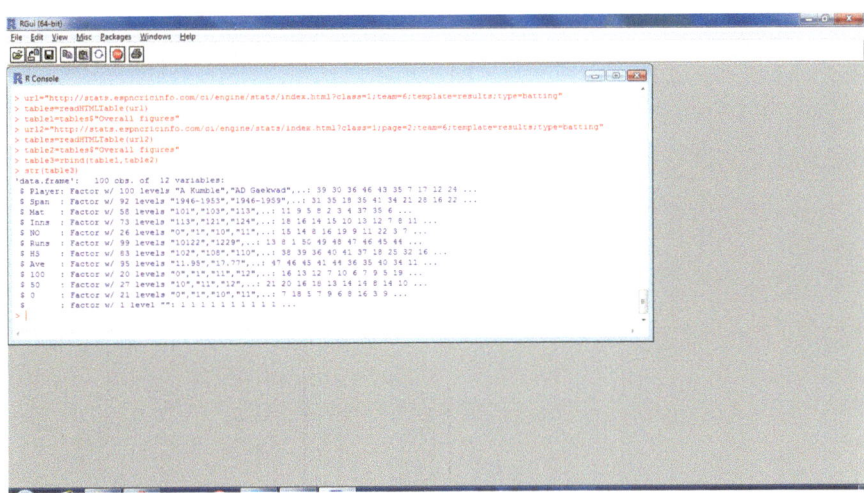

#Now see this—since I only got 50 results in each page, I look at the url of next
page

table1=tables$"Overall figures"

url2= "http:// stats.espncricinfo.com/ci/engine/stats/index.html?class=1;
***page=2**;team=6;template=results;type=batting"*

tables=readHTMLTable(url)
table2=tables$"Overall figures"
#Now I need to join these two tables vertically
table3=rbind(table1,table2)

Now the data is within R, and we can use something like Deducer to visualize.
Additionally we can use a browser plug-in like IMacros for web scraping.

5.4   Social Media and Web Analytics Using R

Some tutorials for social media analytics are given below.

5.4.1   Facebook Network Analytics Using R

A tutorial for analysing Facebook Networks using R is given below. Note this can be replicated by anyone—and you can theoretically be able to create adjacency matrix (friend of friends) of all people who have given permission into your app—thus maybe a network analysis of people to some group (like R Facebook group https://www.facebook.com/groups/rusers/?fref=ts or even FOASStat https://www.facebook.com/groups/foastat/?fref=ts is possible).

While traditional marketing and targeting focusses on variables like demographics and psychographics, social network analysis lets you tap into influential people within communities with the right offer and then let the free retweet, reshare as proxy free ads. The hypothesis being that people in similar network clusters have similar consumer behaviours (not just in similar demographic or psychographics). This should ideally be able to capture changing consumer behaviour faster for better targeting.

- Go to https://developers.facebook.com/apps and create a new app.
- An example is given here to help the reader understand the various options in this step, https://developers.facebook.com/apps/241634542707615.

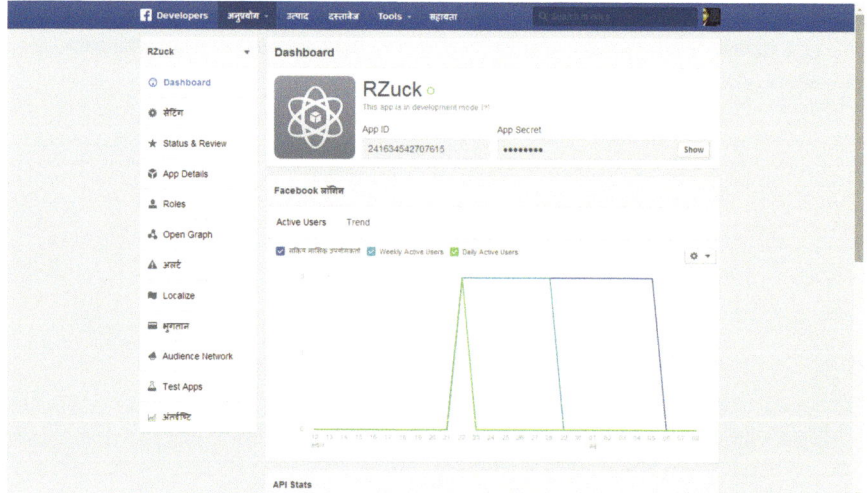

- Change url in settings (to http://localhost:1410) (the first tab below Dashboard in the left margin). (*The author wishes to apologize for the mild inconvenience since Hindi is his first language—he uses that on Facebook*)

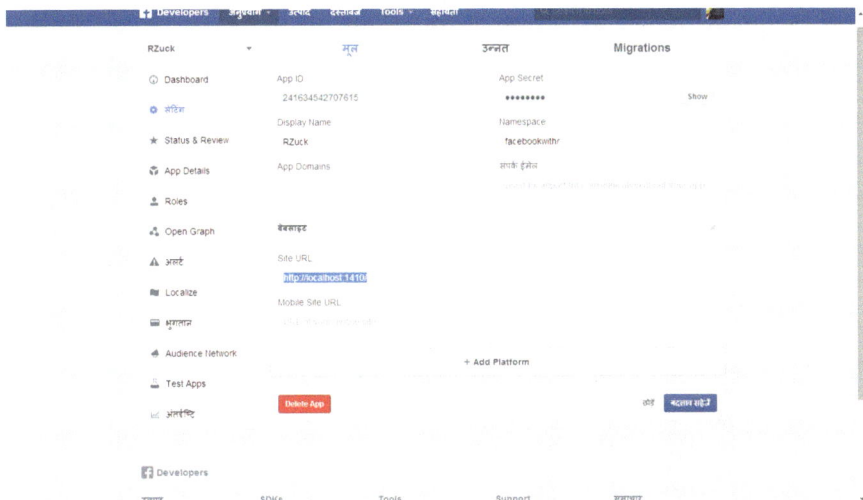

- Copy the secret keys from the dashboard (the App ID and the App Secret). These help in secure authentication later—Example https://developers.facebook.com/ apps/241634542707615/dashboard/.

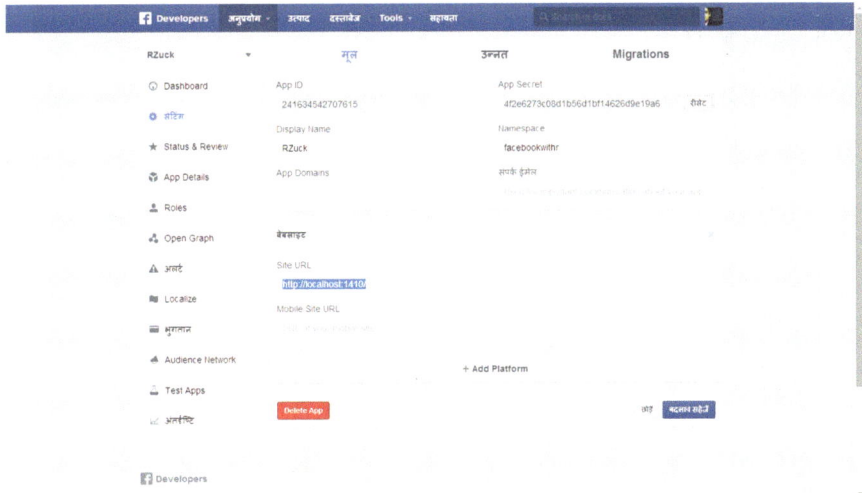

- Using the Rfacebook package we can use the following code (modified with the secret keys above) to create a connection from our R session to our newly created Facebook App and save those credentials for later use.

install.packages("Rfacebook") #Installs the package Rfacebook

install.packages("httpuv") #Installs the package httpuv

library(Rfacebook) #Loads the package Rfacebook

library(httpuv) #Loads the package httpuv

#This code creates the secure oauth connection fbOAuth(app_id, app_secret, extended_permissions = TRUE)

fb_oauth=fbOAuth("241634542707615",   "4f2e6273c08d1b56d1bf14626d9e 19a6", extended_permissions = TRUE)

#Do change the App ID to your ID and also it is a good practiise to periodically change your app secret especially after you have shared it

#fb_oauth   <-   fbOAuth(app_id="123456789",   app_secret="1A2B3C4D"). The following screenshots show a successful authentication

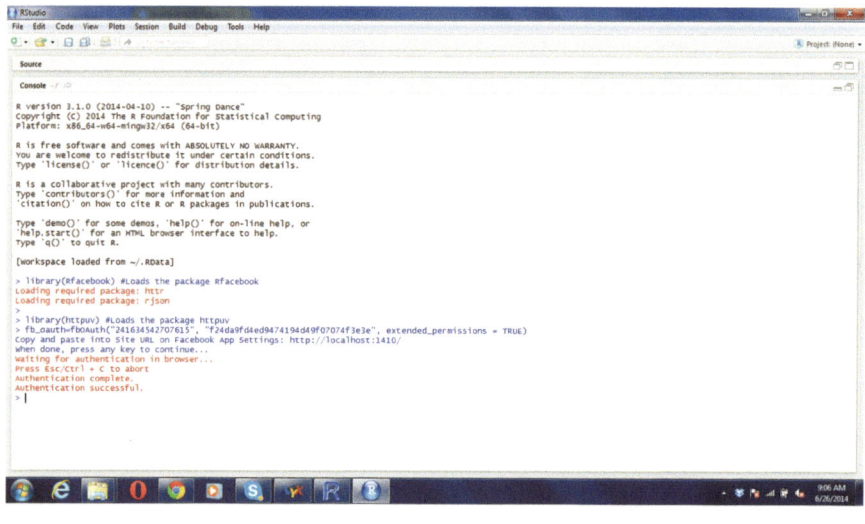

save(fb_oauth, file= "fb_oauth") #saves the oauth connection credentials to a file
getwd() #looks at which is the current working directory to help us locate the
oauth credential files for use later on
dir() #lists all the files within the current working directory.

- Now we have a fb oauth object and we can just load it up. We use the following code and it can then be modified at will to get a basic demographic analysis

library(Rfacebook)
library(httpuv)
library(RColorBrewer)
load("fb_oauth")
me <- getUsers("me", token=fb_oauth)
#getFQL(query, token)
my_friends <- getFriends(token=fb_oauth, simplify=F)
str(my_friends) table(my_friends$relationship_status)

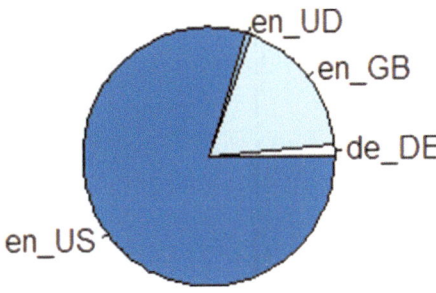

pie(table(my_friends$relationship_status),col=brewer.pal(5, "Set1")) table(my_friends$location)

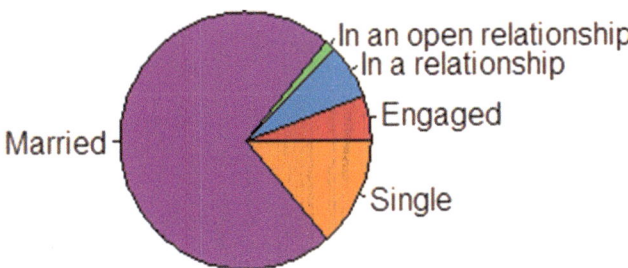

pie(table(my_friends$location),col=brewer.pal(20, "Greens"))

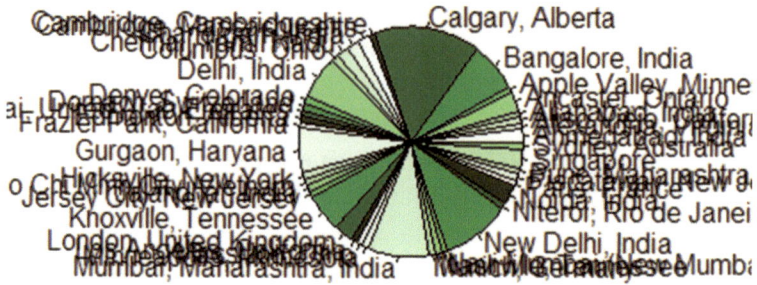

- Now we do a basic network analysis to get clusters and determine relationships between my friends

```
load("fb_oauth")
    mat <- getNetwork(token=fb_oauth, format="adj.matrix")
    library(igraph)
    network <- graph.adjacency(mat, mode="undirected")
    getwd()
    setwd("C:/Users/dell/Desktop")
    pdf("network_plot.pdf")
    plot(network, vertex.size=5, vertex.label=NA, vertex.label.cex=0.45, edge.arrow.
size=1, edge.curved=TRUE,) dev.off()
```

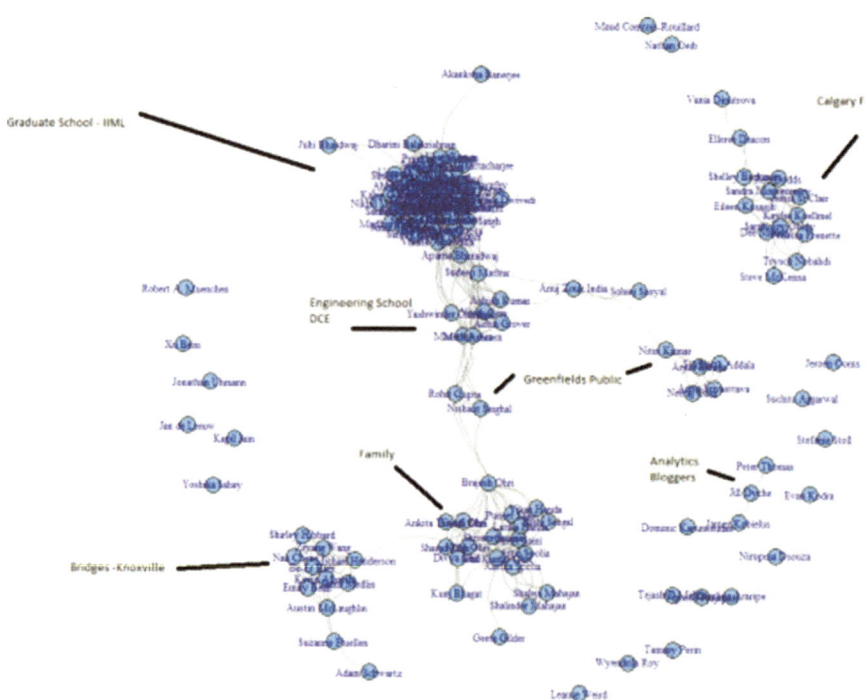

This following is an adjacency matrix and it is the basic building block for a social network analysis—you can use it for turning your Fb friends into a 1-0 matrix based on their relationships. One more thing—the more Facebook friends the reader has the more interesting this analysis.

row.names	Vivek Gera	Emily Bean	Michael Henderson	Shirley Hibbard	Adam Schwartz	Siddharth Addala	Jeena Medlin	Tammy Penn	Nan Chen	Karthik Parthasarathy	Brajesh
1 Vivek Gera	FALSE	FALSE	FALSE	FALSE	FALSE	FALSE	FALSE	FALSE	FALSE	FALSE	FALSE
2 Emily Bean	FALSE	FALSE	TRUE	TRUE	FALSE	FALSE	FALSE	FALSE	TRUE	FALSE	FALSE
3 Michael Henderson	FALSE	TRUE	FALSE	TRUE	FALSE	FALSE	TRUE	FALSE	TRUE	FALSE	FALSE
4 Shirley Hibbard	FALSE	TRUE	TRUE	FALSE	FALSE	FALSE	FALSE	FALSE	TRUE	FALSE	FALSE
5 Adam Schwartz	FALSE	FALSE	FALSE	FALSE	FALSE	FALSE	FALSE	FALSE	FALSE	FALSE	FALSE
6 Siddharth Addala	FALSE	FALSE	FALSE	FALSE	FALSE	FALSE	FALSE	FALSE	FALSE	FALSE	FALSE
7 Jeena Medlin	FALSE	FALSE	TRUE	FALSE	FALSE	FALSE	FALSE	FALSE	FALSE	FALSE	FALSE
8 Tammy Penn	FALSE	FALSE	FALSE	FALSE	FALSE	FALSE	FALSE	FALSE	FALSE	FALSE	
9 Nan Chen	FALSE	TRUE	TRUE	TRUE	FALSE	FALSE	FALSE	FALSE	FALSE	FALSE	FALSE
10 Karthik Parthasarathy	FALSE	FALSE	FALSE	FALSE	FALSE	FALSE	FALSE	FALSE	FALSE	FALSE	FALSE
11 Brajesh Ohri	FALSE	FALSE	FALSE	FALSE	FALSE	FALSE	FALSE	FALSE	FALSE	FALSE	FALSE
12 Sohini Sanyal	FALSE	FALSE	FALSE	FALSE	FALSE	FALSE	FALSE	FALSE	FALSE	FALSE	FALSE
13 Chetan Verma	FALSE	FALSE	FALSE	FALSE	FALSE	FALSE	FALSE	FALSE	FALSE	TRUE	FALSE
14 Shuchi Suri	FALSE	FALSE	FALSE	FALSE	FALSE	FALSE	FALSE	FALSE	FALSE	TRUE	FALSE
15 Harneet Singh	FALSE	FALSE	FALSE	FALSE	FALSE	FALSE	FALSE	FALSE	FALSE	TRUE	FALSE
16 Saurabh Kumar	FALSE	FALSE	FALSE	FALSE	FALSE	FALSE	FALSE	FALSE	FALSE	FALSE	FALSE
17 Anirban Paul	FALSE	FALSE	FALSE	FALSE	FALSE	FALSE	FALSE	FALSE	FALSE	TRUE	FALSE
18 Sandra Montgomery	FALSE	FALSE	FALSE	FALSE	FALSE	FALSE	FALSE	FALSE	FALSE	FALSE	FALSE
19 Anuj Zouk India	FALSE	FALSE	FALSE	FALSE	FALSE	FALSE	FALSE	FALSE	FALSE	FALSE	FALSE
20 Avnish Anand	FALSE	FALSE	FALSE	FALSE	FALSE	FALSE	FALSE	FALSE	FALSE	FALSE	FALSE
21 Ashish Kumar	TRUE	FALSE	FALSE	FALSE	FALSE	FALSE	FALSE	FALSE	FALSE	FALSE	FALSE
22 Shounak Sadra	FALSE	FALSE	FALSE	FALSE	FALSE	FALSE	FALSE	FALSE	FALSE	FALSE	FALSE
23 Arun Spolia	FALSE	FALSE	FALSE	FALSE	FALSE	FALSE	FALSE	FALSE	FALSE	FALSE	TRUE
24 Peter Thomas	FALSE	FALSE	FALSE	FALSE	FALSE	FALSE	FALSE	FALSE	FALSE	FALSE	FALSE
25 Divya Ohri	FALSE	FALSE	FALSE	FALSE	FALSE	FALSE	FALSE	FALSE	FALSE	FALSE	TRUE
26 Jeroen Ooms	FALSE	FALSE	FALSE	FALSE	FALSE	FALSE	FALSE	FALSE	FALSE	FALSE	FALSE

133 observations of 133 variables

Note—We can also do likes analysis which is of some use to marketing companies trying to get likes (Facebook likes) for their page. We can use the following code and your own username (Example—I have used mine since I am the only one who has allowed the app permissions!)

likes=getLikes(user="byebyebyer",n=500,token=fb_oauth)

Additional Note—An excellent presentation on social network analysis using R is here http://www.openfoundry.org/en/download/doc_download/1720-david--social-network-analysis-using-r-data-science-with-r

Other packages for Social Media Analysis are Twitter and Google Plus

5.4.2   Twitter Analysis with R

An excellent resource for learning everything about Twitter Analytics and R is at http://decisionstats.com/2013/09/11/using-twitter-data-with-r/ and https://sites.google.com/site/miningtwitter/questions/sentiment/analysis.

The code for Twitter Analysis is here

install.packages("twitteR")
library(twitteR)
reqURL <- "https://api.twitter.com/oauth/request_token"
accessURL <- "https://api.twitter.com/oauth/access_token"
authURL <- "https://api.twitter.com/oauth/authorize"
consumerKey <- "rR16FxDLkTYmuVhqH4s4EQ"

```
consumerSecret <- "xrGr71kTfdT3ypWFURGxyJOC4Oqf46Rwu4qxyxoEfM"
twitCred    <-    OAuthFactory$new(consumerKey=consumerKey,   consumer-
Secret=consumerSecret, requestURL=reqURL, accessURL=accessURL, authURL
=authURL)
twitCred$handshake() #Pause here for the Handshake Pin Code
registerTwitterOAuth(twitCred) #Wait till you see True
a=searchTwitter("#rstats", n=2000) #Get the Tweets
tweets_df = twListToDF(a) #Convert to Data Frame
install.packages(c("tm", "wordcloud"))
library(tm) library(wordcloud)
b=Corpus(VectorSource(tweets_df$text),  readerControl  =  list(language  =
"eng"))
b<- tm_map(b, tolower) #Changes case to lower case
b<- tm_map(b, stripWhitespace) #Strips White Space
b <- tm_map(b, removePunctuation) #Removes Punctuation
inspect(b)
tdm <- TermDocumentMatrix(b)
m1 <- as.matrix(tdm)
v1<- sort(rowSums(m1),decreasing=TRUE)
d1<- data.frame(word = names(v1),freq=v1)
wordcloud(d1$word,d1$freq)
```

For doing sentiment analysis a good project has been created by one of my students Kaify at http://www.slideshare.net/ajayohri/twitter-analysis-by-kaify-rais.

5.4.3 Google Analytics API with R

• We download the r-google-analytics package in .zip format from https://code. google.com/p/r-google-analytics/ (Note this is NOT a CRAN package hence the installation procedure is a bit different.)

- We install it using the local zip files package option in R in Windows and navigating to the location of the download in previous step.

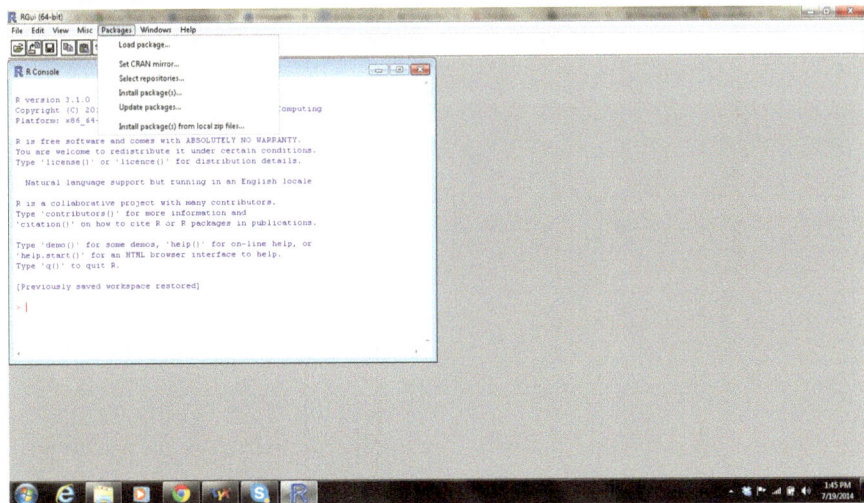

- We load the package using library command

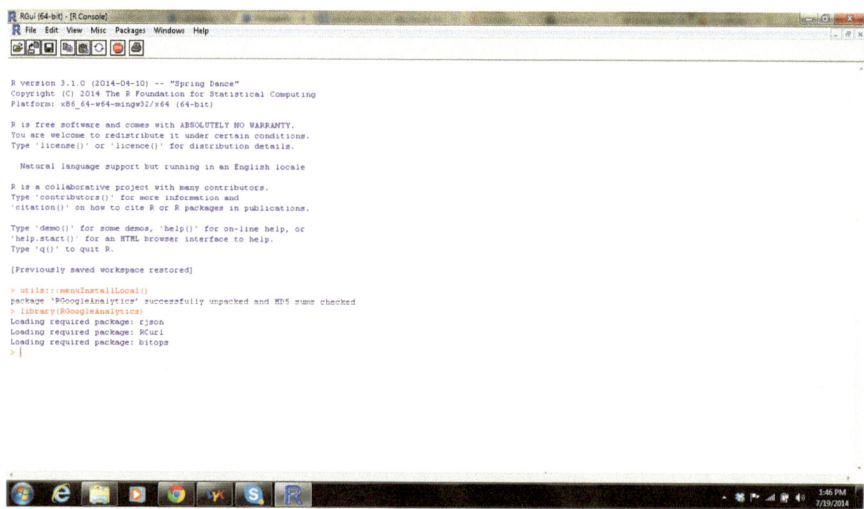

- • We authenticate our session by copying and pasting the right code in the R
  Session Window from the OAuth2.0 Playground. This is how it works—we use
  the QueryBuilder and the query$Authorize commands

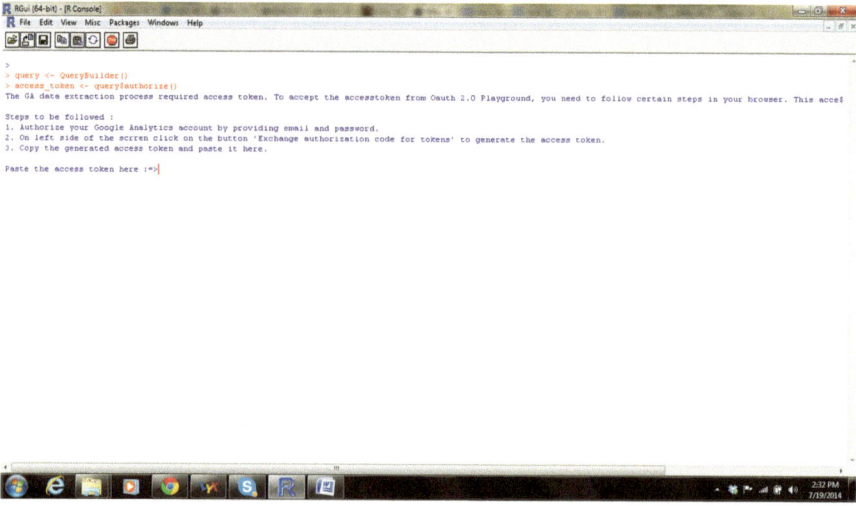

- The OAuth2 playground is at https://developers.google.com/oauthplayground/ and it generates tokens for enabling access to various APIs within Google APIs. The first time it will ask us for permission (provided we are already logged into our Google Account. If not please do login).

- Note we need to paste the **access token** and NOT authorization code within the R window

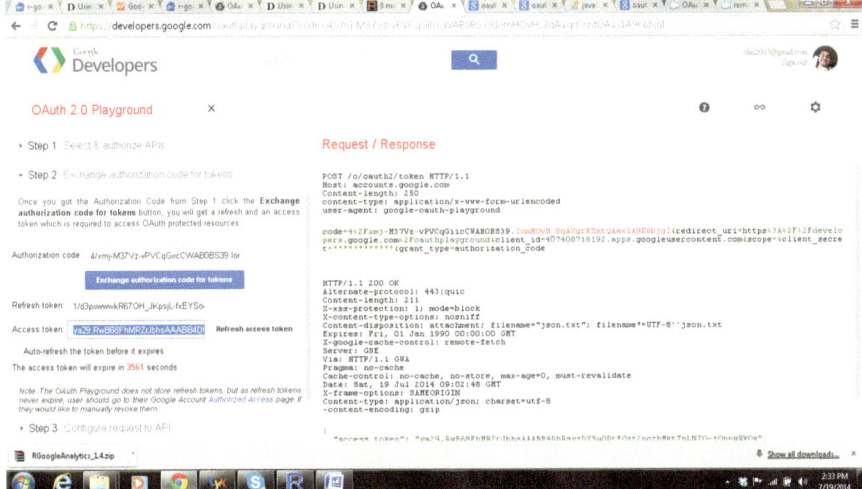

- Now we paste the authorization token and test if it is working by using the conf command as shown below. Retrieving the accounts successfully shows that our session is now working.

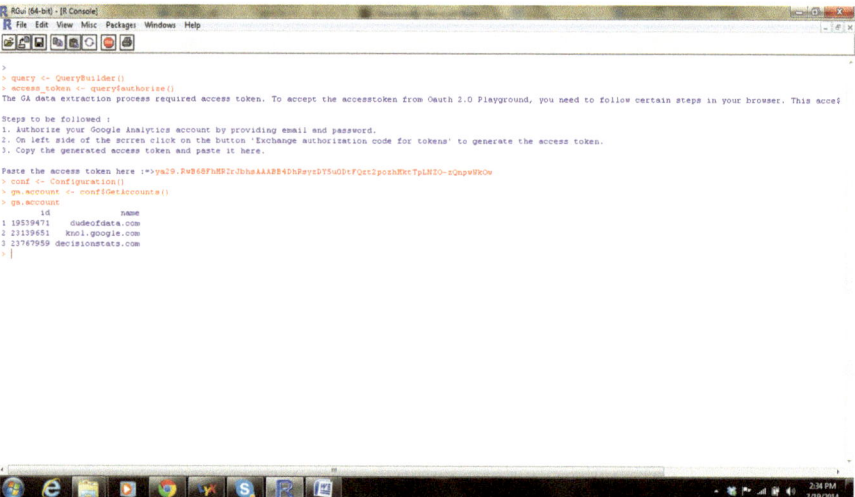

- If there is any error, you can repeat the query and access token step again
- We now need to run the ga object to get the profiles data (which is different from account data). We set up the input parameters and make the query for getting data from within API.

The following code helps us execute this. Note that we have chosen the 3 rd profile here in this line *profile <- ga.profiles$id[3] (so this should be modified to whatever website you choose)*

```
>ga <- RGoogleAnalytics()
>ga.profiles <- ga$GetProfileData(access_token)
> profile <- ga.profiles$id[3]
> startdate <- "2011-06-18"
> enddate <- "2011-06-28"
> dimension <- "ga:date"
> metric <- "ga:visitors"
> sort <- "ga:date"
> maxresults <- 990
query$Init(start.date = startdate,
+ end.date = enddate,
+ dimensions = dimension,
+ metrics = metric,
+ max.results = maxresults,
+ table.id = paste("ga:",profile,sep="",collapse=","),
+ access_token=access_token)
> ga.data <- ga$GetReportData(query)
```

- In the following screenshot we change the end-date parameter and note the two different results shown by R. We then use the head command to inspect the object.

- By changing the start and end dates, we can narrow down the time period for analysis. By changing the max rows, we can increase the breadth of analysis. For deeper analysis please refer to the Dimensions and Metrics options in https://developers.google.com/analytics/devguides/reporting/core/dimsmets?csw=1
- We can then use the lubridate package for manipulating the format of the date.

The ymd function helps in making this change.

> *install.packages(lubridate)*

> *library(lubridate)*

> *ga.data$date2=ymd(ga.data$date)*

- We can finally plot the line graph of the web analytics data.

Here type= l helps make a line graph, while par(bg="grey) changes the background to grey, and col= "blue changes the line color to blue.

```
>par(bg="grey")
> plot(ga.data[,3],ga.data[,2],type="l",col="blue")
```

- Additionally I use xlab and ylab parameters to change the labels of the X axis and Y Axis.

```
>plot(ga.data[,3],ga.data[,2],type="l",col="blue",xlab="Date", ylab=
"Visitors")
```

- To plot two graphs in the same window I can use the par(mfrow) option.

Here I am plotting two rows and one column (hence 2,1).

```
> par(mfrow=c(2,1))
> par(bg="grey")
> plot(ga.data[,3],ga.data[,2],type="l",col="blue",xlab="Date",ylab=
"Visitors")

> plot(ga.data[,3],ga.data[,2],type="l",col="blue")
```

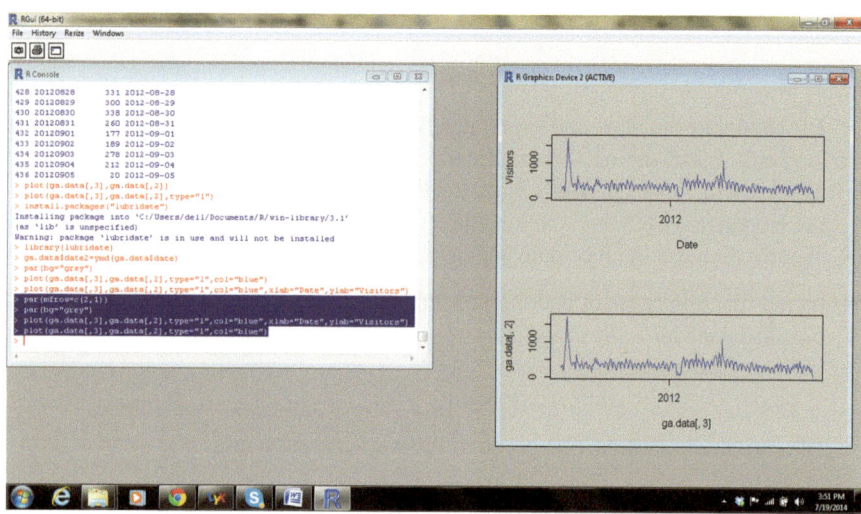

- To further look at two different periods in different graphs but within the same screen, I can use the square bracket notation of R.

Here we are looking at the last six months of 2011 versus the first six months of 2012.

```
> plot(ga.data[1:187,3],ga.data[1:187,2],type="l",col="blue",xlab="Date",
ylab="Visitors")

>plot(ga.data[188:436,3],ga.data[188:436,2],type="l",col="blue",xlab=
"Date",ylab="Visitors")
```

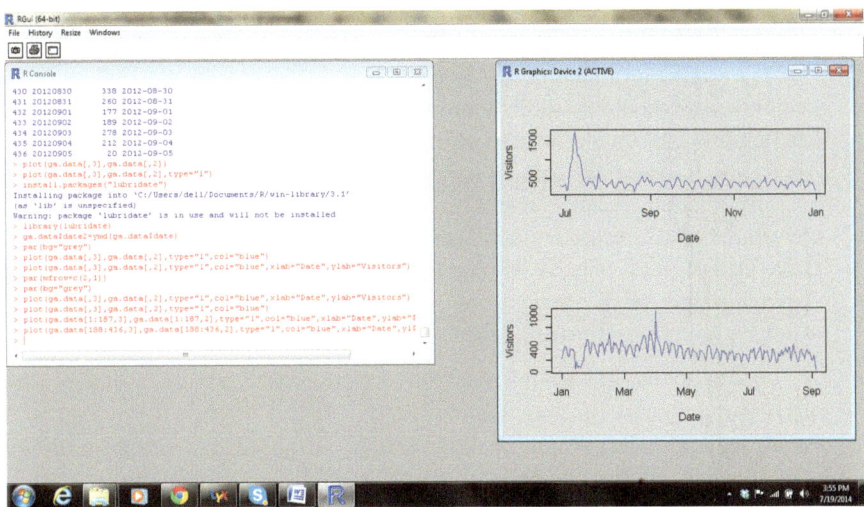

Note this can be misleading—the scales of the Y axis are different ! The analyst must thus be careful in harnessing R's power and flexibility and understanding the various options and parameters. (See lie factor in Section on Data Visualization of Chap. 5).

- These data can now be used for calendar heat maps, time series forecasting, association analysis, and other advanced statistical techniques not available for Google Analytics user.

5.4.4 R for Web Analytics

We can use the Google Analytics API and other APIs for Web Analytics. A great resource for using R for Web Analytics based on Google Analytics is here http://www.tatvic.com/blog/category/r/.

5.5 Doing Data Visualization Using R

Data Visualization is defined as the visual representation of data, including aggregated and segmented data, to give analytical insights to the user. Data visualization is much more than pretty graphs. Good data visualization is accurate and truthful and helps decision making by the insights it helps generate. The Anscombe quartet is the best example of the importance of graphing data. This can be further referenced at http://en.wikipedia.org/wiki/Anscombe%27s_quartet.

Key concepts presented by the work of Edward Tufte have helped push the fields of data visualization.

- The representation of numbers, as physically measured on the surface of the graphic itself, should be directly proportional to the quantities represented. See **Lie factor**—http://www.infovis-wiki.net/index.php?title=Lie_Factor.
- Above all else show the data: A **large share of ink** on a graphic should present data-information, the ink changing as the data change. See **Data-ink ratio** http://www.infovis-wiki.net/index.php/Data-Ink_Ratio.
- **Data Density**—A portion of the total size of the graph that is dedicated displaying data. High density in most graphs can be shrunk way down without losing legibility or information data density of a graphic.

Also see—http://thedoublethink.com/2009/08/tufte%E2%80%99s-principles-for-visualizing-quantitative-information/.

For R, seminal to its acceptance as the leading advanced data visualization software has been the work in grammar of graphics and its subsequent implementation by Hadley Wickham.

The layered grammar defines the components of a plot as:
– A default dataset and set of mappings from variables to esthetics,
– One or more layers, with each layer having one geometric object, one statistical transformation, one position adjustment, and optionally, one dataset and set of aesthetic mappings,
– One scale for each esthetic mapping used,
– A coordinate system,
– The facet specification

5.5.1 Using Deducer for Faster and Better Data Visualization in R

We showcase easier data visualization using the GUI package Deducer. One more alternative to using a menu driven GUI for enhanced Graphical Visualization is the KMggplot2 plug-in for RCommander which includes histograms, line graphs, density plots et al (http://cran.r-project.org/web/packages/RcmdrPlugin.KMggplot2/index.html).

- Download a dataset from http://archive.ics.uci.edu/ml/datasets.html
- We choose the adult dataset.
- We start by using JGR—package.

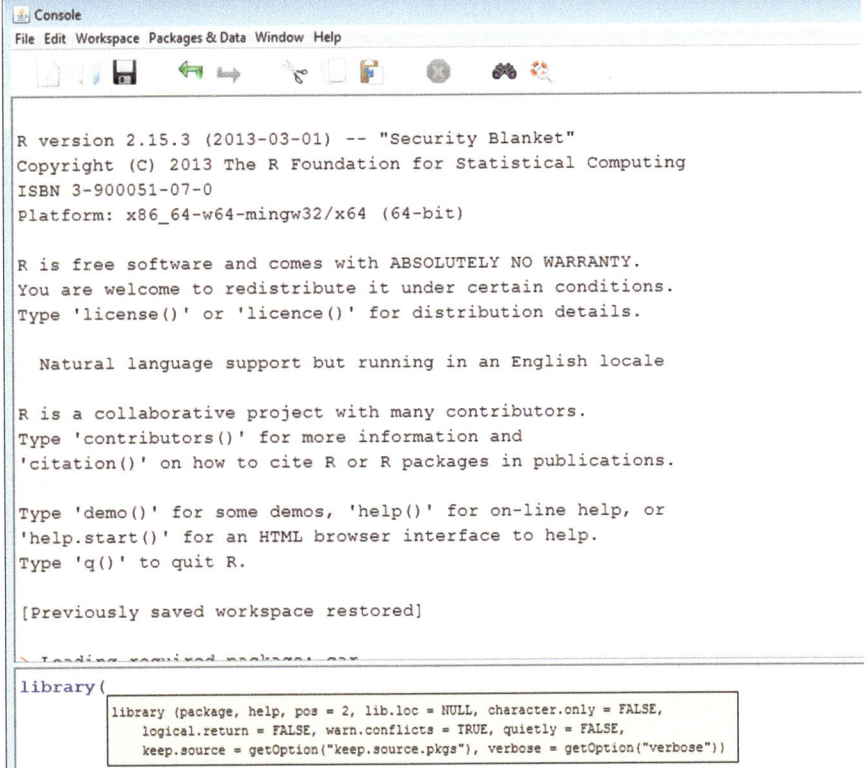

We then load Deducer from within JGR console. Note the JGR console suggests syntax as we type.

We then see the revised menu within JGR due to Deducer—including the Data, Analysis, Plots menus.

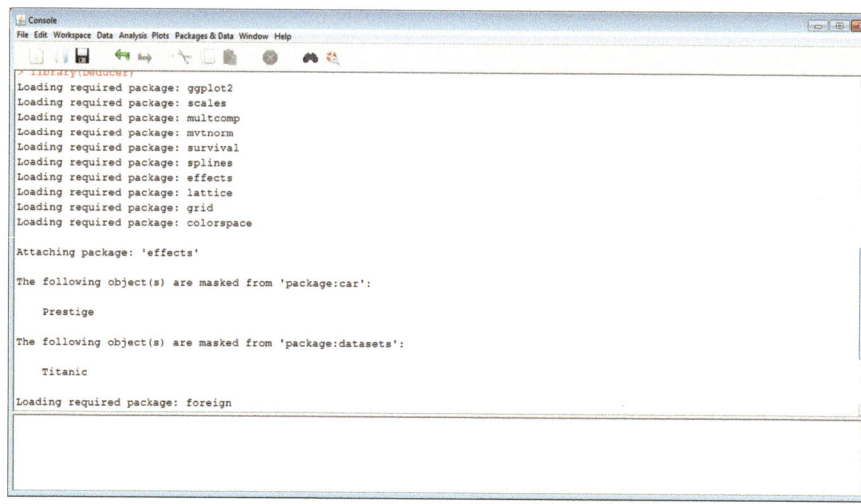

This is the Data Viewer—which we use for viewing and inputting data. We click on Open Data to open a new dataset (from a text file). We navigate to the location of the dataset adult downloaded from the repository.

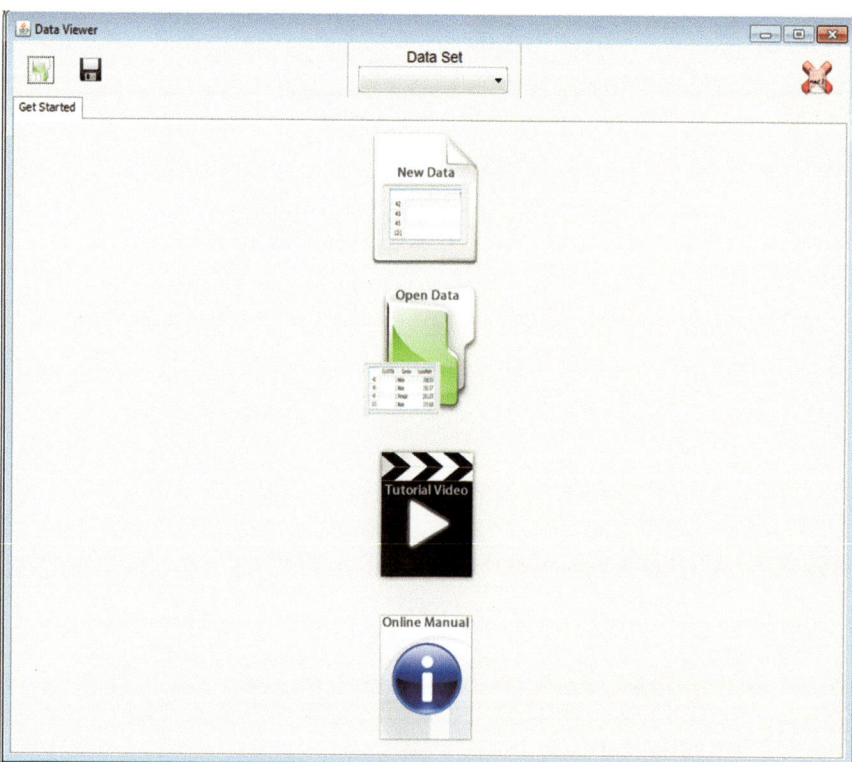

And we fill in the options for reading the data correctly, including delimiter (what separates the data), header (if first row contains variable names)

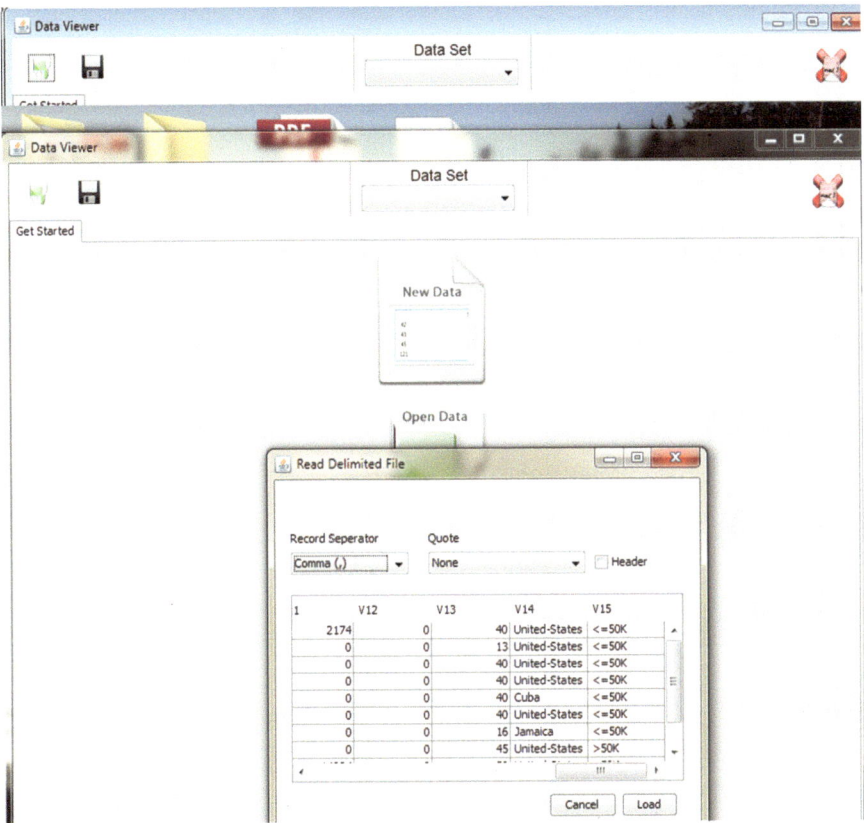

Once the data is input, we change from **Data View** tab to **Variable View** Tab, and change the names of variables by typing in the relevant names from dataset description url. Note the Variable **Type** and **Factor Levels** have been automatically populated by Deducer.

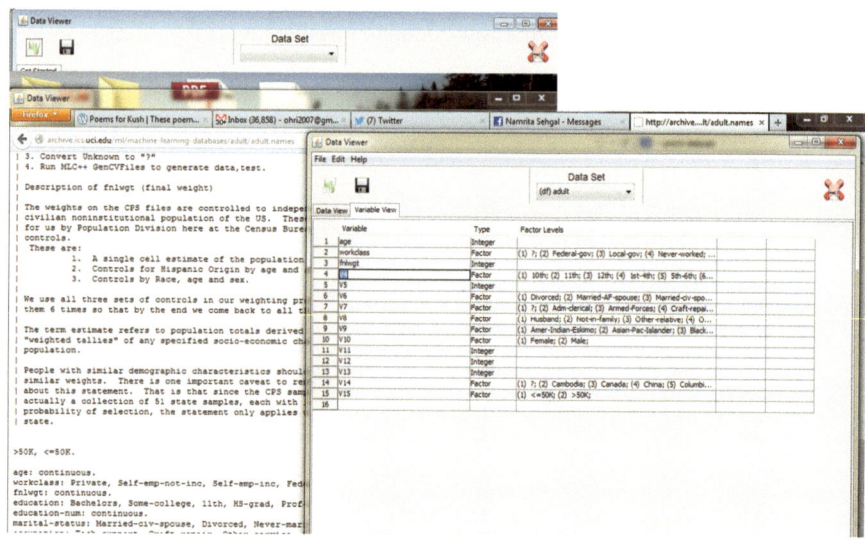

And we see the final input data.

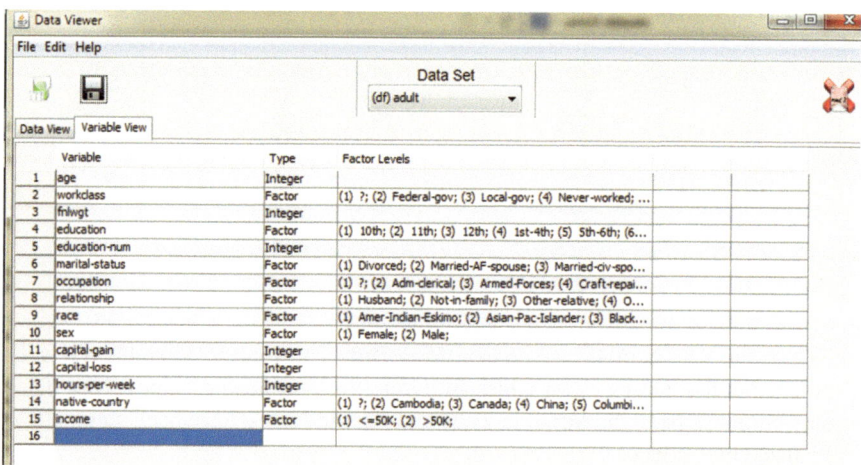

Now we switch to the **Plots** menu and the **Plot Builder** Sub-Menu from the **JGR-Deducer console**.

This is how the Deducer Plot Builder looks like.

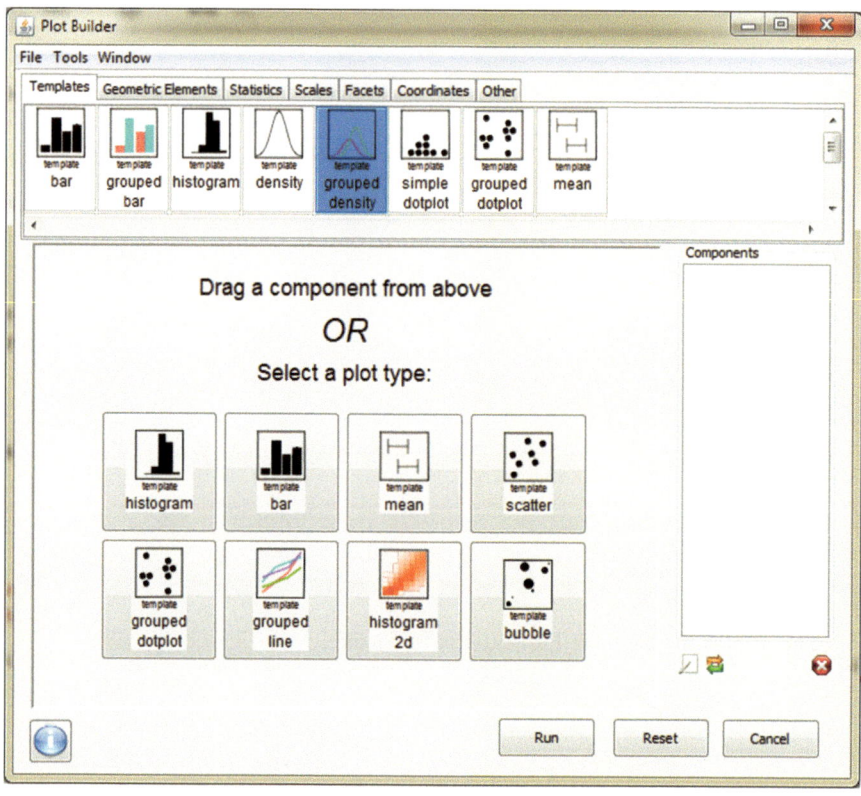

We showcase a couple of examples here of plots. We simply drag and drop a plot-type—(**grouped density**) to the menu on right. It asks us what variables we want to see and what variables we want to group by. We are trying to analyse how age is distributed across income levels (<50 K, or >50 K). Accordingly we select variables using the mouse and move them to the right using the blue directional buttons (we can click on them again to remove the variables).

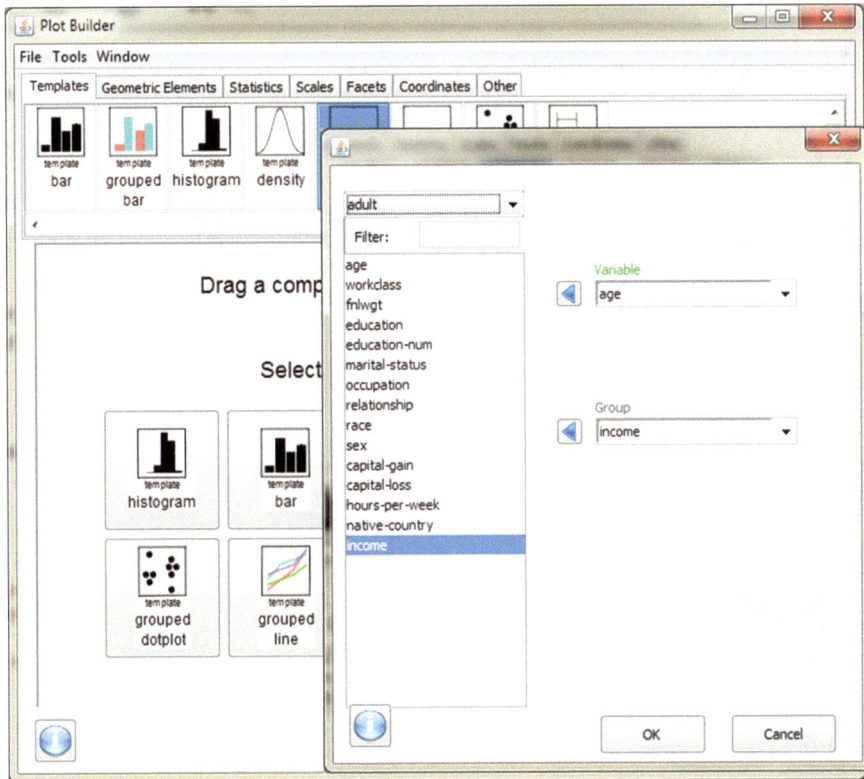

This is what comes when we click **OK**. Clearly, younger people have lower income levels.

OR people in the lower income bracket are younger (in median age).

Is there a better way to explain the graph below?

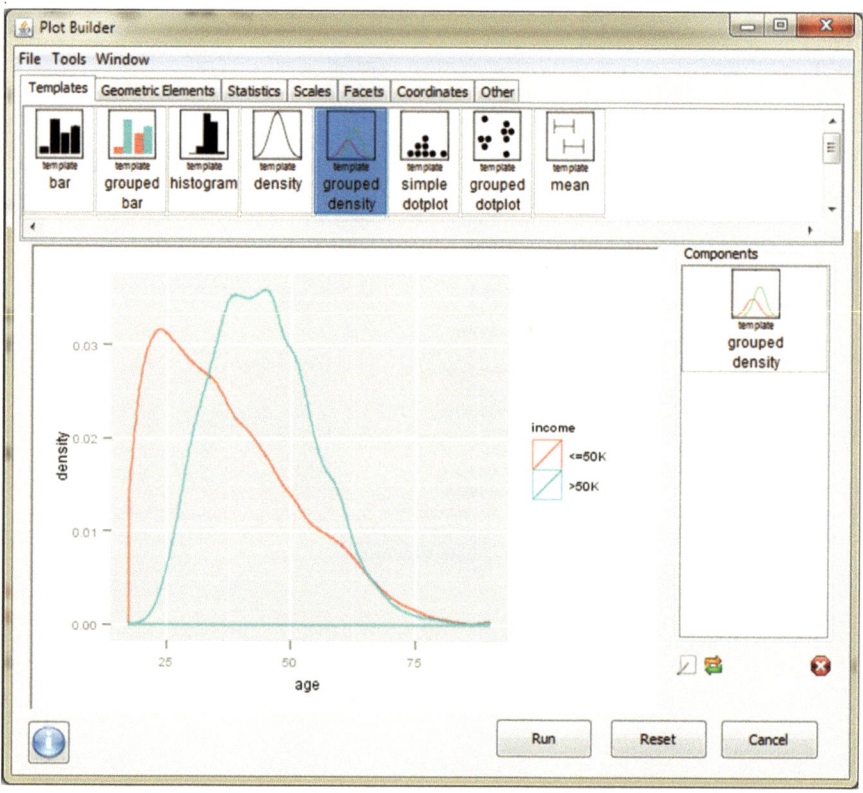

let us **grouped bar** (plot type) with comparing **marital status** with **income.**

Note we are still using the **Templates** tab in the top margin of the **Deducer Plot Builder**.

The partial screenshot (cropped due to size and clarity) is as follows. Red shows below <50 K and Blue shows >50 K.

Are married people more likely to have higher incomes?

OR are people with higher incomes more likely to get and stay married?

Then we move to the **Facets** tab in the top margin of **Plot Builder.**

We choose **wrap** and we choose the **sex** variable to see comparisons on how the two graphs compare when next to each other.

Let us see the effect of race and sex on income.

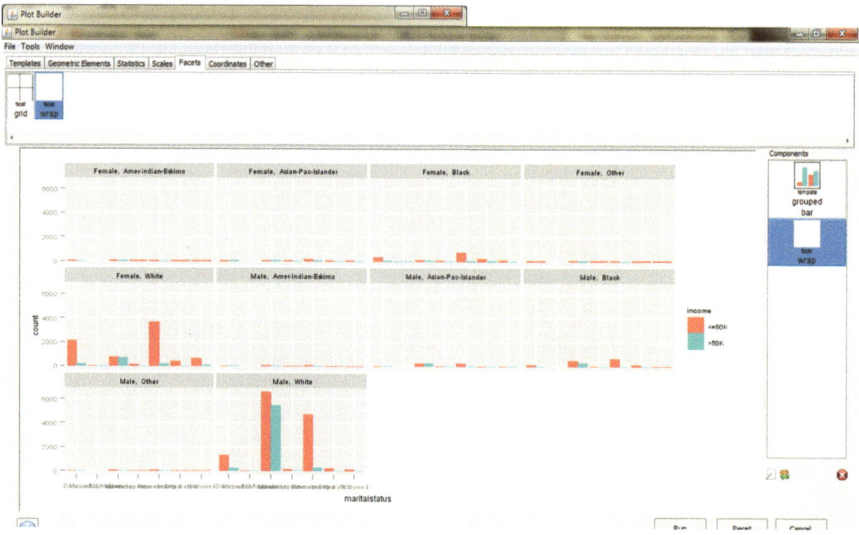

Are there more graphs we can use readily from **Templates** within **Deducer Plot Builder** ?

Are these graphs interchangeable? Yes! It depends on your data.

Yes! A group boxplot—compare this with the grouped density plot earlier

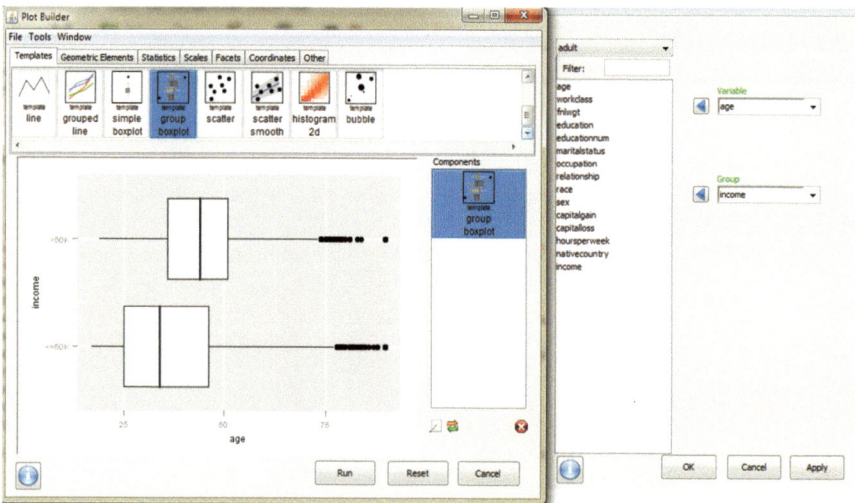

Now let us see this with **Facets** to compare mens and women's income

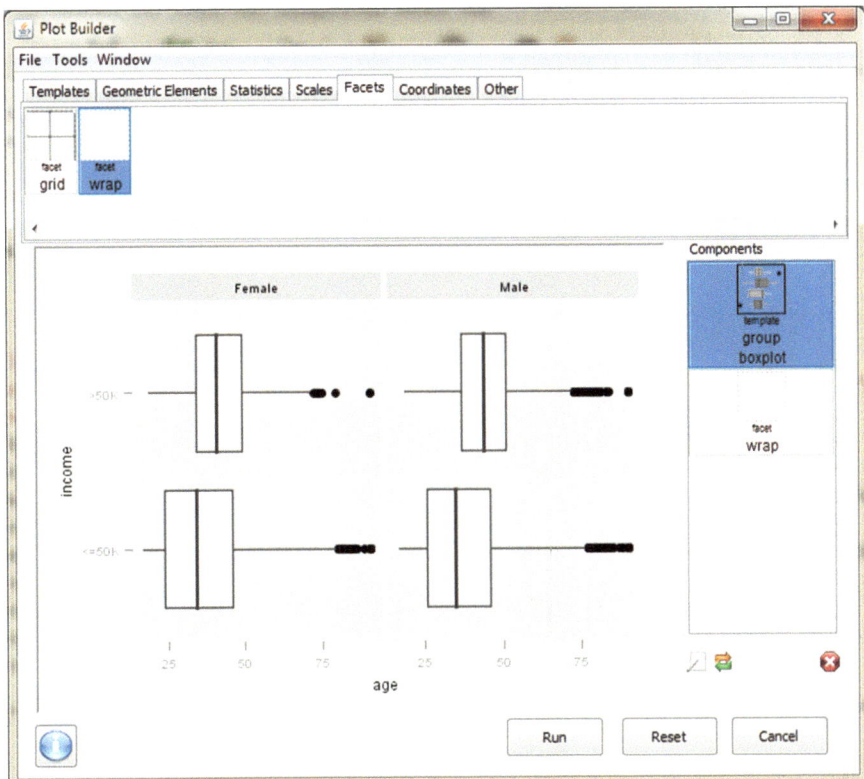

and the effect of relationships as well.

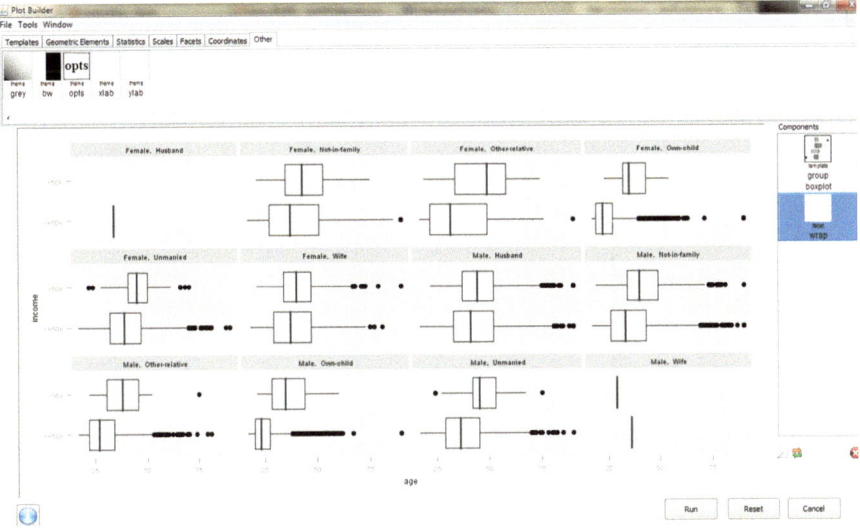

Now if we want to see the code behind all this, we go to **Tools** in the top menu and see what functions have been called.

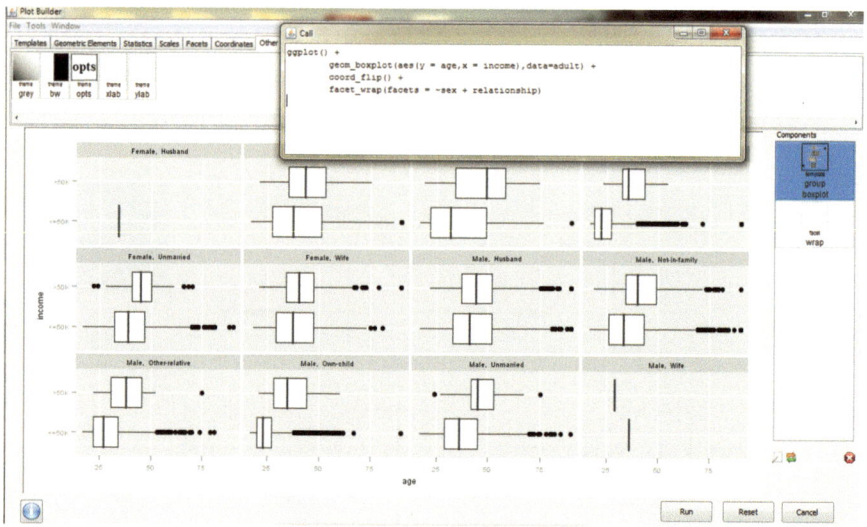

That's how we can build very good analytical data visualization using R without writing any code at all!

5.5.2 R for Geographical Based Analysis

ggmap—This is a great R package for spatial analysis. Note we are using geocode and ggmap for quick encoding and visualization of spatial data

library(ggmap)

geocode("Calgary")

Information from URL : http://maps.googleapis.com/maps/api/geocode/json?address=Calgary&sensor=false Google Maps API Terms of Service : http://developers.google.com/maps/terms lon lat 1 -114.0581 51.04532

qmap("Calgary Canada")

Map from URL : http://maps.googleapis.com/maps/api/staticmap?center=Calgary+Canada&zoom=10&size=%20640x640&scale=%202&maptype=terrain&sensor=false Google Maps API Terms of Service : http://developers.google.com/maps/terms Information from URL : http://maps.googleapis.com/maps/api/geocode/json?address=Calgary+Canada&sensor=false Google Maps API Terms of Service : http://developers.google.com/maps/terms

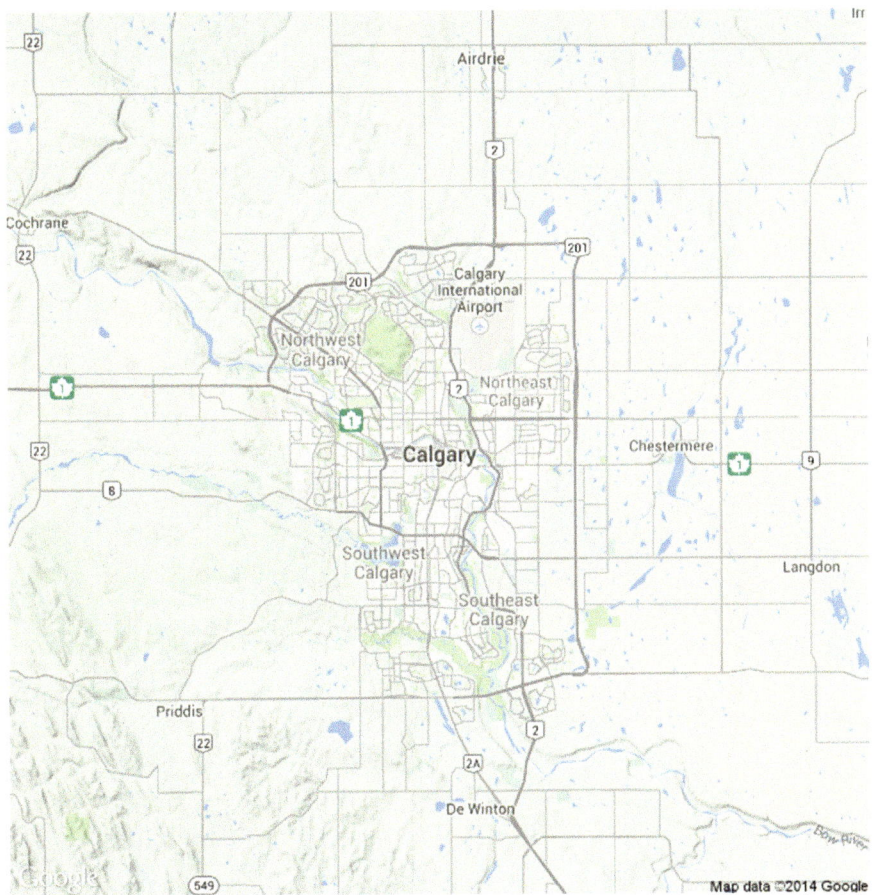

> *qmap("Calgary Canada",zoom=15)*

Map from URL : http://maps.googleapis.com/maps/api/staticmap?center= Calgary+Canada&zoom=15&size=%20640x640&scale=%202&maptype=terrain& sensor=false Google Maps API Terms of Service : http://developers.google. com/maps/terms Information from URL : http://maps.googleapis.com/maps/api/ geocode/json?address=Calgary+Canada&sensor=false Google Maps API Terms of Service : http://developers.google.com/maps/terms

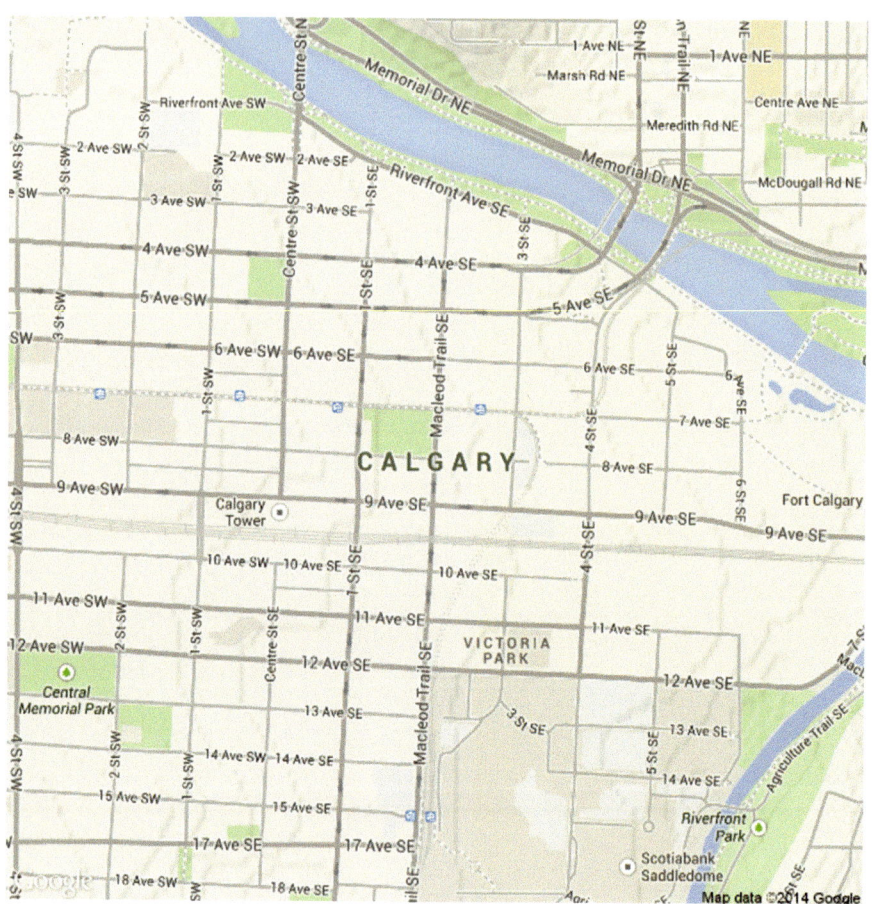

We can also use raster package and gadm database (which had administrative boundaries of the world) to create base layers for spatial data.

library(raster)

gadm<- getData('GADM', country = "IND", level=3)

head(gadm)

table(gadm$NAME_1)

gadm_GUJ=subset(gadm,gadm$NAME_1== "Gujarat")

length(gadm_GUJ)

Now we generate dummy data using sample function and use it as a factor variable

gadm_GUJ$f = factor(sample(1:5,214,replace=T),labels=letters[1:5])

gadm_GUJ$g = factor(sample(1:5,214,replace=T),labels=letters[1:5])

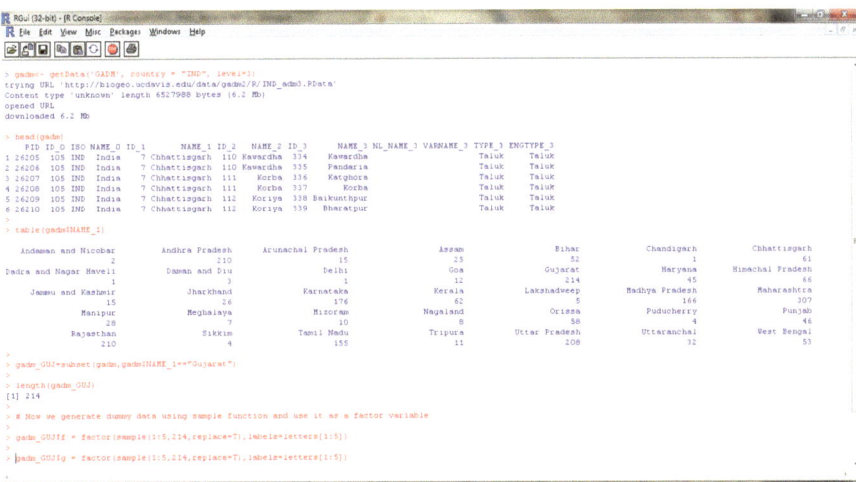

library(RColorBrewer) # We use the RColorBrewer package for nice color palette

spplot(gadm_GUJ, c("f","g"), col.regions=brewer.pal(5, "Set3"), scales=list (draw = TRUE))

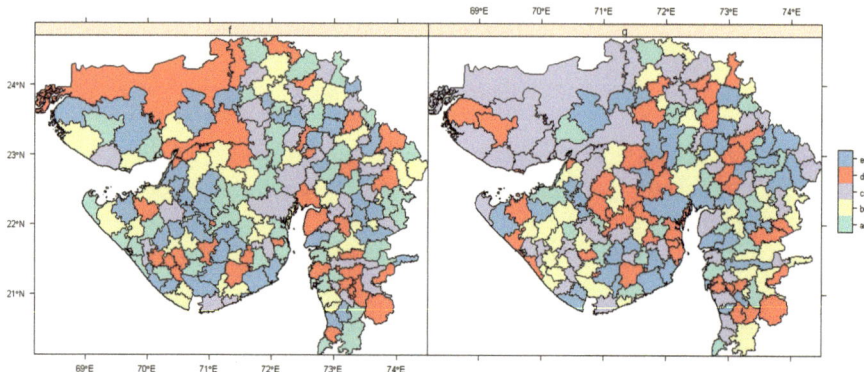

Note this is a much more elegant and easy to understand method of seeing how numerical quantities have changed across time in a single geographic region.

5.6   Creating a Basic Forecasting Model with R

The following diagram explains the statistical process of creating a forecasting model. It is created by Rob Hyndman (see References at the end of this chapter).

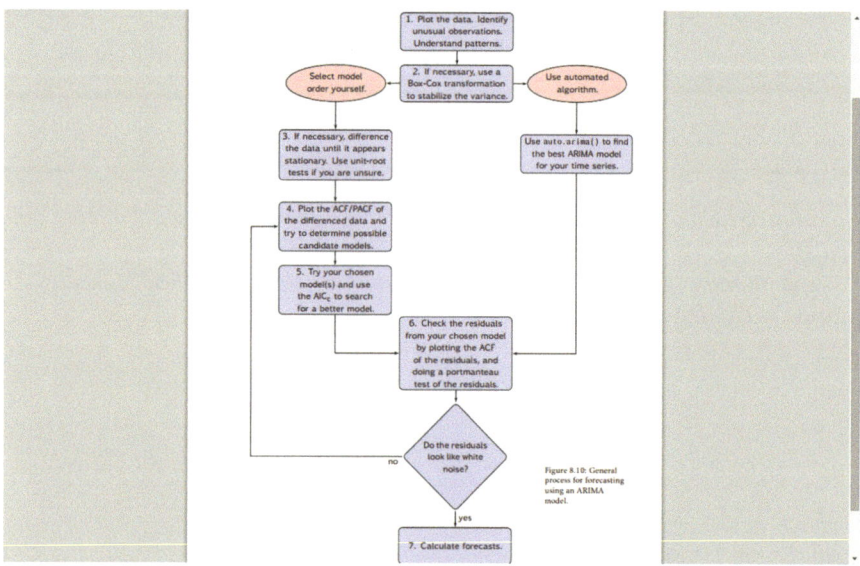

Figure 8.10: General process for forecasting using an ARIMA model.

The diagram shows auto.arima() function in R. This is available from the forecast package in R. A GUI for making Time Series is the Rcommander Epack plug-in. We need to load the Rcmdr package and then load the epack plug-in from within Rcmdr (it will restart the GUI and add a few menus). Using Bulkfit you can fit various ARMA models to dataset and choose based on minimum AIC.

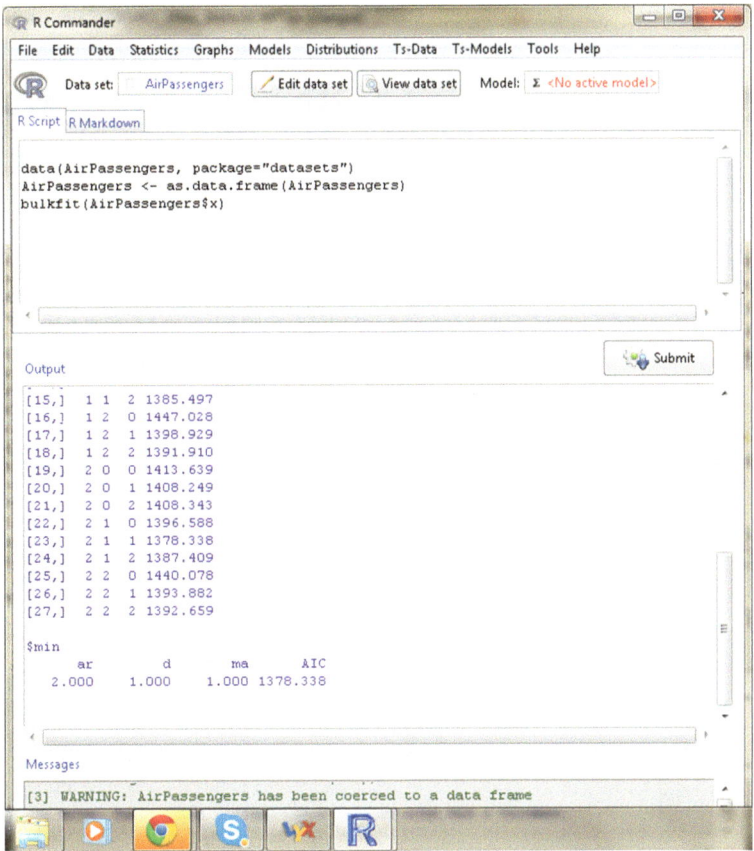

This is further elaborated in the article http://decisionstats.com/2010/10/22/doing-time-series-using-a-r-gui/.

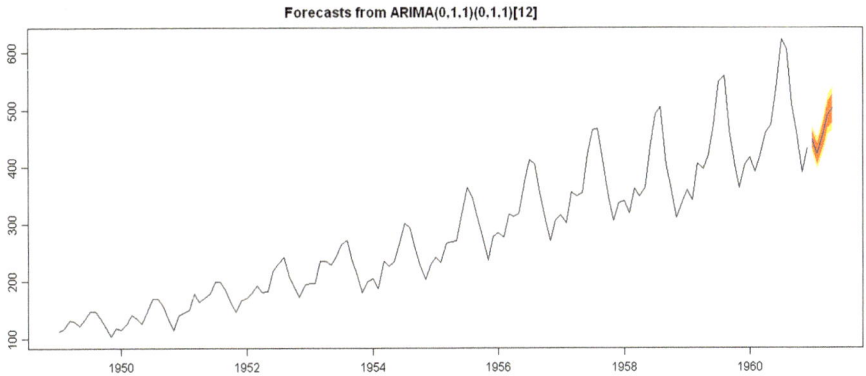

Forecasts from ARIMA(0,1,1)(0,1,1)[12]

5.7   Easy Updating R

We can use the installr package to easily update R

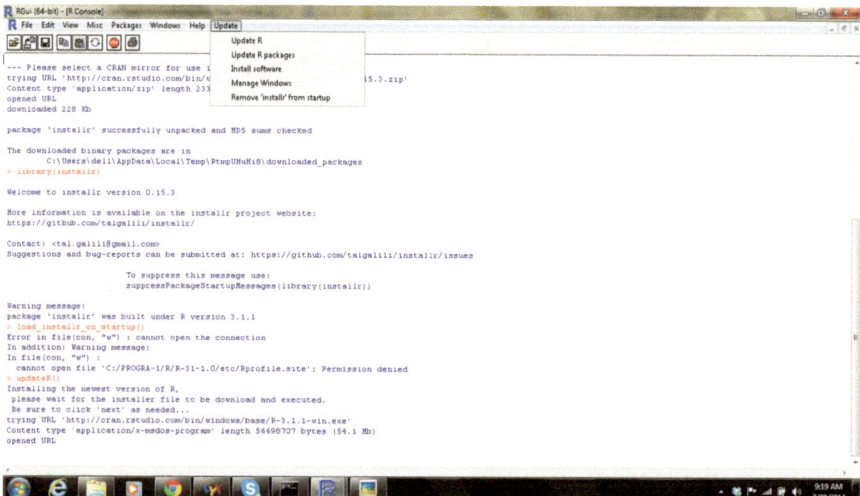

This easily helps us update R (by using the Update R option). It also copies your old packages to the new version of R and updates them. Updating open source R is thus simplified almost like a professional enterprise software.

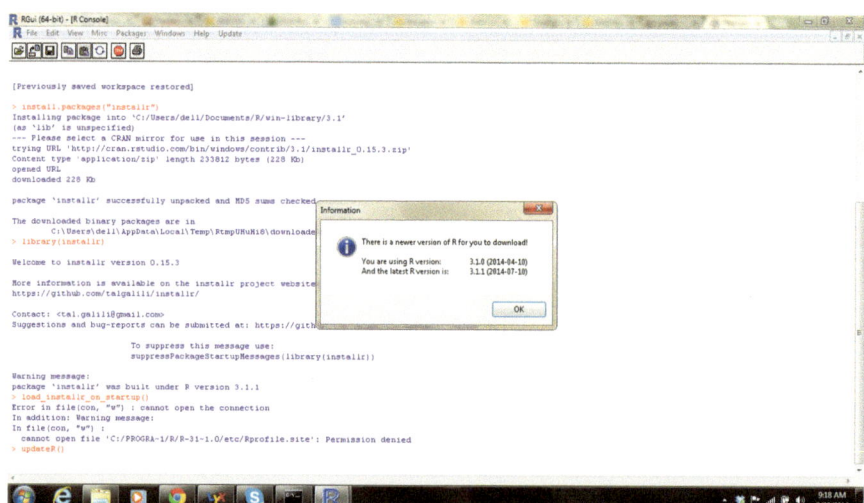

The best thing is you can also install other software from a single location within R (using the Install Software option).

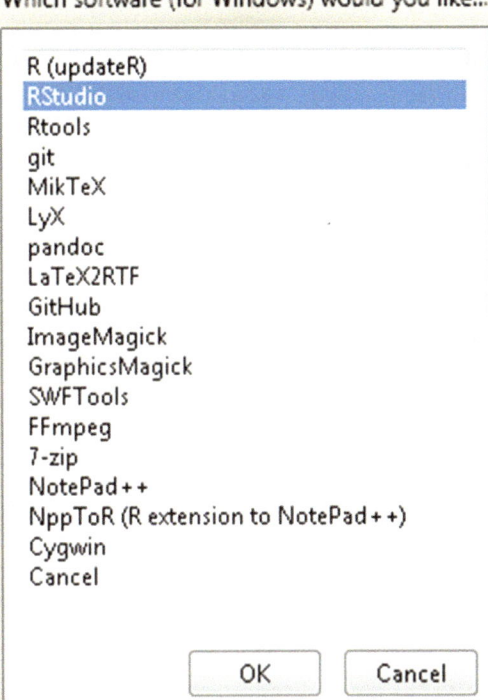

5.8   Other R on the Web Projects

Some older projects for R integrated with the Web are available at http://cran.r-project.org/doc/FAQ/R-FAQ.html#R-Web-Interfaces.

5.8.1   Concerto

Concerto is a web-based, adaptive testing platform for creating and running rich, dynamic tests. It combines the flexibility of HTML presentation with the computing power of the R language, and the safety and performance of the MySQL database. It is totally free for commercial and academic use, and it is an open source. The testing platform allows users to create various online assessment tools, from simple surveys to complex IRT-based Adaptive Tests. It is available at https://code.google.com/p/concerto-platform/ and http://www.psychometrics.cam.ac.uk/newconcerto/options. This enables a custom platform especially for market research industry.

Using Concerto

- You can create a free Concerto account on the server http://www.psychometrics. cam.ac.uk/newconcerto/options (software as a service).
- Alternatively, you can launch an Amazon Machine Image with Concerto v4 pre-installed.
- You can also download Concerto and install it on your own server

An interview with its creator is reproduced below:

Ajay—What was the motivation behind building Concerto?

Michal—We deal with a lot of online projects at the Psychometrics Centre—one of them attracted more than 7 million unique participants. We needed a powerful tool that would allow researchers and practitioners to conveniently build and deliver online tests.

Also, our relationships with the website designers and software engineers that worked on developing our tests were rather difficult. We had trouble successfully explaining our needs, and each little change was implemented with a delay and at significant cost. Not to mention the difficulties with embedding some more advanced methods (such as adaptive testing) in our tests.

So we created a tool allowing us, psychometricians, to easily develop psychometric tests from scratch and publish them online. And all this without having to hire software developers.

Ajay—Why did you choose R as the background for Concerto? What other languages and platforms did you consider? Apart from Concerto, how else do you utilize R in your center, department, and University?

Michal—R was a natural choice as it is open-source, free, and nicely integrates with a server environment. Also, we believe that it is becoming a universal statistical and data processing language in science. We put increasing emphasis on teaching R to our students and we hope that it will replace SPSS/PASW as a default statistical tool for social scientists.

Ajay—What all can Concerto do besides a computer adaptive test?

Michal—We did not plan it initially, but Concerto turned out to be extremely flexible. In a nutshell, it is a web interface to R engine with a built-in MySQL database and easy-to-use developer panel. It can be installed on both Windows and Unix systems and used over the network or locally.

Effectively, it can be used to build any kind of web application that requires a powerful and quickly deployable statistical engine. For instance, I envision an easy to use website (that could look a bit like SPSS) allowing students to analyse their data using a web browser alone (learning the underlying R code simultaneously). Also, the authors of R libraries (or anyone else) could use Concerto to build user-friendly web interfaces to their methods.

Finally, Concerto can be conveniently used to build simple non-adaptive tests and questionnaires. It might seem to be slightly less intuitive at first than popular questionnaire services (such us my favorite Survey Monkey), but has virtually unlimited flexibility when it comes to item format, test flow, feedback options, etc. Also, it is free.

Ajay—How do you see the cloud computing paradigm growing? Do you think browser-based computation is here to stay?

Michal—I believe that cloud infrastructure is the future. Dynamically sharing computational and network resources between online service providers has a great competitive advantage over traditional strategies to deal with network infrastructure. I am sure the security concerns will be resolved soon, finishing the transformation of the network infrastructure as we know it. On the other hand, however, I do not see a reason why client-side (or browser) processing of the information should cease to exist—I rather think that the border between the cloud and personal or local computer will continually dissolve.

About

Michal Kosinski is associated with the University of Cambridge Psychometrics Centre as its Deputy Director. In the past he has been one of the leading researchers at the Psychometrics Centre and a researcher at Microsoft Research. You can read more about him at http://www.michalkosinski.com/.

5.8.2   Rapporter

A startup in the R ecosystem with a promising product is RApporter (http://rapporter.net/). It has actually been there for some time, but with the launch of their new product we ask them the trials and tribulations of creating an open source startup in the data science field.

What Rapporter.net does is use precreated templates for usage of the user. For example if a business user wants to create K Means clustering, you can simply upload the dataset, and specify the variables. The output is a report, not just the statistical output that standard analytics software produces. Here is an example

Step 1 Choose Template

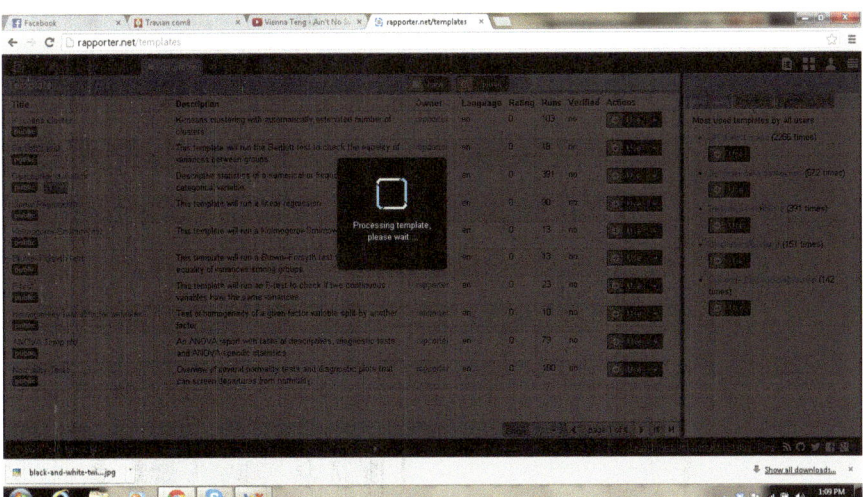

Step 2 Choose Dataset and Variables

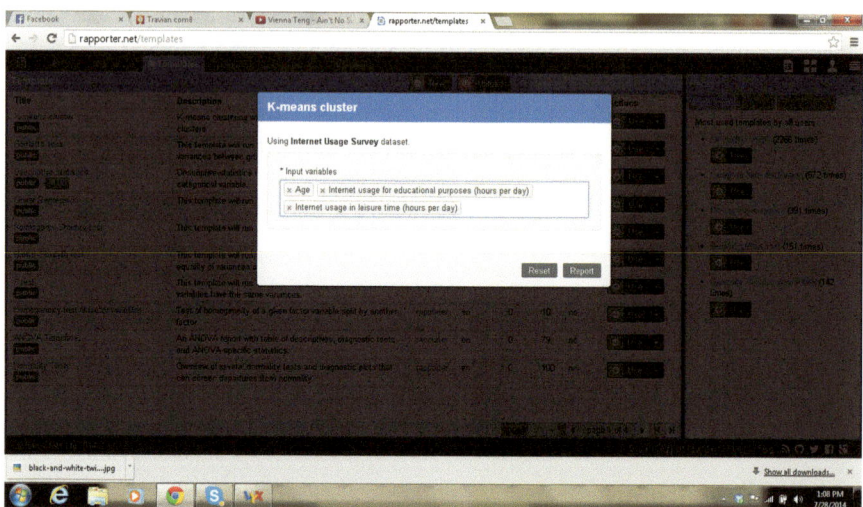

Step 3 Review the generated Report

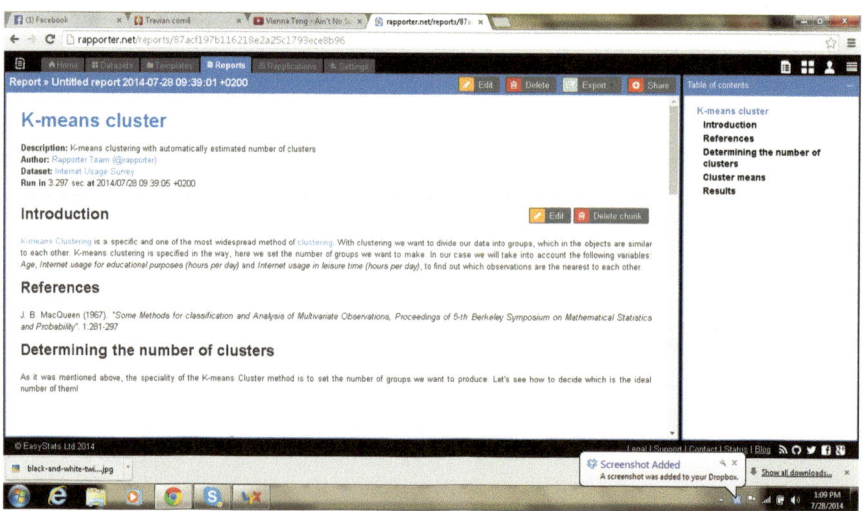

We scroll down to review the standardized output

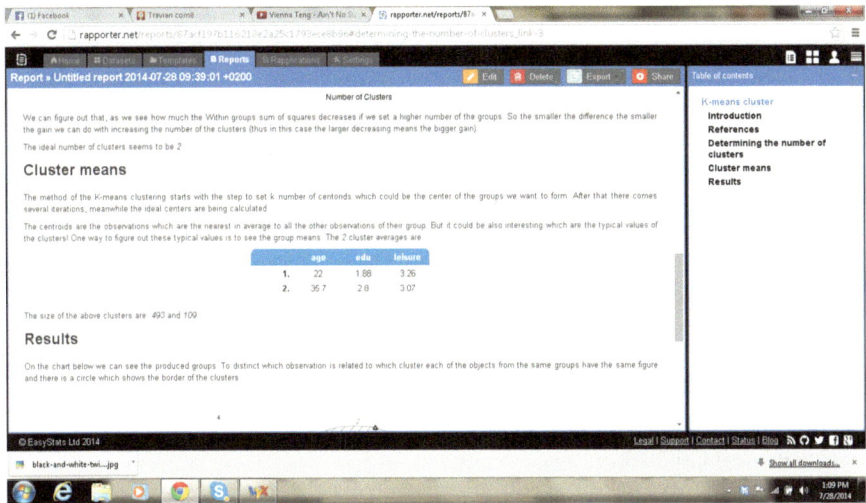

Statistical reports creation is just a few clicks away! So much for the hype on the indispensability of data scientists!

This is part of the interview with Gergely Dar'czi, co-founder of the Rapporter project.

Ajay—Describe the journey of Rapporter till now, and your product plans for 2013.

Greg—The idea of Rapporter presented itself more than 3 years ago while giving statistics, SPSS, and R courses at different Hungarian universities and also creating custom statistical reports for a number of companies for a living at the same time. Long story short, the three Hungarian co-founder faced similar problems at both sectors: students, just like business clients, admired the capabilities of R and the wide variety of tools found on CRAN, but were not eager at all to get into learning how to use that. So we tried to make up some plans how to let the non-R users also build on the resources of R, and we came up with the idea of an intuitive web-interface as an R front-end.

The real development of a helper R package (which later become "rapport") started in the January of 2011 by Aleksandar Blagoti and met in our spare time and rather just for fun, as we had a dream about using "annotated statistical templates" in R after a few conversations on StackOverflow. We also worked on a front-end in the means of an Rserve driven PHP engine with MySQL—to be dropped and completely rewritten later after some trying experiences and serious benchmarking.

We have released "rapport" package to the public at the end of 2011 on GitHub, and after a few weeks on CRAN too. Despite the fact that we did our best with creating a decent documentation and also some live examples, we somehow forgot to spread the news of the new package to the R community, so "rapport" did not attract any serious attention.

Even so, our enthusiasm for annotated R "templates" did not wane as time passed, so we continued to work on "rapport" by adding new features and also Aleksandar started to fortify his Ruby on Rails skills. We also dropped Rserve with MySQL back-end, and introduced Jeffrey Horner's awesome RApache with some NoSQL databases. To be honest, this change resulted in a one-year delay of releasing Rapporter and no ends of headaches on our end, but in the long run, it was a really smart move after all, as we own an easily scalable and a highly available cluster of servers at the moment.

But back to 2012.

As "rapport" got too complex as time passed with newly added features, Aleksandar and I decided to split the package, which move gave birth to "pander". At that time "knitr" got more and more familiar among R users, so it was a brave move to release "another" similar package, but the roots of "pander" were more then one year old, we used some custom methods not available in "knitr" (like capturing the R object beside the printed output of chunks), we needed tweakable global options instead of chunk options and we really wanted to build on the power of Pandoc—just like before.

So we had a package for converting R objects to Pandoc's markdown with a general S3 method, another package to automatically run that and also capture plots and images a brew-like document with various output formats—like pdf, docx, odt, etc. In the summer, while Aleksandar dealt with the web interface, I worked on some new features in our packages: (a) automatic and robust caching of chunks with various options for performance reasons, (b) automatically unifying "base", "lattice" and "ggplot2" images to the same style with user options—like major/minor grid colour, font family, colour palette, margins etc. (c) adding other global options to "pander", to let our expected clients later personalize their custom report style with a few clicks.

At the same time, we were searching for different options to prevent running malicious code in the parallel R sessions, which might compromise all our users' sensitive data. Unfortunately no full blown solution existed at that time, and we really wanted to stand clear of running some Java-based interpreters in our network. So I started to create a parser for R commands, which was supposed to filter out malicious R commands before evaluation, and a handful flu got me some spare time to implement "sandboxR" with an open and live "hack my R server" demo, which ended up in a great challenge on my side, but proved to really work after all. I also had a few conversations with Jeroen Ooms (the author of the awesome OpenCPU), who faced similar problems on his servers and was eager to prevent the issues with the help of AppArmor. The great news of "RAppArmor" did make "sandboxR" needless (as AppArmor just cannot regulate inner R calls), but we started to evaluate all user specified R commands in a separate hat, which allowed me to make "sanboxR" more permissive with black-filtered functions. In the middle of the summer, I realized that we have an almost working web application with any number of R workers being able to serve tons of users based on the flexible NoSQL database backends, but we had no legal background to release such a service, nor had I any solid financial background to found one—moreover the Rapporter project already took huge amount from my family budget.

As I was against of letting some venture capital to dominate the project, and did not found any accelerator that would take on a project with a maturing, almost market-ready product, me and a few associates decided to found a UK company on our own and having confidence in the future and God.

So we founded Easystats Ltd, the company running rapporter.net, in July, and decided to release the first beta and pretty stable version of the application to the public at the end of September. At that time users could: upload and use text or SPSS sav data sets, specify more than 20 global options to be applied to all generated reports (like plot themes, table width, date format, decimal mark and number of digits, separators and copula in vectors, etc.), create reports with the help of predefined statistical "templates", "fork" (clone) any of our templates and modify without restriction, or create new statistical templates from scratch, edit the body or remove any part of the reports, resize images with the mouse or even with finger on touch-devices, and export reports to pdf, odt, or docx formats.

A number of new features were introduced since then:

OpenBUGS integration with more permissive security profiles, users can create custom styles for the exported documents (in LaTeX, docx, and odt format) to generate unique and possibly branded reports, to share public or even private reports with anyone without the need for registering on rapporter.net by a simple hyperlink, and to let our users to integrate their templates in any homepage, blog post, or even HTML mail, so that let anyone use the power of R with a few clicks building on the knowledge of template authors and our reliable back-end. Although 2 years ago I was pretty sure that this job would be finished in a few months and that we would possibly have a successful project in a year or two, now I am certain, that bunch of new features will make Rapporter more and more user-friendly, intuitive, and extensible in the next few years. Currently, we are working hard on a redesigned GUI with the help of a dedicated UX team at last (which was a really important structural change in the life of Rapporter, as we can really assign and split tasks now just like we dreamed of when the project was a two-men show), which is to be finished no later than the first quarter of the year. Beside design issues, this change would also result in some new features, like ordering the templates, data sets and reports by popularity, rating or relevance for the currently active data set; and also letting users to alter the style of the resulting reports in a more seamless way.

The next planned tasks for 2013 include: (a) a "data transformation" front-end, which would let users to rename and label variables in any uploaded data set, specify the level of measurement, recode/categorize or create new variables with the help of existing ones and/or any R functions, (b) edit tables in reports on the fly (change the decimal mark, highlight some elements, rename columns, and split tables to multiple pages with a simple click), (c) a more robust API to let third-party users temporary upload data to be used in the analysis, option to use multiple data sets in a template and to let users merge or connect data online, (d) and some top-secret surprises.

Beside the above tasks, which was made up by us, our team is really interested in any feedback from the users, which might change the above order or add new tasks with higher priority, so be sure to add your two cent on our support page.

And we will have to come up with some account plans with reasonable pricing in 2013 for the hosted service to let us cover the server fees and development expenses. But of course Rapporter will remain free forever for users with basic needs (like analysing data sets with only a few hundreds of cases) or anyone in the academic sector, and we also plan to provide an option to run Rapporter "off-site" on any Unix-like environment.

Ajay—What are some of the Big Data use cases I can do with Rapporter?

Greg—Although we have released Rapporter beta only a few months ago, we already heard some pretty promising use cases from our (potential) clients.

But I must emphasize that at first we are not committed to deal with Big Data in the means of user contributed data sets with billions of cases, but rather concentrating on providing an intuitive and responsive way of analysing traditional, survey-like data frames up to about 100,000 cases.

Anyway, to be on topic: a really promising project of Optimum Dosing Strategies has been using Rapporter's, API for a number of weeks even in 2012 to compute optimal doses for different kind of antibiotics based on Monte-Carlo simulation and Bayesian adaptive feedback among other methods. This collaboration lets the ID-ODS team develop a powerful calculator with full-blown reports ready to be attached to medical records—without any special technical knowledge on their side, as we maintain the R engine and the integration part, they code in R. This results in pleased clients all over the world, which makes us happy too.

We really look forward to ship a number of educational templates to be used in real life at several (multilingual) universities from September 2013. These templates would let teachers show customizable and interactive reports to the students with any number of comments and narrative paragraphs, which statistical introductory modules would provide a free alternative to other desktop software used in education.

In the next few months, a part of our team will focus on spatial analysis templates, which would mean that our users could not just map, but really analyse any of their spatially related data with a few clicks and clear parameters.

Another feature request of a client seems to be a really exciting idea. Currently, Google Analytics and other tracking services provide basic options to view, filter, and export the historical data of websites, blogs, etc. As creating an interface between Rapporter and the tracking services to be able to fetch the most recent data is not beyond possibility any more with the help of existing API resources, so our clients could generate annotated usage reports of any specified period of time— without restrictions. Just to emphasize some potential add-ons: using the time-series R packages in the analysis or creating realtime "dashboards" with optional forecasts about live data.

Of course you could think of other kind of live or historical data instead of Google Analytics, as creating a template for, e.g., transaction data or gas usage of a household could be addressed at any time, and please do not forget about the above referenced use-cases in the 3 rd question ("[...]Rapporter can help: [...]").

But wait: the beauty of Rapporter is that you could implement all of the above ideas by yourself in our system, even without any help from us.

Ajay—What are some of things that can be easily done with Rapporter than with your plain vanilla R?

Greg—Rapporter is basically developed for creating reproducible, iterative, and annotated statistical modules (a.k.a. "templates"), which means the passing a data set and the list of variables with some optional arguments would end up in a full-blown written report with automatically styled tables and charts.

So using Rapporter is like writing "Sweave" or "knitr" documents, but you write the template only once, and then apply that to any number of data sets with a simple click on an intuitive user interface.

Beside this major objective: as Rapporter is running in the cloud and sharing reports and templates (or even data sets) with collaborators or with anyone on the Internet is really easy, our users can post, share any R code for free and without restrictions, or release the templates with specified license and/or fees in a secured environment.

This means that Rapporter can help:

scholars sharing scientific results or methods with reproducible and instantly available demo and/or dedicated implementation along with publications, teachers to create self-explanatory statistical templates which would help the students internationalize the subject by practice, any R developer to share a live and interactive demo of the implemented features of the functions with a few clicks, businesses could use a statistical platform without restrictions for a reasonable monthly fee instead of expensive and non-portable statistical programs, governments, and national statistical offices to publicize census or other Big Data with a scientific and reliable analytic tool with annotated and clear reports while insuring the anonymity of the respondents by automatically applying custom methods (like data swapping, rounding, micro-aggregation, PRAM, adding noise, etc.) to the tables and results, etc. And of course, do not forget about one of our main objectives to let us open up the world of R to non-R users too with an intuitive, driving user interface. .

About

Gergely Dar'czi is coordinating the development of Rapporter and maintaining their R packages. Beside he tries to be active in some open-source projects and on StackOverflow, he is a PhD candidate in sociology and also a lecturer at Corvinus University of Budapest and Pázmány Péter Catholic University in Hungary

Rapporter is a web application helping you to create comprehensive, reliable, statistical reports on any mobile device or PC, using an intuitive user interface.

5.8.3   R Service Bus

Here is an interview with Tobias Verbeke, Managing Director of Open Analytics (http://www.openanalytics.eu/). Open Analytics is doing cutting edge work with R in the enterprise software space. Their flagship project is R Service Bus. The R Service Bus is a Swiss army knife that allows you to plug R into your processes independently of the technology used by other software applications.

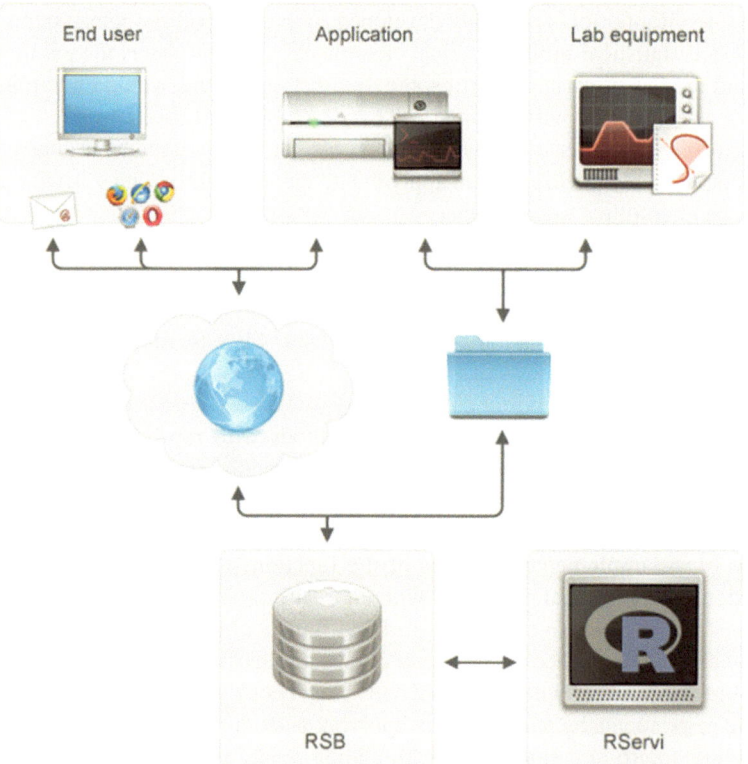

Ajay—What is RSB all about—what needs does it satisfy—who can use it?
Tobias—RSB stands for the R Service Bus and is communication middleware and a work manager for R jobs. It allows to trigger and receive results from R jobs using a plethora of protocols such as RESTful web services, e-mail protocols, sftp, folder polling, etc. The idea is to enable people to push a button (or software to make a request) and have them receive automated R based analysis results or reports for their data.

Ajay—What is your vision and what have been the challenges and learning so far in the project?
Tobias—RSB started when automating toxicological analyses in pharmaceutical industry in collaboration with Philippe Lamote. Together with David Dossot, an exceptional software architect in Vancouver, we decided to cleanly separate

concerns, namely to separate the integration layer (RSB) from the statistical layer (R) and, likewise, from the application layer. As a result any arbitrary R code can be run via RSB and any client application can interact with RSB as long as it can talk one of the many supported protocols. This fundamental design principle makes us different from alternative solutions where statistical logic and integration logic are always somehow interwoven, which results in maintenance and integration headaches. One of the challenges has been to keep focus on the core task of automating statistical analyses and not deviating into features that would turn RSB into a tool for interaction with an R session, which deserves an entirely different approach. Rservice-diagram

Ajay—Computing seems to be moving to an heterogeneous cloud, server, and desktop model. What do you think about the R and Cloud Computing— current and future?

Tobias—From a freedom perspective, cloud computing and the SaaS model are often a step backwards, but in our own practice we obviously follow our customer's needs and offer RSB hosting from our data centres as well. Also, our other products, e.g., the R IDE Architect are ready for the cloud and use on servers via Architect Server. As far as R itself concerns in relation to cloud computing, I foresee its use to increase. At Open Analytics we see an increasing demand for R-based statistical engines that power web applications living in the cloud.

Ajay—You recently released RSB version 6. What are all the new features? What is the planned roadmap going forward Tobias—RSB 6.0 is all about large-scale production environments and strong security. It kicked off on a project where RSB was responsible for spitting 8500 predictions per second. Such large-scale production deployments of RSB motivated the development of a series of features. First of all RSB was made lightning fast: we achieved a full round trip from REST call to prediction in 7 ms on the mentioned use case. In order to allow for high throughput, RSB also gained a synchronous API (RSB 5.0 had an asynchronous API only). Another new feature is the availability of client-side connection pooling to the pool manager of R processes that are ready to serve RSB. Besides speed, this type of production environments also need monitoring and resilience in case of issues. For the monitoring, we made sure that everything is in place for monitoring and remotely querying not only the RSB application itself, but also the pool of R processes managed by RServi.

(Note from Ajay—RJ is an open source library providing tools and interfaces to integrate R in Java applications. RJ project also provides a pool for R engines, easy to setup, and manage by a web-interface or JMX. One or multiple client can borrow the R engines (called RServi) see http://www.walware.de/it/rj/ and https://github.com/walware/rj-servi).

Also, we now allow to define node validation strategies to be able to check that R nodes are still functioning properly. If not, the nodes are killed and new nodes are started and added to the pool. In terms of security, we are now able to cover a very wide spectrum of authentication and authorization. We have machines up and running using openid, basic http authentication, LDAP, SSL client certificates, etc. to serve everyone from the individual user who is happy with openid authentication for his RSB app to large investment banks who have very strong security requirements. The next step is to provide tighter integration with Architect, such that people can release new RSB applications without leaving the IDE.

Ajay—Describe the open source ecosystem in general and R ecosystem in particular for Europe. How does it compare with other locations in your opinion?

Tobias—Open source is probably a global ecosystem and crosses oceans very easily. Dries Buytaert started off Drupal in Belgium and now operates from the US interacting with a global community. From a business perspective, there are as many open source models as there are open source companies. I noticed that the major US R companies (Revolution Analytics and RStudio) cherished the open source philosophy initially, but drifted both into models combining open source and proprietary components. At Open Analytics, there are only open source products and enterprise customers have access to exactly the same functionality as a student may have in a developing country. That being said, I do not believe this is a matter of geography, but has to do more with the origins and different strategies of the companies.

5.9   The Difference Between Open Source and Closed Source Enterprise Software

Here is an interview with Christoph Waldhauser a noted researcher and the Founder, CEO at KDSS K Data Science Solutions, which is a R based Analytics advisory firm. In a generous and insightful interview, Christoph talks of the perceptions around open source, academia versus startups, Europe and North America for technology, and his own journey through it all.

Ajay Ohri (AO)—Describe your career in science. At what point did you decide to become involved in open source projects including R?

Chrisoph Waldhauser (CW)—When I did my second course on quantitative social science, the software we used was SPSS. At that time, the entire social science curriculum was built around that package. There were no student versions available, only a number of computer labs on campus that had SPSS installed. I had previously switched from Windows to Linux to cut on licensing costs (as a student you are constantly short on money) and to try something new. So I was willing to try out the same with R. In the beginning I was quite lost, having to work with survey weighted data and only rudimentary exposure to Perl before that. That was in a time long before RStudio and I started out with Emacs and ESS. As you might imagine, I landed in a world full of metaphorical pain. But in due time I was able to replicate all of the things we did in class.

Even more, I was able to do them much more efficiently. And while my colleagues were only interpreting SPSS output, I was understanding where those numbers came from. This epiphany was then guiding me for the remainder of my scientific career. For instance, instead of Word I'd use LaTeX (back then a thing unheard of at my department) and even put free/libre/open source software in the focus of my research for my master thesis. Continuing down that path, I eventually started working at WU Vienna University of Economics and Business and that had led me to one of the centres of R development. There, most of every day's work was revolving around Free Software. The people there had a great impact on my understanding of Free Software and its influence on how we do research.

AO—Describe your work in social media analytics including package creation for Google Plus and your publication on Twitter

CW—Social media analytics is a very exciting field. The majority of research focuses on listening to the garden hose of social media data, that is, analysing the communication revolving around certain keywords or communities. For instance, linking real-world events to the #euromaidan hashtag in Ukraine. I tread down a different path: instead of looking at what all users have to say on a certain topic, I investigate how a certain user or class of users communicates across all topics they bring up. So instead of following a top–down approach, I chose to go bottom–up.

Starting with the smallest building blocks of a social network has a number of advantages and leads to Google+ eventually. The reason behind this is, that the utility of social media for Google is different from say Twitter or Facebook. While classical social media is used to engage followers, say a lottery connected to the Facebook page of a brand, Google+ has an additional purpose: enlist users to help Google produce better, more accurate search results. With this in mind, focus shifts naturally from many users on one topic to how a single user can use Google+ to optimize the message they get across and manage the search terms they are associated with. This line of argument has fueled my research in Google+ and Twitter:

Which messages resonate most with the followers of a certain user? We know that each follower aims at resharing and liking messages she deems interesting. What precisely is interesting to a follower depends on her tastes. And if that will eventually lead to a reshare or not depend also on other factors like time of day and chance. For this, I have created a simulation framework that is centred on the preferences of individual users and their decision to reshare a social media message. In analyses of Twitter and Google+ content, we have found interesting patterns. For instance, there are significant differences in the types of message that are popular among followers of the US Democrats' and Republicans' Twitter accounts. I am currently investigating if these observations can also be found in Europe. In the world of brand marketing, we have found significant differences in the wording of messages between localized Google+ pages. For instance, different mixtures of emotions in BMW's German and US Google+ pages are key to increased reshare rates.

AO—What are some of the cultural differences in implementing projects in academia and in startups?

CW—This is a very hard question, mainly due to the fact that there is no one academia. Broadly speaking, quantitative academia can always be broken down in two classes that I like to refer to as science vs. engineering. Within this framework, science is seeking to understand why something is happening, often at the cost of practical implementability. The engineering mindset on the other hand focuses on producing working solutions and is less concerned about understanding why something behaves the way it does. Take for instance neural networks that are currently enjoying somewhat of a renaissance due to deep learning approaches. In science, neural networks are not really popular because they are black boxes. You can use a neural network to produce great classifiers and use them to filter, e.g., the picture of cats out of a stack of pictures. But even then it is not clear what factors are the defining essence of a cat. So while engineers might be happy to have found a useful classifier, scientists will not be content. This focus on understanding precludes many technological options to science. For instance, Big Data analyses aim at finding patterns that hold for most cases, but accept if the patterns do not apply to every case. This is fine for engineering, but science would require theoretical explanations for each case that did not match the pattern. To me, this "rigor" has few practical benefits. In startups, there is little place for science. The largest part of startups is being financed by some sort borrowed capital. And these lenders are only interested in return on their investment, and not insights or enlightenment. So, to me, there are few difference between academic engineering and startups. But I find that startups that want to do science properly, will have a very hard time getting off to good start. That is not to say it is impossible, just more difficult.

AO—What do you think of the open access publishing movement as represented by http://arxiv.org/ and JSS? What are some of the costs and benefits for researchers that prevent whole-scale adoption of the open access system and how can these be addressed?

CW—I think it is important to differentiate open access and preprints like arxiv.org. Open access merely means that articles are accessible without paying for accessing them. As most research that is published has been paid for by the taxpayer anyway, it should also be freely accessible to them. Keeping information behind paywalls is a moral choice, and I think it is self-evident which side we as a scientific community should choose. I would also question the argument of publishing houses that their services are costly. Which services? Copy-editing? Marketing stunts at conferences? I fail to see how these services are important to academia. Turning to preprints, one must note that academic publishing is currently plagued by two flaws.

One is the lack of transparency that leads to poor reviews.

The other one is academia's using of publications as a quantitative indicator of academic success. This led to a vast increase of results being submitted for publication: a publishing house that had to review hundreds of articles before is now facing thousands. Therefore, it is not uncommon today for authors having to wait for multiple years until a final decision has been made by the editors. And the longer the backlog of articles gets, the lower the quality of the reviews will become. This is unacceptable. Preprints are a way around this deadlock. Findings can be accessed by fellow researchers even before a formal review has been completed. In an ideal world with impeccable review quality, this would lead to a watering down of the quality of research being available. This certainly poses a risk, but today's reviews are from flawless. More often than not, reviews fail to discover obvious flaws in research design and barely ever do reviewers check if data actually do lead to the results published. So, relying on preprints or reviewed articles, researchers always need to use common sense anyway: If five independent research groups come to the same conclusion, the papers are likely to be solid. This heuristic is somewhat similar to Wikipedia: it might not always be correct, but most of the time it is.

AO—What are some of the differences that you have encountered in the ecosystem in funding, research, and development both in academia and tech startups as compared to Europe versus North America?

CW—Living and working in a country that is increasingly being affected by the aftershocks of the Great Depression of 2007—2009 has left me somewhat disillusioned. In face of the economic problems in Europe at the moment, most of public funding has come to a full stop. Private capital is somewhat still available, but also here risk management has led to an increased focus on business plans and marketability. As pointed out above, this is less of a problem for engineering approaches (even though writing convincing business plans is challenging to scientists and engineers alike). But it is outright deadly to science. From what I see, North America has a different tradition. There, engineering generates so much revenue that part of that revenue goes back to science. An attitude we certainly lack in Europe is what Tim O'Reilly terms the makers' mindset. We could use some more of that. **AO-In enterprise software people often pay more for software that is bad compared to software that is open source. What are your thoughts on this?**

CW—I have just had an interesting discussion with the head of a credit risk unit in a major bank. The unit is switching from SAS to SPSS for modeling credit risk. R, an equally capable or perhaps even superior free software solution, was not even considered. The rationale behind that is simple: in case the software is faulty, there is a company to blame and hold liable. Free software in general does not have software companies that back it in that way. So this appears to be the reason behind the psychological barrier to use free software. But I think it is a false security. Suppose every bank in the world uses either SAS or SPSS for credit risk modeling. And at one point, a fatal flaw in one of those two packages is being discovered. This flaw is then likely to affect most of the banks that chose it. So within 24 hours of that flaw being discovered, the company backing the product will have to file for bankruptcy.

It is somewhat ironic that people responsible for credit risk management do not see that the high correlation introduced due to all banks relying on the same software company does not mitigate but greatly inflate their risk. For example, some years ago a SAS executive said, she would feel more comfortable to fly in a plane that has been developed using closed source and not open source software, because closed source would provide increased quality. That line of argument has been thoroughly refuted. However, there is some truth in the fact that an investor might be more comfortable in putting money in a aircraft company that relies on closed source software for reasons of liability. Should a plane go down because of a closed source software bug, then the software company and not the aircraft company could be held liable.

So any lawsuits against the aircraft company would be redirected to the software company. But at the end of the day, again, the software company will go out of business, leaving the aircraft company with the damage none the less. So the trade off between poorly designed or implemented, expensive closed source software and superior free software is made due to questions of liability. But the truth is, that this is a false sense of security. I would therefore always argue in favor of free software.

About—KDSS is a bleeding edge state of the art data science advisory firm. You can see more of Christoph's work at https://github.com/tophcito.

Chapter 6
Using R with Data and Bigger Data

What is Big Data? Data that is huge and humongous, that is not readily processed by traditional techniques is called Big Data. It is characterized by the three Vs (volume, variety and, velocity), and invariably involves both cloud computing (hardware) and specialized software (like the Hadoop ecosystem). We have covered the three V's before in Chap. 1.

6.1 Big Data Interview

An interview with James G Kobielus, who is the Senior Program Director, Product Marketing, Big Data Analytics Solutions at IBM.

Ajay—What are the specific parts of the IBM Platform that deal with the three layers of Big Data—variety, velocity, and volume

James—Well first of all, let's talk about the IBM Information Management portfolio. Our Big Data platform addresses the three layers of Big Data to varying degrees either together in a product, or two out of the three or even one of the three aspects. We don't have separate products for the variety, velocity, and volume separately.

Let us define these three layers—Volume refers to the hundreds of terabytes and petabytes of stored data inside organizations today. Velocity refers to the whole continuum from batch to real-time continuous and streaming data.

Variety refers to multi-structure data from structured to unstructured files, managed and stored in a common platform analysed through common tooling.

For Volume—IBM has a highly scalable Big Data platform. This includes Netezza and Infosphere groups of products, and Watson-like technologies that can support petabytes volume of data for analytics. But really the support of volume ranges across IBM's Information Management portfolio both on the database side and the advanced analytics side.

© Springer Science+Business Media New York 2014   193
A Ohri, *R for Cloud Computing*, DOI 10.1007/978-1-4939-1702-0__6

For real-time Velocity, we have real-time data acquisition. We have a product called IBM Infosphere, part of our Big Data platform, that is specifically built for streaming real-time data acquisition and delivery through complex event processing. We have a very rich range of offerings that help clients build a Hadoop environment that can scale.

Our Hadoop platform is the most real time capable of all in the industry. We are differentiated by our sheer breadth, sophistication and functional depth and tooling integrated in our Hadoop platform. We are differentiated by our streaming offering integrated into the Hadoop platform. We also offer a great range of modeling and analysis tools, pretty much more than any other offering in the Big Data space.

Ajay—How integral are acquisitions for IBM in the Big Data space (Netezza, Cognos, SPSS, etc.). Is it true that everything that you have in Big Data is acquired or is the famous IBM R and D contributing here? (See a partial list of IBM acquisitions at http://www.ibm.com/investor/strategy/acquisitions.html)

Jim—We have developed a lot on our own. We have the deepest R and D of anybody in the industry in all things Big Data.

For example—Watson has Big Insights Hadoop at its core. Apache Hadoop is the heart and soul of Big Data (see http://www-01.ibm.com/software/data/infosphere/hadoop/). A great deal that makes Big Insights so differentiated is that not everything has been built by the Hadoop community.

We have built additions out of the necessity for security, modeling, monitoring, and governance capabilities into BigInsights to make it truly enterprise ready. That is one example of where we have leveraged open source and we have built our own tools and technologies and layered them on top of the open source code.

Yes of course we have done many strategic acquisitions over the last several years related to Big Data Management and we continue to do so. This quarter we have done 3 acquisitions with strong relevance to Big Data. One of them is Vivisimo (http://www-03.ibm.com/press/us/en/pressrelease/37491.wss).

Vivisimo provides federated Big Data discovery, search and profiling capabilities to help you figure out what data is out there, what is relevance of that data to your data science project—to help you answer the question which data should you bring in your Hadoop Cluster.

We also did Varicent, which is more performance management and we did TeaLeaf, which is a customer experience solution provider where customer experience management and optimization is one of the hot killer apps for Hadoop in the cloud. We have done great many acquisitions that have a clear relevance to Big Data.

Netezza already had a massively parallel analytics database product with an embedded library of models called Netezza Analytics, and in-database capabilities to massively parallelize Map Reduce and other analytics management functions inside the database. In many ways, Netezza provided capabilities similar to that IBM had provided for many years under the Smart Analytics Platform (http://www-01.ibm.com/software/data/infosphere/what-is-advanced-analytics/).

There is a differential between Netezza and ISAS.

ISAS was built predominantly in-house over several years. If you go back a decade ago IBM acquired Ascential Software, a product portfolio that was the heart and soul of IBM InfoSphere Information Manager that is core to our Big Data platform. In addition to **Netezza**, IBM bought **SPSS** two years back. We already had data mining tools and predictive modeling in the InfoSphere portfolio, but we realized we needed to have the best of breed, SPSS provided that and so IBM acquired them.

Cognos—We had some BI reporting capabilities in the InfoSphere portfolio that we had built ourselves and also acquired for various degrees from prior acquisitions. But clearly Cognos was one of the best BI vendors, and we were lacking such a rich tool set in our product in visualization and cubing and so for that reason we acquired Cognos.

There is also **Unica**—which is a marketing campaign optimization which in many ways is a killer app for Hadoop. Projects like that are driving many enterprises.

Ajay—How would you rank order these acquisitions in terms of strategic importance rather than data of acquisition or price paid?

Jim—Think of Big Data as an ecosystem that has components that are fitted to particular functions for data analytics and data management. Is the database the core, or the modeling tool the core, or the governance tools the core, or is the hardware platform the core? Everything is critically important. We would love to hear from you what you think has been most important. Each acquisition has helped play a critical role to build the deepest and broadest solution offering in Big Data. We offer the hardware, software, professional services, the hosting service. I don't think there is any validity to a rank order system.

Ajay—What are the initiatives regarding open source that Big Data group have done or are planning?

Jim—What we are doing now—We are very much involved with the Apache Hadoop community. We continue to evolve the open source code that everyone leverages. We have built BigInsights on Apache Hadoop. We have the closest, most up-to-date in terms of version number to Apache Hadoop (Hbase,HDFS, Pig, etc.) of all commercial distributions with our BigInsights 1.4.

We have an R library integrated with BigInsights. We have an R library integrated with Netezza Analytics. There is support for R Models within the SPSS portfolio. We already have a fair amount of support for R across the portfolio.

Ajay—What are some of the concerns (privacy, security, regulation) that you think can dampen the promise of Big Data?

Jim—There are no showstoppers, there is really a strong momentum. Some of the concerns within the Hadoop space are immaturity of the technology, the immaturity of some of the commercial offerings out there that implement Hadoop, the lack of standardization for formal sense for Hadoop.

There is no Open Standards Body that declares, ratifies the latest version of Mahout, Map Reduce, HDFS, etc. There is no industry consensus reference framework for layering these different sub-projects. There are no open APIs. There are no certifications or interoperability standards or organizations to certify different vendors interoperability around a common API or framework.

The lack of standardization is troubling in this whole market. That creates risks for users because users are adopting multiple Hadoop products. There are lots of Hadoop deployments in the corporate world built around Apache Hadoop (purely open source). There may be no assurance that these multiple platforms will interoperate seamlessly. That's a huge issue in terms of just magnifying the risk. And it increases the need for the end user to develop their own custom integrated code if they want to move data between platforms, or move map-reduce jobs between multiple distributions.

Also governance is a consideration. Right now Hadoop is used for high volume ETL on multi structured and unstructured data sources, or Hadoop is used for exploratory sand boxes for data scientists. These are important applications that are a majority of the Hadoop deployments. Some Hadoop deployments are stand-alone unstructured data marts for specific applications like sentiment analysis.

Hadoop is not yet ready for data warehousing. We don't see a lot of Hadoop being used as an alternative to data warehouses for managing the single version of truth of system or record data. That day will come but there needs to be out there in the marketplace a broader range of data governance mechanisms, master data management, data profiling products that are mature that enterprises can use to make sure their data inside their Hadoop clusters is clean and is the single version of truth. That day has not arrived yet.

One of the great things about IBM's acquisition of Vivisimo is that a piece of that overall governance picture is discovery and profiling for unstructured data, and that is done very well by Vivisimo for several years.

What we will see is vendors such as IBM will continue to evolve security features inside of our Hadoop platform. We will beef up our data governance capabilities for this new world of Hadoop as the core of Big Data, and we will continue to build up our ability to integrate multiple databases in our Hadoop platform so that customers can use data from a bit of Hadoop, some data from a bit of traditional relational data warehouse, maybe some noSQL technology for different roles within a very complex Big Data environment.

That latter hybrid deployment model is becoming standard across many enterprises for Big Data. A cause for concern is when your Big Data deployment has a bit of Hadoop, bit of noSQL, bit of EDW, bit of in-memory, there are no open standards or frameworks for putting it all together for a unified framework not just for interoperability but also for deployment.

There needs to be a virtualization or abstraction layer for unified access to all these different Big Data platforms by the users/developers writing the queries, by administrators so they can manage data and resources and jobs across all these disparate platforms in a seamless unified way with visual tooling. That grand scenario, the virtualization layer is not there yet in any standard way across the Big Data market. It will evolve, it may take 5–10 years to evolve but it will evolve.

So, that's the concern that can dampen some of the enthusiasm for Big Data Analytics.

A tutorial by IBM is available for free at http://bigdatauniversity.com/bdu-wp/bdu-course/using-r-with-databases/ and you can learn how to perform data analysis using R when your data is stored in DB2 and BLU Acceleration for Cloud while an article on using R with Databases is available at http://www.ibm.com/developerworks/data/library/techarticle/dm-1402db2andr/index.html?ca=drs

6.2   The Hadoop Paradigm

As data has scaled up, enterprises needed to find a solution to create fault tolerant systems at a very low cost. The website for Hadoop is at http://hadoop.apache.org/ and it remains the best and most credible source of information on Hadoop, uncluttered by competing claims.

The following components help explain the Hadoop Ecosystem. Note Hadoop is not one software—it is a suite of many software working together.

6.2.1   What Is Hadoop All About

Official Definition (from http://hadoop.apache.org/#What+Is+Apache+Hadoop %3F)—The Apache Hadoop software library is a framework that allows for the distributed processing of large data sets across clusters of computers using simple programming models. It is designed to scale up from single servers to thousands of machines, each offering local computation and storage. Rather than rely on hardware to deliver high availability, the library itself is designed to detect and handle failures at the application layer, so delivering a highly-available service on top of a cluster of computers, each of which may be prone to failures.

Key to the hadoop paradigm is the concept called MapReduce. The following diagram is taken from the original Mapreduce paper by Dean, Ghemawat at https://www.usenix.org/legacy/event/osdi04/tech/full_papers/dean/dean.pdf which is quite possibly one of the most influential papers regarding scientific computing in the modern era.

MapReduce is a programming model and an associated implementation for processing and generating large data sets. Users specify a map function that processes a key/value pair to generate a set of intermediate key/value pairs, and a reduce function that merges all intermediate values associated with the same intermediate key.

6.2.2   The Ecosystem of Hadoop

The following software constitute the Hadoop Ecosystem as of 2014. I am putting the bold font to emphasize the difference. The project includes these modules:

• Hadoop Common: The common utilities that support the other Hadoop modules.

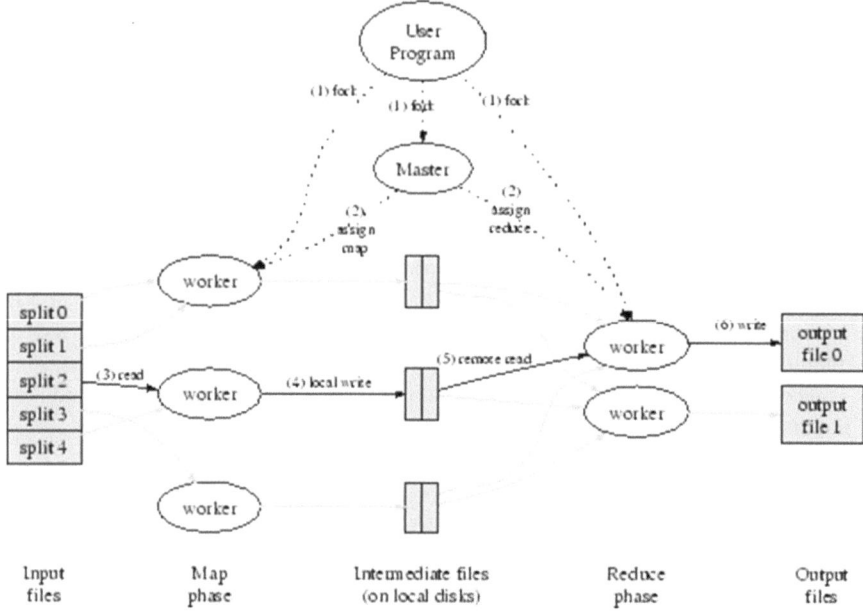

- Hadoop Distributed File System (HDFS): A **distributed file system** that provides high-throughput access to application data.
- Hadoop YARN: A framework for **job scheduling** and cluster resource management.
- Hadoop MapReduce: A YARN-based system for **parallel processing of large data sets.**
- Other Hadoop-related projects at Apache include:
- Ambari: A **web-based tool for provisioning, managing, and monitoring** Apache Hadoop clusters which includes support for Hadoop HDFS, Hadoop MapReduce, Hive, HCatalog, HBase, ZooKeeper, Oozie, Pig, and Sqoop. Ambari also provides a dashboard for viewing cluster health such as heatmaps and ability to view MapReduce, Pig, and Hive applications visually along with features to diagnose their performance characteristics in a user-friendly manner.
- Avro: A data serialization system.
- Cassandra: A **scalable multi-master database with no single points of failure**.
- Chukwa: A data collection system for managing large distributed systems.
- HBase: A scalable, **distributed database** that supports structured data storage for large tables. Use Apache HBase when you need random, real-time read/write access to your Big Data. This project's goal is the hosting of very large tables— billions of rows X millions of columns—atop clusters of commodity hardware. Apache HBase is an open-source, distributed, versioned, non-relational database model after Google's Bigtable: A Distributed Storage System for Structured Data by Chang et al. Just as Bigtable leverages the distributed data storage provided by the Google File System, Apache HBase provides Bigtable-like capabilities on top of Hadoop and HDFS. http://hbase.apache.org/

- Hive: A data warehouse infrastructure that provides **data summarization and ad hoc querying.** Hive provides a mechanism to project structure onto this data and query the data using an SQL-like language called HiveQL. At the same time this language also allows traditional map/reduce programmers to plug in their custom mappers and reducers when it is inconvenient or inefficient to express this logic in HiveQL.
- Mahout: A Scalable **machine learning** and data mining library.
- Pig: A high-level **data-flow language** and execution framework for parallel computation.
- Spark: A **fast and general compute engine** for Hadoop data. Spark provides a simple and expressive programming model that supports a wide range of applications, including ETL, machine learning, stream processing, and graph computation.
- Tez: A generalized data-flow programming framework, built on Hadoop YARN, which provides a powerful and flexible engine to execute an arbitrary DAG of tasks to process data for both batch and interactive use-cases. Tez is being adopted by Hive, Pig, and other frameworks in the Hadoop ecosystem, and also by other commercial software (e.g., ETL tools), to replace Hadoop MapReduce as the underlying execution engine.
- ZooKeeper: A high-performance **coordination service** for distributed applications.

Other commonly used terms within the Hadoop Space-

- HCatalog—Apache HCatalog is a table and storage management layer for Hadoop that enables users with different data processing tools—Apache Pig, Apache MapReduce, and Apache Hive—to more easily read and write data on the grid. HCatalog's table abstraction presents users with a relational view of data in the Hadoop Distributed File System (HDFS) and ensures that users need not worry about where or in what format their data is stored. HCatalog displays data from RCFile format, text files, or sequence files in a tabular view. It also provides REST APIs so that external systems can access these tables' metadata. http://hortonworks.com/hadoop/hcatalog/. Following HCatalog's merge with Hive (in March of 2013) HCatalog is now released as part of Hive
- Hue-Hue is a Web interface for analysing data with Apache Hadoop. http://gethue.com/
- Impala—Cloudera Impala is the industry's leading massively parallel processing (MPP) SQL query engine that runs natively in Apache Hadoop. The Apache-licensed, open source Impala project combines modern, scalable parallel database technology with the power of Hadoop, enabling users to directly query data stored in HDFS and Apache HBase without requiring data movement or transformation. http://www.cloudera.com/content/cloudera/en/products-and-services/cdh/impala.html
- Storm—Apache Storm is a distributed real-time computation system for processing fast, large streams of data. Storm adds reliable real-time data processing capabilities to Apache Hadoop® 2.x. (see http://hortonworks.com/hadoop/storm/)

- Sqoop—Apache Sqoop(TM) is a tool designed for efficiently transferring bulk data between Apache Hadoop and structured datastores such as relational databases. http://sqoop.apache.org/
- Thrift—The Apache Thrift software framework, for scalable cross-language services development, combines a software stack with a code generation engine to build services that work efficiently and seamlessly between C++, Java, Python, PHP, Ruby, Erlang, Perl, Haskell, C#, Cocoa, JavaScript, Node.js, Smalltalk, OCaml, and Delphi and other languages http://thrift.apache.org/

Additional Note—The Apache LuceneTM project develops open-source search software including Solr. Solr is a high performance search server built using Lucene Core, with XML/HTTP and JSON/Python/Ruby APIs, hit highlighting, faceted search, caching, replication, and a web admin interface.

You can see all the tope level Apache Projects for Big Data at http://projects.apache.org/indexes/category.html#big-data

The following graphic from explains the various components better to a new learner.

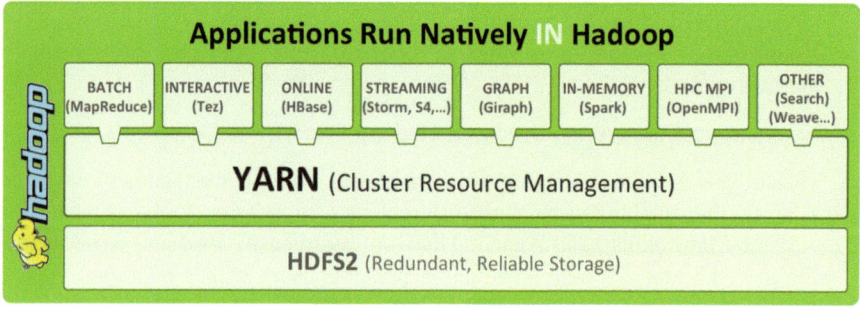

6.2.3   Current Developments in Hadoop

The following diagram from Hortonworks explains the current dynamics in motion in the Hadoop Ecosystem. Source-http://hortonworks.com/hadoop/tez/

Apache Spark is one of the newest and most promising projects in Hadoop for analytics—It is based out of http://spark.apache.org/. It is said to be much faster and it has the following constituents.

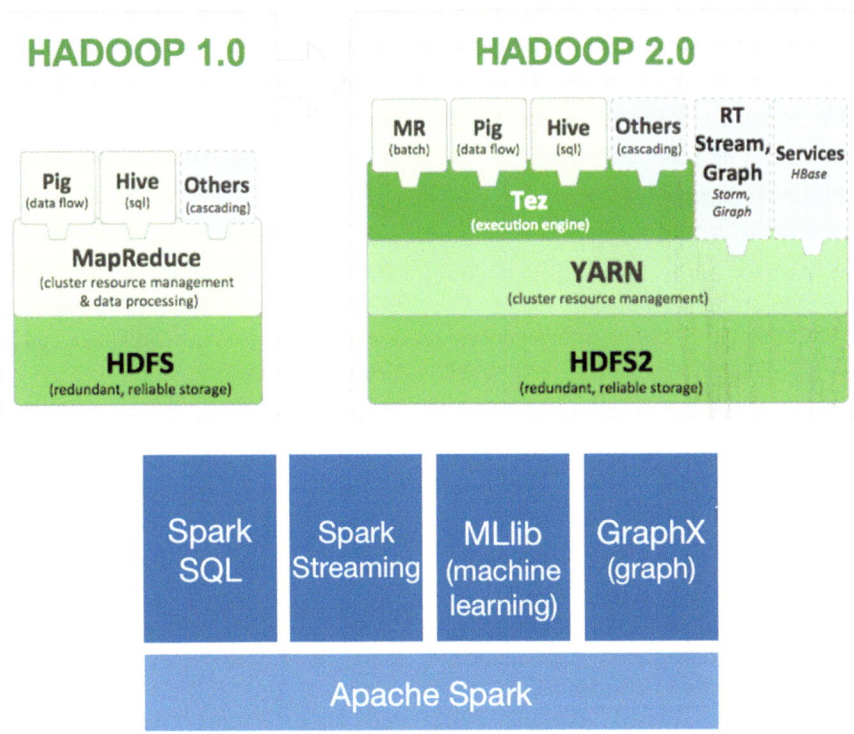

6.3 Commercial Distributions of Hadoop

The following are the most widely used distributions of Apache Hadoop by software vendors.

1. Cloudera is one of the leading vendors of Hadoop. http://www.cloudera.com/content/support/en/downloads.html. Cloudera's Distribution for Hadoop (CDH) can be run on Amazon Ec2. Please see the documentation here https://ccp.cloudera.com/display/CDH2DOC/CDH+Cloud+Scripts+%28CDH2%29. You can also run it within the browser at http://go.cloudera.com/cloudera-live.html
2. Hue is a Web interface for analysing data with Apache Hadoop. It is available at http://gethue.com/ and you can even test it at http://demo.gethue.com/
3. IBM distributes Infosphere BigInsights http://www-01.ibm.com/software/data/infosphere/biginsights/. IBM 's cloud offering is called Softlayer (it shut down its earlier offering SmartCloud for retail customers, but it is still open for Enterprise Customers). You can see hadoop deployments on the IBM Softlayer cloud at http://www.softlayer.com/cloudera-hosting
4. Greenplum has its own distribution of Apache Hadoop at http://www.greenplum.com/products/greenplum-hd

5. MapR's distribution of ApacheHadoop is available at http://www.mapr.com/ products/only-with-mapr. It has been used by Google for its Compute Engine http://www.mapr.com/partners/partner/google-compute-engine-and-mapr

6.3.1   Hadoop on the Cloud as a Service

1. Amazon has its Elastic Map Reduce for Hadoop as a service http://aws.amazon. com/elasticmapreduce
2. HDInsight is Microsoft's Hadoop-based service in the cloud and is available at http://azure.microsoft.com/en-us/services/hdinsight/
3. You can run Hadoop on Google's cloud at https://cloud.google.com/solutions/ hadoop/

6.3.2   Learning Hadoop

1. You can run the tutorials by Hortonworks in its sandbox at http://hortonworks. com/products/hortonworks-sandbox/ and http://hortonworks.com/products/ hortonworks-sandbox/#tutorial_gallery
2. Cloudera's virtual machine helps you learn Hadoop faster at http:// www.cloudera.com/content/dev-center/en/home/developer-admin-resources/ quickstart-vm.html and http://www.cloudera.com/content/cloudera-content/ cloudera-docs/HadoopTutorial/CDH4/Hadoop-Tutorial.html
3. IBM has a very lucid tutorial at http://www.ibm.com/developerworks/data/ library/techarticle/dm-1209hadoopbigdata/

One of the very few releases of Hadoop for Windows is from Hortonworks and can be referenced at http://hortonworks.com/blog/install-hadoop-windows-hortonworks-data-platform-2-0/.

6.4   Learning Hadoop

A very good resource on Learning MapReduce is available at http://www.mapr.com/ resources/videos/intro-mapreduce. One of the best training resources for Hadoop is http://www.cloudera.com/content/cloudera/en/training/courses/data-science-training.html and others are http://hortonworks.com/training/class/applying-data-science-using-apache-hadoop/ (note it uses Python and not R).

The most commonly used method is to download the virtual machine from Hortonworks (sandbox) and do the tutorials http://hortonworks.com/products/ hortonworks-sandbox/.

6.5   RHadoop and Other R Packages

The following four packages constitute RHadoop project sponsored by Revolution Analytics. They can be available at https://github.com/RevolutionAnalytics/RHadoop/wiki

* plyrmr—higher level plyr-like data processing for structured data, powered by rmr
* rmr2—functions providing Hadoop MapReduce functionality in R https://github.com/RevolutionAnalytics/rmr2
* rhdfs—functions providing file management of the HDFS from within R
* rhbase—functions providing database management for the HBase distributed database from within R https://github.com/RevolutionAnalytics/rhbase

A step-by-step tutorial is available at http://www.rdatamining.com/tutorials/rhadoop and http://home.mit.bme.hu/~ikocsis/notes/2013/10/23/(r)hadoop-sandbox-howto/
Some more R packages associated with Hadoop are included below-

* **SparkR** is an R package that provides a lightweight front-end to use Apache Spark from R. SparkR exposes the Spark API through the RDD class and allows users to interactively run jobs from the R shell on a cluster. http://amplab-extras.github.io/SparkR-pkg/
* **RHive** http://nexr.github.io/RHive/ RHive is an R extension facilitating distributed computing via HIVE query. RHive allows easy usage of HQL(Hive SQL) in R, and allows easy usage of R objects and R functions in Hive.
* **Rhipe**   http://cran.r-project.org/web/packages/RHive/index.html   DDR   with R—Rhipe
* **RImpala** http://www.datadr.org/ RImpala A package to connect and run queries on Cloudera Impala (thanks to Mu Sigma) http://cran.r-project.org/web/packages/RImpala/index.html
* **RCassandra**: This package provides a direct interface (without the use of Java) to the most basic functionality of Apache Cassanda such as login, updates, and queries. http://cran.r-project.org/web/packages/RCassandra/index.html
* a plug-in package to **tm** called **tm.plugin.dc** implementing a distributed corpus class which can take advantage of the Hadoop MapReduce library for large-scale text mining tasks. http://www.r-project.org/conferences/useR-2009/slides/Theussl+Feinerer+Hornik.pdf and http://www.jstatsoft.org/v51/i05/paper
* **solr**: General purpose R interface to Solr This package provides a set of functions for querying and parsing data from Solr endpoints (local and remote), including search, faceting, highlighting, stats, etc. http://cran.r-project.org/web/packages/solr/index.html

Also read http://hortonworks.com/blog/using-r-and-other-non-java-languages-in-mapreduce-and-hive/

6.6   Interview with Antonio Piccolboni, Consultant on RHadoop

Here is an interview with Antonio Piccolboni, a consultant on Big Data analytics who has most notably worked on the RHadoop project for Revolution Analytics. Here he tells us about writing better code, and the projects he has been involved with.

DecisionStats(DS)—Describe your career journey from being a computer science student to one of the principal creators for RHadoop. What motivated you, what challenges did you overcome? What were the turning points? (You have $3500+$ **citations. What are most of those citations regarding?)**

Antonio (AP)—I completed my undergrad in CS in Italy. I liked research and industry didn't seem so exciting back then, both because of the lack of a local industry and the Microsoft monopoly, so I entered the PhD program. After a couple of false starts I focused on bioinformatics. I was very fortunate to get involved in an international collaboration and that paved the way for a move to the USA. I wanted to work in the USA as an academic, but for a variety of reasons that didn't work out. Instead I briefly joined a new proteomics department in a mass spectrometry company, then a research group doing transcriptomics, also in industry, but largely grant-funded. That's the period when I accumulated most of my citations. After several years there, I realized that bioinformatics was not offering the opportunities I was hoping for and that I was missing out on great changes that were happening in the computer industry, in particular Hadoop, so after much deliberation I took the plunge and worked first for a web ratings company and then a social network, where I took the role of what is now called a "data scientist"İ, using the statistical skills that I acquired during the first part of my career. After taking a year off to work on my own idea I became a free lance and Revolution Analytics one of my clients, and I became involved in RHadoop. As you can see there were several turning points. It seems to me one needs to seek a balance of determination and flexibility, both mental and financial, to explore different options, while trying to make the most of each experience. Also, be at least aware of what happens outside your specialty area. Finally, the mandatory statistical warning: any generalizations from a single career are questionable at best.

DS—What are the top five things you have learnt for better research productivity and code output in your distinguished career as a computer scientist?

AP-1. Keep your code short. Conciseness in code seems to correlate with a variety of desirable properties, like testability and maintainability. There are several aspects to it and I have a linkblog about this (asceticprogrammer.info). If I had said "simple," different people would have understood different things, but when you say "short"İ it's clear and actionable, albeit not universally accepted.

2. Test your code. Since proving code correct is unfeasible for the vast majority of projects, development is more like an experimental science, where you assemble programs and then corroborate that they have the desired properties via experiments. Testing can have many forms, but no testing is no option.

3. Many seem to think that programming is an abstract activity somewhere in between mathematics and machines. I think a developer's constituency are people, be them the millions using a social network or the handful using a specialized API. So I try to understand how people interact with my work, what they try to achieve, what their background is and so forth.

4. Programming is a difficult activity, meaning that failure happens even to the best and brightest. Learning to take risk into account and mitigate it is very important.

5. Programs are dynamic artifacts. For each line of code, one may not only ask if it is correct but for how long, as assumptions shift, or how often it will be executed. For a feature, one could wonder how many will use it, and how many additional lines of code will be necessary to maintain it.

6. Bonus statistical suggestion: check the assumptions. Academic statistics has an emphasis on theorems and optimality, bemoaned already by Tukey over sixty years ago. Theorems are great guides for data analysis, but rely on assumptions being met, and, when they are not, consequences can be unpredictable. When you apply the most straightforward, run of the mill test or estimator, you are responsible for checking the assumptions, or otherwise validating the results. "It looked like a normal distribution" won't cut it when things go wrong.

DS—Describe the RHadoop project—especially the newer plyrmr package. How was the journey to create it?

AP—Hadoop is for data and R is for statistics, to use slogans, so it's natural to ask the question of how to combine them, and RHadoop is one possible answer. We selected a few important components of Hadoop and provided an R API. plyrmr is an offshoot of rmr, which is an API to the mapreduce system. While rmr has enjoyed some success, we received feedback that a simplified API would enable even more people to directly access and analyse the data. Again based on feedback we decided to focus on structured data, equivalent to an R data frame. We tried to reduce the role of user-defined functions as parameters to be fed into the API, and when custom functions are needed they are simpler. Grouping and regrouping the data is fundamental to mapreduce. While in rmr the programmer has to process two data structures, one for the data itself and the other describing the grouping, plyrmr uses a very familiar SQL-like "group"ï function. Finally, we added a layer of delayed evaluation that allows to perform certain optimizations automatically and encourages reuse by reducing the cost of abstraction. We found enough commonalities with the popular package plyr that we decided to use it as a model, hence the tribute in the name. This lowers the cognitive burden for a typical user.

DS—Hue is an example of making interfaces easier for users to use Hadoop, so are sandboxes and video trainings. How can we make it easier to create better interfaces to software like RHadoop et al?

AP—It's always a trade-off between power and ease of use, however I believe that the ability to express analyses in a repeatable and communicable way is fundamental to science and necessary to business and one of the key elements in the success of R. I haven't seen a point and click GUI that satisfies these requirements yet, albeit it's not inconceivable. For me, the most fruitful effort is still on languages and APIs. While some people write their own algorithms, the typical data analyst needs a large repertoire of algorithms that can be applied to specific problems. I see a lot of straightforward adaptations of sequential algorithms or parallel algorithms that work at smaller scales, and I think that's the wrong direction. Extreme data sizes call for algorithms that work within stricter memory, work and communication constraints than before. On the other hand, the abundance of data, at least in some cases, offers the option of using less powerful or efficient statistics. It's a trade-off whose exploration has just started.

DS—What do you think is the future of R as an enterprise and research software in terms of computing on mobile, desktop, cloud and how do you see things evolve from here?

AP—One of the most interesting things that are happening right now is the development of different R interpreters. A successful language needs at least two viable implementations in my opinion. None of the alternatives is ready for prime time at the moment, but work is ongoing. Some implementations are experimental but demonstrate technological advances that can be then incorporated into the other interpreters. The main challenge is transitioning the language and the community to the world of parallel and distributed programming, which is a hardware-imposed priority. RHadoop is meant to help with that, for the largest data sets. Collaboration and publishing on the web is being addressed by many valuable tools and it looks to me the solutions exist already and it's more a problem of adoption. For the enterprise, there are companies offering training, consulting, licensing, centralized deployments, database APIs, you name it. It would be interesting to see touch interfaces applied to interactive data visualization, but while there is progress on the latter, touch on desktop is limited to a single platform and R doesn't run on mobile, so I don't see it as an imminent development.

About—Antonio Piccolboni is an experienced data scientist with industrial and academic backgrounds currently working as an independent consultant on Big Data analytics. His clients include Revolution Analytics.

6.7 Big Data R Packages

Big Data packages in R are as follows.

- **data.table** : Extension of data.frame Fast aggregation of large data (e.g., 100GB in RAM), fast ordered joins, fast add/modify/delete of columns by group using no copies at all, list columns and a fast file reader (fread). Offers a natural and flexible syntax, for faster development. http://cran.stat.ucla.edu/web/packages/data.table/index.html

- **sqldf**: Manipulate R data frames using SQL. http://cran.stat.ucla.edu/web/packages/sqldf/index.html
- **ff package**—http://cran.r-project.org/web/packages/ff/index.html ff package gives memory-efficient storage of large data on disk and fast access functions

The ff package provides data structures that are stored on disk but behave (almost) as if they were in RAM by transparently mapping only a section (pagesize) in main memory—the effective virtual memory consumption per ff object. Beyond basic access functions, the ff package also provides compatibility functions that facilitate writing code for ff and ram objects and support for batch processing on ff objects (e.g., as.ram, as.ff, ffapply). ff interfaces closely with functionality from package 'bit': chunked looping, fast bit operations and coercions between different objects that can store subscript information ('bit,' 'bitwhich,' ff 'boolean,' ri range index, hi hybrid index). This allows to work interactively with selections of large datasets and quickly modify selection criteria.

- **ffbase** Basic (statistical) functionality for package ff http://cran.stat.ucla.edu/web/packages/ffbase/index.html
- **filehash** Simple key-value database http://cran.r-project.org/web/packages/filehash/index.html and http://cran.r-project.org/web/packages/filehash/vignettes/filehash.pdf
- **MonetDB.R**: Connect MonetDB to R Allows to pull data from MonetDB into R http://cran.r-project.org/web/packages/MonetDB.R/index.html
- **track** http://cran.stat.ucla.edu/web/packages/track/Automatically stores objects in files on disk so that files are rewritten when objects are changed, and so that objects are accessible but do not occupy memory until they are accessed. Keeps track of times when objects are created and modified, and caches some basic characteristics of objects to allow for fast summaries of objects. Also provides a command history mechanism that saves the last command to a history file after each command completes

Big Memory (http://www.bigmemory.org/) This project extends the R statistical programming environment.

- **big memory** http://cran.stat.ucla.edu/web/packages/bigmemory/ It helps to create, store, access, and manipulate massive matrices. Matrices are allocated to shared memory and may use memory-mapped files. Packages biganalytics, bigtabulate, synchronicity, and bigalgebra provide advanced functionality. The R package **biganalytics** provides extended functionality for working with matrices provided by bigmemory and regular R matrices too. The R package **bigtabulate** provides table()-like, split()-like, and tapply()-like functionality for working with matrices provided by bigmemory. The R package **synchronicity** can be useful on its own for streaming data analyses, but exists primarily to complement the shared-memory capabilities of bigmemory. The R package **bigalgebra** provides cutting-edge linear algebra functionality for use both with regular R matrices and with matrices from bigmemory. **biglm**: bounded memory linear and generalized linear models. Regression for data too large to fit in memoryhttp://cran.stat.ucla.edu/web/packages/biglm/

- **speedglm**: Fitting Linear and Generalized Linear Models to large data sets, http://cran.stat.ucla.edu/web/packages/speedglm/index.html
- **bigrf:** Big Random Forests: Classification and Regression Forests for Large Data Sets—This is an implementation of Leo Breiman's and Adele Cutler's Random Forest algorithms for classification and regression, with optimizations for performance and for handling of data sets that are too large to be processed in memory. Forests can be built in parallel at two levels. First, trees can be grown in parallel on a single machine using for each. Second, multiple forests can be built in parallel on multiple machines, then merged into one. For large data sets, disk-based big.matrix's may be used for storing data and intermediate computations, to prevent excessive virtual memory swapping by the operating system. http://cran.stat.ucla.edu/web/packages/bigrf/index.html
- **biglars**: Scalable Least-Angle Regression and Lasso—Least-angle regression, lasso and stepwise regression for numeric datasets in which the number of observations is greater than the number of predictors. The functions can be used with the ff library to accommodate datasets that are too large to be held in memory. http://cran.stat.ucla.edu/web/packages/biglars/index.html

Other packages can be seen at CRAN View http://cran.stat.ucla.edu/web/views/HighPerformanceComputing.html

- **bigvis** package The bigvis package provides tools for exploratory data analysis of large datasets (10–100 million obs). The aim is to have most operations take less than 5 seconds on commodity hardware, even for 100,000,000 data points. https://github.com/hadley/bigvis
- **tabplot**: Tableplot, a visualization of large datasets. A tableplot is a visualization of a (large) dataset with a dozen of variables, both numeric and categorical. Each column represents a variable and each row bin is an aggregate of a certain number of records. Numeric variables are visualized as bar charts, and categorical variables as stacked bar charts. Missing values are taken into account. Also supports large ffdf datasets from the ff package. See http://cran.r-project.org/web/packages/tabplot/index.html and http://cran.r-project.org/web/packages/tabplotd3/index.html

6.8   Databases and CAP Theorem

Database systems have been driven by the CAP theorem. It was created by Brewer. Eric Brewer is a professor at the University of California, Berkeley, and the co-founder and Chief Scientist of Inktomi.

In theoretical computer science, the CAP theorem, also known as Brewer's theorem, states that it is impossible for a distributed computer system to simultaneously provide all three of the following guarantees

- Consistency (all nodes see the same data at the same time)
- Availability (a guarantee that every request receives a response about whether it was successful or failed)
- Partition tolerance (the system continues to operate despite arbitrary message loss or failure of part of the system)

A common view is to aim for two out of the three things above.

6.8.1   CAP Theorem Visually

A visual guide to CAP Theorem applied to NoSQL Systems is here http://blog.nahurst.com/visual-guide-to-nosql-systems

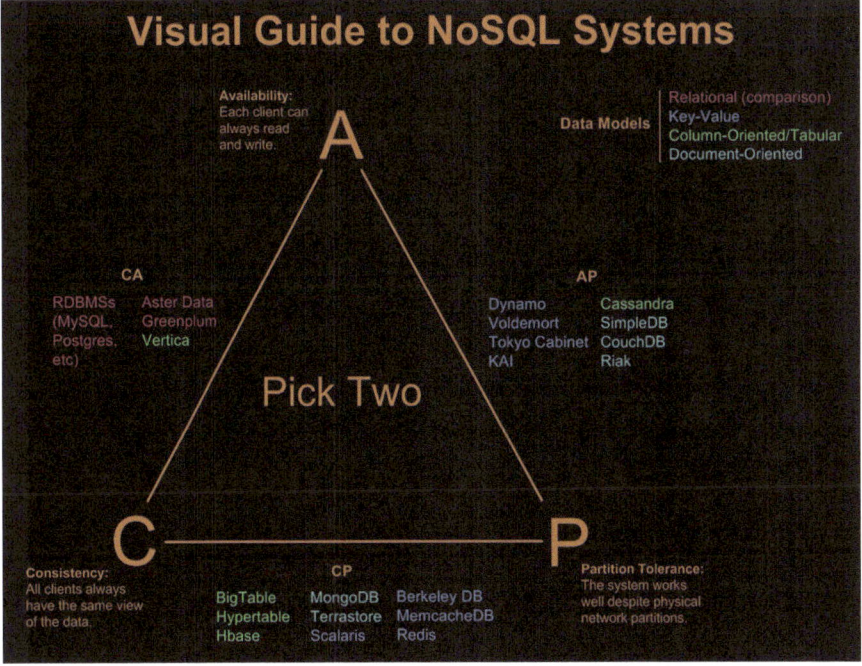

6.9   ACID and BASE for Databases

In computer science, ACID (Atomicity, Consistency, Isolation, Durability) is a set of properties that guarantee that database transactions are processed reliably. As per http://databases.about.com/od/specificproducts/a/acid.htm

- *Atomicity states that database modifications must follow an "all or nothing" í rule. Each transaction is said to be "atomic." í If one part of the transaction fails, the entire transaction fails.*
- *Consistency states that only valid data will be written to the database. If, for some reason, a transaction is executed that violates the database's consistency rules, the entire transaction will be rolled back and the database will be restored to a state consistent with those rules.*
- *Isolation requires that multiple transactions occurring at the same time not impact each other's execution. For example, if Joe issues a transaction against a database at the same time that Mary issues a different transaction, both transactions should operate on the database in an isolated manner. Durability ensures that any transaction committed to the database will not be lost.*
- *Durability is ensured through the use of database backups and transaction logs.*

For a more detailed basis also see http://en.wikipedia.org/wiki/ACID

However another model is often used in database systems especially in distributed ones and it is called BASE. As per http://en.wikipedia.org/wiki/Eventual_consistency

Eventually consistent services are often classified as providing BASE (Basically Available, Soft state, Eventual consistency) semantics, in contrast to traditional ACID (Atomicity, Consistency, Isolation, Durability) guarantees. Eventual consistency is a consistency model used in distributed computing that informally guarantees that, if no new updates are made to a given data item, eventually all accesses to that item will return the last updated value. Eventual consistency is widely deployed in distributed systems.

To ensure replica convergence, a system must reconcile differences between multiple copies of distributed data. This process, often known as anti-entropy, requires exchanging versions of data between servers Timestamps and vector clocks are often used to detect concurrency between updates.

Read repair: The correction is done when a read finds an inconsistency. This slows down the read operation.

Write repair: The correction takes place during a write operation, if an inconsistency has been found, slowing down the write operation.

Asynchronous repair: The correction is not part of a read or write operation.

6.10 Using R with MySQL

A brief screenshot by screenshot tutorial is given at http://decisionstats.com/2011/10/16/using-r-with-mysql/ for using the RODBC package for connecting to MySQL. The RODBC package is the standard package for connecting to relational databases.

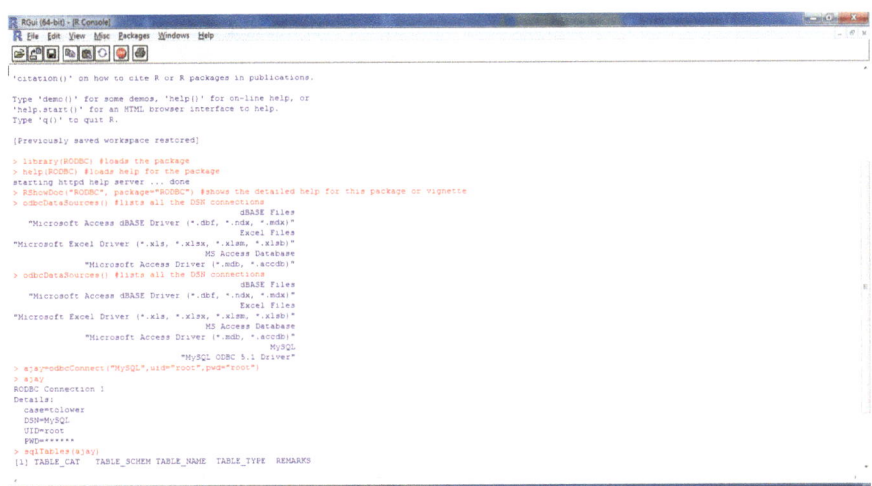

6.11   Using R with NoSQL

For non-relational new generation (not only SQL) or NoSQL databases, we can use R.

6.11.1   MongoDB

It is the leading NoSQL database. For unstructured data we can use MongoDB collections. A brief list of features is shown here:

- Document-Oriented Storage—JSON-style documents with dynamic schemas
- Full Index Support—Index on any attribute
- Replication & High Availability—Mirror across LANs and WANs
- Auto-Sharding
- Querying—Rich, document-based queries.
- Map/Reduce—Flexible aggregation and data processing.
- GridFS—Store files of any size without complicating your stack.

However some people may be confused between JSON and BSON.

BSON is a binary version of JSON which adds two things to the mix, lengths, and types. JSON documents are easy to encode as BSON and BSON can easily, with caveats, be turned back to JSON. The length information is added in BSON so that when we look at BSON data, we can see how long this current data item is and if we need to skip it, do it much more efficiently. The length itself is encoded as a 32 bit integer giving a notional 4GB capacity, but MongoDB caps the maximum document size at 16MB to avoid giant documents swamping memory.

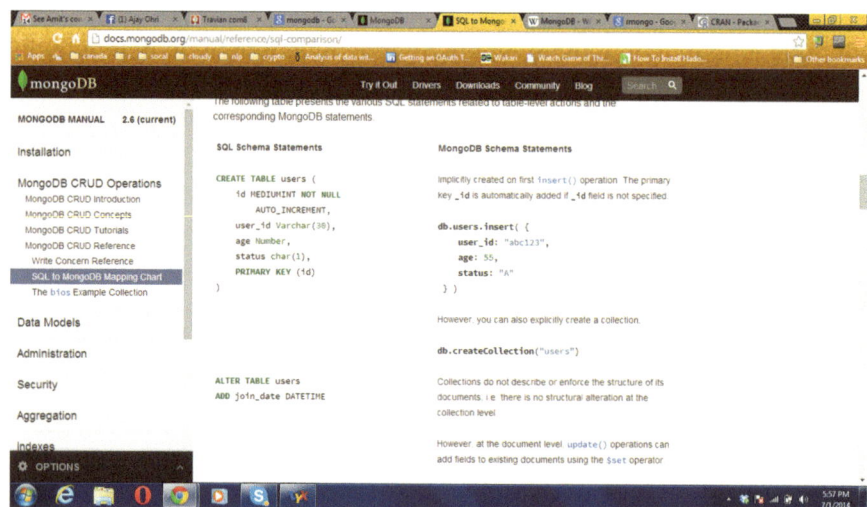

There are two principal ways of using R with MongoDB:

- RMongo—MongoDB Database interface for R. The interface is provided via Java calls to the mongo-java-driver. http://cran.r-project.org/web/packages/RMongo/index.html
- rmongodb—an interface to the NoSQL MongoDB database using the MongoDB C-driver version 0.8. http://cran.r-project.org/web/packages/rmongodb/index.html

In the following example we will use RMongo for some initial operations. Reference manual is at http://cran.r-project.org/web/packages/RMongo/RMongo.pdf

- We download and install MongoDB from http://www.mongodb.org/downloads and using instructions from http://docs.mongodb.org/manual/tutorial/install-mongodb-on-windows/
- Note we need to run the server before we make the connection! This is done by the mongod.exe file within the bin folder
- Now we move to R

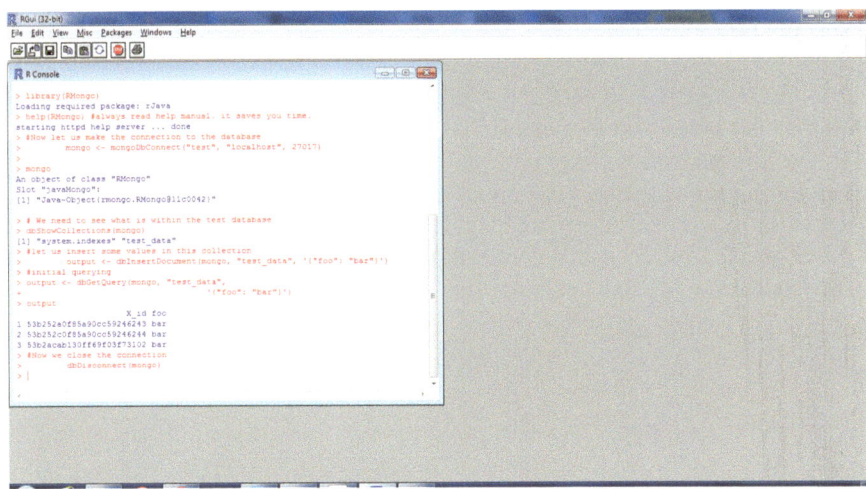

To use rmongodb, a very good tutorial has been given at https://www.mongosoup.de/blog-entry/rmongodb-using-the-MongoDB-Aggregations-Framework.html

6.11.2   jsonlite (prettify)

jsonlite is a package for simplifying the json import process in R. You can read about it here http://arxiv.org/abs/1403.2805. Here is an example using a dataset provided by MongoDB website.

> *json = fromJSON(paste("[",paste(readLines("http://media.mongodb.org/zips.json"),collapse=","), "]"))*

Warning message:

In readLines("http://media.mongodb.org/zips.json"): incomplete final line found on 'http://media.mongodb.org/zips.json'

> *head(json) city loc pop state _id*
1 ACMAR −86.51557, 33.58413 6055 AL 35004
2 ADAMSVILLE −86.95973, 33.58844 10616 AL 35005
3 ADGER −87.16746, 33.43428 3205 AL 35006
4 KEYSTONE −86.81286, 33.23687 14218 AL 35007
5 NEW SITE −85.95109, 32.94145 19942 AL 35010
6 ALPINE −86.20893, 33.33116 3062 AL 35014

6.11.3   CouchDB

Apache CouchDB is a database that uses JSON for documents, JavaScript for MapReduce indexes, and regular HTTP for its API

The R4CouchDB package provides a collection of functions for basic database and document management operations such as add and delete. Every cdbFunction() gets and returns a list() containing the connection setup. Such a list (in the documentation mostly called cdb) can be generated by cdb <- cdbIni(). Then cdb also contains some function resp. functionality, e.g., cdb$baseUrl().http://cran.r-project.org/web/packages/R4CouchDB/index.html

6.11.4   MonetDB

MonetDB is a column-store database management system.

- Download and Install MonetDB SQL Installer x86_64 (for Windows Server 2008 64 bit) from http://dev.monetdb.org/downloads/..
- Install package **MonetDB. R** from CRAN, and load it.
- You may get an error message if you try to connect to MonetDB since the port 50000 is the default port for MonetDB and permissions for opening ports needs to be handled separately on the cloud. Instead of making a batch file, we simply start MonetDB manually rather than start it from R. Start MonetDB server from Windows (Start Menu-All Programs-MonetDB—Server)
- Connect to MonetDB from within R using the code shown

conn <- dbconnect (MonetDB.R(),"monetdb://localhost/demo")

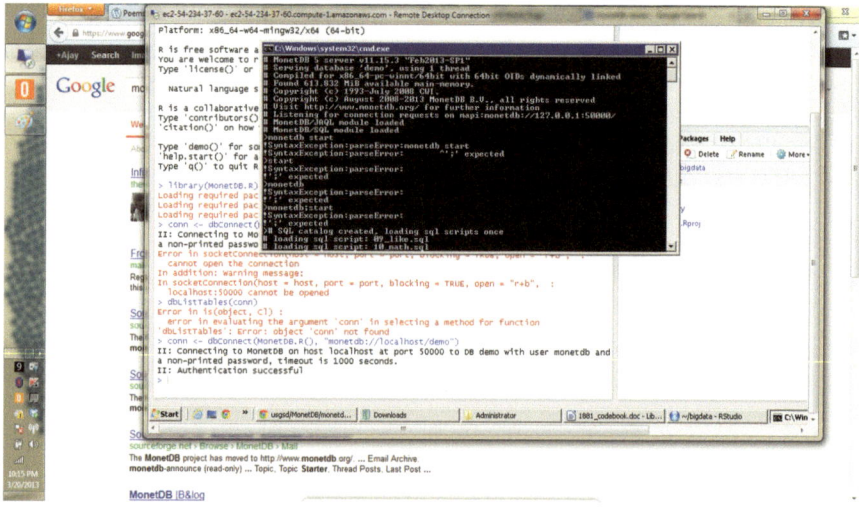

6.12 Big Data Visualization

Some packages for visualizing large amounts of data are

- **HistogramTools: Utility Functions for R Histograms**—This package provides a number of utility functions useful for manipulating large histograms. This includes methods to trim, subset, merge buckets, merge histograms, convert to CDF, and calculate information loss due to binning. It also provides a protocol buffer representations of the default R histogram class to allow histograms over large data sets to be computed and manipulated in a MapReduce environment. It is available at http://cran.r-project.org/web/packages/HistogramTools/index. html
- **Bigvis**—This provides exploratory data analysis for large datasets (10–100 million observations). https://github.com/hadley/bigvis

Lastly you can use the popular enterprise software Tableau with R. The tutorial for that is given at http://www.tableausoftware.com/about/blog/2013/10/tableau-81-and-r-25327

You can also see some code for Big Data analysis using RevoScaleR from Revolution Analytics at https://gist.github.com/joseph-rickert/4742529

Chapter 7
R with Cloud APIs

Our basic R tutorial discussed ways to get data from spreadsheets in R in Chap. 5. Here we deal with much more heterogenous kinds of data formats which are typically use for Big Data Analytics enabled by the cloud. We will talk of APIs that are basically how machines talk to each other. As the concept of Internet of Things and Machine to Machine data hosts up, we will see more and more APIs to exchange data, and consequently more need of R or another analytical tool to directly deal with APIs rather than use an intermediate tool to parse the data into a manageable analytical format.

7.1 Everything Has an API

What exactly is an API—An API is an application programming interface. It is how computer programs talk to each other and fetch data back and forth. Just as human languages have rules of grammar, spelling, and pronunciation, APIs follow certain rules to ensure that we get accurate, consistent, and same results with the same program call. Using APIs basically turns the Internet itself into a programmable web, as a source of data.

CRAN View—Web Technologies (http://cran.r-project.org/web/views/WebTech nologies.html) provides many packages for accessing Web Services using R

- JSON and XML—The two basic formats which APIs use to transfer data are JSON and XML.

  - Extensible Markup Language, abbreviated XML, describes a class of data objects called XML documents and partially describes the behaviour of computer programs which process them. XML is an application profile or restricted form of SGML, the Standard Generalized Markup Language [ISO 8879]. By construction, XML documents are conforming SGML documents.

© Springer Science+Business Media New York 2014   217
A Ohri, *R for Cloud Computing*, DOI 10.1007/978-1-4939-1702-0__7

- XML documents are made up of storage units called entities, which contain either parsed or unparsed data. Parsed data is made up of characters, some of which form character data, and some of which form markup.

```xml
<?xml version="1.0"?>
<quiz>
 <qanda seq="1">
  <question>
   Who was the forty-second
   president of the U.S.A.?
  </question>
  <answer>
   William Jefferson Clinton
  </answer>
 </qanda>
 <!-- Note: We need to add
   more questions later.-->
</quiz>
```

- An example of XML is shown
- JSON is increasingly the more widely used format. JSON (JavaScript Object Notation) is a lightweight data-interchange format. It is easy for humans to read and write. It is easy for machines to parse and generate. It is based on a subset of the JavaScript Programming Language.
- JSON is built on two structures:

  • A collection of name/value pairs. In various languages, this is realized as an object, record, struct, dictionary, hash table, keyed list, or associative array. An ordered list of values. In most languages, this is realized as an array, vector, list, or sequence.

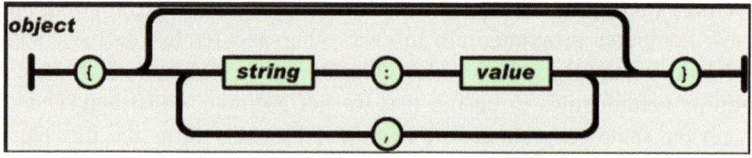

  • An example of JSON and comparison with XML is shown (from http://json.org/example)

7.2   REST

Representational state transfer or REST is an architecture style for designing networked applications. The idea is that, rather than using complex mechanisms simple HTTP is used to make calls between machines. In many ways, the World Wide Web itself, based on HTTP, can be viewed as a REST-based architecture.

This page shows examples of messages formatted using JSON (JavaScript Object Notation).

```
{
    "glossary": {
        "title": "example glossary",
            "GlossDiv": {
            "title": "S",
                "GlossList": {
                "GlossEntry": {
                    "ID": "SGML",
                                    "SortAs": "SGML",
                                    "GlossTerm": "Standard Generalized Markup Language",
                                    "Acronym": "SGML",
                                    "Abbrev": "ISO 8879:1986",
                                    "GlossDef": {
                                    "para": "A meta-markup language, used to create markup languages such as DocBook.",
                                                "GlossSeeAlso": ["GML", "XML"]
                    },
                                    "GlossSee": "markup"
                }
            }
        }
    }
}
```

The same text expressed as XML:

```
<!DOCTYPE glossary PUBLIC "-//OASIS//DTD DocBook V3.1//EN">
 <glossary><title>example glossary</title>
  <GlossDiv><title>S</title>
   <GlossList>
    <GlossEntry ID="SGML" SortAs="SGML">
     <GlossTerm>Standard Generalized Markup Language</GlossTerm>
     <Acronym>SGML</Acronym>
     <Abbrev>ISO 8879:1986</Abbrev>
     <GlossDef>
      <para>A meta-markup language, used to create markup
languages such as DocBook.</para>
      <GlossSeeAlso OtherTerm="GML">
      <GlossSeeAlso OtherTerm="XML">
     </GlossDef>
     <GlossSee OtherTerm="markup">
    </GlossEntry>
   </GlossList>
  </GlossDiv>
 </glossary>
```

RESTful applications use HTTP requests to post data (create and/or update), read data (e.g., make queries), and delete data. Thus, REST uses HTTP for all four CRUD (Create/Read/Update/Delete) operations.

- REST is thus a lightweight alternative to mechanisms like RPC (Remote Procedure Calls) and Web Services (SOAP, WSDL, et al.). A REST service is:

  - Platform-independent
  - Language-independent
  - Standards-based (runs on HTTP), and
  - Can be used easily in the presence of firewalls.

  A tutorial for learning REST is given at http://rest.elkstein.org/

7.3   rOpenSci

At rOpenSci developers are creating packages that allow access to data repositories through the R statistical programming environment that is already a familiar part of the workflow of many scientists. These tools not only facilitate drawing data

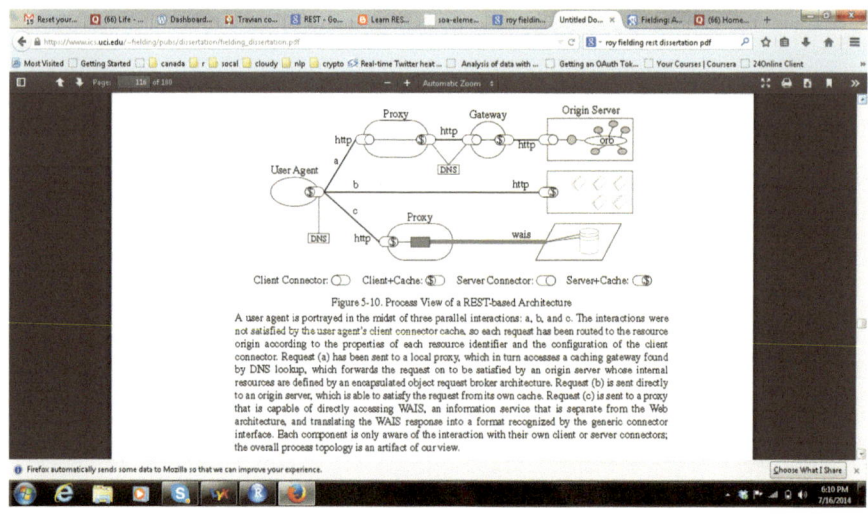

Figure 5-10. Process View of a REST-based Architecture

A user agent is portrayed in the midst of three parallel interactions: a, b, and c. The interactions were not satisfied by the user agent's client connector cache, so each request has been routed to the resource origin according to the properties of each resource identifier and the configuration of the client connector. Request (a) has been sent to a local proxy, which in turn accesses a caching gateway found by DNS lookup, which forwards the request on to be satisfied by an origin server whose internal resources are defined by an encapsulated object request broker architecture. Request (b) is sent directly to an origin server, which is able to satisfy the request from its own cache. Request (c) is sent to a proxy that is capable of directly accessing WAIS, an information service that is separate from the Web architecture, and translating the WAIS response into a format recognized by the generic connector interface. Each component is only aware of the interaction with their own client or server connectors; the overall process topology is an artifact of our view.

into an environment where it can readily be manipulated, but also one in which those analyses and methods can be easily shared, replicated, and extended by other researchers. The website http://ropensci.org/ gives a complete list of all available rOpenSci packages. Packages are grouped by ones that acquire data, full-text of journal articles, altimetrics, data-publication, reproducibility, and data visualization.

An extract from an interview with its co-creator-Karthik Ram.

Ajay—What was the motivation in creating rOpenSci?

Karthik—I've long been frustrated by not having easy access to data that was supposed to be freely available or being able to reproduce findings from a study. This frustration got me started on the open science track. Around the same time I found Carl and Scott talking about several of the same issues on Twitter. We then decided to pool our resources together and start rOpenSci. Our initial goal was to start building bridges to existing data sources so we could inspire not just researchers to be more open about their work, but also to nudge data providers to freeing up more data and accelerate scientific discovery.

Ajay—Why are REST APIs important for statistical and scientific research, in your opinion?

Karthik—Although industry has readily embraced the data revolution, the uptake in most sciences has been fairly slow. I believe that opening up programmatic access to data is really important for advancing science. RESTful APIs make it exceedingly easy to develop tools for programmatic access to data. This allows researchers to make their findings reproducible by sharing just a few lines of code. Not only does this increase transparency and allows other to verify findings, but also makes it easy for anyone to build upon existing work. Many new insights in science will be data-driven, and will likely emerge from leveraging multiple data sources. RESTful APIs are one way to speed up that discovery process.

7.4 What Is Curl

curl is a command line tool for transferring data with URL syntax, supporting DICT, FILE, FTP, FTPS, Gopher, HTTP, HTTPS, IMAP, IMAPS, LDAP, LDAPS, POP3 et al (http://curl.haxx.se/docs/features.html). It is thus similar to wget. (http://www.gnu.org/software/wget/). The package to use curl in R is RCurl.

How to turn curl POST method using R and the RCurl package?

curl -k -u myusername:mypassword -d '{"text":"Hello World!","level": "Noob"}' -H "Content-Type: application/json" -H "Accept: application/json" "http://api.website/v1/access?"

We use the postForm method in RCurl.

library(RCurl)

library(RJSONIO)

postForm("http://api.website/v1/access?", .opts = list(postfields = toJSON (list(text = "Hello World!", level = "Noob")), httpheader = c('Content-Type' = 'application/json', Accept = 'application/json'), userpwd = "Username:Password", ssl.verifypeer = FALSE))

The httr package uses the POST Method just like the postForm method in RCurl.

Trouble shooting Curl issues

In case you have trouble authenticating, the following code helps with the certificate in curl authentication.

download the file needed for authentication

download.file(url="http://curl.haxx.se/ca/cacert.pem", destfile="cacert.pem")
set the curl options

curl <- getCurlHandle() options(RCurlOptions = list(capath = system.file ("CurlSSL", "cacert.pem", package = "RCurl"), ssl.verifypeer = FALSE))
curlSetOpt(.opts = list(proxy = 'proxyserver:port'), curl = curl)

7.5 Navigating oAuth2

oAuth2 is an open system for authentication. Most service providers have shifted to the next generation of authentication called OAuth2. This following flow chart from the Salesforce website is one of the lucid ways to explain the authentication system. This understanding is critical as many time people find it difficult to authenticate their applications with the API.

RForcecom provides the connection to Force.com and Salesforce.com from R. The package is available at http://cran.r-project.org/web/packages/RForcecom/

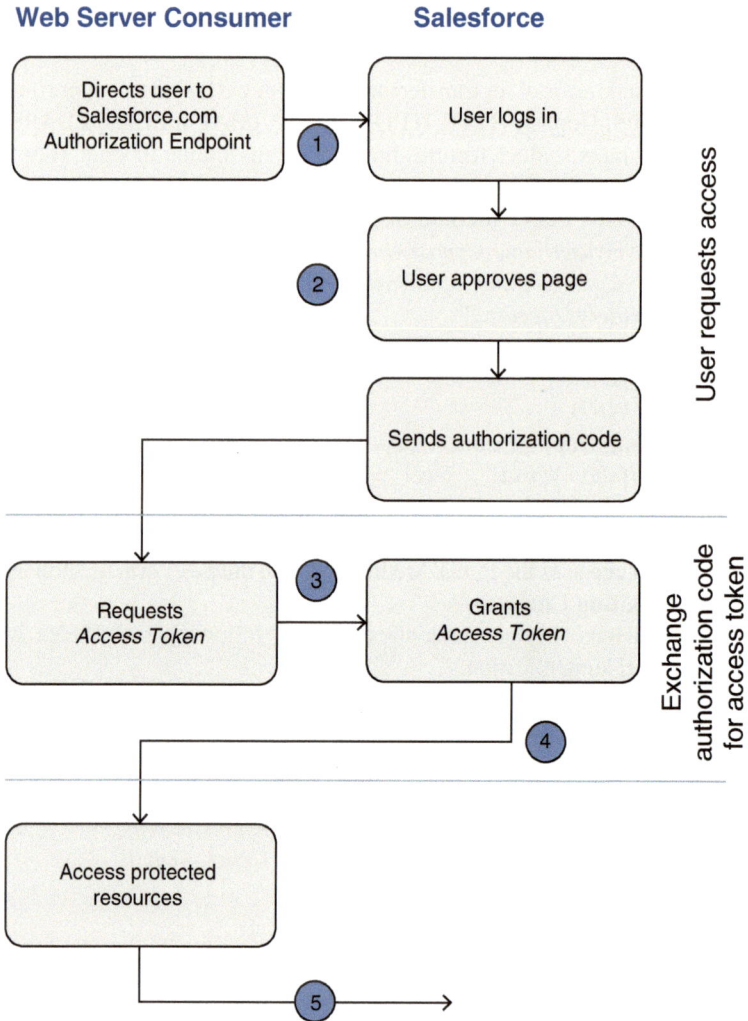

7.6   Machine Learning as a Service

Rather than build your own models, you can choose machine learning as a service from many cloud providers.

7.6.1   *Google Prediction API and R*

Google's cloud-based machine learning tools can help analyse your data. This is present as an API from https://developers.google.com/prediction/. Chapter 4 has a reference to it as well and its corresponding R packages.

7.6.2   BigML with R

BigML.com offers an API as well as a web interface for making decision tree models as well as clusters. The R package is available at https://github.com/bigmlcom/bigml-r and you can check out the features at https://bigml.com/whatsnew

7.6.3   Azure Machine Learning with R

Microsoft has introduced Machine Learning as a service at https://azure.microsoft.com/en-us/services/machine-learning/. You can also embed R scripts within the web interface (ML Studio). You can drop existing R code directly—or write your own in ML Studio, which supports almost 350 R packages as of now.

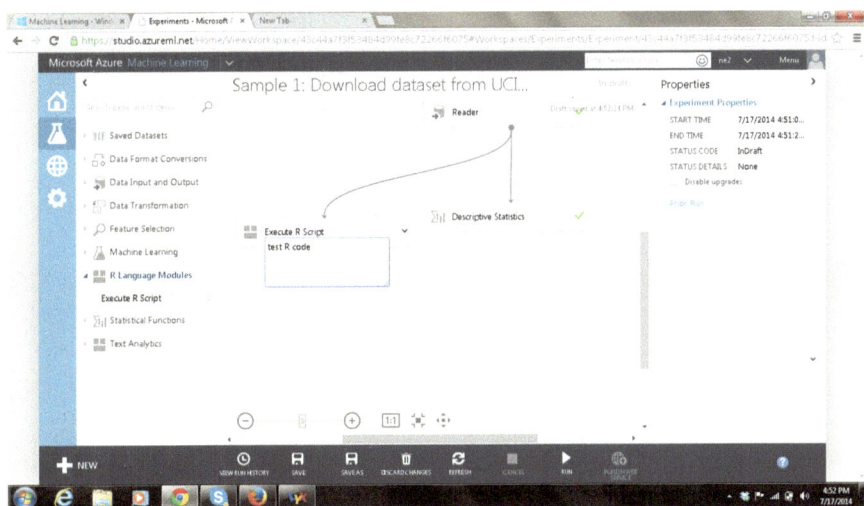

7.7   Examples of R with APIs

7.7.1   Quandl with R

Quandl collects numerical data published by hundreds of different sources, and hosts them on a single easy-to-use website at Quandl.com. You can download the time series data directly into your R session using the Quandl Package from CRAN (http://cran.r-project.org/web/packages/Quandl/). The package interacts directly with the Quandl API to offer data in a number of formats usable in R.

We take our Quandl Authorization Key from our account at http://www.quandl. com/users/edit.

> *Quandl.auth("4irCy8SETmrzLNPgzqy7")*

> *mydata = Quandl("NSE/OIL", start_date="2000-01-01", end_date="2014-07-19")*

> *head(mydata)*

```
In Quandl("NSE/OIL", start_date = "yyyy-mm-dd", end_date = "yyyy-mm-dd") :
  It would appear you aren't using an authentication token. Please visit http://www.quandl.com/he
>
> Quandl.auth("4ir        _        " jzqy7")
> mydata = Quandl("NSE/OIL", start_date="2000-01-01", end_date="2014-07-19")
> head(mydata)
        Date   Open   High    Low   Last  Close Total Trade Quantity Turnover (Lacs)
1 2014-07-18 577.95 580.95 571.00 575.00 573.95               239847         1377.06
2 2014-07-17 579.80 584.75 573.15 578.05 578.90               198773         1150.43
3 2014-07-16 588.50 589.50 576.15 580.50 579.55               222160         1293.31
4 2014-07-15 573.05 584.90 573.05 584.90 580.95               256944         1490.98
5 2014-07-14 574.70 575.05 560.05 572.05 572.20               153277          874.18
6 2014-07-11 582.00 586.80 570.10 571.20 571.75               610452         3506.37
> str(mydata)
'data.frame':   1199 obs. of  8 variables:
 $ Date                : Date, format: "2014-07-18" "2014-07-17" "2014-07-16" "2014-07-15" ...
 $ Open                : num  578 580 588 573 575 ...
 $ High                : num  581 585 590 585 575 ...
 $ Low                 : num  571 573 576 573 560 ...
 $ Last                : num  575 578 580 585 572 ...
 $ Close               : num  574 579 580 581 572 ...
 $ Total Trade Quantity: num  239847 198773 222160 256944 153277 ...
 $ Turnover (Lacs)     : num  1377 1150 1293 1491 874 ...
```

7.7.2 Data Visualization APIs with R

7.7.2.1 Plotly

We install the plotly package from github using devtools. Note this is a different method of installing packages as compared to CRAN or a local zip file.

We then navigate to http://plot.ly, create an account using a social login (like google account), and then navigate to Settings to get our token or API key.

We can then use the following code.

And our data visualization is ready in the cloud. It is automatically generated at a url (https://plot.ly/UserName/ChartNo/X-vs-Y/)

A partial extract from interview with Plot.ly founder by the author (A Ohri) done for ProgrammableWeb.

PW—How do the Plotly APIs work? What are its uses for someone already using Tableau, ggplot2, or matplotlib?

Matt Sundquist (MS)—We love and have been inspired by those tools. Plotly is different because it's web-based. Our goal is for people to have one place to analyse and visualize their data, and do so collaboratively and online. The Plotly APIs

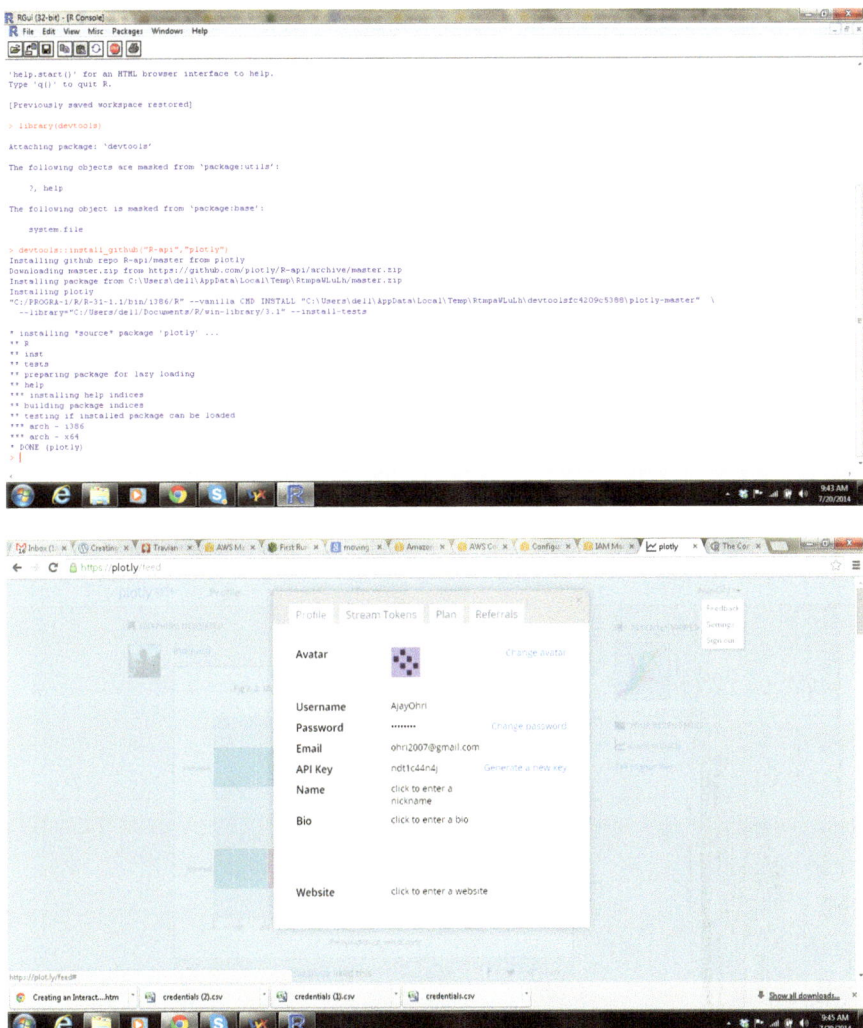

allow you to create an interactive, shareable graph online. You can do so from your language of choice with our APIs (Python, R, MATLAB, REST, Julia, Perl, Rest, and Arduino). You can stream and import data (including from Arduino). Plotly also reads dates and times, and can be used with NumPy, pandas, and Datetime. You send your script to Plotly to make a graph, then Plotly returns a URL where you can access a graph.

Plotly gives you **total control of the graph**, so you can style, colour, and format everything from the API or GUI. Plotly has bubble charts, box plots, line charts, scatter plots, histograms, 2D histograms, and heatmaps. We also support log axes, error bars, date axes, multiple axes, subplots, and LaTeX. Here is the Plotly gallery, which shows some of the graph types you can make (https://plot.ly/feed)

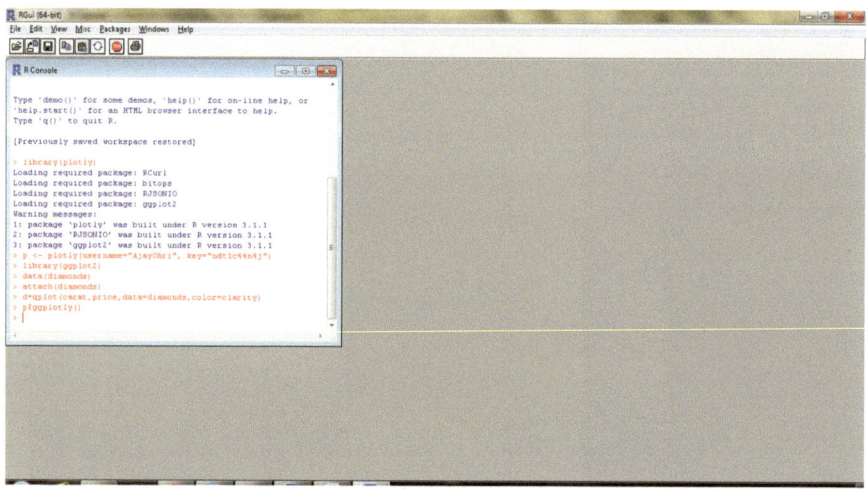

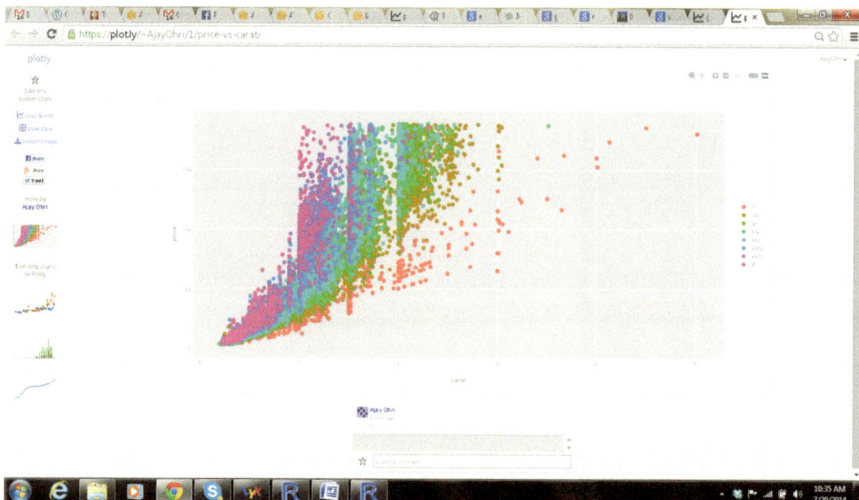

Plotly lets you keep your graphs private, share publicly with a URL or share with your team.

Invites others to collaborate with you Lets teams analyse together with stats, fits, and functions. Lets others style graphs with you. That means others can comment on the graph and data right where it lives. That means no more emailing data and spreadsheets around, having to download graphs or take static screenshots and put them in a deck or email you can't access anymore. You can simply send a Plotly URL to your team or share your project with them so you can edit together.

Plotly lets you add data to an existing graph. So if you already have a graph you want to add data to, or make a new plot with, you can simply add onto that file. Normally, if you have a graph already created in a PDF, that would not be possible.

But with web-based Plotly files, you can make a copy of your original graph, add new data and style away, creating two graphs. For example:

You can also interplay between the API and GUI. Let's say you start off by making your graph with R, and code it how you want. Then, you want to explore a different layout, graph type, legend placement, etc. Normally, you would need to code it again. But with Plotly, you can change your graph with the GUI instead of code. It's fast and easy to find out "how would this look if it were a [graph type]"?

More broadly, Plotly has other features.

You can do your analysis and graphing with Plotly, because the Plotly grid offers stats, fits, functions, and more, so you can analyse and graph your data with Plotly. Plotly is interactive. When you share a graph, others can access the data and graph by clicking through to Plotly, zooming, or hovering on the graph. That means you're viewing the data and graph together, painting a richer picture of your work. Or, you can embed in an article, like in the Washington Post or an IPython Notebook. Plotly allows you to save, create, and apply custom filters to your data. That means you can, with just one click apply any filter to your data to create a beautiful, styled graph. Plotly gives you a profile, so you can keep all your work in one place where others can access what you're working on.

PW—What future do you see for statistical analysis, data mining and data visualization on the cloud? What technologies are leading the trend?

MS—Speaking only for myself, I think the future of analysis will revolve around creating accessible, collaborative, and powerful tools. Two broader trends that seem to be happening in technology are (1) taking things that happen locally into the cloud; and (2) making things that you normally do alone social. Those trends will harness the real power of people and the cloud by making data and tools:

Accessible, meaning that anyone can access the power of scientific computing without needing to code.

Collaborative, meaning I can work with others to manipulate and analyse data, code, and graphs with others at the same time.

Proactive, as in I am much less likely to "miss" something because my suite of tools is mining data and events.

Read more: http://www.programmableweb.com/news/plot.lys-plot-to-visualize-more-data/2014/01/22.

An additional package is the googleVis package Interface between R and Google Charts.

7.7.2.2 googleVis

It provides an interface between R and the Google Charts API. It allows users to create web pages with interactive charts based on R data frames, using the Google Charts API and to display them either via the local R HTTP help server or within their own sites, without uploading the data to Google. Let us use one modified example from

install.packages("googleVis")
library(googleVis)
set.seed(123)
datHist=data.frame(Alpha=rnorm(100,   10,10),   Bravo=rnorm(100,   5,10),
Charlie=rnorm(100, 10,5))

Hist   <- gvisHistogram(datHist, options=list(legend="{ position: 'top',
maxLines: 2 }", colors="['#5C3292', '#1A8763', '#871B47']", width=400,
height=360))
plot(Hist)

As you can see the output is within the browser as a html page. Additionally you can see the tutorial at http://decastillo.github.io/googleVis_Tutorial/ in which this method is combined with the shiny package for making interactive visualizations.

7.7.2.3   tabplotd3

A tableplot is a visualization of a (large) dataset with a dozen of variables, both numeric and categorical. This package contains an interactive version of tableplot working in your browser. http://cran.r-project.org/web/packages/tabplotd3/index.html

> *library(ggplot2)*
> *data(diamonds)*
> *library(tabplotd3)*
> *itabplot(diamonds)*

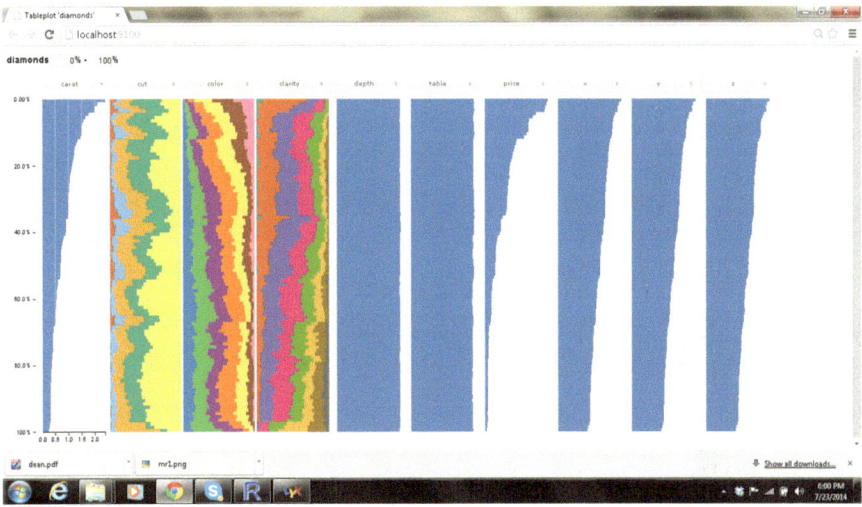

7.7.2.4 Yhat and R

Yhat allows you to host models on the cloud using R. You can see this at https://docs.yhathq.com/r/tutorial

7.7.3 OpenCPU and R

OpenCPU is a system for embedded scientific computing and reproducible research. The OpenCPU HTTP API is a middle layer to R that works like SQL for data analysis. The OpenCPU system exposes an HTTP API for scientific computing to build scalable analysis and visualization modules for use in systems, pipelines, and web applications. You can either use the public servers or host your own. It is available at https://www.opencpu.org/.

A very good reproducible demo is shown at https://www.opencpu.org/posts/scoring-engine/. This post explains how to use the OpenCPU system to set-up a scoring engine for calculating real-time predictions. The example uses the predict.gam function from the mgcv package to make predictions based on a generalized additive model. This is a useful example especially for industry which has been over reliant on logistic regression using proprietary software—particularly the financial services (marketing and risk models) and the telecom industries (attrition models)

As per the example, the process consists of four steps:

• Building a model
• Create an R package containing the model and a scoring function

- Install the package on your OpenCPU server
- Remotely call the scoring function through the OpenCPU API

You can read the details including the code at https://www.opencpu.org/posts/scoring-engine/.

7.7.3.1 Interview Jeroen Ooms OpenCPU

Below an interview with Jeroen Ooms, a pioneer in R and web development. Jeroen contributes to R by developing packages and web applications for multiple projects.

Ajay—What are you working on these days?

Jeroen—My research revolves around challenges and opportunities of using R in embedded applications and scalable systems. After developing numerous web applications, I started the OpenCPU project about 1.5 years ago, as a first attempt at a complete framework for proper integration of R in web services. As I work on this, I run into challenges that shape my research, and sometimes become projects in their own. For example, the RAppArmor package provides the security framework for OpenCPU, but can be used for other purposes as well. RAppArmor interfaces to some methods in the Linux kernel, related to setting security and resource limits. The github page contains the source code, installation instructions, video demos, and a draft of a paper for the journal of statistical software. Another example of a problem that appeared in OpenCPU is that applications that used to work were breaking unexpectedly later on due to changes in dependency packages on CRAN. This is actually a general problem that affects almost all R users, as it compromises reliability of CRAN packages and reproducibility of results. In a paper (forthcoming in The R Journal), this problem is discussed in more detail and directions for improvement are suggested. A preprint of the paper is available on arXiv: http://arxiv.org/abs/1303.2140.

I am also working on software not directly related to R. For example, in project Mobilize we teach high school students in Los Angeles the basics of collecting and analysing data. They use mobile devices to upload surveys with questions, photos, gps, etc. using the ohmage software. Within Mobilize and Ohmage, I am in charge of developing web applications that help students to visualize the data they collaboratively collected. One public demo with actual data collected by students about snacking behaviour is available at: http://jeroenooms.github.com/snack. The application allows students to explore their data, by filtering, zooming, browsing, comparing, etc. It helps students and teachers to access and learn from their data, without complicated tools or programming. This approach would easily generalize to other fields, like medical data or BI. The great thing about this application is that it is fully client side; the backend is simply a CSV file. So it is very easy to deploy and maintain.

Ajay—What's your take on difference between OpenCPU and RevoDeployR?

Jeroen—RevoDeployR and OpenCPU both provide a system for development of R web applications, but in a fairly different context. OpenCPU is open source and written completely in R, whereas RevoDeployR is proprietary and written in Java. I think Revolution focusses more on a complete solution in a corporate environment. It integrates with the Revolution Enterprise suite and their other Big Data products, and has built-in functionality for authentication, managing privileges, server administration, support for MS Windows, etc. OpenCPU, on the other hand, is much smaller and should be seen as just a computational backend, analogous to a database backend. It exposes a clean HTTP api to call R functions to be embedded in larger systems, but is not a complete end-product in itself.

OpenCPU is designed to make it easy for a statistician to expose statistical functionality that will used by web developers that do not need to understand or learn R. One interesting example is how we use OpenCPU inside OpenMHealth, a project that designs an architecture for mobile applications in the health domain. Part of the architecture are so-called Data Processing Units, aka DPU's. These are simple, modular I/O units that do various sorts of data processing, similar to unix tools, but then over HTTPS. For example, the mobility dpu is used to calculate distances between gps coordinates via a simple http call, which OpenCPU maps to the corresponding R function implementing the harversine formula.

Ajay—What are your views on Shiny by RStudio?

Jeroen—RStudio seems very promising. Like Revolution, they deliver a more full featured product than any of my projects. However, RStudio is completely open source, which is great because it allows anyone to leverage the software and make it part of their projects. I think this is one of the reasons why the product has gotten a lot of traction in the community, which has in turn provided RStudio with great feedback to further improve the product. It illustrates how open source can be a win-win situation. I am currently developing a package to run OpenCPU inside RStudio, which will make developing and running OpenCPU apps much easier.

Ajay—Are you still developing excellent RApache web apps (which IMHO could be used for visualization like business intelligence tools?)

Jeroen—The OpenCPU framework was a result of those webapps (including ggplot2 for graphical exploratory analysis, lme4 for online random effects modeling, stockplot for stock predictions and irttool.com, an R web application for online IRT analysis). I started developing some of those apps a couple of years ago, and realized that I was repeating a large share of the infrastructure for each application. Based on those experiences I extracted a general purpose framework. Once the framework is done, I'll go back to developing applications :)

Ajay—You have helped build web apps, openCPU, RAppArmor, Ohmage, Snack, mobility apps. What's your thesis topic on?

Jeroen—My thesis revolves around all of the technical and social challenges of moving statistical computing beyond the academic and private labs, into more public, accessible, and social places. Currently statistics is still done to mostly manually by specialists using software to load data, perform some analysis, and produce results that end up in a report or presentation. There are great opportunities to leverage the open source analysis and visualization methods that R has to offer as part of open source stacks, services, systems, and applications. However, several problems need to be addressed before this can actually be put in production. I hope my doctoral research will contribute to taking a step in that direction.

Ajay—R is RAM constrained but the cloud offers lots of RAM. Do you see R increasing in usage on the cloud? why or why not?

Jeroen—Statistical computing can greatly benefit from the resources that the cloud has to offer. Software like OpenCPU, RStudio, Shiny, and RevoDeployR all provide some approach of moving computation to centralized servers. This is only the beginning. Statisticians, researchers, and analysts will continue to increasingly share and publish data, code, and results on social cloud-based computing platforms. This will not only address some of the hardware challenges but also contribute towards reproducible research and further socialize data analysis, i.e. improve learning, collaboration and integration.

That said, the cloud is not going to solve all problems. You mention the need for more memory, but that is only one direction to scale in. Some of the issues we need to address are more fundamental and require new algorithms, different paradigms, or a cultural change. There are many exciting efforts going on that are at least as relevant as big hardware. Gelman's mc-stan implements a new MC method that makes Bayesian inference easier and faster while supporting more complex models. This is going to make advanced Bayesian methods more accessible to applied researchers, i.e. scale in terms of complexity and applicability. Also Javascript is rapidly becoming more interesting. Performance of Google's javascript engine V8 outruns any other scripting language at this point, and the huge Javascript community provides countless excellent software libraries. For example, D3 is a graphics library that is about to surpass R in terms of functionality, reliability, and user base. The snack viz that I developed for Mobilize is based largely on D3. Finally, Julia is another young language for technical computing with lots of activity and very smart people behind it. These developments are just as important for the future of statistical computing as Big Data solutions.

About—You can read more on Jeroen and his work at http://jeroenooms.github. com/ and reach out to him here http://www.linkedin.com/in/datajeroen

7.8   RForcecom by Takekatsu Hiramura

RForcecom—An R package provides the connection between R and Sales- force.com

This article was created by Takekatsu Hiramura

1. About this article

In this section, I'll introduce an R package RForcecom and its usage. As you may know, R statistical computing environment is the most populous statistical computing software, and Salesforce.com is the world's most innovative cloud- computing based SaaS (Software-as-a-Service) CRM package. RForcecom enables you to connect to Salesforce.com from R. It is provided as an add-on package of R and its source code is available at github.

2. **Preparing the environment**

    To use RForceccom, you should download the latest R statistical computing environment from the R-Project website. As of Jul 2014, Salesforce.com offers 30-days free trial and free environment for Salesforce developers. If you have not already had an account for Salesforce.com, you can create account by using this trial or free environment.

3. **Salesforce.com and Force.com**

    "Salesforce.com" is one of the most famous SaaS (Software-as-a-Service) based CRM (Customer Relationship Management) service. "Force.com" is an application platform of Salesforce.com, and it is specifically called PaaS (Platform-as-a-Service). The figure below is overview of the Salesforce.com/Force.com. Salesforce.com has CRM specific feature and its application platform. Force.com has only an application platform of Salesforce.com; it allows developers to create custom application.

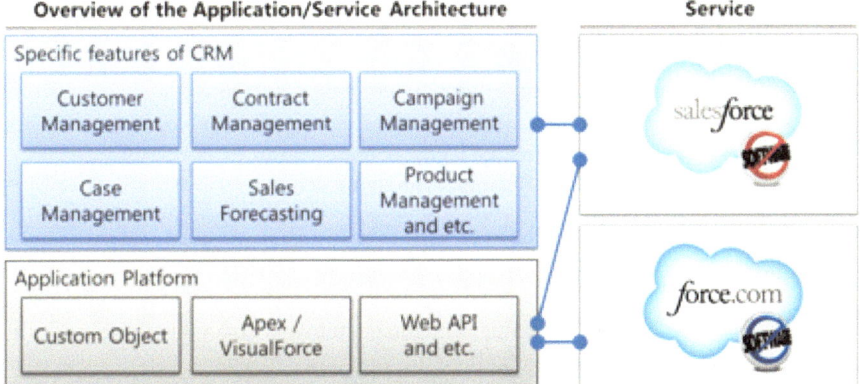

4. **Install and load the RForcecom**

    Type the commands from your R console to install and load the RForcecom.
    install.packages("RForcecom") library(RForcecom)

5. **Sign in to Force.com or Salesforce.com**

    To sign in to the Salesforce.com, use rforcecom.login() function. Set your username, password, instance URL, API version as follows. Note: DO NOT FORGET your security token in password field.

Your security token can be retrieved from your Force.com home page. Click your name displayed in right top and select "Setup"ï. Then select "Personal Setup"ï > "My Personal Information"ï > "Reset My Security Token"ï and click "Reset security token"ï button to retrieve your security token.

    username <- "yourname@yourcompany.com"
    password <- "YourPasswordSECURITY_TOKEN"
    instanceURL <- "https://na14.salesforce.com/"
    apiVersion <- "26.0"
    (session <- rforcecom.login(username, password, instanceURL, apiVersion))

6. **Retrieving records**

   To retrieve the dataset, use rforcecom.retrieve() function. Set parameters as follows.

   objectName <- "Account"

   fields <- c("Id", "Name", "Phone")

   rforcecom.retrieve(session, objectName, fields)

7. **Execute an SOQL**

   To retrieve the dataset using SOQL (Salesforce Object Query Language), userforcecom.query() function. Set parameters as follows.

   soqlQuery <- "SELECT Id, Name, Phone FROM Account WHERE AnnualRevenue > 50000 LIMIT 5"

   rforcecom.query(session, soqlQuery)

8. **Create a record**

   To Create a record, use rforcecom.insert() function.

   objectName <- "Account"

   fields <- c(Name="R Analytics Service Ltd", Phone="5555-5555-5555")

   rforcecom.create(session, objectName, fields)

9. **Retrieve a server timestamp**

   To retrieve a server timestamp from Salesforce.com server, use rforcecom.getServerTimestamp() function. rforcecom.getServerTimestamp(session)

10. **Example of the analysis using RForcecom**

    Visualizing consumers' voice—The demo scenario and the objective of the analysis is to visualizing customers' voice. Assume you are a manager at a company and want to know the consumers' voice from CRM. Consumers' voices are stored in Salesforce.com which registered by their call centre staff.

1. Concept of the example analysis. The image below is conceptual diagram of the example analysis. First step, call centre operators register customer voice into Salesforce.com. Second step, Salesforce.com manages many kinds of consumer data and provides API. Third step, R works as API client to retrieve dataset from cloud, and conduct NLP (Natural Language Processing) algorithm and visualize the data as word cloud. Last step, the managers receive the Analysis report generated by R to grasp consumer voice.

2. Crawling Twitter data. It is difficult to use actual dataset, so we crawled Delta Airline's Twitter account (@DeltaAssist) and stored tweets to Salesforce.com instead of actual dataset. Crawling twitter, twitteR package would work in the case. For detailed usage about twitteR package, refer to http://cran.r-project.org/web/packages/twitteR/index.html

To store retrieved dataset into Salesforce.com, Data Loader developed by Salesforce.com does work in this case. This tool provides the function for importing/exporting to and from Salesforce.com. For more information about Data Loader, see Data Loader Guide (https://developer.salesforce.com/page/Data_Loader).

The framework might be applied for conducting a sentiment (negative/positive) analysis and for analysing customer feedback for specific product or service to improve customer satisfaction. You can also merge the data within the CRM with external data with social media.

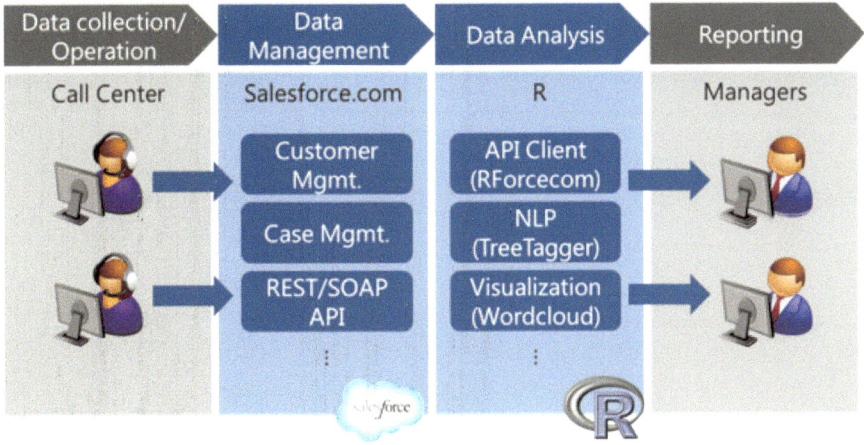

To see the complete case study please refer to http://hiratake55.wordpress.com/2013/03/28/rforcecom/

Chapter 8
Securing Your R cloud

Analytics deals with huge amounts of confidential data. For regulatory and business continuity, it is preferable that analytical environments be secure from operational risk including cyber threats. Some veteran IT administrators may think that their certifications in Networking and Legacy Operating Systems Engineering are not relevant in the cloud environment, but the basic principles remain the same.

8.1 Ensuring R Code Does not Contain Your Login Keys

Occasionally we have to connect to services from R that ask for login details, such as databases but you may not want to store your login details in the R source code file, instead the user would prefer to enter the my login details when I execute the code. The following code can do that https://gist.github.com/mages/2aed2a053e355e3bfe7c#file-getlogindetails-r while the corresponding note is at http://lamages.blogspot.be/2014/07/simple-user-interface-in-r-to-get-login.html

getLoginDetails <- function(){
Based on code by Barry Rowlingson
http://r.789695.n4.nabble.com/tkentry-that-exits-after-RETURN-tt854721.html#none
require(tcltk)
tt<-tktoplevel()
tkwm.title(tt, "Get login details")
Name <- tclVar("Login ID")
Password <- tclVar("Password")
entry.Name <-tkentry(tt,width="20",textvariable=Name)
entry.Password <-tkentry(tt,width="20", show="",textvariable=Password)*
tkgrid(tklabel(tt,text="Please enter your login details."))
tkgrid(entry.Name)
tkgrid(entry.Password)

© Springer Science+Business Media New York 2014
A Ohri, *R for Cloud Computing*, DOI 10.1007/978-1-4939-1702-0_8

```
OnOK <- function() {
tkdestroy(tt)
}
OK.but <-tkbutton(tt,text=" OK ",command=OnOK)
tkbind(entry.Password, "<Return>",OnOK)
tkgrid(OK.but)
tkfocus(tt)
tkwait.window(tt)
invisible(c(loginID=tclvalue(Name), password=tclvalue(Password)))
}
credentials <- getLoginDetails()
## Delete credentials
##rm(credentials)
```

8.2   Setting Up Access Control (User Management Rights)

For a network to be secure, different users need to have different rights based on their need to know, their potential for administrative overlap, and their job functions. Accordingly we give the example of user management in the AWS cloud.

8.2.1   Amazon User Management

- Go to the IAM console (https://console.aws.amazon.com/iam/home).

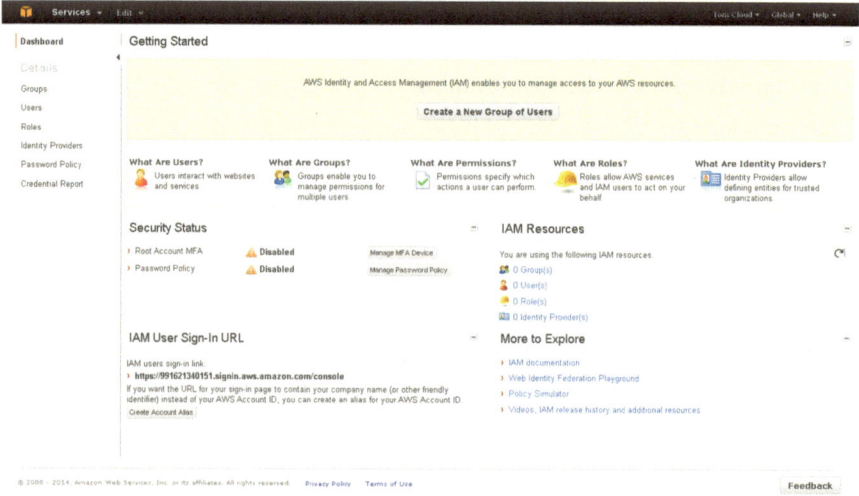

- From the navigation menu, click Users.

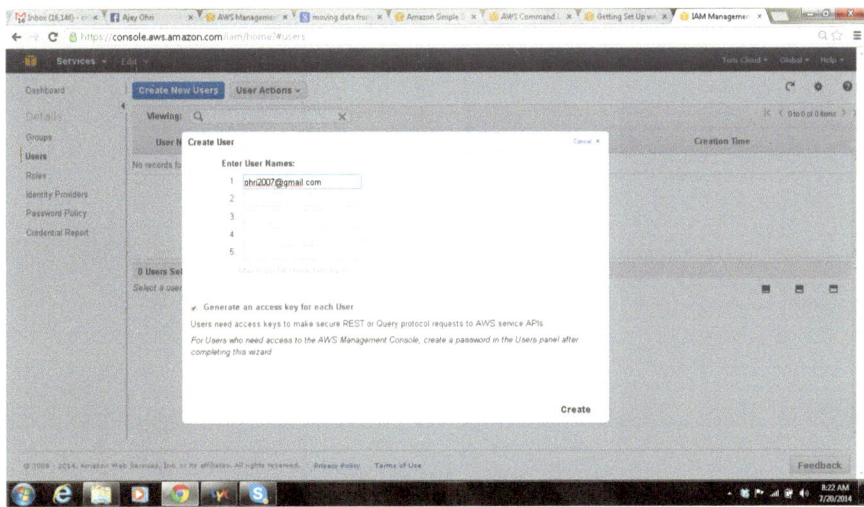

- Select your IAM user name.
    - Click User Actions, and then click Manage Access Keys.
- Click Create Access Key. Your keys will look something like this:
    - Access key ID example: AKIAIOSFFORE7EXAMPLE

    Secret access key example: wJalrXUtnYETAK7MDENG/bPxRfiCYEX-AMPLEKEY

- Click Download Credentials, and store the keys in a secure location.
- You can deactivate these keys (using Manage Access Keys from Security Credentials) and easily Delete Users as well once your project requirements are over.

- If you or your users prefer that they login to your AWS management console, this can be done as follows:
    - For ease of the users we can make the sign in page to a custom url

- Password can be auto generated (which sometimes creates problems). We can specify the password also.

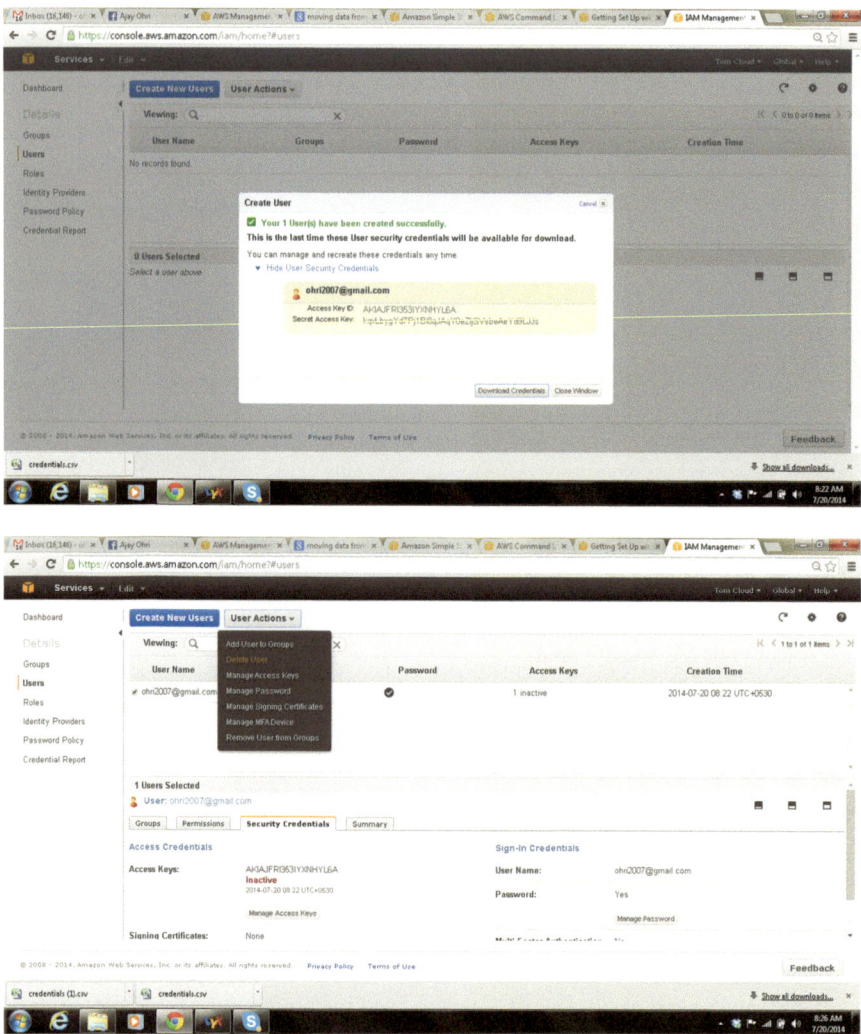

8.3 Setting Up Security Control Groups for IP Address Level Access (Security Groups)

To truly secure your network, it should allow logins from certain IP addresses only, even if the security key and password credentials are given. This is of particular use in case of laptop theft.

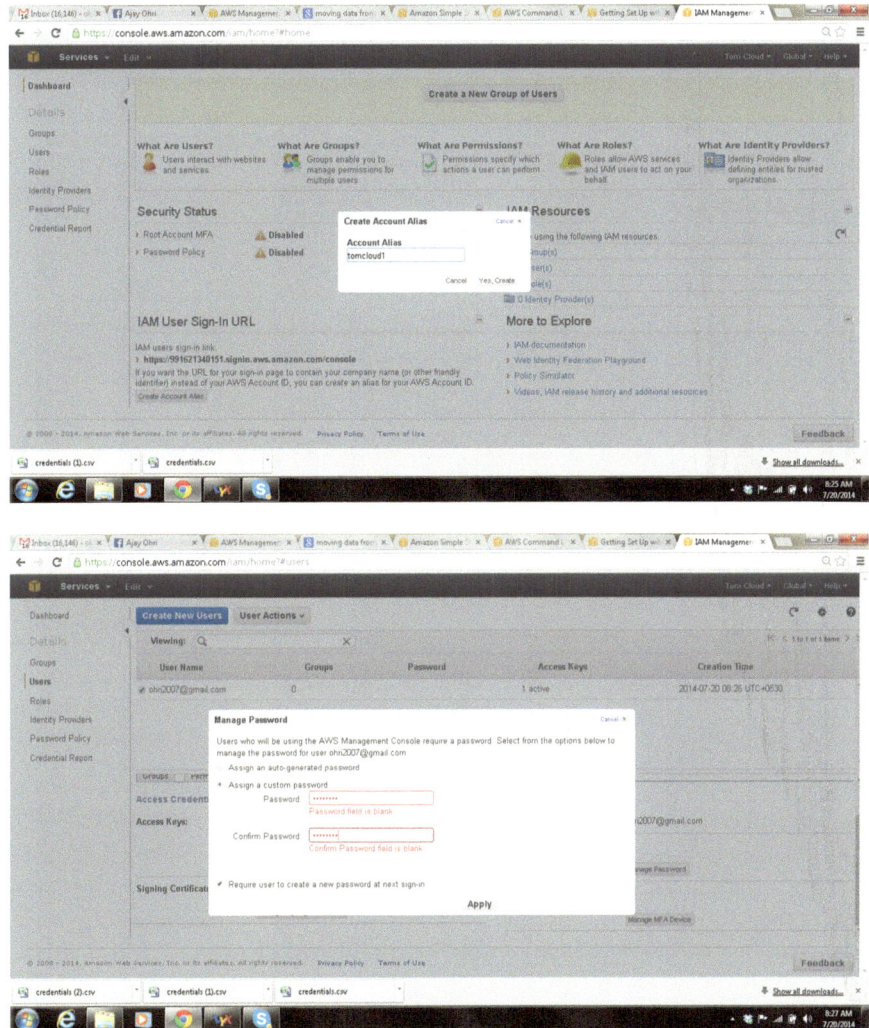

8.3.1 A Note on Passwords and Passphrases

A passphrase is easier to memorize and has more entropy (randomness) than a password which uses a combination of uppercase, lowercase, numbers, special symbols. A lucid example is given here to demonstrate this—perhaps you can share it with your IT administrator.

A salt is random data that is used as an additional input to a one-way function that hashes a password or passphrase. Salts also combat the use of rainbow tables

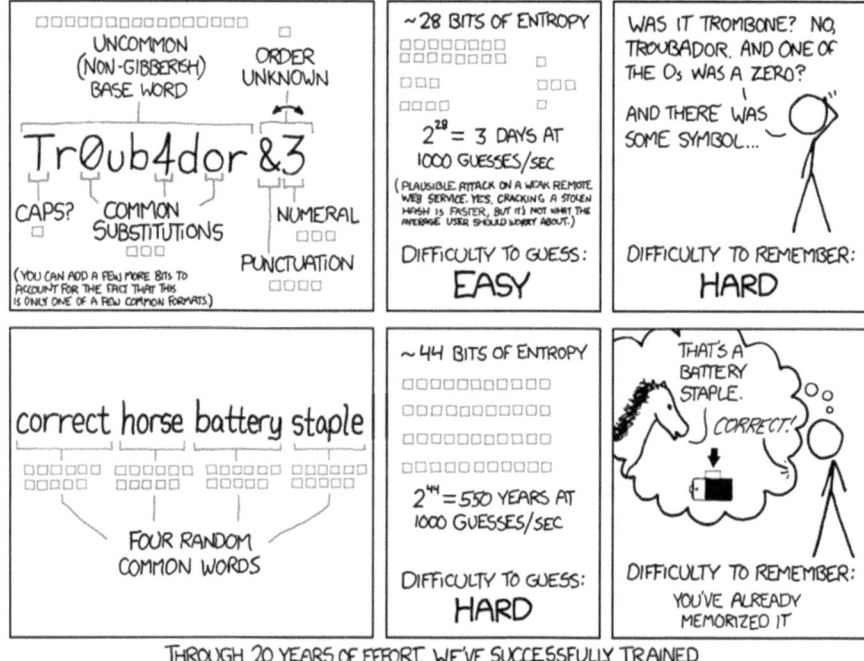

THROUGH 20 YEARS OF EFFORT, WE'VE SUCCESSFULLY TRAINED
EVERYONE TO USE PASSWORDS THAT ARE HARD FOR HUMANS
TO REMEMBER, BUT EASY FOR COMPUTERS TO GUESS.

for cracking passwords. A rainbow table is a large list of pre-computed hashes for commonly used passwords. A dictionary attack is a technique for defeating encryption by trying to determine its decryption key or passphrase by trying hundreds or sometimes millions of likely possibilities, such as words in a dictionary.

8.3.2 A Note on Social Media's Impact on Cyber Security

Social media has basically created a lot more websites for where human users need to manually create and remember passwords. Unfortunately this has led to a lot more lax security as people basically use the same password in repeated locations, thus opening up places they can be attacked or breached by.

8.4   Monitoring Usage for Improper Access

Web analytics to monitor resource usage in the network and statistical tools to detect outliers in such activity is one solution. Anomaly/outlier detection systems looks for deviation from normal or established patterns within given data. In case of network security any threat will be marked as an anomaly.

You can use **wireshark** to capture network data (http://www.wireshark.org/download.html). A demo model to check for network intrusion (good or bad) is given by bigml at https://bigml.com/user/bigml/gallery/model/4f8a88921552687841000000

A public dataset for training purposes is the DARPA Intrusion Detection Data Set. http://www.ll.mit.edu/mission/communications/cyber/CSTcorpora/ideval/data/)

8.5   Basics of Encryption for Data Transfer (PGP- Public Key, Private Key)

As a data scientist, we should know how to protect and defend our data. For sensitive data, it is best to encrypt it before transmission or storage. A public key is used to encrypt text, and a private key is used to decrypt text (we saw this earlier when we ran Puttygen to make keys before we transmit data for the cloud).

Here is a more lucid way of explaining how encryption works.

8.5.1   Encryption Software

Software such as GNU PGP and openssl can help with encryption. GNU PGP is available at https://www.gnupg.org/ and the windows version is available at http://www.gpg4win.org/ GnuPG is a complete and free implementation of the OpenPGP standard as defined by RFC4880 (also known as PGP). GnuPG allows to encrypt and sign your data and communication, features a versatile key management system as well as access modules for all kinds of public key directories.

The OpenSSL Project is a collaborative effort to develop a robust, commercial-grade, full-featured, and Open Source toolkit implementing the Secure Sockets Layer (SSL v2/v3) and Transport Layer Security (TLS v1) protocols as well as a full-strength general purpose cryptography library. It is available at https://www.openssl.org/ and windows version is downloadable at http://slproweb.com/products/Win32OpenSSL.html

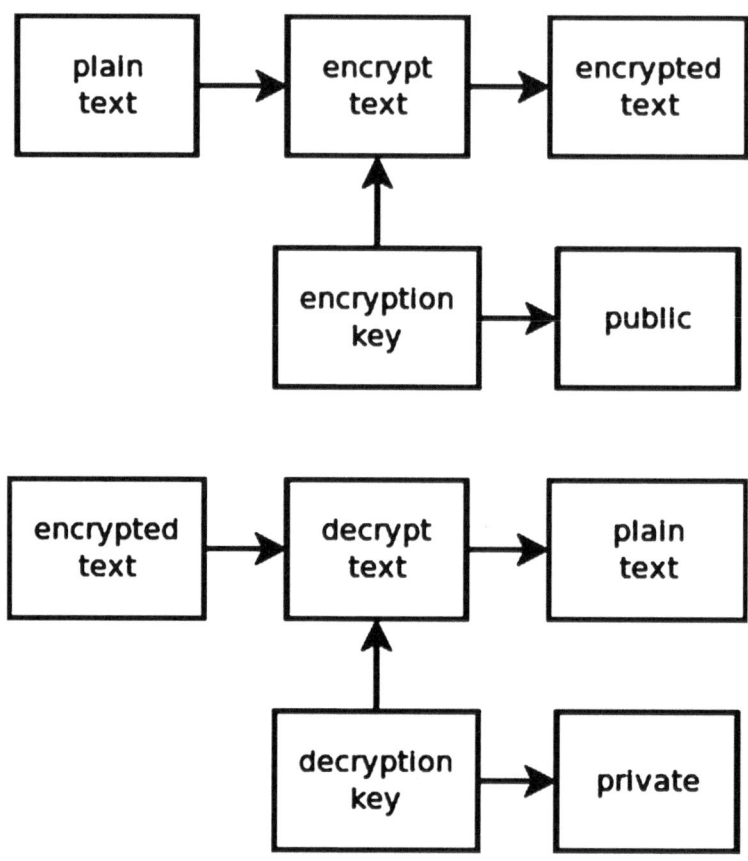

The digest package in R (http://cran.r-project.org/web/packages/digest/index.html) helps create hash digests of arbitrary R objects (using the md5, sha-1, sha-256 and crc32 algorithms) permitting easy comparison of R language objects, as well as a function 'hmac()' to create hash-based message authentication code.

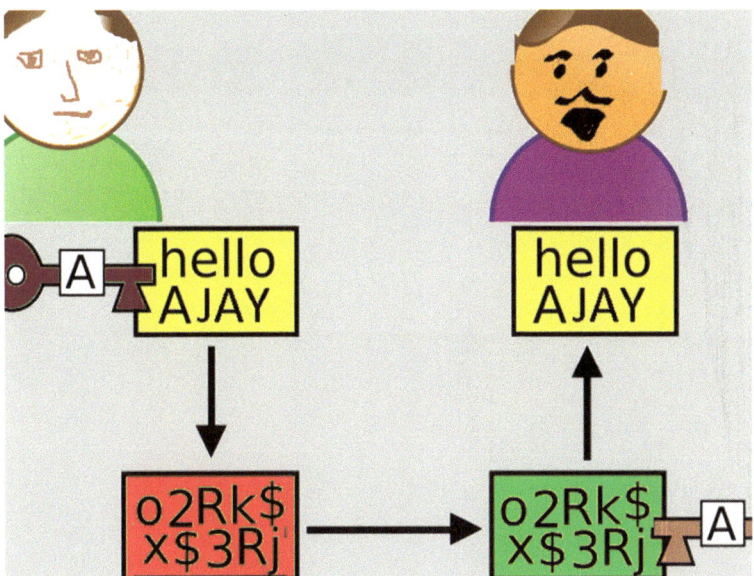

Chapter 9
Training Literature for Cloud Computing and R

9.1 Challenges and Tips in Transitioning to R

Unlike procedure driven languages that used to dominate the world of business analytics, R is an object oriented language. This shift can cause early beginners to the language some difficulties in moving to R. Following are some of the difficulties the author has faced while trying to learn R. These have been augmented by his experience in teaching R for the past 3 years or so to hundreds of industry professionals using online education.

The key challenges in transitioning to R in your organization are-

1. Keeping pace with rapid developments and changes in the R environment. This is actually a problem and an opportunity. The problem exists that largest number of package creators act independently of each other with the R Core Team acting more like a mentor and visionary than a central supervisor or head of Research and Development. The opportunity exists that cutting-edge algorithms almost inevitably are published in R.
2. A dense and sometimes turgid documentation (official manuals) with lack of professional look and feel. This is because of legacy reasons as R came out from the academic world (like other statistical languages did) but it was in incubation for a much longer period within academia before it came to be adopted by industry
3. A non-attractive non-user friendly official website at www.r-project.org. While companies like Datacamp, RStudio, and Revolution Analytics have all tried to give a much more modern look to R Documentation, the sheer size and legacy of the distributed CRAN system prevents major overhauls in aesthetics including projects to use CSS and Markdown to upgrade the current website.

© Springer Science+Business Media New York 2014
A Ohri, *R for Cloud Computing*, DOI 10.1007/978-1-4939-1702-0_9

4. Multiple ways to do the same thing including packages, functions, and syntax without a credible way to learn which is best for a particular use case. There can be 5 different packages that do the same clustering method. How does one choose the best package in a production environment?

5. A over reliance on fragmented sources of information including blogs, email lists, websites. This is partly due to the open source nature and partly due to a lack of effort to upgrade the sources of documenting on troubleshooting this software and very high volunteer support levels vis a vis official or commercial support levels.

Following are some of the best practices the author has seen in people learning and teaching R

1. Keeping up to date of latest developments in the R ecosystem by

  a. following leading package creators on Github where they protype their packages before releasing to CRAN (the Comprehensive R Archive Network is a global collection of 70+ servers offering the official download of R. R (thanks to the design of CRAN) is thus designed to be never offline even in today's world of cyber attacks and Distributed Denial of Service Attacks. Github.com is the leading website for programmers to share collaborate and build software in a distributed version controlled manner using the version control software kit). An example is shown here

    • the Github page for the most prolific package creator Dr Hadley Wickham, also the chief scientist for RStudio.

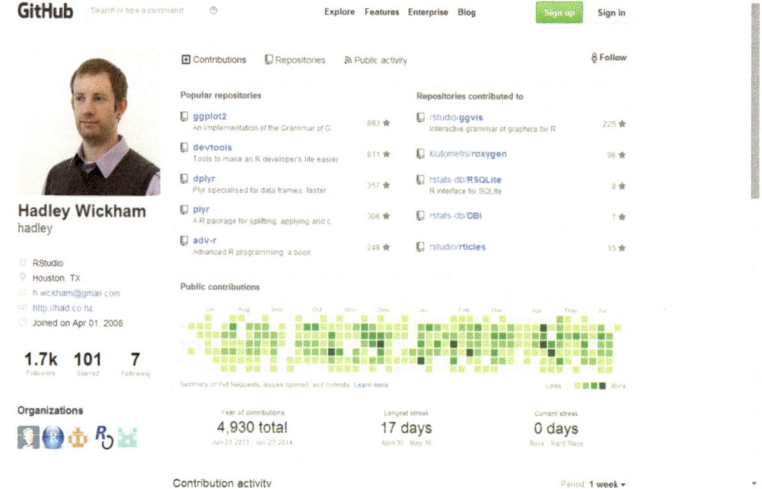

- Another example the latest edition of RHadoop package which is a great piece of Research and Development donated to the community by Revolution Analytics https://github.com/RevolutionAnalytics/RHadoop/wiki

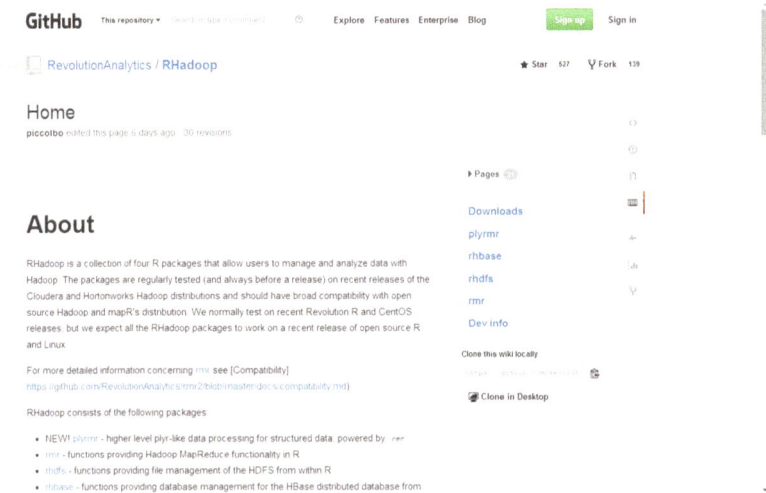

- The official website has a wealth of information (notice the difference in user interface). For example, the CRAN website for packages http://cran.r-project.org/web/packages/

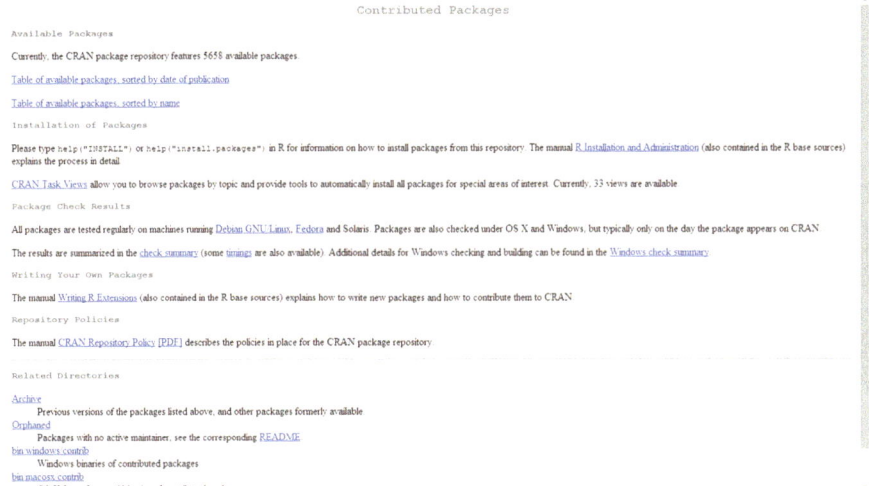

- Subscribing to both R-Bloggers and other blogs that may not be present there. R-Bloggers.com is a blog aggregator that uses Wordpress plugins and RSS feeds for presenting more than 550 blogs in a single newsletter/website thus cutting down on Internet browsing time or searching time for the user.

- By creating Google alerts for specific keywords we can be updated on specific events in real time. This website at http://www.google.com/alerts enables a user to create alerts when certain keywords come up across the Internet.

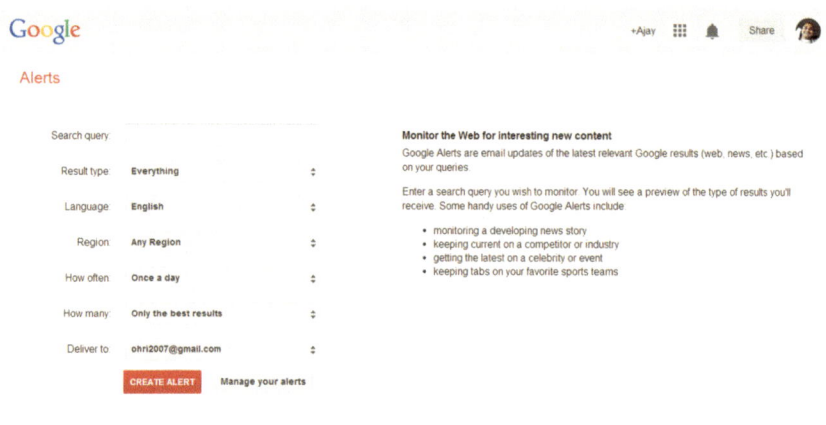

- Interacting and meeting with R developers and users both virtually and face to face in Meetups and unconferences. Meetup.com facilitates these face to face informal gatherings. Example http://r-users-group.meetup.com/ shows the user Meetups groups on R across the world.

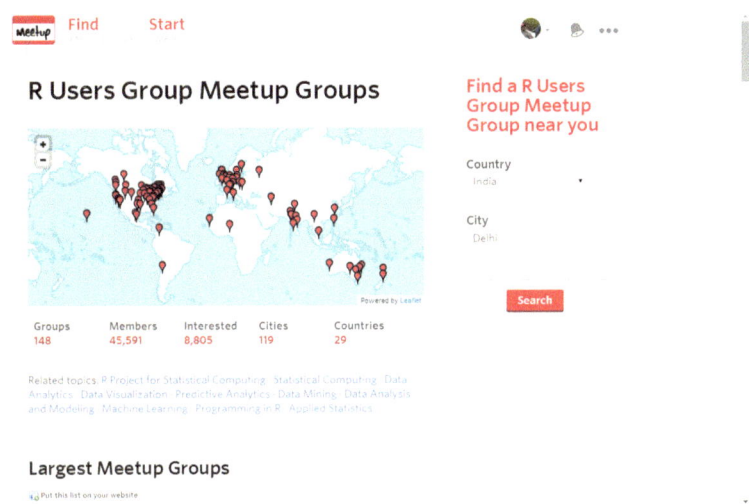

- Be proactive in pointing out defects or commenting on confusing things. This adds your visibility and emphasizes your contribution to the community. However you may want to search for the correctness of your technical view to avoid the perception of spamming or repeating yourself.

2. Documentation—Use better formatted documentation like Inside R (http://www.inside-r.org/) and R Documentation (http://www.rdocumentation.org/). The latter website lists R documentation of 6694 R packages and 136481 R functions including the leading non-CRAN R Package repositories of Github and Bioconductor.

3. A few good Websites—By finding and establish best practise websites for specific categories

   a. Quick R website for beginners syntax http://statmethods.net/
   b. Rattle Website for data mining http://rattle.togaware.com/
   c. A free textbook for Time Series Forecasting https://www.otexts.org/fpp. Time series forecasting is most oftenly used in Demand Forecasting for predicting consumer demand.
   d. Use CRAN Views a lot for finding more on packages by using http://cran.r-project.org/web/views/. CRAN Views act as clusters of packages for specific use cases.

4. Checking and validating code using both Google Search Engine and Stack Overflow (http://stackoverflow.com/questions/tagged/randstats.stackexchange.com) to find alternatives to do the same thing. This will sometimes give you links to http://cran.r-project.org/doc/contrib/andevenhttp://en.wikibooks.org/wiki/m

9.2   Learning R for Free Online

The following sources can help you cut down your training costs while transitioning to R based analytics

Academics—UCLA has a list of resources to help you learn and use R at http://www.ats.ucla.edu/stat/r/.

Videos—If you want to learn about R through videos, you can see this collection of links at http://jeromyanglim.blogspot.in/2010/05/videos-on-data-analysis-with-r.html.

Online Courses—The following are online courses to learn R. Many of them can be categorized as MOOCs (Massive Open Online Course) because they can have unlimited participants and have open access. The unlimited access part is due to the scalability available due to the cloud.

• Computing for Data Analysis https://www.coursera.org/course/compdata. This course is about learning the fundamental computing skills necessary for effective data analysis. You will learn to program in R and to use R for reading data, writing functions, making informative graphs, and applying modern statistical methods.
• Data Analysis https://www.coursera.org/course/dataanalysis. The course is an overview of how to organize, perform, and write-up data analyses and covers some of the most popular and widely used statistical methods like linear regression, principal components analysis, cross-validation, and p-values. The course helps you to apply these techniques to real data using the R statistical programming language, interpret the results, and diagnose potential problems in analysis.
• Statistics One https://www.coursera.org/course/stats1. It is designed to be a friendly introduction to very simple, very basic, fundamental concepts in statistics. Statistics One also provides an introduction to the R programming language. All the examples and assignments will involve writing code in R and interpreting R output.
• CodeSchool—Try R (http://tryr.codeschool.com/) is another easy and free online course for R. It is self paced unlike Coursera's courses.
• Datacamp (https://www.datacamp.com/courses) has a nice and new way for creating and learning courses for R.

Swirlstats is an R package for learning R (http://swirlstats.com/). It is a package so it runs locally.

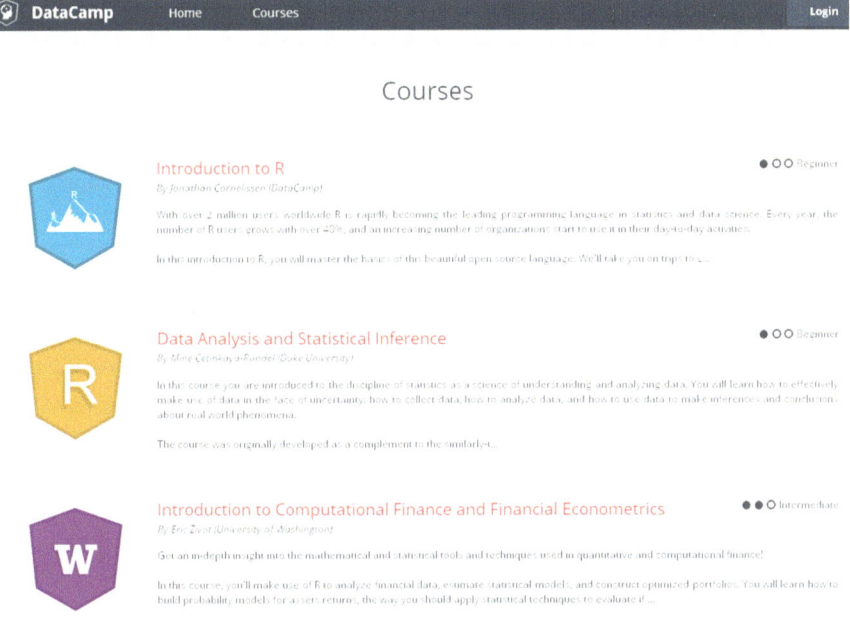

9.3 Learn More Linux

The cloud computing environment heavily relies on the Linux Operating System, unlike the Desktop era which relied on the Windows Operating System mostly. With Red Hat and Ubuntu, enterprises need not worry about open source operating systems being something that is technically too tough for end users. Here are some commonly used Linux commands for people used to a Windows environment.

- ls—directory listing
- cd dir—change directory to dir
- mkdir dirname—makes a directory named dirname
- cd—change to home
- sudo—gives super user or admin rights
- sudo bash—changes to root
- pwd—shows present working directory
- rm filename—removes file named filename
- cat > filename—puts standard output in a file
- cp filename1 filename2—copies filename1 to filename2
- mv filename1 filename2—moves filename1 to filename2
- cd—change directory

For a complete reference card, the reader is directed to http://www.linuxstall.com/linux-command-line-tips-that-every-linux-user-should-know/

9.4   Learn Git

Git is a version control system that is the most popular software used within software and it outmatches other version control systems. Github is where code is hosted and shared. Think of Github as a Facebook for data scientists. LEarnign version control is key to a distributed code project with multiple authors and creating reproducible research.

You can learn Git from https://try.github.io and refer to the reference card here http://overapi.com/static/cs/git-cheat-sheet.pdf

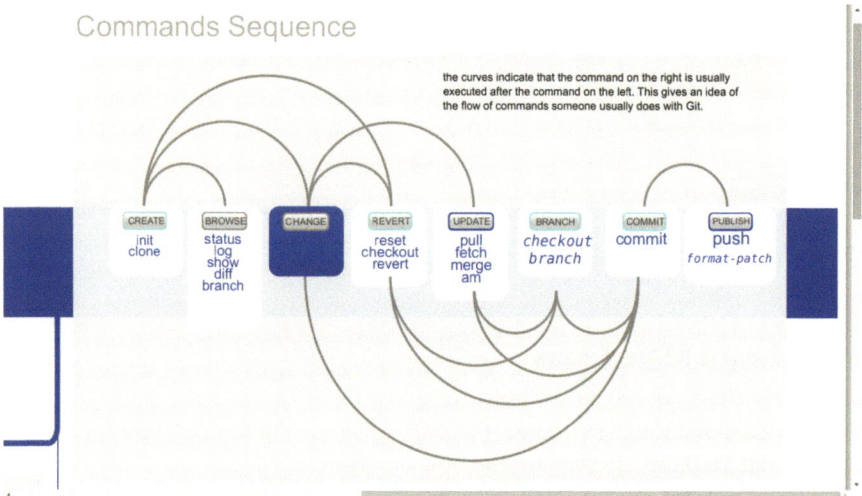

9.5   Reference Cards for Data Scientists

A list of reference cards for data scientists is given by the author at http://www.slideshare.net/ajayohri/cheat-sheets-for-data-scientists and the accompanying article is at http://www.kdnuggets.com/2014/05/guide-to-data-science-cheat-sheets.html. Reference cards are also known as cheat sheets and usually put the most frequently used language syntax on one page to help people learn and refer to commands faster. Note for the data scientist he/she needs to know how to query and store and analyse data so multiple platforms may be needed.

The complete list can also be referenced here as follows:

- **Cheat Sheets for Python**

  - Python

    · www.astro.up.pt/~sousasag/Python_For_Astronomers/Python_qr.pdf

- NumPy, SciPy and Pandas

  · 3.amazonaws.com/quandl-static-content/Documents/Quandl+,+Pandas, +SciPy,+NumPy+Cheat+Sheet.pdf

- **Cheat Sheets for R**

  - Short Reference Card cran.r-project.org/doc/contrib/Short-refcard.pdf
  - R Functions for Regression Analysis cran.r-project.org/doc/contrib/Ricci-refcard-regression.pdf
  - Time Series cran.r-project.org/doc/contrib/Ricci-refcard-ts.pdf
  - Data Mining

    · cran.r-project.org/doc/contrib/YanchangZhao-refcard-data-mining.pdf
    · r-data-miningQuandl s3.amazonaws.com/quandl-static-content/Documents /Quandl+-+R+Cheat+Sheet.pdf

- **Cross Reference between R, Python (and Matlab)**

  - mathesaurus.sourceforge.net/matlab-python-xref.pdf

- **Cheat Sheets for SQL**

  - SQL

    · www.codeproject.com/Articles/33052/Visual-Representation-of-SQL-JoinsSQL and
    · http://bensresearch.com/downloads/SQL.pdf

  - Hive hortonworks.com/wp-content/uploads/downloads/2013/08/Hortonworks. CheatSheet.SQLtoHive.pdf

- **Additional Cheat Sheets for Java**

  - introcs.cs.princeton.edu/java/11cheatsheet/

- **Linux Cheat Sheet**

  - www.linuxstall.com/linux-command-line-tips-that-every-linux-user-should-know/

- **Hadoop Cheat Sheet**

  - https://github.com/michiard/CLOUDS-LAB/blob/master/C-S.md

9.6   Using Public Datasets from Amazon

Many datasets are available for research and training on Big Data and Cloud Computing at http://aws.amazon.com/public-data-sets/

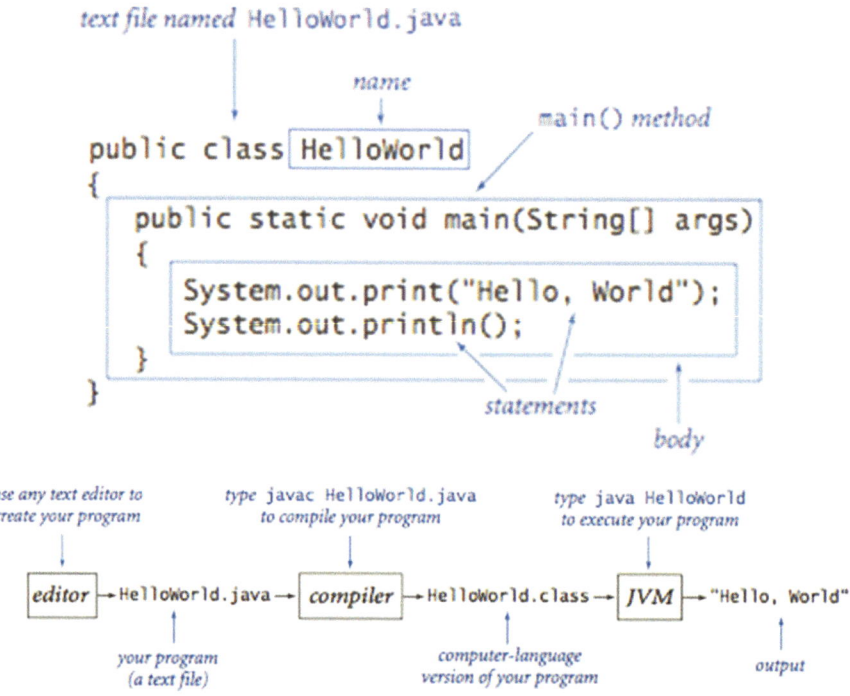

NOTE—For data from Amazon public datasets—Use data from snapshot (an AWS terminology for storage). Copy this Snapshot into your region AND your availability zone, create volume (using Volumes from Management Console), and attach volume (using Volumes from Management Console) finally mount volume—

lsblk—lists all volumes (the/notation shows volume is mounted)
ubuntu@ip-172-31-22-51:/data/AdditionalFiles$ lsblk
NAME MAJ:MIN RM SIZE RO TYPE MOUNTPOINT
xvda 202:0 0 8G 0 disk
xvda1 202:1 0 8G 0 part /
xvdf 202:80 0 10G 0 disk /data
mkdir to make a directory for mountpoint (here /data)
sudo mount /dev/xvdf /data for mounting the volume

9.7   Interview Vivian Zhang Co-founder SupStat

Here is an interview with a noted R training provider.

DecisionStats(DS)—What is the state of open source statistical software in China? How have you contributed to R in China and how do you see the future of open source evolve there?

Vivian Zhang(VZ)—People love R and embrace R. In May 2014, we helped to organize and sponsor the R conference in Beijing, with 1400 attendants. See our blog post for more details: http://www.r-bloggers.com/the-7th-china-r-conference-in-beijing/

We have helped organize two R conferences in China in the past year, Spring in Beijing and Winter in Shanghai. And we will do a Summer R conference in Guangzhou this year. That's three R conferences in one year!

DS—Describe some of your work with your partners in helping sell and support R in China and USA.

VZ—Revolution Analytics and RStudio are very respected in the R community. We are glad to work and learn from them through collaboration.

With Revolution, we provide services to do proof-of-concept and professional services including analytics and visualization. We also sell Revolution products and licenses in China. With RStudio, we sell Rstudio Server Pro and Shiny and promote training programs around those products in NYC. We plan to sell these products in China starting this summer. With Transwarp, we offer the best R analytic and paralleling experience through the Hadoop/Spark ecosystem.

DS—You have done many free workshops in multiple cities. What has been the response so far.

VZ—Let us first talk about what happened in NYC.

I went to a few meetups before I started my own meetup group. Most of the presentation/talks were awesome but they were not delivered and constructed in a way that attendants could learn and apply the technology right away. Most of the time, those events didn't offer source code or technical details in the slides.

When I started my own group, my goal was "whatever cool stuff we showed you, we will teach you how to do it". The majority of the events were designed as hands-on workshops while we hosted a few high profile speakers' talks from time to time (including the chief data science scientist for the Obama Campaign).

My workshops cover a wide range of topics, including R, Python, Hadoop, D3.js, data processing, Tableau, location data query, open data, etc. People are super excited and keep saying "oh wow oh wow", "never thought that I could do it"Ï, "it is pretty cool".Ï Soon our attendants started giving back to the group by teaching their skills and fun projects, offering free conference room, and sponsoring pizzas.

We are glad we have built a community of sharing experience and passion for data science. And I think this is a very unique thing we can do in NYC (due to the fact everything is close to half-hour subway distance). We host events 2–3 times per week and have attracted 1900 members in one year.

In other cities such as Shanghai and Beijing, we do free workshops for college students and scholars every month. We promise to go to the colleges as far as within 24 hours distance by train from Beijing. Through partnerships with Capital of Statistics and DataUnion, we hosted entrepreneur sharing events with devoted speeches and lighting talks.

In NYC, we typically see 15 to 150 people per event. U.S. sponsors have included McKinsey & Company, Thoughtworks, and others. Our Beijing monthly tech event sees over 500 attendees and gains attraction from event co-hosts including Baiyu, Youku, and others.

DS—What are some interesting projects of Supstat that you would like to showcase?

VZ—Let me start with one interesting open data project on Citibike data done by our team. The blog post, slides, and meetup videos can be found at http://nycdatascience.com/meetup/nyc-open-data-project-ii-my-citibike/

Citibike provides a public bike service. There are many bike stations in NYC. People want to take a bike from a station with at least one available bike. And when they get to the destination, they want to return their bike to a station with at least one available slot. Our goal was to predict where to rent and where to return Citibikes. We showed the complete workflow including data scraping, cleaning, manipulation, processing, modeling, and making algorithms into a product.

We built a program to scrape data and save it to our database automatically. Using this data we utilized models from time series theory and machine learning to predict bike numbers in all the stations. Based on the models, we built a website for this citibike system. This application helps users of citibike arrange their trips better. We also showed a few tricks such as how to set up cron job on Linux, Windows, and Mac machines, and how to get around RAM limitations on servers with PostgreSQL.

We've done other projects in China using R to solve problems ranging from Telecommunications data caching to Cardiovascular disease prevention. Each of these projects has required a unique combination of statistical knowledge and data science tools, with R being the backbone of the solution. The commercial cases can be found at our website: http://www.supstat.com/consulting/

About—SupStat is a statistical consulting company specialized in statistical computing and graphics using state-of-the-art technologies.

9.8   Interview EODA

This is an interview with Heiko Miertzsch, founder EODA (http://www.eoda.de/en/). EODA is a cutting-edge startup. Recently they launched a few innovative products that made me sit up and pay attention. In this interview, Heiko talks on the startup journey and the vision of analytics.

DecisionStats (DS)—Describe the journey of your startup eoda. What made you choose R as the platform for your software and training? Name a few turning points and milestones in your corporate journey.

Heiko Miertzsch (HM)—eoda was founded in 2010 by Oliver and me. We both have a strong background in analytics and Information Technology industry. So we observed the market a while before starting the business. We saw two trends: First, a lot of new Technologies and Tools for data analysis appeared and second Open Source seemed to become more and more important for several reasons. Just to name one the easiness to share experience and code in a broad and professional community. Disruptive forces seem to change the market and we just don't want back the wrong horse.

From the beginning on we tested R and we were enthusiastic. We started choosing R for our projects, software development, services and build up a training program for R. We already believed in 2010 that R has a successful future. It was more flexible than other statistic languages, more powerful in respect of the functionality, you could integrate it in an existing environment and much more.

DS—You make both Software products and services. What are the challenges in marketing both?

HM—We even do more: We provide consulting, training, individual software, customizing software and services. It is pure fun for us to go to our customers and say "hey, we can help you solving your analytical problems, no matter what kind of service you want to buy, what kind of infrastructure you use, if you want to learn about forest trees or buy a SaaS solution to predict your customers revenues". In a certain way we don't see barriers between these delivery models because we use analytics as our basis. First of all, we focus on the analytical problem of our customers and then we find the ideal solution together with the customer.

DS—Describe your software tableR. How does it work, what is the pricing and what is the benefit to user? Name a few real life examples if available for usage.

HM—Today the process of data collection, analysis and presenting the results is characterized by the use of a heterogeneous software environment with many tools, file formats, and manual processing steps. tableR supports the entire process from design a questionnaire, share a structured format with the CAXI software, import the data and doing the analysis and plot the table report with only one single solution. The base report comes with just one click and if you want to go more into detail you can enhance your analysis with your own R code.

tableR is used in a closed beta at the moment and the open beta will in start next weeks.

(It is available at http://www.eoda.de/en/tableR.html)

DS—Describe your software translateR (http://www.eoda.de/en/translateR. html). How does it work, what is the pricing and what is the benefit to user. Name a few real life examples if available for usage.

HM—Many companies realized the advantages of the open source programming language R. translateR allows a fast and inexpensive migration to R—currently from SPSS code.

The manual migration of complex SPSS® scripts has always been tedious and error-prone. translateR will help here and the task of translating by hand becomes a thing of the past. The beta test of translateR will also start in the next weeks.

DS—How do you think we can use R on the cloud for better analytics?

HM—Well, R seems to bring together the best "Data Scientists" of the world with all their different focuses on different methods, vertical knowledge, technical experience and more. The cloud is a great workplace: It holds the data—a lot of data and it offers a technical platform with computing power. If it succeeds to bring these two aspects together, we could provide a lot of knowledge to solve a lot of problems—with individual and global impact.

9.9   Rpubs

RPubs—enables easy web publishing from R. You can write code in R. Create the Markdown documents in RStudio. Share them on RPubs Website https://rpubs.com/).

It is the best way for reproducible research using R (apart from gists in github!)

Appendix

A.1 Creating a Graphical Cloud Desktop on a Linux OS

1. We can configure a Cloud Desktop using Linux if we install additional software. Launch a Ubuntu Server instance first. Then install desktop environment on it, and access the headless server instance via VNC remote desktop (or XRDP from http://www.xrdp.org/). Do enable X11 forwarding (which is slow). This can be potentially very problematic for the non-expert Linux User (and can be avoided by simply using the RStudio Server Option)

   a. Use this command using your PuTTY terminal window to download Ubuntu Desktop *sudo apt-get install ubuntu-desktop or sudo apt-get install xfce4 or* Use this *sudo apt-get install gnome-session-fallback*
   b. Use this for xrdp *sudo apt-get install xrdp*
   c. Run xrdp using *sudo /etc/init.d/xrdp start*
   d. Enable remote desktop protocol in security groups by opening the port

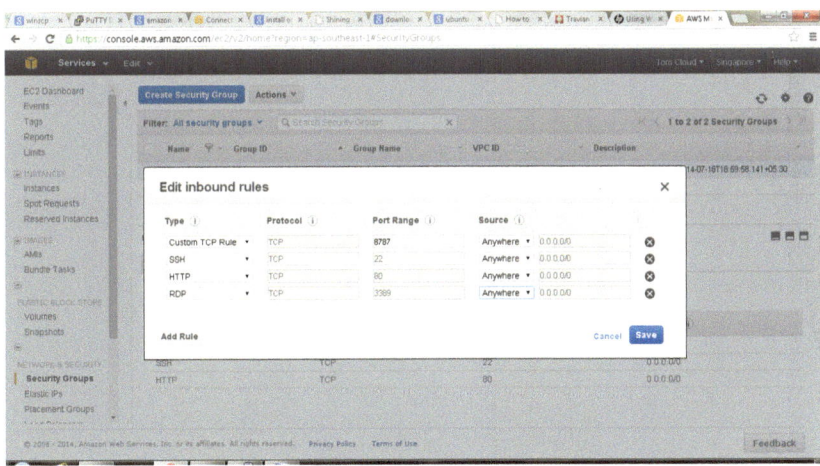

© Springer Science+Business Media New York 2014
A Ohri, *R for Cloud Computing*, DOI 10.1007/978-1-4939-1702-0

e. Make a new user running this command in the terminal *sudo adduser xrdp1*

    i. You can give super user rights to this user by *sudo adduser xrdp1 sudo*

f. Run Windows Remote Desktop using mstsc

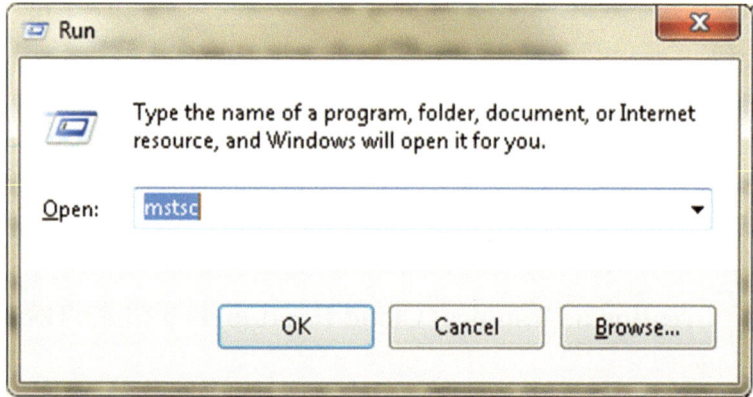

g. Login using credentials created above
h. su USERNAME Create a file called .xsession:
i. Change permissions to make it editable *sudo chmod 777 .xsession*
j. To edit the file *sudo nano .xsession* populate this file with this data: *gnome-session–session=Ubuntu-2d*
k. For shutdown use *sudo shutdown*, and for reboot *sudo reboot*

References

1. Cramming More Components onto Integrated Circuits GORDON E. MOORE, LIFE FELLOW, IEEE http://www.cs.utexas.edu/~fussell/courses/cs352h/papers/moore.pdf
2. R Core Team (2014). R: A language and environment for statistical computing. R Foundation for Statistical Computing, Vienna, Austria. http://www.R-project.org/.
3. http://www.nist.gov/itl/cloud/ The NIST Definition of Cloud Computing Authors: Peter Mell and Tim Grance Version 15, 10-7-09 National Institute of Standards and Technology, Information Technology Laboratory csrc.nist.gov/publications/nistpubs/800-145/SP800-145.pdf
4. Duncan Temple Lang (2013). XML: Tools for parsing and generating XML within R and S-Plus.. R package version 3.98-1.1. http://CRAN.R-project.org/package=XML
5. Interview Jan de Leeuw Founder JSS http://decisionstats.com/2014/07/14/interview-jan-de-leeuw-founder-jss/
6. Resources to help you learn and use R. UCLA: Statistical Consulting Group. from http://www.ats.ucla.edu/stat/r/ (accessed February 27, 2013).
7. Videos on Data Analysis with R: Introductory, Intermediate, and Advanced Resources http://jeromyanglim.blogspot.in/2010/05/videos-on-data-analysis-with-r.html
8. 50 functions in R http://decisionstats.com/2013/11/24/50-functions-to-clear-a-basic-interview-for-business-analytics-rstats/
9. Modelling Infuence in a Social Network: Metrics and Evaluation Behnam Hajian and Tony White School of Computer Science Carleton University July, 2011 http://people.scs.carleton.ca/~bhajian/sna.pdf
10. Journal of Statistical Software February 2008, Volume 24, Issue 6. http://www.jstatsoft.org/ Social Network Analysis with sna Carter T. Butts University of California, Irvine
11. McFarland, Daniel, Solomon Messing, Michael Nowak, and Sean J. Westwood. 2010. "Social Network Analysis Labs in R." Stanford University.
12. IaaS, PaaS and SaaS Terms Clearly Explained and Defined http://www.silverlighthack.com/post/2011/02/27/iaas-paas-and-saas-terms-explained-and-defined.aspx
13. http://channel9.msdn.com/posts/Windows-Azure-Jump-Start-01-Windows-Azure-Overview
14. What is Cloud Computing? http://aws.amazon.com/what-is-cloud-computing/?nc1=f_cc
15. David Chiu (Qiuyou Wei) -Social Network Analysis Using R (Data Science With R) http://www.openfoundry.org/en/download/doc_download/1720-david--social-network-analysis-using-r-data-science-with-r
16. Nicole Leaper A visual guide to CRISP DM http://exde.wordpress.com/2009/03/13/a-visual-guide-to-crisp-dm-methodology/
17. Jeffrey Horner (2013). rApache: Web application development with R and Apache. http://www.rapache.net/

18. Rob J Hyndman with contributions from George Athanasopoulos, Slava Razbash, Drew Schmidt, Zhenyu Zhou, Yousaf Khan, Christoph Bergmeir and Earo Wang (2014). forecast: Forecasting functions for time series and linear models. R package version 5.3. http://CRAN. R-project.org/package=forecast
19. SAS, Base SAS, SAS/ACCESS, SAS/AF, SAS/CONNECT, SAS/GRAPH, SAS/IntrNet, SAS/STAT and SAS/TOOLKIT are trademarks of the SAS Institute. SAS and all other SAS Institute Inc. product or service names are registered trademarks or trademarks of SAS Institute Inc. in the USA and other countries. ® indicates USA registration.
20. RcmdrPlugin.epack: Rcmdr plugin for time series This package provides an Rcmdr "plug-in" based on the time series functions. Contributors: G. Jay Kerns, John Fox, and Richard Heiberger. http://cran.r-project.org/web/packages/RcmdrPlugin.epack/index.html
21. Interview BigML.com http://decisionstats.com/2012/05/01/interview-bigml-com/
22. Drew Conway, John Myles White Machine Learning for Hackers O'Reilly Publishing.
23. http://decisionstats.com/2012/07/24/interview-john-myles-white-machine-learning-for-hackers/
24. http://decisionstats.com/2012/03/25/book-review-machine-learning-for-hackers/
25. Google analytics data extraction in R Vignesh Prajapati | 03.12.2012 http://www.tatvic.com/blog/ga-data-extraction-in-r/
26. Servers http://en.wikipedia.org/wiki/Server_(computing)
27. ETL http://en.wikipedia.org/wiki/Extract,_transform,_load
28. Amazon DynamoDB — a Fast and Scalable NoSQL Database Service Designed for Internet Scale Applications http://www.allthingsdistributed.com/2012/01/amazon-dynamodb.html
29. Ramnath Vaidyanathan http://ramnathv.github.io/pycon2014-r/explore/tidy.html
30. Hadley Wickham- Tidy Data http://vita.had.co.nz/papers/tidy-data.pdf
31. Hadley Wickham The Split-Apply-Combine Strategy for Data Analysis Journal of Statistical Software April 2011, Volume 40, Issue 1. http://www.jstatsoft.org/v40/i01/paper
32. Graham Williams (2011). Data Mining with Rattle and R: The Art of Excavating Data for Knowledge Discovery, Springer, Use R!.
33. About Twitter https://about.twitter.com/company
34. About Facebook https://newsroom.fb.com/company-info/
35. Datasift http://datasift.com/platform/datasources/
36. Graham Williams, One Page R: A Survival Guide to Data Science with R http://onepager. togaware.com/
37. Data Mining Algorithms In R http://en.wikibooks.org/wiki/Data_Mining_Algorithms_In_R
38. Brett Lantz, Machine Learning with R, Packt Publishing (http://www.packtpub.com/machine-learning-with-r/book)
39. Genetic K-Means Algorithm K. Krishna and M. Narasimha Murty http://eprints.iisc.ernet.in/2937/1/genetic-k.pdf
40. A K-Means Clustering Algorithm Author(s): J. A. Hartigan and M. A. Wong Reviewed work(s): Source: Journal of the Royal Statistical Society. Series C (Applied Statistics), Vol. 28, No. 1 (1979), pp. 100–108 http://www.labri.fr/perso/bpinaud/userfiles/downloads/hartigan_1979_kmeans.pdf
41. K-means clustering http://en.wikipedia.org/wiki/K-means_clustering
42. Ordinary least squares http://en.wikipedia.org/wiki/Ordinary_least_squares
43. William H. Greene, On the Asymptotic Bias of the Ordinary Least Squares Estimator of the Tobit Model Econometrica Vol. 49, No. 2 (Mar., 1981), pp. 505–513 http://www.jstor.org/stable/1913323
44. M. Stone; R. J. Brooks Continuum Regression: Cross-Validated Sequentially Constructed Prediction Embracing Ordinary Least Squares, Partial Least Squares and Principal Components Regression Journal of the Royal Statistical Society. Series B (Methodological), Vol. 52, No. 2. (1990), pp. 237–269. http://www.jstor.org/stable/2345437
45. K-nearest neighbors algorithm http://en.wikipedia.org/wiki/K-nearest_neighbors_algorithm
46. Rakesh Agrawal Ramakrishnan Srikant Apriori Algorithm http://www.cs.uvm.edu/~xwu/kdd/Slides/Apriori-Faloutsos.pdf

47. Ingo Steinwart, Andreas Christmann Support Vector Machines Springer Science & Business Media, 15-Sep-2008
48. Support Vector Machines—The Interface to libsvm in package e1071 by David Meyer http://stuff.mit.edu/afs/athena.mit.edu/software/r/current/arch/i386_ubuntu1104/lib/R/library/e1071/doc/svmdoc.pdf
49. Marti A. Hearst Support vector machines http://pages.cs.wisc.edu/~jerryzhu/cs540/handouts/hearst98-SVMtutorial.pdf
50. Bayes Theorem http://en.wikipedia.org/wiki/Bayes'_theorem
51. Neural Networks for Machine Learning https://www.coursera.org/course/neuralnets
52. Andrew Ng, Machine Learning https://www.coursera.org/course/ml
53. CRISP-DM Process Diagram CC BY-SA 3.0 Kenneth Jensen
54. A Proposed Data Mining Methodology and its Application to Industrial Procedures Seyyed Soroush Rohanizadeha,*, Mohammad Bameni Moghadama Journal of Industrial Engineering 4 (2009) 37–50
55. Chapman, J. Clinton, R. Kerber, T. Khabaza, T. Reinartz, C. Shearer, And R. Wirth, CRISP-DM 1.0, Step by Step data mining guide. USA, SPSS Inc.,35–45, 2000.
56. NoSQL http://en.wikipedia.org/wiki/NoSQL#NoSQL_databases_on_the_cloud
57. Tal Galili (2014). installr: Using R to install stuff (such as: R, Rtools, RStudio, git, and more!). R package version 0.15.3. http://CRAN.R-project.org/package=installr
58. Rserve A Fast Way to Provide R Functionality to Applications Simon Urbanek Proceedings of the 3rd International Workshop on Distributed Statistical Computing (DSC 2003) March 20—22, Vienna, Austria ISSN 1609-395X Kurt Hornik, Friedrich Leisch & Achim Zeileis (eds.) http://www.ci.tuwien.ac.at/Conferences/DSC-2003/
59. A simple web application using Rook by Ben Ogorek http://anythingbutrbitrary.blogspot.in/2012/12/a-simple-web-application-using-rook.html
60. Jeffrey Horner (2013). Rook: Rook - a web server interface for R. R package version 1.0-9. http://CRAN.R-project.org/package=Rook
61. Jeffrey Horner (2013). rApache: Web application development with R and Apache. http://www.rapache.net/
62. Simon Urbanek (2013). Rserve: Binary R server. R package version 1.7-3. http://CRAN.R-project.org/package=Rserve
63. http://decisionstats.com/2013/11/18/interview-christian-mladenov-ceo-statace-excellent-and-hot-rstats-startup/
64. , http://decisionstats.com/2013/12/03/interview-dr-jonathan-cornelissen-ceo-datamind-rstats/
65. http://decisionstats.com/2013/02/02/interview-jeff-allen-trestle-technology-rstats-rshiny/
66. Justin Talbot, Zachary DeVito,Pat Hanrahan- Riposte: a trace-driven compiler and parallel VM for vector code in R. PACT '12 Proceedings of the 21st international conference on Parallel architectures and compilation techniques Pages 43–52 http://dl.acm.org/citation.cfm?id=2370825
67. Install R and R Studio server using instructions from http://decisionstats.com/2013/03/11/running-r-on-red-hat-linux-rhel-rstats/
68. Bioconductor: open software development for computational biology and bioinformatics-Genome Biology 2004, 5:R80 Robert C Gentleman, Vincent J Carey, Douglas M Bates, Ben Bolstad, Marcel Dettling, Sandrine Dudoit, Byron Ellis, Laurent Gautier, Yongchao Ge, Jeff Gentry, Kurt Hornik, Torsten Hothorn, Wolfgang Huber, Stefano Iacus, Rafael Irizarry, Friedrich Leisch, Cheng Li, Martin Maechler, Anthony J Rossini, Gunther Sawitzki, Colin Smith, Gordon Smyth, Luke Tierney, JeanYH Yang and Jianhua Zhang
69. http://docs.aws.amazon.com/AWSEC2/latest/UserGuide/AmazonS3.html
70. GOOGLE CLOUD SQL: RELATIONAL DATABASE ON THE CLOUD Ajay Ohri Aug. 13 2012 ProgrammableWeb http://www.programmableweb.com/news/google-cloud-sql-relational-database-cloud/2012/08/13
71. Hadley Wickham. A layered grammar of graphics. Journal of Computational and Graphical Statistics, vol. 19, no. 1, pp. 3—28, 2010.

72. Michael Pearmain, Nicolas Remy, Nick Mihailovski and Vignesh Prajapati (2013). RGoogle-Analytics: R Handler for importing Google Analytics information from the Google Analytics API. R package version 1.4.

73. Fox, J. (2005). The R Commander: A Basic Statistics Graphical User Interface to R. Journal of Statistical Software, 14(9): 1–42.

74. Williams, G. J. (2011), Data Mining with Rattle and R: The Art of Excavating Data for Knowledge Discovery, Use R!, Springer.

75. Flow chart for forecasting is reproduced with permission from Hyndman and Athanasopolous (2014) "Forecasting: principles and practice", OTexts: Melbourne, Australia. www.otexts.org/fpp/8/7/.

76. The Mediawiki is the software behind the Wikipedia. The R extension allows to run R programs within the Mediawiki and to display graphics, HTML output and raw output in the Wiki pages http://www.mediawiki.org/wiki/Extension:R

77. Definition of CAP Theorem http://en.wikipedia.org/wiki/CAP_theorem

78. Brewer's Conjecture and the Feasibility of Consistent, Available, Partition-Tolerant Web Services http://lpd.epfl.ch/sgilbert/pubs/BrewersConjecture-SigAct.pdf

79. Towards Robust Distributed Systems http://www.cs.berkeley.edu/~brewer/cs262b-2004/PODC-keynote.pdf

80. James Long (2012). segue: A segue into parallel processing on Amazon's Web Services. Includes a parallel lapply function for the Elastic Map Reduce (EMR) engine. R package version 0.05. http://code.google.com/p/segue/

81. Duncan Temple Lang (2013). RCurl: General network (HTTP/FTP/...) client interface for R. R package version 1.95–4.1. http://CRAN.R-project.org/package=RCurl

82. Interview James G Kobielus IBM Big Data http://decisionstats.com/2012/07/13/interview-james-g-kobielus-ibm-big-data/

83. ECMA - 404 1 st Edition / October 2013 The JSON Data Interchange Format http://www.ecma-international.org/publications/files/ECMA-ST/ECMA-404.pdf

84. Extensible Markup Language (XML) 1.0 (Fifth Edition) W3C Recommendation 26 November 2008 http://www.w3.org/TR/xml/

85. Architectural Styles and the Design of Network-based Software Architectures by Roy Thomas Fielding University of California, Irvine, 2000

86. Learn REST: A Tutorial A fast-training course for REST - Representational State Transfer, a new approach to systems architecture and a lightweight alternative to web services Dr. M. Elkstein http://rest.elkstein.org/

87. MongoDB http://www.mongodb.org/

88. From JSON to BSON and Back DJ WALKER-MORGAN http://blog.mongohq.com/from-json-to-bson-and-back/

89. Interview with James Kobielus http://decisionstats.com/2012/07/13/interview-james-g-kobielus-ibm-big-data/

90. ACID http://databases.about.com/od/specificproducts/a/acid.htm

91. Jeffrey Dean and Sanjay Ghemawat. MapReduce: Simplified data processing on large clusters. In OSDI'04, 6th Symposium on Operating Systems Design and Implementation, pages 137—150, 2004. https://www.usenix.org/legacy/publications/library/proceedings/osdi04/tech/full_papers/dean/dean_html/index.html

92. I. Feinerer, K. Hornik, and D. Meyer Text mining infrastructure in R Journal of Statistical Software, 25(5):1—54, March 2008 ISSN 1548-7660 URL http://www.jstatsoft.org/v25/i05

93. A tm Plug-In for Distributed Text Mining in R I. Feinerer, K. Hornik, Stefan Theu'l Journal of Statistical Software November 2012, Volume 51, Issue 5. http://www.jstatsoft.org/v51/i05/paper

94. Jeroen C.L. Ooms (2010). yeroon.net/ggplot2: A web interface for the R package ggplot2. Version 0.2. http://www.yeroon.net/ggplot2

95. H. Wickham. ggplot2: elegant graphics for data analysis. Springer New York, 2009.

96. Quandl http://www.quandl.com/help/r

97. Markus Gesmann and Diego de Castillo. Using the Google Visualisation API with R. The R Journal, 3(2):40–44, December 2011.

98. Edwin de Jonge and Martijn Tennekes (2013). tabplotd3: Tabplotd3, interactive inspection of large data. R package version 0.3.3. http://CRAN.R-project.org/package=tabplotd3

99. Interview Concerto http://decisionstats.com/2012/02/28/interview-michal-kosinski-concerto-web-based-app-using-rstats/.

100. http://www.programmableweb.com/news/pw-interview-karthik-ram-ropensci-wrapping-all-science-apis/2013/03/20

101. http://cran.r-project.org/web/packages/RForcecom/RForcecom.pdf

102. Package 'RForcecom' Takekatsu Hiramura <thira@plavox.info>

103. http://imgs.xkcd.com/comics/password_strength.png

104. http://en.wikipedia.org/wiki/Salt_(cryptography)

105. R Bloggers http://www.r-bloggers.com/data-mining-for-network-security-and-intrusion-detection/

106. http://www.blackwasp.co.uk/SaltedPasswordHashing.aspx

107. Dirk Eddelbuettel with contributions by Antoine Lucas, Jarek Tuszynski, Henrik Bengtsson, Simon Urbanek, Mario Frasca, Bryan Lewis, Murray Stokely, Hannes Muehleisen and Duncan Murdoch. (2013). digest: Create cryptographic hash digests of R objects. R package version 0.6.4. http://CRAN.R-project.org/package=digest

108. https://crackstation.net/hashing-security.htm